Chaves

- general urban sociology discussion
47 - "communities of limited liability"
48 - corps change the city

Religion and Community in
the New Urban America

49 - relative rarity of "neighborhood" corps — large issue of
    how corps relate to immediate environment
52 - 9 variables influency urban impact — but really
    11, including neighborhood — area — metro +
    internal/external orientation
55 - adapting or resisting corps.
    — 6 types of corp. action (not a bad list)
113 - urban geog. forces firm place for Muslim neighborhood
120 - inherently shift towards more civic engagement by mosque —
    as e.g. Americanizing its form?
129 - mosques as magnets for Muslim residents
131 - clergy acting as role legal authority adjudicating
135 - mosques more ethnicals divorce from most churches —
         disputes
    — e.g. of immigrant religion forced to find a common
      identity. ≈ 30% in Chicago are diverse;
    about rate of diversity in RC churches, probably for
    similar reasons — large, parish-like structure + identity
    that spans different ethnic groups.

Religion and Community in the New Urban America

PAUL D. NUMRICH

AND

ELFRIEDE WEDAM

OXFORD
UNIVERSITY PRESS

OXFORD
UNIVERSITY PRESS

Oxford University Press is a department of the University of
Oxford. It furthers the University's objective of excellence in research,
scholarship, and education by publishing worldwide.

Oxford   New York

Auckland   Cape Town   Dar es Salaam   Hong Kong   Karachi
Kuala Lumpur   Madrid   Melbourne   Mexico City   Nairobi
New Delhi   Shanghai   Taipei   Toronto

With offices in

Argentina   Austria   Brazil   Chile   Czech Republic   France   Greece
Guatemala   Hungary   Italy   Japan   Poland   Portugal   Singapore
South Korea   Switzerland   Thailand   Turkey   Ukraine   Vietnam

Oxford is a registered trademark of Oxford University Press
in the UK and certain other countries.

Published in the United States of America by
Oxford University Press
198 Madison Avenue, New York, NY 10016

Cataloging-in-Publication data is on file at the Library of Congress
ISBN 978–0–19–938684–0 (hbk.); 978–0–19–938685–7 (pbk.)

1 3 5 7 9 8 6 4 2
Printed in the United States of America
on acid-free paper

From both authors: In memory of the late Director of the Religion in Urban America Program, Lowell W. Livezey (1943–2007), to whom we owe so much.

From Numrich: For Christine, who has explored some of the world's great cities with me.

From Wedam: For my immigrant parents, whose urban experiences shaped the next generation.

Contents

Foreword

CHICAGO HAS BEEN the primary focus for the study of the city for just short of a hundred years. Through that time many individuals and teams, from many different disciplines, have focused on the structures of the city, on the lives of its inhabitants, and on the way in which the people impact on the city and the city impacts on its people. From the very start Robert Park emphasized the need to focus both on the "ecology" of the city, its social and physical structures, and on the "moral order" of the urban community. For many in sociology, history, urban studies, and urban planning, the first of these has predominated over the second. In focusing, once again, on Chicago, and in this case taking into account the wider metropolis, Elfriede Wedam and Paul Numrich have attempted to redress the balance. They explore the relationship between religion and the city, both historically in the academic literature, and more significantly on the ground in various neighborhoods, suburbs, and intersections within the metropolis.

This book has grown out of the work of the Religion in Urban America Program that was established by Lowell Livezey in Chicago in the early 1990s. I have been privileged and honored to play a very small part in the development of that project and to provide an international comparator in my own work in the British city of Birmingham. Over those twenty years we have witnessed a paradigm shift in the study of the city, and in the study of religion. In urban studies the focus has moved to the "global city," "transnationalism," "globalization" in one direction, and to the recognition of diversity, multiculturalism and, more recently, superdiversity in the other. In terms of religion, academic concerns have moved away from a focus on the world religions, secularization, and on Europe and the United States to more emphasis on everyday, or lived, religion, religious diversity, and the interaction between the secular and the religious. In this text we see both these paradigm shifts in action as Wedam and Numrich draw on an extensive range of theory, in both urban studies and the study of religion, to situate the work of the Religion in Urban America Program over the last twenty years, but more importantly to understand and articulate the nature and impact of the congregations that have been the main focus of that study. Through the careful application of theory and the meticulous attention to ethnographic detail, the stories told within this book speak directly to the changes in religion, society, the city, and the study of all three.

Looking in from Birmingham there are a number of features of the study that highlight important differences and, by implication, the value of studies that focus on very specific contexts. If I were to undertake a study of the impact of religion on the city of Birmingham, or of the city on religion, I would not begin with the idea of the congregation. We sometimes forget the way in which religious organizations and expressions change, albeit very subtly, in different parts of the world. There are, of course, many congregations, of many different religions, within Birmingham and I can easily recognize those in our own city that match the examples so clearly illuminated in this study. However, the wider context, the relationship between the city's leaders and the faith leaders, the nature of the religious populations across the city, and, in the news during the writing of this book, the importance of religion in relation to education, all add something different to the situation in Birmingham to that in Chicago. This is not to challenge the findings of this book—far from it; it is to stress the value and importance of local studies, of learning from the specific and using that to ask new and important questions of other localities. That is what I would suggest this particular book does so well.

I have continued to admire the work of the Religion in Urban America Program and the insights on religion and the city that are still coming out of Chicago. There is so much still to learn, and so many questions that still need to be asked, but in the light of so much change, in religion, in the urban environment and in the study of both, it is vital to have studies such as this to illuminate important relationships and influences and which point the way to new means of studying, new questions, and new challenges in the future.

Martin D. Stringer
Professor of Liturgical and Congregational Studies
University of Birmingham, UK

Preface and Acknowledgments

AS WE PUT the finishing touches on this book, a working group of sociologists published a manifesto on "why American sociology has had difficulty taking religion seriously" (C. Smith et al. 2013, 905). More than two decades prior, the Religion in Urban America Program (RUAP) began taking the religion factor seriously in order to redress a comparable scholarly myopia in contemporary urban studies (see introduction).

Our initial judgment that religion *matters* in the new metropolis evolved into ever fuller understandings of *how* religion matters. In our 1996 research report, we documented "many different ways religious organizations are responding to the contemporary challenges of urban life and interacting with the other actors that shape it" (L. W. Livezey 1996a, 1). In our first book, *Public Religion and Urban Transformation: Faith in the City*, in an introductory chapter titled "The New Context of Urban Religion," we noted that "the institutions of urban religion are made up of people whose frames of reference have been shaken by some combination of structural and cultural change" (L. W. Livezey 2000b, 21). The present book pulls together our two main research topics from these previous works, namely, the kinds of congregational communities being created in new urban contexts and the role of religion (through congregations) in shaping those new contexts.

The latter topic, religion's role in shaping the new metropolis, should be neither understated nor overstated. Whereas urban scholars may tend to underappreciate the religion factor, religion scholars sometimes overestimate it. In his epilogue to our first book, sociologist R. Stephen Warner (2000, 298) predicted that "RUAP's findings will likely disappoint those who expect urban churches to be activist cadres dedicated to social change." But Warner goes on to explain the importance of our findings in that book, namely, how "Americans are inclined to use their religious institutions to build community in the face of social change" generally (298) and how the congregations of Chicago "devote themselves to building cultural coherence and social bonds in the face of powerful individualizing currents" specifically (306). The present book picks up where our previous works left off as we continue to document congregational community-building and offer a measured assessment of the role of congregations in the new urban America and beyond.

It seems fitting that a research project about religion in a restructuring metropolis would itself undergo major restructuring during its long tenure. RUAP began in 1992 with generous grants from the Lilly Endowment and the Louisville Institute. The project had a series of institutional homes over the next three decades, at each stop transformed by those who welcomed us and the resources they provided us.

In *Public Religion and Urban Transformation* (L. W. Livezey 2000c, ix–xii), we thanked the many individuals involved in our project while it was housed in the Office of Social Science Research at the University of Illinois at Chicago. Two deserve mention again: John Gardiner for his able direction of OSSR and R. Stephen Warner for his ongoing encouragement of RUAP in particular and our professional careers generally. Angela McHenry adeptly managed the office during our final two years at UIC. We reiterate our gratitude to the Lilly Endowment for its generous financial support during those early years. We note with great sadness two untimely deaths: RUAP researcher Peter D'Agostino in 2005 and, in 2007, RUAP director Lowell W. Livezey, to whom this volume is dedicated. We owe our greatest debt, of course, to Livezey, who, when initially armed with a Lilly Endowment planning grant, wanted to explore "something more" about the role of religion in a changing late modern urbanscape. We are grateful that Livezey's hunch and leadership pushed the project beyond the venerable tradition of Protestant urban ministry (his roots) into this broader arena of the reciprocal influence of urban structures and cultures with the multireligious actors of late twentieth-century Chicago.

After *Public Religion* was published, four members of the original twelve-person RUAP research team, Livezey, David D. Daniels, III, Paul D. Numrich, and Elfriede Wedam, signed on to write this volume. By that time we all worked at different institutions and lived in different cities. When Livezey became ill and died of pancreatic cancer in New York City in 2007, Numrich and Wedam committed to finishing the manuscript while Daniels continued as an advisor. We thank Daniels for his perceptive grasp of many of the project's thorny issues, globalization, racialization, denominational histories and their historical context, and his ability to articulate their connections to our central questions.

Between 2004 and 2005 McCormick Theological Seminary became RUAP's next institutional home. We are indebted to the president of the seminary at the time, Cynthia Campbell, dean of the faculty, David Esterline, and the administrative assistant to Dean Esterline, Carol Beisadecki, for generously permitting RUAP to house its voluminous files and provide comfortable working space for researchers.

RUAP's final institutional home beginning in 2007 was the McNamara Center for the Social Study of Religion, Department of Sociology, Loyola University Chicago. We were fortunate to work under two supportive department chairs, Fred Kniss and Rhys H. Williams. Williams was particularly helpful in bringing the present book to fruition. We are very grateful to the map makers who worked on this project. The initial maps were produced by University of Illinois at Chicago sociology graduate student Hermann Maiba, who first taught us how to appreciate ArcView. The next generation of maps was produced by Melissa Gesbeck Howell with refinements and additions by David J. Treering, GIS analyst in Loyola's Institute for Environmental Studies. Howell's work was supported by grants from the Graduate School and the McNamara Center for the Social Study of Religion, both of Loyola University Chicago. Treering's work was funded by research grants from the Society for the Scientific Study of Religion and Trinity Lutheran Seminary, Columbus, Ohio. All the map makers were souls of patience as we repeatedly scrutinized and reconsidered what we wanted to communicate with this complex form of data presentation and we were continually impressed with their creativity and attention to detail. Several Loyola colleagues read partial drafts and made significant recommendations: Marilyn C. Krogh, Rhys H. Williams, and Judith Wittner. We are glad we followed them, although perhaps not as fully as we might have. We also thank Deborah H. Kapp for helping us avoid some substantial errors and Frank E. Fortkamp for casting his clarifying eye over several chapters. Over the years, we have benefited repeatedly from Lois Gehr Livezey's many perceptive observations on religion in the city. We mourn with her the loss of Lowell. We are most fortunate that Martin B. Stringer of the University of Birmingham, UK, agreed to write the foreword. We value both his astute critical view and his global perspective on urban religion.

Various RUAP team members published articles and made conference presentations independently while also pursuing a collective analysis. In the present book, the plural "we" sometimes refers to the research and publications of other team members. The chapter notes track the publication record of the entire team; here we mention only our own previous publications and presentations.

Wedam (1996; 2000a; 2000b) contributed chapters on Catholic parishes on Chicago's Southwest and Near West Sides to RUAP's 1996 *Research Report* and 2000 book, *Public Religion*. Wedam and Livezey (2004) published some early ideas from the research in "Religion in the City on the Make" in *Religion and Public Life in the Midwest: America's Common Denominator?*, part of the Religion by Region series edited by Philip Barlow and Mark Silk. Wedam (2005) published an early and partial version of chapter 3 in " 'If We Let the Market Prevail, We Won't Have a Neighborhood Left': Religious Agency and Urban Restructuring on Chicago's Southwest Side" in *City and Society*. Some initial ideas developed in chapter 2 were published by Wedam (2008) as "Structure, Agency, and Adaptation in Congregations" in *Cross Currents*. In 2011, 2012, and 2013, Wedam made presentations at the Religious Research Association annual meetings, the *Instituto Superior de Estudio Ecclesiásticos* conference in Mexico City, and the meetings of the International Society for the Sociology of Religion.

Numrich (1996; 2000a; 2000b; Numrich and Peterman 1996) contributed chapters on Chicago's Rogers Park community area, Naperville, and religious diversity across metropolitan Chicago to RUAP's 1996 *Research Report* and 2000 book, *Public Religion*. Numrich published an article on immigrant religions in the *Journal of Cultural Geography* (1997), contributed a chapter on Calvary Church to *Tending the Flock: Congregations and Family Ministry* edited by K. Brynolf Lyon and Archie Smith, Jr. (1998), and made presentations to the Association for the Sociology of Religion Annual Meeting in 1995, the Council for a Parliament of the World's Religions in 1995, the Religious Research Association Annual Meeting in 1997, and the Naperville Ministerium in 2000.

Oxford University Press has our enduring gratitude for supporting the idea of this book and expertise in publishing it. Religion editor Cynthia Read, a consummate professional, encouraged us at every turn. Numrich offers special thanks as this was his third book shepherded into print under Read's guidance. Marcela Maxfield, our editorial assistant, gave us timely and precise advice throughout the production process. We are indebted to three anonymous reviewers who suggested significant redirections in our analysis. Each brought pointed criticisms while also confirming the general thrust of our ideas. This book would have looked much different and, we are convinced, would be less solid without their acute observations. We may not have, but are nonetheless hopeful that we met their expectations.

With so many supporters throughout the RUAP years, we ask forgiveness of any we may have neglected to mention here, especially family, friends, and colleagues with whom we had many rewarding conversations. We lift up the following for special recognition. Numrich could not have persevered without Christine's patience and the institutional backing of Methodist Theological School in Ohio and Trinity Lutheran Seminary. Wedam is grateful that her daughters, Sabine and Elise, never seemed to doubt that their mother would finish this project, despite how long it took. Their support was unfailing. Many colleagues at Loyola were encouraging while graciously urging us to get on with it in equal measure. It should go without saying that the authors thank each other, but since the kind of collegiality we enjoyed is not a given in academia, we must say it explicitly. We also note that the alphabetical ordering of our names indicates equal contributions to this book.

Lastly, we acknowledge our research sites and subjects, without whom the Religion in Urban America Program could not have existed. Unlike many scholars and other observers of the new urban era, they "get the religion thing" (see introduction and chapters 3, 8). They understand religion's role in the ensemble of forces creating the new metropolis, as well as how the new metropolis affects their faith communities in both positive and negative ways. We offer this book as a gift to them in the hope that it will enhance their understanding of the religion thing.

Paul D. Numrich
Elfriede Wedam

Religion and Community in the New Urban America

Introduction

THE NEW URBAN ERA AND THE RELIGION FACTOR

The New Urban Reality. The Global City. The Informational City. Edge City. The Inverted Metropolis. Prismatic Metropolis. Postmetropolis. Megalopolis. Since Megalopolis. Technopolis. The Metropolitan Revolution. Public Religion and Urban Transformation.

TITLES SPEAK VOLUMES. The key words, images, and metaphors reach for meaning and markets at the same time. A stream of books announces that something radically new is happening both *in* cities and *to* cities. The rhetoric is fresh, perhaps pretentious at times, but a growing consensus among scholars and other observers suggests that urban life has been undergoing a fundamental transformation since at least the late 1960s (Soja, Morales, and Wolff 1983; Soja 2000; Abu-Lughod 1999). Because place matters, the particulars of this transformation are not precisely the same everywhere (Abu-Lughod 1999; Molotch, Freudenburg, and Paulsen 2000), but deep restructuring or reconfiguration of the contemporary metropolis is a global phenomenon.

More than 80 percent of Americans consider themselves religious to some degree (Newport 2007) and religious organizations ubiquitously dot the American urbanscape. Religious life cannot escape the changes this new urban era is provoking. One purpose of this book is to explore the effects of urban change on urban religion through an in-depth study of selected congregations in the Chicago region.

But we propose to do more than that. In this book we offer an assessment of the religion factor in urban change. Analyzing urban religion as a dependent variable, that is, how religion is affected by the urban context, will produce important insights, but it is a rather conventional approach. Instead, we will engage in a bidirectional investigation of religion in the new urban era, adding the more surprising claim that religion has also been an independent variable, that it has played a role in recent urban restructuring. In other words, congregations are both shaped by and shape their metropolitan environments. The latter insight has largely escaped scholars and other observers of the new urban era who generally "don't get the religion thing," to paraphrase a Chicago activist's opinion of local business leaders.

The Meaning of Urban

By "urban" we mean the configuration of dense, complex, organized human settlement that emerged ten thousand or more years ago. According to Edward Soja (2000), the Third Urban Revolution in the nineteenth century created the modern "metropolis," an industrial capitalist configuration epitomized by Manchester and Chicago. Soja suggests that we have entered a Fourth Urban Revolution, the harbinger of a "postmetropolis" era that has yet to receive a consensus label. While agreeing with Soja and others about the new urban era, we use "metropolis" and its adjectival form "metropolitan" ("metro" for short) in a less restrictive sense to refer to the integrated configuration of a large city and the suburbs, satellite cities, "edge cities" (Garreau 1991), exurbs (A. Nelson and Dueker 1990; Berube et al. 2006), and other urban entities in its orbit.

Symbolically, "the city" can refer to urban life, experiences, and contexts generally. Technically, a "city" is an urban place smaller than a metropolis—it can either stand alone or be part of a metropolis—but it differs both quantitatively and qualitatively from even smaller settlements like towns or villages, which are not considered urban. The transformation of a town or village into a city involves increases in size, density, and intensity (Pile 1999, 21). Interpreting the urban historian Lewis Mumford's description of a city as a "geographic plexus," Steve Pile (1999, 16–17) explains that a city is the site of multiple networks connecting internally and reaching beyond its borders. As a result, possibilities for new kinds of social exchanges are created that include both personal and social dramas and that heighten creativity as well as disharmony. Mumford (1938, 6) referred to this as "purposive social complexity," leading to a higher level of achievement than can be gained in smaller agglomerations.

Expanding beyond the classical city is the "global city," better labeled a "global metropolis," which differs from other metropolises by virtue of its geographic vastness, dominance in worldwide economic and other systems, and extreme stratification of rich and poor residents (Sassen 2001). Following Janet Abu-Lughod (1999) and Saskia Sassen (2004), we consider Chicago to be one of America's global metropolises. Already in the 1930s, Mumford doubted "the desirability and the sustainability of ever-spreading cities," arguing for attention to planning that benefited the intensity, creativity, and vibrancy of urban life (Pile 1999, 17). We share his keen interest in the quality of life in the new urban era. (See Orum and Chen 2003 for an overview of cities and urban theories.)

Much of the literature on the new metropolis emphasizes economics as the driving force of urban restructuring. Soja's (2000) neo-Marxist analysis, for example, foregrounds the symptoms of a global economy transitioning away from industrial capitalism. Other observers foreground politics as the primary dynamic in urban transformation. Terry Nichols Clark (2004) contrasts the approach of the Los Angeles School of urbanism to that of the neo-Chicago School of urban sociology, which he advocates: "Politics is barely mentioned in the LA School accounts. We by contrast see politics as far more central."

Despite a predilection for privileging economics or politics, most observers of the new urban era recognize that "places comprise an ensemble of forces that somehow must be examined together," as Molotch, Freudenburg, and Paulsen (2000, 792) put it in their comparative study of Santa Barbara and Ventura Counties in California. They note a trend in urban studies to include culture in the ensemble of forces, a trend we place within the larger "cultural turn" in American sociology since the early 1980s that no longer contrasts the "soft" factor of culture to "hard" economic or political factors. Culture is now recognized as an instigator of social change, not merely a consequence of change in other domains. Thus, sociological analysis can now examine the full range of religion's ideational and symbolic components, instead of focusing only on values and religion's role in values integration. Therewith, urban theory can now consider the influence of religious ideas and actors in shaping the city. The cultural turn in sociology also provided a vocabulary and a technique for discussing a different form of sociological explanation: the interpretive mode, a non-predictive, non-positivistic, and primarily qualitative-based analytical stance in which the experience of the subject is particularly salient. This approach permitted analysts to move from understanding religion as a mere consequence of other, more powerful forces to that of a force in its own right.

Religion as Part of the Ensemble of Forces Shaping the New Metropolis

Although the question of religion's role in the new metropolis seems unavoidable, it is often ignored or under-analyzed in urban studies (e.g., Castells 1989; Massey 1994; Abu-Lughod 1999; Soja 2000; Massey and Jess 2000; Champion 2001; Ihlanfeldt and Scafidi 2002; Keating 2002; Bruch and Mare 2006). This may be a residual effect of ideological biases against religion that have permeated the social sciences for decades, such as Marxism and secularization theory (Warner 1998; Kniss and Numrich 2007). Writing just after we began our research in Chicago, Kathleen Neils Conzen (1996, 109) confessed her own "deficiency" in relegating the religion variable to secondary status behind her "primary objects of inquiry" (such as race and class) in researching Milwaukee in the 1970s. "In effect," she argued, "American urban history has accepted an implicit secularization thesis without really examining its assumptions or implications" (110). She urged urban historians to understand religion "more specifically as a city-building factor and more broadly as an ideology and a cultural matrix" (111). Conzen concluded in compelling fashion: "But first and foremost, the urban historian must simply recognize that religion has been and remains a structuring and enculturating factor in American urban life and to ignore its power is to risk both misrepresentation and irrelevance" (114). In like manner, we claim that religion, exemplified by congregations, is part of the ensemble of forces creating the new American metropolis. We will test this claim by using metropolitan Chicago as our urban laboratory.

We use the term "congregation" generically to designate a relatively small, face-to-face, geographically situated community whose character and activities are primarily religious in nature. Early in our project we recognized the privileging of Protestant churches in the congregational studies literature but found the conceptual extension of the term beyond Protestant (and Jewish) cases to be useful (L. W. Livezey 2000b, 17–18; cf. Warner and Wittner 1998; Ebaugh and Chafetz 2000). Designations for a congregation that are specific to religious traditions include church (Christianity), parish (especially Catholicism), mosque or *masjid* (Islam), synagogue (Judaism), and temple (Buddhism, Hinduism, and Judaism).

Congregations are by definition religious communities. "Religious" and "religion" refer to a worldview grounded in perceptions of a reality that both transcends the material world and imbues it with sacred meaning and purpose. We did not consider possible distinctions between "religion" and "spirituality" when we named our project the *Religion* in Urban America Program—that discussion was just beginning in scholarly circles in the early 1990s (see Zinnbauer et al. 1997; Marler and Hadaway 2002). In retrospect, we are pleased with our choice, since, according to consensus usage today, religion is a more institutionalized expression of a transcendent worldview than the typically individualized expressions of spirituality.

Our choice of the congregation as our unit of study followed common practice of the time (e.g., Roozen, McKinney, and Jackson 1984; Hopewell 1987; Wind and Lewis 1994; Ammerman 1997; Warner and Wittner 1998; Ebaugh and Chafetz 2000), but it also made methodological sense, since congregations are the most prevalent institutional expression of religion in the United States and they epitomize key issues surrounding the role of local associational religion in the new metropolis. We are aware of the value of augmenting the congregational study approach with systematic research on other kinds of lived urban religion, for instance in homes and workplaces (cf. Vasquez 2005; Cadge and Ecklund 2007). We caught glimpses of what is occurring in such venues and encourage other researchers to investigate how those might be similar to or different from the congregation-centered religious life described in this book.

We recognize how urban religion differs from the kinds of religion found in non-urban settings. As historian of religions Robert Orsi (1999, 43) explains, "Urban religion is what comes from the dynamic engagement of religious traditions . . . with specific features of the industrial and post-industrial cityscapes and with the social conditions of city life." One important feature that Orsi emphasizes is the demographic "heterogeneity of even the most restricted and isolated urban worlds" (58). Religion's dynamic engagement with the city results in "distinctly and specifically urban forms of religious practice, experience, and understanding" (43), complex and creative ways of shaping the lives of people affected by the mobility, diversity, challenges, and opportunities of urban contexts.

Our particular interest in the congregation has to do with its participation in forming and nurturing "community" in the new metropolis. We use this term in two ways. The first refers to social-geographic units like neighborhoods or the official "community areas" of metropolitan

Chicago. In cities, the intensity of community feelings has always tended to diminish as one moves outward toward progressively larger social-geographic units. In the new metropolis, the intensity of community feelings has been challenged at all levels. Urbanists have acknowledged the centrality of community as the "least well defined [institution] but most authentically expressive of the people of the city at large" (LeGates and Stout 2011, 87).

We also use the term community in a cultural sense that may or may not be integrally dependent on a geographic location. Cultural communities engage in common activities and share an identity based on beliefs, values, social intimacy, and personal concern and loyalty. The identity of a cultural community can be largely congruent with the social-geographic community in which it is located or it can stand in tension with it. We are most interested in the cultural communities created by urban congregations and how they relate to the social-geographic communities around them, especially the neighborhood and the local community area.

How does the religious life and work of congregations contribute to the formation of particular and diverse forms of community, thereby affecting various urban structures, especially race/ethnicity, class, moral authority, and even religious systems themselves? Do congregations embody alternative visions of community, associational life, and interpersonal ties, or are they complicit in creating the fragmented and polarized milieu of the new metropolis? Do congregations resist the forms of injustice in the new metropolis, perhaps by helping to "morph" current practices into more just ones, or do they create and sustain the status quo? Are unjust racial/ethnic and class differences perpetuated or dissipated in and through congregations? Do congregations represent the interests and claims of diverse groups in new ways in light of the challenges of the new urban configurations? What systems of moral authority within congregations might prepare members to weigh in on disputed aspects of urban restructuring?

Interrelated Restructurings

Our analytical endeavor is complicated by the fact that both the metropolis and religion have entered an era of global restructuring. We see these as interrelated, wherein urban restructuring affects religions and religious restructuring affects the new urban configurations. To the surprise of many observers, the late modern (what some label "postmodern") period has not become progressively more secular. Notwithstanding recent increases in the non-affiliated and nonreligious or "nones" category (Kosmin et al. 2009; " 'Nones' on the Rise"), religions today evidence increasing vitality, as expressed, for instance, through conservatism, revivalism, indigenous traditions, new religious movements, and religious rebellion against secular nationalism (e.g., Berger 1999; Juergensmeyer 2008). Moreover, religious groups are increasingly transnational in membership and influence, functioning much like multinational corporations and international political actors (Levitt 2001; 2007).

In the late 1980s, Robert Wuthnow (1988) heralded the "restructuring of American religion," pointing to the devolution of authority and resources from denominations to congregations; deepening theological and ideological divisions within (not only between) denominations and faith traditions; a hegemonic shift from mainline Protestant and (to a lesser extent) Roman Catholic denominations to evangelical, Pentecostal, and independent churches; and an increase in the number, diversity, and independence of religious voluntary associations and special purpose organizations. A host of scholars since the early 1990s have documented the diversification of American religious affiliations through three main demographic and social processes: differential birth rates across religious groups, including higher rates as religiosity increases (Hayford and Morgan 2008); recent immigration, which has both de-Europeanized American Christianity and increased the number of non-Christian groups (Warner 2006; Kniss and Numrich 2007); and a growing trend of shopping the spiritual marketplace (Wuthnow 1998; Roof 2001).

In the conventional wisdom about US cities, religious organizations are commonly seen as resilient in the face of urban change, anchors of urban neighborhoods, including those in decline, and the last best hope for the poor and oppressed. Religion in the United States blatantly defies secularization theory, while religious groups, whether motivated by the demands for material justice or spiritual concerns, have helped to alleviate the most negative consequences of urban excesses and contradictions. The presumption of religion's social efficacy provided a rationale for the Charitable Choice provisions of the US welfare reform legislation of 1996 and was regularly cited by the second Bush administration in support of its Faith-Based Initiative. But while it is quite evident that religious organizations often adapt to changing urban structures in more or less passive fashion, little attention has been given to whether they might also be agents in the restructuring process. If our claim is true that religion and the metropolis are undergoing interrelated restructurings, observers interested in urban restructuring must pay attention to religious restructuring, for it is one of the constitutive forces of the new urban era.

About This Book

This book draws upon ethnographic research conducted since 1992 by the Religion in Urban America Program, originally housed in the Office of Social Science Research at the University of Illinois at Chicago. Our research pool included 105 congregations across various religious traditions and locations; we gathered significant data for more than half of this pool (55 of the 105; see L. W. Livezey 2000c, 309–18 for a partial list of the congregations in our research pool). We also studied twelve other organizations, all religiously based except the Greater Southwest Development Corporation. Our primary research periods were the 1990s and early 2000s, but we have updated our knowledge of the fifteen major congregational case studies featured in this book, shown in Figure I.1 along with the cities or community areas of the city of Chicago in which they are located. Census data (especially at the tract level) cited in this book come from the 2000 census and subsequent Census Bureau estimates prior to the 2010 census, thus correlating with the period during which we gathered congregational data. Our investigation was highly inductive, attentive to the life and work of each congregation without prejudicing what aspects might be most salient in the new urban configuration (see the appendices for a full discussion of our research methods).

We made previous analytical passes through our data in a research report (L. W. Livezey 1996c) and the book *Public Religion and Urban Transformation: Faith in the City* (L. W. Livezey 2000c). Although some overarching themes in those works inform the present book, here we frame a more comprehensive and systematic analysis of the data, particularly with regard to congregational communities in the new metropolitan Chicago.

The two chapters of Part I establish the theoretical and conceptual framework of the book. Chapter 1 offers an overview of Chicago's history, showing how the often overlooked religion factor has intersected with political, socioeconomic, and racial/ethnic urban structures. Chapter 2 examines the notion of "community" in general, explores the nature of urban communities (especially congregations) in the new urban era, and posits three key factors that affect a congregation's impact on the urban

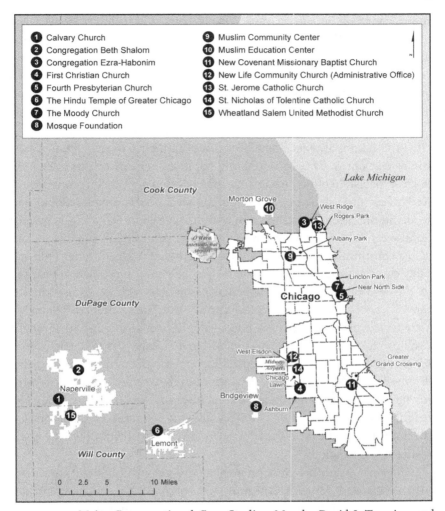

1. Calvary Church
2. Congregation Beth Shalom
3. Congregation Ezra-Habonim
4. First Christian Church
5. Fourth Presbyterian Church
6. The Hindu Temple of Greater Chicago
7. The Moody Church
8. Mosque Foundation
9. Muslim Community Center
10. Muslim Education Center
11. New Covenant Missionary Baptist Church
12. New Life Community Church (Administrative Office)
13. St. Jerome Catholic Church
14. St. Nicholas of Tolentine Catholic Church
15. Wheatland Salem United Methodist Church

FIGURE I.I. Major Congregational Case Studies. Map by David J. Treering and Melissa Gesbeck Howell, Loyola University Chicago.

environment: spatial type ("neighborhood," "area," or "metro," based on the residential distribution of constituents), congregational community traits, and congregational action. Taking these factors into account, we are able to array our fifteen congregations along a continuum that measures their impact from weak to moderate to strong.

The five chapters of Part II are organized according to congregational spatial type, with three neighborhood congregations featured in chapter 3, nine area congregations in chapters 4 through 6, and three metro congregations in chapter 7. Each case study includes an overview of the congregation's urban context and descriptions of its identity, traits, and actions, thus illustrating the variety of ways in which congregational community is created in the new metropolis. The chapters of Part II also assess each congregation's urban impact using the weak-moderate-strong continuum.

All three neighborhood congregations in chapter 3 are located in the city of Chicago. St. Nicholas of Tolentine Catholic Church, situated in a contested Southwest Side neighborhood, invokes its history as a "cosmopolitan" parish in efforts to serve the diversifying population around it. St. Nick's has also participated in religious and secular organizational networks in order to effect change in both its neighborhood and the greater Southwest Side. St. Jerome Catholic Church is located in the diverse but stable community area of Rogers Park on the city's North Side. This stability came at the price of heavy white Catholic out-migration that resulted in the loss of St. Jerome's parochial elementary school. Subsequently, the Chicago Archdiocese created a multi-campus Catholic academy in a contested process of pan-parochial identity construction. St. Jerome's response to the challenges of neighborhood change was to participate in a larger geographic strategy of education and membership. Chapter 3 also discusses the efforts of First Christian Church to create a multiracial/ethnic neighborhood congregation on the diversifying Southwest Side. The neighborhood congregations in this chapter have maintained place-based communities and exerted moderate to strong urban influence on their restructured locations.

Chapter 4 examines Muslim area congregations in both city and suburban locations. Muslim Community Center (MCC) and its suburban facility, Muslim Education Center, helped to diversify two major transit and development corridors on the north and northwest sides of metropolitan Chicago. MCC's case is particularly intriguing in that its early dream of creating a Muslim neighborhood in the city was not realized, yet its dual site operation now serves a congregational community living across a much wider geographic expanse. Mosque Foundation similarly helped to diversify a major transit and development corridor on the southwest side of metropolitan Chicago, its single site facility serving as a magnet attracting Arab Muslim settlement. The area congregations in this chapter rise to the stronger end of the urban impact continuum. Chapter 4 also discusses the particularities of Islamic beliefs and practices that favor the creation of area mosques.

Chapter 5 brings together three very different area congregations in very different locations in the city of Chicago. New Covenant Missionary Baptist Church is situated in the middle of Chicago's predominantly black South Side, a racially and culturally bounded area under great stress from the restructuring economy. Fourth Presbyterian Church stands on the famous Magnificent Mile of North Michigan Avenue, "the most prestigious address in the city" (Stamper 2005), but also within blocks of the now-demolished Cabrini-Green Homes public housing project, perhaps the most (in)famous symbol of black urban plight in the country. Much as these two area congregations differ, they share a common desire to create communities of resistance to the most deleterious aspects of the new metropolis. Congregation Ezra-Habonim, an area congregation founded by Holocaust survivors, is located in a Jewish enclave within the diverse West Ridge community area of Chicago. Ezra-Habonim contributed to Chicago's racialized history when its precursor body relocated from its racially changing neighborhood to then-all-white West Ridge. But West Ridge's Jewish enclave emerged for religious as much as racial reasons, namely, the need for a residential and institutional infrastructure that can support strict adherence to Jewish law. The area congregations in this chapter fall along the entire urban impact continuum from weak to strong.

Chapter 6 discusses area congregations in one of the metropolitan region's most attractive locations, the west suburban boom town of Naperville. We describe how these cases offer place-dependent congregational communities in an increasingly transient urban era and also explain why they have relatively little impact on their urban context, Congregation Beth Shalom (a nonaffiliated synagogue) exerting slightly more influence than either Calvary Church (a Pentecostal megachurch) or Wheatland Salem United Methodist Church (an evangelical mainline congregation). Chapter 6 also discusses selected Catholic parishes in order to explore the roles played by religious identity, choice, and mobility in the creation of congregational communities in places like Naperville.

Chapter 7 considers variations on the metropolitan or metro congregation type. One variation is represented by immigrant congregations that create ethno-religious enclaves near the expressway interchanges of the new American metropolis, such as The Hindu Temple of Greater Chicago located in southwest suburban Lemont. Our discussion of this congregation leads into an excursus on entities near expressway interchanges, including shopping malls, megachurches, and megatemples. Chapter 7 also discusses The Moody Church and New Life Community Church, describing their congregational communities and explaining why they contribute more to urban change than The Hindu Temple.

Part III synthesizes the theoretical and conceptual framework from Part I with our findings from the case studies of Part II. Chapter 8 examines the need for urban community and the kind of community offered by congregations in the new urban era. The chapter also discusses the continuum of congregational urban impact based on variables of spatial type, traits, and action, and makes a reasonable case for why urban scholars and other observers should pay more attention to religion's role in the new metropolis. An afterword addresses the issue of representativeness: How much can we generalize from our research? How representative is the new Chicago and its congregations? Drawing upon evidence from Los Angeles, New York, and Boston, we argue that the new urban experience is sufficiently similar across American metropolises despite local variations. We argue further that our Chicago congregational cases are generalizable to the extent that they reveal certain processes, phenomena, mechanisms, tendencies, types, relationships, dynamics, or practices found in congregations of the new urban era. Finally, we describe our research methods in a set of appendices.

Stating—Not Overstating—Our Case

As noted, we make the case that religion has played a role in the ensemble of forces creating the new American metropolis and that congregations shape their urban contexts as well as being shaped by them. In our desire to compensate for the analytical myopia in urban studies, we will not overstate our case for religion's role. Congregational impact is never nil by virtue of the very existence of congregations on the landscape, but neither is congregational impact always strong. Previews of two of our congregational case studies make the point.

The pastor of Wheatland Salem United Methodist Church (chapter 6) once made an offhand remark that revealed an intuitive grasp of his congregation's role in the recent reconfiguration of the suburbanscape. By 1980, his old farming community church had been so decimated by out-migration that it was scheduled to close, but over the next decade it burst at the seams with members newly arrived to the area. Rather than expand its physical plant, the congregation decided to build a multimillion dollar facility about a mile away.

The pastor saw the move as the faithful thing to do. The old farm church, he remarked to us, would stick out like "a retrograde sore thumb" among the impending self-serve gas stations, commercial strips, and residential subdivisions. The church could have closed but instead adapted to the new environment, both recreating itself and contributing to the recreation of its social-geographic area.

Mosque Foundation (chapter 4) has also contributed to the reconfiguration of Chicago's suburbanscape. The first Arab mosque in the region (est. 1954), Mosque Foundation relocated from the city of Chicago to a newly built facility in southwest suburban Bridgeview in 1982. The principal of one of Mosque Foundation's Islamic schools once made a remark that revealed his intuitive grasp of this congregation's role in the recent reconfiguration of the setting: "The area surrounding the mosque has become a core, a center for south-west suburban Arabs" (McKinney 2001). The decision to relocate largely had to do with land prices and geographic proximity, but it set in motion the dramatic diversification of the area over the next decades.

Wheatland Salem Church and Mosque Foundation both contributed to the ensemble of forces creating their new (sub)urban contexts. Wheatland Salem's role was adaptive, whereas Mosque Foundation's was agentive. Thus, Wheatland Salem falls on the weak end of our urban impact continuum, Mosque Foundation on the strong end. The difference can be summarized in this way: had Wheatland Salem closed in the 1980s, suburban Naperville would look the same today; had Mosque Foundation not relocated in the 1980s, southwest suburban Chicago would look very different today.

Such congregational stories provide the analytical grist for this book. Some are more or less dramatic, some congregations persist against strong odds, others make surprisingly self-defeating decisions—the variations are numerous and interesting, but the key questions remain: How does the new American metropolis impact its congregations? How do congregations participate in the ensemble of forces creating the new American metropolis?

PART I

Theoretical and Conceptual Framework

I

Adding Religion to Chicago's Story

FROM A FORBIDDING marshland that indigenous peoples refused to set-tle, the old Chicago became an industrial powerhouse less than a century after its incorporation in 1837. The new Chicago is a global metropolis that retains its down-to-earth Midwestern character and a reputation as "the city that works," more of a hybrid of modernity and late modernity than New York or Los Angeles, though it shares the strains of urban restruc-turing with its sister cities on the coasts.

Driving along Chicago's expressways today, one can easily spot the steeples, spires, and domes of its myriad congregations. Some abut the overpasses and ramps oddly close, bringing traffic noise and exhaust fumes right up to the stained glass windows. To Mark Girouard's (1985, 319) historical eye, Chicago's flat landscape with frequently spaced reli-gious peaks has a "curiously medieval effect," but Chicago's religionscape is thoroughly contemporary, increasingly diverse, and globalized. From the beginning, religion has been a part of Chicago's story, a part that deserves telling particularly as it intersects with political, socioeconomic, and racial/ethnic urban structures.

Early Settlement and Industrial Development, 1600s to 1930s

The first European incursion into the region that came to be called Chicago included a religious presence in the person of the French Jesuit mis-sionary Jacques Marquette, who accompanied trader Louis Jolliet on his inland exploration of the continent in 1673. Jean Baptiste Point DuSable, son of a French frontiersman and a former African slave, built his fur trading cabin by the mid-1780s, while Fort Dearborn was established in 1803 nearby at the confluence of the Chicago River with Lake Michigan, the corner of today's Michigan Avenue and Wacker Drive. Presbyterians, Catholics, Methodists, and Baptists were the first to organize local congregations. By the 1850s, they were joined by Episcopalians, Unitarians, Lutherans, Jews, and others (Richesin 1988, 153).

The first churches and the first synagogue in the city were erected in today's central business district (CBD) or the Loop (L. W. Livezey and Bouman 2004, 691). Such siting was typical of nineteenth-century American cities, marking the active role of religion in the commercial and public life of young Chicago. Today, only First United Methodist Church at the Chicago Temple—on West Washington Street and across from the city/county building—remains on its original site, all the others having receded to residential places beyond the Loop. Historians contend that this geographic and civic shift resulted from cultural, political, and ideological pressures, a combination of the retreat of religious authority and efforts by the political and economic elite to separate public and private life (D. Bluestone 1991, 79). Even so, we argue that religion has continued to influence the urban context, if not as obviously as it once did via its presence in the Loop.

Metropolitan Chicago developed in the skeletal pattern characteristic of many American cities, with five major transit and development corridors radiating outward from the Loop, which took its name from the ring of elevated public transit tracks completed in 1897 (Danzer 2004). The five corridors have featured intense and varied land use as well as multiple types of transportation, from early pathways, roadways, canals, and rail lines to later expressways and public rapid transit routes. These "high-accessibility corridors are an important structuring element in the overall economic and social vitality of the Chicago region" ("Alternatives Analysis" 1982, I-1, II-3). Figures 1.1 and 1.2 show the urban dimensions of metropolitan Chicago and the city of Chicago mentioned in this chapter. Note the broad outlines of the five corridors comprising the skeletal structure of metropolitan Chicago in Figure 1.1.

In the early 1800s, water transportation seemed the way of the future given Chicago's strategic location between the Great Lakes and the Mississippi River. Following the southwest corridor, the Illinois and Michigan Canal connected the Chicago River to the Illinois River, which then flowed into the Mississippi. But rail lines soon eclipsed the canals, the first laid to the west by the Galena and Chicago Union Railroad in

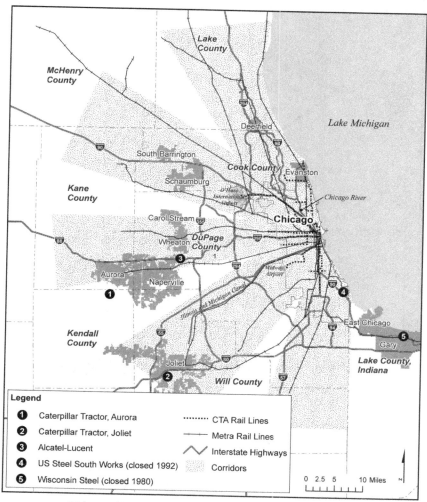

FIGURE I.I. Urban Dimensions of Metropolitan Chicago. Map by David J. Treering and Melissa Gesbeck Howell, Loyola University Chicago.

1848, the same year the I&M Canal was completed. By the 1860s, multiple rail lines served the Chicago region, including one to Naperville in western DuPage County, creating the structural skeleton for rapid economic expansion and positioning Chicago to become an industrial giant by the end of the nineteenth century (Hudson 2004; Grant 2004). As Henry Binford (2004, 550) explains, "Although Chicago also began its life as a water-oriented town, the process of fitting the city around a railroad skeleton began almost immediately and with few obstacles, either man-made

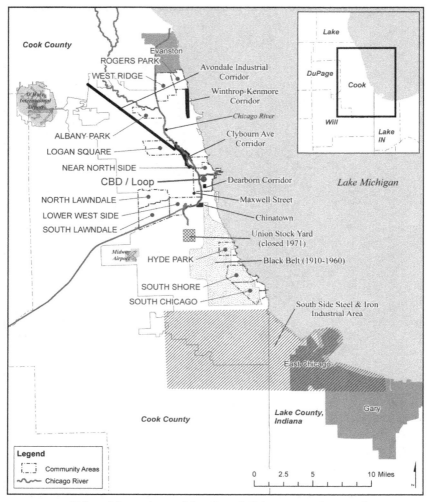

FIGURE I.2. Urban Dimensions of the City of Chicago. Map by David J. Treering and Melissa Gesbeck Howell, Loyola University Chicago.

or natural. In this sense, the city was 'born modern'—and also born to sprawl." The corridor skeleton supported railroad commuter suburbs, recreational towns, industrial suburbs, and satellite industrial cities on the urban fringes. It also brought the agricultural hinterlands into the metropolitan economic orbit, including numerous farm communities, churches, and schools established by German immigrants (Cronon 1991; Keating 2004; Keating and Conzen 2004). By the end of the nineteenth century, "A centripetal metropolitan world pulsating on a daily basis had begun to emerge" (M. Conzen 2004, 341).

Chicago's spectacular urban development, as well as attendant economic and social strains, was marked by two world's fairs, the World's Columbian Exposition in 1893 and the Century of Progress Exposition in 1933–1934. The first was held between the 1886 Haymarket Square bombing and the 1894 Pullman Strike, iconic expressions of the Industrial Revolution's class divide, while the second fair was held in the midst of the Great Depression. Both also exposed the structural racism, particularly against blacks, that marked the period between Reconstruction and the civil rights movement (Rydell 2004a; 2004b).

Chicago's early industrial configuration of a manufacturing, commerce, and management core surrounded by concentric residential zones provided approximate geographic markers of class boundaries. Segregation by race/ethnicity was added with the establishment of the Jewish ghetto around Maxwell Street followed by the Black Belt south of the central business district (Wirth 1928; Drake and Cayton 1945; Spear 1967). While the Jewish population became increasingly assimilated and mobile, the black population grew exponentially as a result of the Great Migration that began during World War I (Grossman 2004) but continued to be restricted to the areas of the South and West Sides of Chicago proper, which Arnold Hirsch (1983) called the Second Ghetto.

The Black Belt became the home of southern blacks seeking better economic fortunes in industrial Chicago. The Great Migration brought blacks from southern states who established a variety of Protestant congregations, and found grudging acceptance in a few Catholic parishes. Southern blacks were used as strikebreakers by the packinghouse industry during the especially harsh strikes of 1904 and 1921, thus establishing a conflictual relationship with immigrant European groups almost from the beginning of their association. Nonetheless, black migration and employment expanded rapidly so that by 1920, Chicago's black population numbered more than one hundred thousand. By 1928, almost 30 percent of the employees in slaughtering and meatpacking were black. By that same year, black churches numbered around three hundred, accounting for about 20 percent of all Chicago churches despite being largely restricted to an area five miles long and four blocks wide (L. W. Livezey and Bouman 2004, 693; Barrett 1987, 39, 48). Today there are more than 1,600 predominantly black houses of worship in Cook County, more than one-third of the total number (Zelinsky and Matthews 2011, 125).

Jews fleeing pogroms in Russia and Poland around the turn of the twentieth century created a new Chicago Jewish population internally divided by class and religious practice. The earlier German Jewish cohort was mostly Reform (and later also Conservative), hailed from urban contexts in Europe, and started businesses in Chicago, whereas the later Jewish immigrants came from predominantly rural areas and small towns in Eastern Europe, had fewer skills, and practiced the more traditional Orthodox Judaism (Cutler 1996). East European Jews developed the Maxwell Street ghetto, which contained more than forty-five synagogues at its height around 1910 (L. W. Livezey and Bouman 2004, 693). Chicago's German Jews established an institutional infrastructure to facilitate the Americanization of the newcomers that included the Jewish Training School (1890), the Maxwell Street Settlement House (1893), the Chicago Hebrew Institute (1903), the Sinai Temple's recreation center (1912), and Michael Reese (1881) and Mount Sinai (1918) hospitals (Gems 2004). Between the two World Wars, most Jewish residents, accompanied by their synagogues, moved five miles to the west into the North Lawndale community area, which by the 1930s included sixty synagogues (fifty-eight of them Orthodox) and a thick infrastructure of Jewish community and social service organizations (Cutler 2004, 437).

The first Asian residents of Chicago, the Chinese, migrated from the US West in the 1870s. A significant number established a so-called Chinatown district along the north side of the central business district, but the others dispersed across the city, fearing hostility against enclavism. Around 1910, Chinatown relocated some twenty blocks south to its present location, which became a center of Chinese business and tourism and has steadily expanded over the decades (Kiang 2004; Steffes 2004).

Significant numbers of Mexicans began arriving in Chicago around 1915. The first Mexican neighborhood emerged near the steelyards in the South Chicago community area. Residential pockets also formed near the stockyards and other industrial sectors of the city, and in satellite industrial cities like Aurora to the west and East Chicago and Gary in Indiana. In addition, Mexican migrant agricultural laborers worked throughout the metropolitan region (Arredondo and Vaillant 2004; Cutler 2006, 177).

At the time of the Great Chicago Fire of 1871, congregations had already been established throughout the region, in outlying farming communities and trading centers as well as in city neighborhoods. Following the Fire, the trend of locating congregations in residential neighborhoods outside of the Loop accelerated rapidly (D. Bluestone 1991, 63). New congregations kept pace with the titanic growth of the population, which increased from three hundred thousand in 1870 (the fifth largest city in the United

States), to more than one million in 1890 (marking it as America's Second City after New York), to more than three million in 1930. The height of classical American immigration occurred between 1880 and the restrictive immigration act of 1924, bringing large numbers of European immigrants to the emerging Chicago metropolis. Immigrant Catholics and Jews and southern blacks of the Great Migration largely provided the infrastructure of cheap labor and businesses for the expanding industrial economy, although the three groups lived in distinct enclaves of the city, with the immigrants subdivided by nationality and religious identity.

Catholic immigrants quickly separated into national parishes, which were permitted by Roman Catholic canon law until 1918 but continued long afterward despite the Americanization efforts of Chicago's George Cardinal Mundelein. Worshipping in one's own language was as crucial to the adjustment process in the classical period of American immigration as it is today. The "huddled masses" of Catholic laborers who built and filled the huge parish churches in countless neighborhoods, along with the priests and bishops who laid out the parish grid of the city, established Chicago as a major Catholic center for the nation. For nearly a century, parish names would serve as the principal and most meaningful designations of place for Catholic Chicagoans. Germans settled along the north branch of the Chicago River and the Irish west and south of the central business district. Poles lived in the southeast near the steel mills, in the southwest near the stockyards, and in the northwest along the Avondale industrial corridor, creating the largest Polish community outside of Warsaw. As these groups rose to better paying jobs, they moved further outward from their original settlement, leaving newer immigrants from southern Europe and southern American blacks to occupy the aging and often shabby quarters (L. W. Livezey and Bouman 2004, 693–94; Girouard 1985, 318). Many Catholic workers participated in labor rights advocacy during these decades, although the Church hierarchy remained mostly uninvolved until Bishop Bernard Sheil threw his support behind the Congress of Industrial Organizations and the packinghouse workers in the 1930s (Rosswurm 2004, 719).

Protestants dominated Chicago business and politics and accounted for the largest number of the region's congregations at the close of the nineteenth century. The self-conscious efforts of white Protestants to develop a coherent vision of moral leadership for Chicago bore different kinds of urban fruit in this period. Like their Catholic and Jewish counterparts, Episcopalians, Presbyterians, Methodists, Lutherans, and the

Swedish Evangelical Covenant Church established hospitals. Theological conservatives took the lead in tending to both the social and the spiritual welfare of the urban poor through the work of the YMCA (1858) and YWCA (1876), Pacific Garden Mission (1877), the Salvation Army (1885), and the precursor body of The Moody Bible Institute called Bible Work of Chicago (1873) (V. Brereton 2004). Theological liberals applied the Social Gospel through initiatives like the Women's Christian Temperance Union (established in Ohio in 1874 but eventually headquartered in the Chicago suburb of Evanston) and the Church Federation of Chicago (1907), the latter seeking "to be for the churches what the Association of Commerce is to the business interests of the city" (Richesin 1988, 154). The Church Federation provided controversial but viable leadership between 1920 and 1960, taking liberal positions on race relations, international peace, and social welfare activism, and supporting local Christian evangelism. The leftward social movements of the 1960s and 1970s, increasingly supported by liberal mainline Protestant churches, deprived the Federation of its conservative Church support and it ceased operations in the 1980s.

Industrial jobs in Chicago increased by more than 50 percent between 1929 and 1946, but these were concentrated in large-scale, relatively inflexible firms located mostly in the South Side industrial districts. The advent of air transportation and the opening of Midway Airport (originally named Chicago Municipal Airport) in 1927 stimulated the local economy. Between 1932 and the ascendancy of O'Hare Airport in the 1960s, Midway was the world's busiest airport (Vaillant 2004). The Great Depression slashed Chicago's industrial jobs by one-fourth before World War II infused new capital into the economy. With the notable exception of Julius Rosenthal, Chicago's industrialists and financiers were calloused to the plight of their hard-pressed workers, who, before the New Deal programs reached the city, were chiefly dependent on their own thinly resourced, race- and ethnicity-specific congregations and group networks (Abu-Lughod 1999, 213–14).

From Industrial to Postindustrial Metropolis, World War II to the Present

The overcrowded Black Belt could not sustain the increasing numbers of southern blacks who found work in Chicago during World War II. By the early 1960s, slum clearance in a decrepit Italian immigrant district in the Near North Side community area evolved into the iconic and virtually all-black Cabrini-Green public housing complex. When racially restricted covenants were successfully challenged in the US Supreme Court in the late 1940s and the federally funded Chicago Public Housing Association began to construct new (though still segregated) housing outside the Black Belt, the suburbanization of white residents increased dramatically. Not to be overlooked was the impact of Federal Housing Administration policies that refused low-interest loans to black homebuyers, creating spatial disparities still evident today. The white population of the city of Chicago had hovered in the ninetieth percentile in every decennial census between 1840 and 1940, but by the 1980 census it had dropped precipitously to 50 percent.

Chicago, both the city proper and the metropolitan region, is today stratified and fragmented in ways that extend and complicate its segregated past. For instance, while Chinese and Mexican populations are still concentrated in Chinatown and the Lower West Side, respectively, they are also widely dispersed throughout the metropolitan region. South Asians, Koreans, Thais, and other Asians live in many parts of the city and the suburbs, with concentrations of the less-well-off in certain Chicago neighborhoods. Even though the geographic segregation and socioeconomic inequality of blacks remain the most intractable aspects of Chicago's stratified structure, given the many other diverse groups and their varying spatial configurations, the meaning of race/ethnicity in Chicago today is oversimplified if framed as a matter of black and white.

Much has changed since the 1960s as a result of the civil rights movement and postindustrial economic restructuring. Resegregated residential patterns now characterize the region as a whole and reflect the multipolarity of the metropolis. Some minorities, especially blacks, are no longer confined to inner-city areas, but many are newly segregated throughout the region. These concentrations are not randomly distributed but they are peripheral to the new economic nodes of the multipolar metropolis. Even so, an analysis of segregation trends in the years 1980–2009 (Hall et al. 2010) found that "residential segregation of all racial groups in Chicago (including blacks) declined" and that "blacks in the Chicago area today live in neighborhoods that have, on average, 4 percentage points fewer blacks than at the start of the decade (from 72 percent to 68 percent)" (Hall 2010). Additionally, as in most metropolises today, the meaning of "minority" is increasingly complex as the firms of the new global economy draw employees from around the world. Because they attract both elites to serve in technical and managerial roles and unskilled workers (many of them undocumented) to serve in poorly paid supportive roles, the racially and ethnically diverse immigrant population adds to the regional economic bipolarization. Thus a new class structure is interwoven with the historic structure of race and ethnicity, creating a social order that is possibly as rigid and constraining as the concentric zones and ghettos of a century ago. In our quest for an image of the new Chicago that is more nuanced than that of the racially segregated city, we have borrowed concepts from the Los Angeles School of urbanism, such as "fractal city" and "acute fragmentation" (chapter 2).

As Robert Bruegmann (1993, 159–61) and Michael Ebner (2004) note, the decentering of metropolitan Chicago, that is, the deconcentration of population and economic wealth from the urban center to the suburbs and periphery, can be traced back to a time long before World War II, but these movements accelerated after World War II due to a combination of factors. Federal mortgage loans to returning military personnel encouraged new home construction and abetted the desire for a better house in a better—and whiter—suburban neighborhood. The Interstate Highway Act of 1956 provided federal dollars to carry forward the plans of the Illinois State Toll Highway Commission for a regional expressway system, thus establishing a new transportation infrastructure that "reworked the logic of growth" of metropolitan Chicago: "Places that had remained rural, or very small, were now drawn closely into the metropolitan web and grew in new ways" (Keating 2004, 530). This included areas along the Edens Expressway/Interstate 94 (1951) and the Kennedy Expressway/Interstate 90 (1960) to the north and northwest, the Eisenhower Expressway/ Interstate 290 (1955–1960) and the East-West Tollway/Interstate 88 (1958) to the west, the Tri-State Tollway/Interstate 294 (1958) as a beltway around the city of Chicago, and the Stevenson Expressway/Interstate 55 (1964) to the southwest (McClendon 2004). Enhanced automobility benefitted the relatively well-off, especially outside the city of Chicago, as businesses followed the expressways, often locating where they intersect (Bruegmann 1993, 159). Forty-two suburban malls were built in the 1950s and the suburban share of metropolitan-wide retail sales rose from approximately 30 percent in 1949 to approximately 60 percent in 1972. The relatively less-well-off suffered further economic losses: from 1960 to 1989, the median family income gap between the metropolitan region's richest and poorest communities nearly doubled. The difficulty of many impoverished people to travel to jobs in outlying areas is indicative of a growing "spatial mismatch" that continues into the twenty-first century (Ebner 2004).

Since the liberalization of immigration laws beginning in 1965, non-European immigrant groups have not only diversified metropolitan Chicago's racial/ethnic profile but its religious landscape as well. These newest immigrants differ from their predecessors not only by religion and culture but also by the postindustrial economy that pulls them here. Many come, not with the hope that their descendants might become professionals and join the middle class, but because many of them are middle-class professionals already and can thus settle immediately in the suburbs and establish the mosques, temples, and other new religious centers that now share the metropolitan religionscape with the earlier churches and synagogues. The three largest "new" religious groups—Muslims, Buddhists, and Hindus—have perpetuated the bimodal economic and dispersed residential patterns of other religious groups in the new Chicago. (Of course, these religions are not completely "new" to Chicago; the significant increase in their adherents since the 1960s, largely through immigration, is new.) As we (Numrich 2000b, 262) wrote previously, "Ethnic residential enclavism, characteristic of the classical period of American immigration, has given way to a socioeconomically determined, bimodal geography, as poorer, less assimilated, and less successful immigrants cluster in depressed and transitional metropolitan areas, while better-off, more assimilated, and more successful immigrants gravitate to attractive city locations or disperse throughout [suburbia and] exurbia." Socioeconomic status, which includes variables of ethnic and religious identity, has become the most salient factor in today's immigrant religious geography (265). Hence we see, for instance, a new kind of ethnic enclavism as immigrants living in dispersed residential locations throughout metropolitan Chicago commute to religious sites near expressway interchanges.

Not surprisingly, recent congregational growth for the "old" religions has occurred primarily in Chicago's suburbs. Jews and Protestants led the march out of the inner city, often taking their synagogues and churches along. The once tightly knit Jewish community around Maxwell Street yielded in a wholesale manner to the need for additional housing for blacks who had been prevented from moving outside the black belt by restrictive real estate covenants. North Lawndale became the new heart of the Jewish community, though not for long. In 1950 87,000 whites lived in North Lawndale, where forty-eight synagogues were active. By 1960, the change was dramatic: only eleven thousand whites remained, one hundred thousand blacks had moved in, and all the synagogues had closed (McGreevy 1996, 102). Jews moved into other community areas of the city, especially Rogers Park, West Ridge, Albany Park, and Logan Square to the north, and Hyde Park and South Shore to the south. But most eventually left the city: whereas 95 percent of the region's Jews lived in the city of Chicago in 1950, 70 percent lived in the suburbs by the 1990s, most having followed the expressways into the north and northwest suburbs (Cutler 2004, 437). The contiguous North Side community areas of Rogers Park and West Ridge currently form the most concentrated Jewish enclave, with an infrastructure of religious and ethnic institutions that support Jewish needs throughout metropolitan Chicago.

The geographic redistribution of Protestants during the twentieth century was nearly as remarkable as that of Jews. White mainline Protestants, being disproportionately represented in management and higher-paying jobs and least attached by theology and tradition to particular places, were the first to move in large numbers to the suburbs. In 1923 nearly two-thirds (65 of 101) of all Presbyterian churches in the region, for instance, were located within the city limits of Chicago; in 2002 only fifteen remained (12 percent of 123 total churches) (L. W. Livezey and Bouman 2004, 692). Southern black Methodists, Baptists, and Pentecostals often purchased the church buildings abandoned by their white Protestant predecessors. Protestant Chicago today is substantially divided along racial/ethnic lines that coincide with city/suburban boundaries, one of several divisions that have "worked to inhibit Protestant influence" in the new metropolis (Marty 2004, 654). Since the clash over modernism in the 1920s, the theological division between conservatives and liberals has widened, symbolized by the two premier Protestant periodicals in the country. The liberal and ecumenically minded *Christian Century* is located in downtown Chicago and the evangelical *Christianity Today* is headquartered in west suburban Carol Stream along with several other evangelical organizations, next door to Wheaton, "the evangelical Vatican" (Marty 2004, 690). The Chicago region also has the distinction of producing one of the archetypal megachurches, Willow Creek Community Church in South Barrington (established 1975), which attracts members and spiritual seekers from across the metropolis. As analysts of religious restructuring point out, Protestant action in the new metropolis is exerted at the congregational level, which was less likely during the industrial era.

Unlike North Lawndale, which was emptying out its white residents, adjacent South Lawndale, dominated by Catholic Poles, Bohemians, and Italians, remained more than 90 percent white through the 1960 census. However, it succumbed to white flight by the 1990 census, which counted only 27 percent white residents (McGreevy 1996, 102; Reed 2004). Catholics were religiously, if not economically, less mobile because the archdiocese owned the church properties (Kantowicz 1983). Moreover, the Catholic parish was the geographic expression of a communal religious identity, knitted together by a church and its parochial school, preferred home ownership within parish boundaries, and the relatively autocratic leadership of priests and nuns (McGreevy 1996). Catholics were on the whole less financially secure than their Protestant and Jewish counter-parts and remained the bedrock of the blue-collar workforce until many in a new generation of Catholics attended college in the 1960s and 1970s. These newly professionalized Catholics increasingly joined Protestants and Jews in suburban subdivisions, often leaving their elderly parents in the "old neighborhood" in the city. Many of the earlier Mexican immi-grants had settled alongside European Catholics near industrial jobs. More recent Hispanic immigrants from a variety of Latin American countries have moved into the old neighborhoods in a southwesterly and northwesterly pattern, largely filling the Catholic churches left behind by the previous white ethnics. The South Lawndale community area, for instance, was 83 percent Hispanic according to the 2000 census, with a significant Mexican enclave in its Little Village neighborhood.

Chicago's religions have long formed and maintained communities highly segregated and structured by socioeconomic inequities. Today, we argue, they extend and complexify this pattern, as well as resist and reme-diate it. This book also considers examples of congregations that include and exclude people based on race/ethnicity and class, that articulate the meaning of race/ethnicity so as to affirm or to critique the new stratifica-tion of the Chicago metropolitan region, and that endorse or challenge the separations and hierarchies of new urban structures. We further argue that racial/ethnic separation is a more explicit concern of congregations than is socioeconomic inequality, but this does not necessarily mean that congregations are more effective in ameliorating racial/ethnic discrimi-natory urban structures.

The immediate post–World War II years brought temporary prosperity for wage earners, but as early as 1948 there were signs of decline in "the great Fordist powerhouse of the Midwest" as the number of industrial firms and workers in Chicago hit its peak in 1947 and the region as a whole declined sharply after 1967 (Abu-Lughod 1999, 219, 323). In the meatpacking sector, for many years an iconic Chicago economic engine—recall Upton Sinclair's novel *The Jungle* and Carl Sandburg's opening line in the poem "Chicago," "HOG Butcher for the World"—most of the packinghouses had closed by 1964, while the Union Stock Yard ceased operations in 1971. The steelworks soon followed suit, Wisconsin Steel going out in 1980, the US Steel South Works facility in 1992. The city of Chicago lost a quarter of a million manufacturing jobs between 1967 and 1982, nearly half of its total (Wievel 1988, 4), while the situation became increasingly contentious for the remaining blue-collar workers. In the mid-1990s, for instance, Caterpillar Tractor, one of the region's largest industrial employers with plants in the satellite cities of Aurora and Joliet, entered into a bitter labor dispute with its United Auto Workers employees, who had worked without a contract for several years under "terms stipulating less overtime, smaller raises, limits on union activity and rules of etiquette" ("Cat to Put More . . ."). Such developments hastened the demise of "big labor" in the postindustrial American economy.

The global shifts in labor, resources, production, and markets that undercut the mass production base of America's industrial urban centers have been felt in Chicago, though not as severely as in other rust belt metropolises. Heavy industry, which once united Chicago with its Midwestern hinterland (Cronon 1991), is now mostly gone, but as the largest intermodal transportation center in the United States, Chicago remains essential to the Midwest's productivity and competitiveness in agriculture, mining, manufacturing, and shipping. Moreover, as Michael Conzen (2004, 344) observes, "Chicago emerged tolerably well to compete in a new environment of diversified, globally positioned, high-tech industries, as well as to develop its financial and corporate services institutions." In metropolitan Chicago, as in other American metropolises, corporate professionals have replaced factory workers as the backbone of a viable regional economy. Yet downsizing and consolidation have become routine, bringing occupational anxiety, long the bane of the factory floor, into corporate hallways. AT&T, for example, a precursor of Alcatel-Lucent and the largest employer in west suburban DuPage County, eliminated nearly 125,000 jobs nationwide in the decade prior to its 1996 dismissal of forty thousand more (S. Franklin 1996). Both the city of Chicago and the state of Illinois suffer from unresolved debt burdens (especially pensions) and the city has been criticized for a variety of administrative inefficiencies that limit the growth of businesses (Renn 2014). At this writing, a global recession has had a chilling effect on wage and salary earners alike across the metropolis.

Still, all things considered, metropolitan Chicago is adapting to the requirements of the new urban era while retaining and benefiting from its characteristics as a modern industrial city. In many ways, Chicago is a hybrid of the industrial and the postindustrial, the early modern and the late modern while other places may better exemplify the "informational city" (Castells 1989). For a milieu of innovation, one might look to the Silicon Valley; for purveyors of advanced business services, to New York and Los Angeles; for cultural industries, to New York, Los Angeles, Boston, and Las Vegas. To all of these, Chicago may be a "Second City" in some ways, but it is competitive and still growing. In a few subsectors, such as futures markets and architecture, it has been both highly innovative and dominant.

Perhaps more important, Chicago's "informational" trajectory did not start from scratch. Chicago is (re)making itself competitively as a producer and as an attractive place to live by building out incrementally—though often conflictually—from the quintessentially modern industrial city that it was until very recently. It is still in the process of change. Thus it exemplifies the benefits, growth, dislocations, and contradictions that many American metropolises, having taken their present form as modern industrial cities in the nineteenth century, will experience as they attempt to prosper in the information age. Moreover, the restructuring that facilitated Chicago's participation in the information-based economy has been enabled in large measure by a political machine characteristic of the older industrial cities. In this respect, Chicago is far more representative of American urban life than "purer" information-age metropolises like Austin and Minneapolis that never based their livelihood mainly in manufacturing and shipping and therefore do not have to transcend the physical, political, and social infrastructures associated with the industrial era. By contrast, Chicago had to fight it out, with older, neighborhood-based and out-lying manufacturing interests competing against new information-based interests for public funds and political favors. Indeed, critics have pointed out that a regional rather than parochial perspective is needed to take on the challenges of a restructured economy (Rusk 1999; Orfield 2002; Moberg 2014).

The new Chicago is not only a city but also a metropolis, and it is the metropolitan region that largely competes in the global information-based economy and participates in the transnational flow of people and ideas. The region is defined in various ways: as the Chicago-Naperville-Joliet, IL-IN-WI Metropolitan Statistical Area by the federal Office of Management and Budget; as the Chicago Bioregion by environmentalists; as the seven-county Chicago region by the Chicago Metropolitan Agency for Planning; as Chicagoland by advertisers. As a restructuring metropolis, it sprawls along the shore of Lake Michigan from the southeast corner of Wisconsin through the city of Chicago to the northwest corner of Indiana. It radiates outward from the Loop along the skeleton of rail lines and expressways, most of the interstitial farmland having given way to residential, commercial, and corporate development. It contains multiple centers of economic and cultural power that function as nodes in global networks. Alongside this global networking, Chicago's sub-regional centers are deeply entwined in mutual symbiotic relationships and with concentrations of information-age firms in the city of Chicago proper. The precursor of Alcatel-Lucent did not build its multi-campus facility in the city of Chicago, but neither did it locate at a randomly selected site in rural Illinois. Rather, it chose far west suburban Naperville because of its strategic location in the region, close to Chicago yet easily accessible to the rest of the nation and the world. The same can said of Motorola in Schaumburg, Abbott Laboratories in "Abbott Park" in Deerfield, and others.

The multipolarity, economic vitality and volatility, and cultural opportunities of the new Chicago encourage a high volume of commuting, in every direction, to and from various centers of employment, consumption, and sociability. A 2004 US Census Bureau report descriptively titled "Commuter Blues" ranked Chicago the second city in the nation (after New York) in time spent commuting to work. Congregations of all religious traditions increasingly position themselves to compete for their constituents' allegiances, assuming they are willing to commute to accommodate their spiritual needs, moral preferences, aesthetic tastes, and various identities (class, cultural, and racial/ethnic). Even the Catholic parishes and Orthodox synagogues that persist as neighborhood congregations cannot avoid the impact of the low-density multipolarity and automobility of the new metropolis. Although their constituents may stay close to home to worship, they and their neighbors often travel outside the neighborhood for other reasons. As a result, both neighborhood-type and more dispersed congregations are often problematically related to the places in which they are located. Congregations are under stress because

their places are being disrupted as the region restructures to accommodate the emerging economic and cultural networks. This problem arises
in one congregation after another in metropolitan Chicago regardless of
their location.

Chicago's multipolarity and commute-everywhere-lifestyle may not be
as extreme as Southern California's, but both reflect an underlying "culture of choice" with national if not global reach. Since the "rights revolu-
tions" of the 1960s and 1970s, mobility in all aspects of life, especially
automobility, has fostered a particular kind of consumerism consistent
with the multipolar structure of the landscapes of goods and services yet
increasingly bewildering to the consumer. "Chicago's world has expanded
exponentially over time, in physical, psychological, symbolic, and practical ways," observes Michael Conzen (2004, 344). "The metropolitan
'neighborhood' of greater Chicago has more people crammed in and
strewn about than ever before; they move about with greater speed and
frequency; there are vastly more things to acquire and aspire to; there is
more choice of what to do and what to be interested in—and greater difficulty in comprehending the complexity of it all." Religion is embedded
in this new urbanscape and acts both to advance and to resist the culture
of choice (cf. Bellah et al. 1985; Hammond 1992).

With its still vibrant central business district, the city of Chicago
proper remains the dominant node in the multipolar region, imposing an order at odds with the theory of the postmodern metropolis (see
chapter 2). The mile-square grids, platted two centuries ago, and the
skeletal transit and development corridors fanning out from the center
tenaciously provide some order amidst even the most "fractal" developments. Other economic corridors continue to command attention in
metropolitan planning circles, some falling within Chicago's city limits,
such as the Winthrop-Kenmore Corridor (Marciniak 1981), the Dearborn
Corridor (R. Miller 1993), the Clybourn Avenue Corridor (Rast 1999),
and the Downtown Corridor along the Chicago River in the Loop (Zotti
1990), others traversing multiple governmental boundaries, like the I-355
Corridor ("I-355 Heritage Corridor") and the I-88 Corridor ("Governor
Announces Opportunity Returns Grant") on the western fringes of the
metropolitan region.

The fragmenting, decentering, and centrifugal qualities that characterize Chicago's participation in the global information economy, the shift
from centralized city to multipolar region, the scattering of racial and
ethnic concentrations, the replacement of place-dependent and ascriptive

communities with voluntary communication networks of likeminded people—all these evidences of late modernity emerged not in a vacuum but in direct tension with the persistently modern city that is Chicago.

Neither did the new Chicago emerge in a religious vacuum. Thus, a full telling of Chicago's story must include attention to the religion factor, as we have done in this chapter. This chapter has also brought Chicago into the new urban era; the next chapter will fill out the portrait of this era, with special attention to community in the new metropolis.

2

Community and Congregations in the New Metropolis

WHAT KINDS OF community do we find in the new urban America? Communities embody both a perduring human desire and a basic social fact. Urban communities persist in the new metropolis even as the challenges to them have escalated. Like other cultural communities, an urban congregation is a collection of people who engage in common activities and share an identity based on beliefs, values, social intimacy, and personal concern and loyalty. Urban congregations are more than merely symbolic or imagined communities—they are situated social facts in a reciprocal relationship with particular urban contexts. Congregations are shaped by, but also help to shape, the new metropolis.

In this chapter we present our understanding of "community" as both a sociological concept and an urban phenomenon that includes congregational forms. We also introduce a spatial typology of urban congregations and a method for measuring congregational impact on the urban environment that will frame our analysis in later chapters.

Community

Community is a multidimensional concept situated within geographic places and interest-based spaces that recognizes the persistent desire to seek mutual aid and social accountability despite perpetual failure to do so fully.

Robert Nisbet (1966, 47) saw community as sociology's most fundamental and far-reaching unit-idea. In theoretical terms, however, C. Wright Mills's (1959) concept of the sociological imagination was more compelling and influential in defining the investigation of social order and social life. The sociological imagination understands private lives in the contexts of history and prevailing social structures. Mills focused on the interaction between individual behavior and large social forces such as economic change, demographic shifts, and political exigencies, not on intermediate structures such as neighborhoods or voluntary associations. The predilection for methodological individualism in sociological research models has also contributed to the tendency to overlook the importance of mediating groups. Even when such groups are examined, the models often focus on individual interconnections, such as in network analysis (B. Wellman 1999), rather than the actions, consequences, and meaning of the group per se.

The conceptualization of community as an intermediary between the individual and large social forces has been problematic. Neither the classical nineteenth-century notion of *Gemeinschaft* nor the American community studies tradition has been sufficiently explanatory of late industrial-era and postindustrial-era forms of relationships. The lack of a singular or unified concept of community originates in part in the tension between a particular and a universal sense of community and poses new difficulties today: the quest for belonging on a global scale while at the same time searching for indigenous roots (Delanty 2010, 7). Moreover, the kinds of communities created in the postindustrial era differ from those formed during the American industrial era, when tight ethnic enclaves often functioned as transplanted Old World villages. The Chicago School of urban sociology (see below) was particularly astute in capturing elements of community building as industrial workers helped to shape their urban surroundings.

Considering the facts of contemporary urban restructuring, it is understandable that scholars have sought new and dynamic ways to conceptualize community. Vered Amit (2002) suggests that community is not comprehensive but contingent; it is partial, changing, and only one of several competing attachments in people's lives. This conforms well with Steven Brint's (2001, 9, emphasis added) contention that community does not require an exclusive "holistic" character or even extremely frequent contact, but only that communal relationships are primarily based on "affect, loyalty, shared values, *or* personal involvement with the lives of others." Thereby, communal relationships retain their emotional quality without being superficial or trivial. Nonetheless, with the move toward voluntary rather than ascribed relationships, many people experience a loss of security as a result. The "ethical community" of the past—sharing such that every member has communal insurance against the inevitable errors and misadventures of individual life—has been replaced by the "aesthetic community" of the present, the latter providing "bonds without consequences" (Bauman 2001, 71–73).

We rightly dismiss sentimentalized notions of *Gemeinschaft* that inform unsophisticated decline-of-community theories, but we must not dismiss all notions of *Gemeinschaft*, since a desire for "community" of some type remains high in the new urban era. In *Ethnic Options*, Mary Waters (1990) argued that ethnic identity stemmed from "a culturally based need for community—community lacking individual cost" (Cerulo 1997, 389). Gerald Suttles (1972, 265–66) suggested that Americans do not desire Tönnies's *Gemeinschaft* as much as Herman Schmalenbach's "communion," a voluntarily chosen social intimacy that is difficult to cultivate in today's communities of limited liability. If their yearning for such communion is not fulfilled in the neighborhood, urban dwellers will seek it elsewhere—Suttles lists student communities, political communities, and business communities. We would add congregational communities.

It is also worth noting the importance of historical context in Tönnies's theorizing about the move away from *Gemeinschaft*. Tönnies rejected a romantic view of the past, arguing that the communal relationships of feudalism were politically dangerous because they led to despotism and tyranny; at the same time, Tönnies criticized modern society for its tendency to construct new forms of domination through the remarkable achievements of a refined rationality (Samples 1988, xx). As John Samples (xxii) summarizes Tönnies, "Community . . . should be founded on duty manifested in an objective law [not custom or habit], which itself was a product of human natural will and rationality," thus rejecting the critique of community as inherently essentialist.

Steven Brint (2001) suggests that an empirical test of the idea of community requires a flexible and disaggregated conceptualization (cf. Calhoun 1980). Adapting Brint, we understand a cultural community most broadly as a collection of people who engage in common activities and share an identity based on beliefs, values, social intimacy, and personal concern and loyalty. This shares much in common with the Chicago School understanding of a social-geographic community (see below) but without the necessary dependence on location. Brint differentiates between geographic and elective bases of social ties, in other words between place-dependent and voluntary associations. A congregation can function as a community of place or a dispersed community based on beliefs or other kinds of shared identity, or it can combine functions.

In recognizing the complexity of human relations, Brint allows that communities possess a dimension of self-interest, although it is not their primary motivation. In this conceptualization, *Gemeinschaft* communities are not necessarily cohesive and supportive, a mistaken notion of some in the American community studies tradition that limits the generalizability of their otherwise rich and informative case studies and opens them up to criticism about nostalgia and sentimentalism (see Day 2006, 34, 47).

Our alternative is to conceive of community relationships as containing variable properties that can be analyzed for their impact on attitudes and behaviors within a group and in turn on the larger social-geographic community. Moreover, instrumental action based on the idea of *Gesellschaft*, the conceptual antithesis to *Gemeinschaft*, always exists as a challenge, a conflictive or opportunistic alternative to any particular event or decision within a group. Brint follows Durkheim's lead of disaggregating the social structural and cultural processes associated with communal relations. Rather than treating communal relations as a single concept, Brint suggests that community is made up of four social structural and two cultural variables that can independently influence behavior and consciousness. In this disaggregated model, the four social structural variables are dense and demanding social ties, social attachments to and involvements in institutions, ritual occasions, and group size. The two cultural variables are perceptions of similarity with the physical characteristics, expressive style, way of life, or historical experience of others, and common beliefs in an idea system, moral order, institution, or group. Below we adapt Brint's analysis to suggest a set of congregational community traits that shape a congregation's impact on its social-geographic space.

Urban Community
Chicago School Insights

Our interest in the social-geographic organization of the new metropolis is influenced by the Chicago School of urban sociology that began in the 1920s with the University of Chicago sociologists Robert Park, Ernest Burgess, and others, who offered a functionalist and relatively deterministic theory of the industrial-era city that nevertheless provided an analytical lens grounded in local context. As Andrew Abbott (1997, 1152, emphasis in original) explains, "the Chicago school thought—and thinks—that one cannot understand social life without understanding the arrangements of particular social actors in particular social times and places. Another way of stating this is to say that Chicago felt that no social fact makes any sense abstracted from its context in social (and often geographic) space and social time. Social facts are *located*."

Park (1925, 115) provided a social-geographic definition of an urban community: "The simplest possible description of a community is this: a collection of people occupying a more or less clearly defined area. But a community is more than that. A community is not only a collection of people, but it is a collection of institutions. Not people, but institutions, are final and decisive in distinguishing the community from other social constellations." In addition to homes, the following institutions typically characterize an urban community: "churches, schools, playgrounds, a communal hall, a local theater, perhaps, and, of course, business and industrial enterprises of some sort."

Chicago School theorists have investigated urban communities of varying geographic sizes down to the street block level (A. Hunter 1974; Sampson 1999). We are particularly interested in neighborhoods and community areas. Neighborhoods are "analytic units with simultaneous social and spatial significance" (Sampson 2012, 56). In operationalizing an idealized spatial size of an urban neighborhood, we draw upon Robert Sampson's (1999, 248) insight that "the lay person's concept of neighborhood" is a relatively small group of street blocks and the conventional notion that a neighborhood comprises a comfortable walking distance of no more than one mile (e.g., Sinha et al. 2007, 248; USDA 2009, 3; Hattori, An, and Sturm 2013, 2).

The Chicago School's notion of a community area developed out of its well-known invasion/succession model based on analogies from plant ecology (McKenzie 1925, 74). Immigrants and other "undesirable invaders" (76) settle first in areas of low resistance in and near the central business district, then "gradually push their way out along business or transportation thoroughfares to the periphery of the community," creating "well-defined areas, each having its own peculiar selective and cultural characteristics," distinct social-geographic enclaves that McKenzie called "natural areas" (76, 77).

Chicago School theorists applied this notion of natural areas or ecological groupings to seventy-five "community areas" within the city of Chicago (the current seventy-seven are shown in Figure 2.1). As the *Local Community Fact Book, 1990* (xvii) explains, "the objective was to define

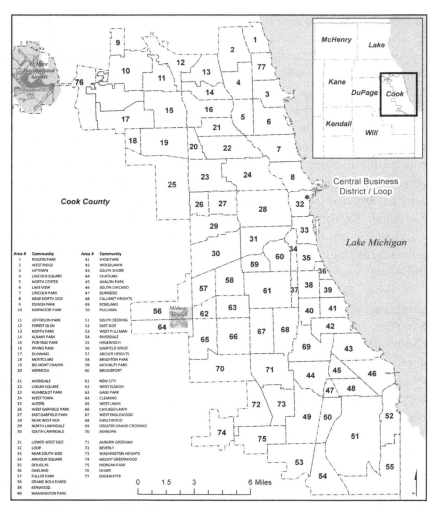

FIGURE 2.1. City of Chicago Community Areas.

Source: www.cityofchicago.org. Map by David J. Treering and Melissa Gesbeck Howell, Loyola University Chicago.

a set of subareas of the city each of which could be regarded as having a history of its own as a community, a name, an awareness on the part of its inhabitants of common interests, and a set of local businesses and organizations oriented to that local community" (cf. A. Hunter 1974, 25).

Following the Chicago School's lead, we see a community area as the largest social-geographic unit in which a meaningful sense of urban community can emerge (A. Hunter 1974, 72–77; Sampson 1999, 247–49;

Local Community Fact Book, 1990, xvii). Like Albert Hunter (1974), we do not restrict our attention to the official community areas within the city of Chicago; we also recognize larger areas like the Black Belt, the South Side, and the West Side (all predominantly black), and the North Side and the Southwest Side (both predominantly white until recently). Likewise, our notion of community areas is not limited to suburban municipalities of a certain population size, as in the *Local Community Fact Book* (beginning with the 1960 edition). We also include counties, relatively large expanses like the western suburbs, the North Shore, and the Fox Valley, and smaller entities like townships and sections of cities. We define a "community area" (or simply "area") as a social-geographic unit of variable size, mid-range between the neighborhood and the metropolis as a whole, with boundaries, a name, a history, and a relatively coherent identity that are recognized by its residents and institutions.

According to Chicago School thinking, the boundaries of an urban community at any level are determined by a combination of physical, structural, historical, social, and individual factors. The simplistic Chicago School notion of "natural areas" created by individual choice has been replaced by an awareness of translocal forces that affect local urban dynamics, such as the political economy (Sampson 1999, 261–63), without losing sight of local actors. As Sampson (267) explains with regard to the urban neighborhood, "Although structural constraints surely operate, so do individual choice and the differential selection of environments."

Sampson (2002, 46) lists "a concern for public affairs and the improvement of community life" as a characteristic Chicago School theme. The Chicago School was thus interested in more than sociology. It "was also a social psychology, a general theory of institutions, and a broad critique of American life" (A. Abbott 2002, 33), and it used the city as a lens for understanding the larger and more nebulous topics of modern life and individual experience in an urban context (35, 36). The Chicago School was concerned about social pathologies and so its "urban analysis had an applied aspect that was believed importantly relevant to virtually all of society's emerging problems" (Molotch 2002, 43). The classical Chicago School saw the city as a place where traditional human relationships and social controls break down, as captured in Louis Wirth's (1938) essay, "Urbanism as a Way of Life."

Wirth's essay was heavily influenced by the work of the German sociologist Georg Simmel, particularly his 1903 essay, "The Metropolis and Mental Life." Simmel's insight was to explain how modern urban people interact socially in different ways from rural and small town people, and how modern urban life creates profound disruptions for individuals and their social relationships, relationships which became "quite remote from the depth of the personality" (Simmel [1903] 1950, 411). For instance, the money economy tends to place calculating needs ahead of personal needs, while social unity loosens as the circle of urban population expands. Like Durkheim, both Tönnies and Simmel incorporated size as a major distinguishing feature of the urban *Gesellschaft*. The concern over the resultant loss of social control was expressed, for instance, through the settlement house work of Mary McDowell and Jane Addams. Furthermore, writing in the 1970s about the persistence of local urban communities in the face of transformations caused by "the increasing scale of modern urban society" (1974, 173), Albert Hunter expressed a basic Chicago School wish that such communities may "continue to humanize modern mass society" (1978, 162).

Hunter (1978) suggested that the classical Chicago School emphasis on social disorganization and pathologies was somewhat unfairly interpreted to support a decline-of-community thesis with roots much farther back in sociological theory. Morris Janowitz and David Street (1978) also challenged simplistic, straight-line decline-of-community models. Urban dynamics such as population deconcentration and increased work commute times do not necessarily weaken community ties; rather, "the local urban community and the neighborhood have specialized their functions" (105).

Janowitz's (1952) notion of communities of limited liability continues to have explanatory power in the new metropolis, as applied, for instance, by Robert Sampson (1999) in a perceptive essay titled "What 'Community' Supplies." Sampson takes on the seemingly ubiquitous appeal to a nostalgic and unsophisticated ideal of community as an "elixir for much of what ails American society" (241). Such utopian wishes ignore the ambivalent reality of neighborhoods and other social-geographic communities that both supply social goods and suffer social conflicts. The notion of communities of limited liability recognizes the increasingly voluntary, contingent, and instrumental commitment residents make to their neighborhoods and other social-geographic communities, as well as the fact that urban dwellers participate in any number of communities "liberated" from propinquity (246). Sampson distinguishes the private and public realms of urban residents' lives and their different relationships to locale. "No longer do we depend on neighborhoods to provide psychological support, religious nourishment, and deep friendships" (270). In fact, such "private and personal needs . . . are best met elsewhere," and even the means to satisfy the more basic "sustenance needs . . . for better or worse appear to be irretrievably dispersed in space" (247).

In the public realm, on the other hand, Sampson (247) argues that "local community remains essential as a site for the realization of common values in support of social goods, including public safety, norms of civility and mutual trust, efficacious voluntary associations, and collective socialization of the young." Sampson sees a significant role for religious and other local voluntary associations in stabilizing urban communities. His dichotomy between the private and public realms of residents' lives anticipates our investigation of congregational investment (or non-investment) in its locale, for it is not a given that congregations will participate in public efforts to provide local social goods. A congregation may instead choose to satisfy the private and personal needs of constituents who disperse themselves across the metropolis.

In our view, the analytical strength of the Chicago School's ecological metaphor is its attempt to account for all entities (actors) in a system (the metropolis) and to explain their complex relationships of competition and interdependence. The limitation of the metaphor is that action is reduced to a Darwinian-like process of natural selection, with survival and dominance the only motivations having explanatory power. We employ a revised notion of urban ecology more cognizant of the nuances of human action, especially religious action, in the metropolitan system. We share the Chicago School emphasis on local geography but we also recognize its weakness in accounting for global economic and political structures underlying the local urban context. Here we take our cues from the Los Angeles School (see below) and other critics of the old urban paradigm, as well as neo-Marxist insights generally (see D. Smith 1995; Walton 1980; Orum and Chen 2003, 32–44; cf. A. Abbott 2002, 34–35).

Other Insights about Urban Community

Although Georg Simmel examined the industrial-era city, recent observers have noted the contemporary relevance of his analysis (Levine 1971; D. Weinstein and M. Weinstein 1989), as in this excerpt from "The Metropolis and Mental Life" (Simmel [1903] 1950, 422):

> Here in buildings and educational institutions, in the wonders
> and comforts of space-conquering technology, in the formations

of community life, and in the visible institutions of the state, is offered such an overwhelming fullness of crystallized and impersonalized spirit that the personality, so to speak, cannot maintain itself under its impact. On the one hand, life is made infinitely easy for the personality in that stimulations, interests, uses of time and consciousness are offered to it from all sides. They carry the person as if in a stream, and one needs hardly to swim for oneself. On the other hand, however, life is composed more and more of these impersonal contents and offerings which tend to displace the genuine personal colorations and incomparabilities.

Simmel's primary interest in cities was dissecting the experience of individual personal freedom that is won at the cost of the security of life in small towns and rural areas. In adapting to the unrelenting crowding and discontinuously flashing images of urban life, people experience impersonality and loneliness and develop a protective shell, indifference, and a blasé outlook toward the strangers they constantly encounter. Furthermore, the division of labor atrophies individual cultural skills and, as a result, city dwellers short-change their individual personalities and become "mere cog[s] in an enormous organization of things and powers which tear from [their] hands all progress, spirituality, and value" (Simmel [1903] 1950, 422). Consequently, people in cities work to develop, even exaggerate, their individuality, all the while striving to overcome the impersonality of city life. Simmel focused on the consequences for the late modern individual in which the "crystallized and impersonalized spirit" of the metropolis foreshadowed the struggle to reconstitute identities and rebuild a coherent social life.

For Simmel, the metropolis is the setting in which new forms of social relating become possible as a result of the increasing size of the social group. As Simmel argues in his 1908 essay "Group Expansion and the Development of Individuality," small and undifferentiated groups have an individual character that stands for the group as a whole. When groups become larger and differentiated, competition occurs, and members become more individuated but only as parts of the whole. Increasing size requires a division of labor that in turn creates structures of activities and roles, but these roles are similar from group to group. Consequently, the larger whole is less individual as a social group (Simmel [1908] 1971, 253). Furthermore, from centripetal forces of the original, egalitarian group, there develop centrifugal forces that connect individuals with other groups, leading to the dissolution of prior fellowships. These differentiating roles lead to more freedom for the person; in other words, one person does not have to do everything and is not confined by being responsible for different functions. Consequently, the development of size leads to individualization and to expansion across a larger geographic territory. As Simmel states, "Individual freedom and the expansion of commercial enterprise are interdependent" (254). So, while the individual in the metropolis is freed from the constraining influences of a small town or, in our case, a small congregation, he or she also loses an autonomy or uniqueness of character. In large congregational communities, individuals are more free but tend to be more alike.

The Los Angeles School of urbanism, to use Michael Dear's (2002b) label, emerged in the 1980s in self-conscious opposition to the Chicago School's industrial-era perspective. A basic LA School tenet is ubiquitous urban restructuring that has created both a new urban geography and a new urban experience (Dear 2002a, 10). LA School insights help to illuminate life and community in the new metropolis, what Edward Soja (2000) calls the emerging "postmetropolis": postindustrialized, polarized, decentered, and perpetually reterritorializing, where attachments to place are weakened at all levels and "the real and imagined problems" of contemporary urban life can be found anywhere (260); a "carceral archipelago" characterized by intensified social and territorial controls and urban fortressing within an "ecology of fear" (299); a "fractal" place with a "restructured social mosaic" and "multiplying and cross-cutting social polarizations" (282). All of this notwithstanding, Soja points out that the new metropolis is also a place where notions of identity, community, and association are being re-formed, where "new forms and combinations of social spatiality and territorial identity" are arising (151–52). It is "also the scene of creative new 'hybridities' and a cultural politics aimed not just at reducing inequalities but also at preserving difference and fostering flexible 'transversal' identities" (155). Thus, "spaces of resistance" have emerged in the new metropolis, "concrete sites for progressive political action" (282).

Despite its emphasis on the dispersed, undifferentiated, and decentralized geography of the new metropolis, the Los Angeles School identifies mid-range demographic and economic areas like racial/ethnic enclaves, edge cities, and industrial or technological districts (Soja 1989, chap. 8; Soja and Scott 1996; R. Weinstein 1996). The LA School's perspective seems to imply that such urban areas increasingly do not function as communities according to Chicago School criteria, since the new metropolis subverts geographically grounded community (Dear and Flusty 2002). But we find the Chicago School notion of social-geographic communities still salient and will examine the role of congregations in both shaping and responding to them in the new urban context, and in creating livable communities within them.

We are justified in selecting pertinent insights from the LA and Chicago schools since no single urban theory can comprehensively explain the new urban era (see Judd 2011, 17–18). Our understanding of the new metropolis and its forms of community has also been informed by observers unaffiliated with either school. Kenneth Jackson (1985) traces the effects of suburbanization and automobility. "A major casualty of America's drive-in culture," Jackson argues, "is the weakened 'sense of community' which prevails in most metropolitan areas. I refer to a tendency for social life to become 'privatized,' and to a reduced feeling of concern and responsibility among families for their neighbors and among suburbanites in general for residents of the inner city" (272). Moreover, the post–World War II interstate highway system contributed to the new urban configuration, continuing "the downward spiral of public transportation and virtually guaranteed that future urban growth would perpetuate a centerless sprawl" (249). The centerless phenomenon has been variously labeled, as in the conceptual thread running from Joel Garreau's (1991) edge cities, through Robert E. Lang's (2003) edgeless cities, to Dolores Hayden's (2003) edge nodes.

Soja (2000, 243–46) criticizes Garreau's (1991) superficial and overly optimistic boosterism of edge cities, but Garreau does make some astute comments about life in the new urban America. He admits that edge cities remain "works in progress" (8). Though they represent the future, the kind of future they portend is unclear: "Are we satisfying our deepest yearnings for the good life with Edge City? Or are we poisoning everything across which we sprawl?" (11–12). Garreau suggests that a key to the quality of life in the edge cities of the future lay in efforts by residents to create community there, not primarily on the basis of geographic propinquity, but through voluntary association with like-minded peers (275, 279). Citing an observation by Tocqueville on the American penchant for forming voluntary associations, Garreau comments: "That is why, to this day, Edge Cities are the places where we invent new institutions to create community, new ways to connect with each other. Community in Edge City is disparate people voluntarily seeking connectedness in a

single whole" (288). Congregations have historically provided such connectedness and wholeness for Americans, yet Garreau asserts that congregations do not fit comfortably into the edge city milieu, their buildings
representing "noncompeting low-density use" to edge city builders, their
perspective about a more abundant spiritual life appearing superfluous in
the midst of material abundance (63–65). Of course, paradoxically, material abundance can just as easily trigger spiritual restlessness: Is that all
there is?

Community in the New Urban Era

We opened this chapter with the question, What kinds of community do
we find in the new urban America? While resisting nostalgic impulses
about the nature of community in industrial-era metropolises, we can
still recognize the pressures on urban community in the postindustrial
era. Communities of limited liability contain inherent constraints on
group identity, ambivalences that work against strong communal feelings, especially in the private realm of urban life that is increasingly liberated from geographic propinquity. The negative characteristics of the new
urban era tend to overshadow the positive possibilities for communal life.
Contemporary urban people have multiple loyalties and identifications.
Their movement within an array of networks, associations, and informal
groups does not necessarily require a coherent or consistent identity (Day
2006, 212). Even so, partial and episodic ties need not be trivial or superficial. Community has become contingent, only one of a number of possible affiliations, while at the same time, the strong emotions attached to
such affiliations continue to surface (Amit 2002, 16–18). Urban people,
too, seek the security of lasting social bonds, and such bonds are essential
to the ongoing construction of a good—or at least better—society. Edward
Soja (2000, 231) notes a potential turn in scholarly discussions of the new
metropolis, which may help "to recenter the specifically urban discourse
not just on the negative impacts of globalization but also on the new
opportunities and challenges provoked by globalization to rethink from a
more explicitly spatial perspective established notions of citizenship and
democracy, civil society and the public sphere, community development
and cultural politics, social justice and the moral order."

Thus, the LA School shares the Chicago School's interest in much
more than sociology, namely, as we saw above, "a concern for public
affairs and the improvement of community life." As Dick Simpson and

Tom Kelly (2011, 365) suggest, "Directly or indirectly, urban scholars tend to agree on a singular principle: we study to advance the goal of a livable, just, and democratic city—or as Jane Addams put it, of a 'socially just city.'" One of our contributions to the discourse on the new metropolis will be to recognize the role played by urban congregations in these and related themes, such as the creation of real and unsentimentalized forms of urban *Gemeinschaft*.

Congregations account for a ubiquitous form of urban community. Like other forms, churches, parishes, synagogues, mosques, and temples are affected by the powerful urban dynamics described above. The chapters of Part II will describe how selected congregations in Chicago create unsentimentalized religious communities in response to those urban dynamics, but also how they change their urban contexts as part of the ensemble of forces creating the new American metropolis. The following sections introduce a theoretical framework for understanding the extent and significance of congregations' impact on their surroundings.

Measuring Congregational Impact on the Urban Environment

Multiple factors must be considered in determining a congregation's influence on its urban context: spatial type, congregational traits, and congregational action. Through a general calculus of these factors we can arrange our congregations along a continuum of weak to moderate to strong urban impact.

A Threefold Spatial Typology of Urban Congregations

Urban congregations can be categorized by a threefold spatial typology based on the residential distribution of their constituents. This typology draws upon Chicago School insights about the social-geographic organization of the metropolis and has implications for the impact of congregations of each type.

A *neighborhood* congregation has a simple majority of constituents living within a one-mile radius of its location. (The term "constituents" is broader than "members"—not all congregations require formal membership.) In this type, there is a significant spatial correspondence between the boundaries of the neighborhood and the residential distribution of the congregational community. An *area* congregation has a simple majority of its constituents living in an area mid-range in size between its neighborhood and the metropolis as a whole. In this type, there may or may not be a significant spatial correspondence between the boundaries of the official social-geographic community area in which it is located and the residential distribution of the congregational community, which may cross several boundaries. A simple majority of a *metropolitan* (or simply *metro*) congregation's constituents is residentially dispersed throughout the metropolitan region.

We were able to categorize fifty-five congregations for which we had sufficient data as follows: nine neighborhood congregations (16 percent), thirty-four area congregations (62 percent), and twelve metro congregations (22 percent). Thus, 84 percent of our pool are non-neighborhood congregations, and nearly three-fourths of these are area congregations. Table 2.1 breaks out the percentages of each spatial type within the total of fifty-five congregations, as well as their locations and religious and racial identities.

All neighborhood congregations are located in the city of Chicago, which helps to account for the large percentage of majority non-white congregations in this spatial type. One-third of the neighborhood congregations are Catholic parishes, yet only 30 percent of the Catholic parishes in our population of fifty-five are neighborhood congregations.

Table 2.1. **Congregational Spatial Types by Location, Religious Identity, and Race (N = 55)**

Spatial type	Neighborhood	Area	Metro	
Location				
City	9 (100%)	15 (44%)	6 (50%)	
Suburb	0	19 (56%)	6 (50%)	
Religious identity				
Protestant	4 (44%)	17 (50%)	5 (42%)	
Catholic	3 (33%)	6 (18%)	1 (8%)	
Non-Christian	2 (22%)	11 (32%)	6 (50%)	
Race				
White	1 (11%)	15 (44%)	6 (50%)	
Non-white	8 (89%)	19 (56%)	6 (50%)	
Totals	9 (16%)	34 (62%)	12 (22%)	55 (100%)

The seeming incongruity that such a small number of Catholic parishes fall within the neighborhood type needs explanation. We recognize that Catholic parish boundaries do not necessarily conform to our definition of a neighborhood congregation due to two patterns at work since the Second Vatican Council: Catholic parishioners have increasingly attended churches outside their residential parishes and suburban parish boundaries (especially in new growth suburbs) typically encompass larger geographic spaces than was the norm in older cities. Even for parishes in which the majority live within the parish boundaries, they may not live within a one-mile radius of the church. Hence, while Catholic city parishes typically qualify as "neighborhood" congregations according to our definition, suburban parishes typically do not, given the larger expanses of the suburbs.

Regarding area congregations, slightly more than half (56 percent) are located in the suburbs; half are Protestant, 18 percent are Catholic, nearly one-third are non-Christian; slightly more than half (56 percent) are majority non-white, including seven black churches and eight Asian congregations. Metro congregations divide half-and-half according to city/suburb location, non-Christian/Christian affiliation (all but one of the Christian churches being Protestant), and race (white/non-white).

The city/suburban distinction is intriguing, even counterintuitive in some respects. The city locations of the neighborhood congregations in our pool can be explained straightforwardly. Neighborhood congregations have difficulty taking root in the suburbs due to high automobility and an emphasis on separation and privacy in residential subdivisions. In contrast, the city's lower automobility, residential density, and tradition of neighborhoods enhance the likelihood of neighborhood congregations. The fact that nearly half of our area and metro congregations are located in the city seems to run counter to this last statement. It is true that cities tend to enhance the likelihood of neighborhood congregations, but they can also produce area and metro congregations due to other factors, especially increased mobility and personal choice. For instance, some metro congregations capitalize on their central location in the city by designating a metro-wide recruitment zone.

Note that area congregations dominate our typology (more than three-fifths of the total). This is significantly influenced by the nature of community areas, which both favors the creation of area congregations and limits the creation of metro congregations. As explained above, a community area has boundaries, a name, a history, and a relatively coherent identity that are recognized by its residents and institutions. These characteristics induce residents to stay within their area when considering congregational affiliation. Area congregations draw their constituents from nearby, from some part of the metropolis, not anywhere. Constituents who affiliated with an area congregation in the city did not experience a "loss" of neighborhood as the city changed; they never had a neighborhood, only an area. Mobility is another limiting factor that favors the area congregation over the metro congregation. People with automobiles may be willing to travel to a congregation they prefer, but there must be good reason to drive a long distance—that is, well beyond their community area. People without automobiles may be able to reach a congregation they prefer within their area via public transportation or ride sharing, but such arrangements become more difficult the farther away the congregation is located.

To sum up, America's urban configurations conduce to different spatial congregational types today. Neighborhood congregations are more likely to be found in the city; area congregations are slightly more likely to be found in the suburbs; and metro congregations can be found anywhere due to the improved transportation infrastructures of the new metropolis. The decline in the number of neighborhood congregations can be detected at least as early as the 1920s (Sinha et al. 2007, 246; Douglass 1924; Hallenbeck 1929). The new urban era favors the creation of area congregations, while making metro congregations more feasible for those motivated and able to make the long urban trek.

A study of more than 1,300 congregations located within the city limits of Philadelphia seems to support our observations about neighborhood, area, and metro congregations. In an article aptly titled "Proximity Matters," Jill Witmer Sinha et al. (2007) report that less than half (42.5 percent) of their pool were neighborhood congregations (which they call "resident congregations"). The other two categories in the study, "city commuter congregations" and "suburban commuter congregations," do not correspond exactly to our area and metro types, but the racial/ethnic breakdown of the Philadelphia study implies the existence of area congregations in the large number of black and Hispanic congregations that fall under the "city commuter" type. The same may be the case with Muslim congregations, 73 percent of which fall under the "city commuter" type and may draw from areas of Philadelphia with high concentrations of Muslim residents. The large percentage of Asian congregations that fall under the "suburban commuter" category implies our metro type. Sinha et al. identify religious affiliation, race/ethnicity, and neighborhood characteristics as key factors in these patterns. Mobility factors are implied in their analysis.

The wider versus narrower residential spread of a congregation's constituents produces different relationships to the urban spaces in which the religious community is located. For instance, we can hypothesize that it is more likely that a neighborhood congregation will invest in the welfare of its neighborhood because its constituents live there than for area and metro congregations to do so because the majority of their constituents are dispersed beyond the neighborhood. The greater the constituent diffusion, the more diffuse the awareness of a congregation's urban context becomes. Thus, we can also hypothesize that area and metro congregations tend to exert relatively weaker urban impact.

Nonetheless, local investment is not solely a consequence of distance. As Ebaugh, O'Brien, and Chafetz (2000, 115) concluded in their study of Houston, "residential dispersion patterns by themselves are insufficient" to assess the extent of neighborhood involvement by what they call "parish" (our "neighborhood" type) and "niche" (commuter) congregations. Even widely scattered constituents of area or metro congregations choose how to manage their time and energy, which may be invested in the congregation's neighborhood. Constituents of neighborhood and area congregations may be less liable to think in larger geographic terms, but they can do so.

Congregational Community Traits

The influence of spatial arrangements is conditioned by internal congregational community traits. Adapting Steven Brint's analysis (see above), we suggest nine congregational community traits, one or more of which help to shape a distinctive congregational life that, in turn, helps to contour that congregation's urban impact: common beliefs, the uniting function of ritual, enforcement of internal norms, mutual support, dense and demanding social ties, internal social similarities, stratification based on status or office, maintenance of boundaries to the outside world, and types of disputes and their resolution. These nine traits vary in their causes and their expressions across congregations. For example, mutual support is relatively consistent in the congregations we studied, but the external challenges that create the opportunity and need for mutual support differ across congregations, from specific neighborhood resistance to broader social and ideological threats. Likewise, the maintenance of boundaries with the outside world as well as internal stratification vary considerably across congregations.

Finally, a congregational trait that implies action by the congregation is whether the group has an internal or external orientation, that is, a greater or lesser tendency to focus primarily on the needs of its constituents vis-à-vis the attention it pays to the needs of its surrounding residents. Each congregation makes specific choices and encounters specific constraints within which it works. These decisions direct and shape where their energies are put, varying considerably from congregation to congregation. We can hypothesize that congregations with a strong focus on internal needs will tend to exert relatively weaker urban influence.

In her research report "Doing Good in American Communities," sociologist Nancy Ammerman (n.d.) details the many ways that congregations serve the needs of both their own constituents and the larger communities in which they are located. Ammerman notes that "While congregations are intimately involved in the good work that is done in every community, their primary task is not the delivery of social services or supporting cultural organizations. Their primary task is the spiritual well-being of their members," which Ammerman summarizes in the phrase "worship and spiritual life." She calls the secondary task of congregations "fellowship": congregations "see themselves as a family, a community of people who care for each other and do things together." Yet congregations also engage in various service or social-change-oriented activities, with much variation among them. Congregations that belong to a beleaguered minority group, for example, may find committing to external activities to be more constraining geographically or interactionally than they desire. Also, external action can be motivated in various ways by congregations, such as engaging the city as a mission field or seeking to improve the life circumstances of their constituents by altering the economic or political structures of the neighborhood, area, or metropolis as a whole. Therefore, how congregations allocate their energies and how their decisions are interconnected to the kinds of community they have built will result in different forms of impact on their environments.

In all of the above, we are not arguing causality, but rather suggesting that internal characteristics have a bearing on the kinds of relationships a congregation forms with other groups and institutions. Furthermore, a congregation's urban context has a bearing on the kind of internal community it forms. In our descriptions of the congregations in Part

II, we will focus on the salient traits that factor into each case's urban impact.

Congregational Action

A congregation's impact is also shaped in part by its action, which must be understood in terms of the structure/action dialectic (for a more detailed discussion of this dialectic, see Wedam 2008). Following the structuration theories of Anthony Giddens (1984), William Sewell (1992), David Rubinstein (2001), and others, we understand urban structures as economic, political, geographic, social, and other constraints on, and opportunities for, action by entities embedded in those same structures. Urban actors, such as congregations, are thus constitutive of urban structures, not somehow outside of or aloof from them. David Rubinstein's multidimensional theoretical model of social action elevates the influence of culture to an equal role with structure and (individual) action. Rubinstein (n.d., 13) understands culture as "not merely adaptive" and points to many examples of "the power of moral rules to override practical [read: structural] interests." To support his multidimensional view of society, Rubinstein argues for a balance among the influences of structures, cultures, and individual dispositions on social action by positing them as interpenetrating forces. Each is constitutive of the others, partially autonomous, partially influential, and dialectically related in three, rather than two, directions. Under certain circumstances, one may dominate the others but no one is theoretically privileged (2001, 155). This perspective is helpful in explaining congregational action in light of constraining circumstances such as economic losses or population shifts.

Molotch, Freudenburg, and Paulsen (2000, 793) explain the structure/action dialectic in this way: "as people take action they make structures, and every action is both enabled and constrained by the prior structures. All this occurs in an unending series of adjacent and recursive choice-point moves." Race/ethnicity, for instance, has been a powerful urban structure imposing constraints and affording opportunities in unequal measure for individuals and groups. Through the actions of civil rights organizations and recent immigrant groups—both significantly informed by religion—racialized urban structures now differ in significant ways from earlier periods, presenting a new set of constraints and opportunities to congregations.

We distinguish two kinds of congregational action: "agency" creates structures or fundamental changes in structures; "adaptation" seeks to fit into existing structures without challenging them. Adaptive congregations are unwilling to challenge problematic structural conditions, such as racial/ethnic disparity or economic inequality. In contrast, congregations that confront unjust systems seek to assert their agency, to be "prophetic" in the language of some religious traditions. We should not make too fine a distinction between adaptation and agency—some congregations choose to be both adaptive and confrontive in order to survive in their urban environment. We should also be realistic about agency—confronting structural conditions does not guarantee the intended change.

We propose six indicators of a congregation's action, whether through adaptation or agency, that factor into its impact on the urban environment, recognizing some overlap among them: territorial claims, jurisdictional claims, public policy advocacy, programs or positions that challenge inequality, racial/ethnic composition, and mission activities. Once again, in our descriptions of the congregations in Part II, we will focus on the salient indicators in each case's urban impact.

Congregations stake territorial claims by contributing to the infrastructure of the built environment, such as places of worship, schools, recreational or community service centers, and parking lots (on territoriality, see Rapoport 2002). Congregations also make jurisdictional claims, that is, temporary and contingent demands on space (cf. Rapoport 2002; Cormack 2007), such as conducting a prison visitation program, a worship service in a retirement home, or a social service program in a facility operated by another organization. The same can be said of demanding kosher, *halal*, vegetarian, or other dietary options in a public school cafeteria. Less obviously, congregations may also claim spiritual and/or moral jurisdiction over the social-geographic communities in which they are located through small group gatherings in homes. When a congregation maps the residential distribution of its own congregational community on the urban landscape, whether mentally or literally, it makes some kind of jurisdictional claim on that portion of the metropolis, for instance the Catholic parish, the Jewish *eruv*, and evangelical mission maps of the city. Of course, congregations vary in the intensity with which they assert their jurisdiction.

Congregations also have a bearing on their urban environments directly through advocating public policy for social change. The impact can be strong when it involves changes in laws and other regulatory mandates. Congregations can indirectly influence their urban surroundings by taking positions on or creating programs that challenge social, political, and economic inequality. Sometimes a congregation's advocacy clashes with other urban actors regarding civic, legal, social, or moral issues (cf. Brower 1980). While religious actors may be moving from a strong form of authority based on traditional prestige to a weaker form based on negotiated arrangements, their influence stems precisely from their unwillingness to be relegated to the confines of their territorial holdings and temporary jurisdictional claims. A congregation can participate with other actors in the ongoing construction of the identity, ethos, character, relationships, and livability of its urban place.

Since the new American metropolis is characterized by racial/ethnic structural stratification, the racial/ethnic composition of an urban congregation necessarily has some level of impact. This is a complicated matter. When congregations create internally diverse communities, they challenge urban stratification, a difficult challenge to sustain as indicated by the typical instability of multiracial congregations (Emerson and Smith 2000; Wedam 1999; 2002). But mono-racial/ethnic congregations provide many benefits for their constituents—comfort, protection from societal stresses, approbation of a particular cultural and religious heritage, solidarity (Kostarelos 1995; T. Nelson 1996; Daniels 2000)—that can challenge urban stratification in a different way, for instance in offering resistance to the dominant society.

Congregations engage in a variety of mission activities, many of them conversion-based. This form of action is the most indirect and least measurable in terms of its "objective" urban impact. On the other hand, many congregations make the argument that changing the person in the direction of positive social and moral behavior reverberates in less visible but still palpable ways in the larger society. Programs that emphasize social service over evangelization may be merely ameliorative but they are widely regarded as evidence of good neighboring and positive civic involvement.

The preceding discussion leads us to an analytical perspective that will frame our remaining chapters. By taking into account *spatial type* (neighborhood, area, metro), *community traits* (common beliefs, the uniting function of ritual, enforcement of internal norms, mutual support, dense and demanding social ties, internal social similarities, stratification based on status or office, maintenance of boundaries with the outside world, types of disputes and their resolution, and internal versus external focus on needs), and *action* (territorial claims, jurisdictional claims,

Table 2.2. **Continuum of Congregational Urban Impact of**
Fifteen Case Studies

Weak	Low moderate	Moderate	High moderate	Strong
Ezra-Habonim (A)	Beth Shalom (A)	St. Jerome (N)	MCC (A)	St. Nicholas (N)
Calvary (A)		First Christian (N)	MEC (A)	Mosque Foundation (A)
Wheatland Salem (A)		New Covenant (A)	New Life (M)	Fourth Presbyterian (A)
HTGC (M)				Moody (M)

Abbreviations: Neighborhood (N), Area (A), Metro (M). Congregations listed in each column by order of appearance in Part II.

public policy advocacy, programs or positions that challenge inequality, racial/ethnic composition, and mission activities), we can measure a congregation's impact on the urban environment along a continuum of weak to moderate to strong. Table 2.2 arranges our fifteen congregational case studies along that continuum. Chapter 8 presents our analysis of the cases and the implications for understanding congregational urban impact generally.

Religion's Role in the New American Metropolis

Our purpose in this book is to understand how congregations are both shaped by and shape their urban environments, how they function as both dependent and independent variables in the new American metropolis. An analysis of contemporary urban restructuring is incomplete at best and misleading at worst if it fails to account for religion as part of the ensemble of forces creating the new urban reality. This is not to deny that religion has often been ineffective vis-à-vis the dynamics of urban restructuring. Religious actors can be passive, go-with-the-flow adapters rather than agents of change.

But the evidence from Chicago supports the important claim that religious actors, particularly congregations and the individuals they influence and empower, do engage urban structures in effective and reciprocal ways. Perhaps more importantly, while congregations function in many respects like secular nonprofit organizations, it is often through their explicitly "religious" work that they make their most profound impact on the new American metropolis, particularly in the kinds of community they create, nurture, and debate.

The chapters of Part II offer case studies organized according to our threefold spatial typology of neighborhood, area, and metro congregations. We will examine the communities these congregations have created in the new Chicago and measure their impact on the new urban environment.

PART II

Congregational Case Studies

3

Neighborhood Parishes and Churches in a Restructuring City

JAMES CAPRARO, A Southwest Side activist and director of a nonprofit economic development organization, was named a "Chicagoan of the Year" by *Chicago* magazine in the mid-1990s (Eastman, Reynolds, and Johnson 1995). He recounted to us a meeting of business leaders discussing an appropriate "brand" for Chicago. When Capraro asked, "What parish are you from?" they stared back blankly. Explained Jim, "Few business leaders are any longer from Chicago," and as a result, "they don't get the church thing." If that were not enough to demonstrate their declining cultural knowledge, he added, "They don't get the neighborhood thing either."

Captains of the economic and political structures of the new Chicago—and other new metropolises—may wish to dismiss congregations and neighborhoods, but they could not be ignored in an earlier period. During the industrial era, Chicago's identity was heavily shaped by the ways European immigrant and southern migrant populations created subcultures within particular—and separate—places. Congregation and neighborhood often grew simultaneously, influencing each other in mutually transformative ways. It is our contention that this interactive process continues in a restructuring Chicago today despite being mostly off the radar screen of secular actors. The congregational cases in this chapter challenge the notion that the new metropolis "eradicates genuine particularity," replacing it with a "vast, virtually undifferentiated territory," a "non-place urban realm" (Sorkin 1992, xii). In vital ways, these neighborhoods and these neighborhood congregations matter.

The two primary cases of this chapter are Catholic parishes on opposite sides of the city of Chicago: St. Nicholas of Tolentine on the Southwest
Side and St. Jerome in Rogers Park on the far North Side. These parishes, historic keepers of neighborhood identity and managers of cultural norms and expectations, adopted the translocal strategies of two
organizations that no longer defer to parish boundaries in the face of the
challenges of urban realignment. The Southwest Organizing Project, a
faith-based community organization, and Northside Catholic Academy,
an archdiocese-initiated, restructured parochial school model, provided
the means for parishes to push back against such realignments in order
to reduce their negative consequences, offering a more inclusive template
for constructing neighborhood life. Through these organizations, St.
Nick's and St. Jerome were able to reshape their local environments as
well as develop new understandings about their relationships with other
parishes.

We will also briefly examine the case of First Christian Church, which
intentionally diversified its congregational community as the Southwest
Side diversified around it, rather than succumb to the white flight syndrome. The Catholic and Protestant cases in this chapter illustrate different processes by which place-based congregational community can be
maintained in the new urban era. They also exemplify how neighborhood
churches can exert moderate to strong urban impact, perhaps to the surprise of urban observers who "don't get the church thing."[1]

Parish as Place

Throughout the late nineteenth and early twentieth centuries, large numbers of Catholics, Protestants, and Jews came to work in the businesses, factories, stockyards, and steelyards of the giant industrial machine growing
in the drained swamps on Lake Michigan's western shore. For Catholics,
the largest of these groups, the adjustment process included establishing
parish communities of ethnic co-religionists. By the mid-twentieth century, urban Catholic parish ties to the neighborhood were concrete expressions of communal "sacred space," which included local home ownership
inside parish boundaries (McGreevy 1996, 78; Skerrett 1993). In his leading study of parish life and race relations in northern industrial cities,
historian John McGreevy (1996, 20) claimed that "American Catholics
frequently defined their surroundings in religious terms." Their parish institutions, under the kindly yet autocratic leadership of priests and

nuns, typically included schools, gymnasiums, auditoriums, rectories and convents, and other buildings that served the various needs of the growing immigrant population. In McGreevy's words, "the Catholic parish itself, because of its size and community base, helped define what neighborhood would mean." In our terminology, the parish's substantial territorial presence and the residential density of its parishioners created a Catholic neighborhood.

This process of neighborhood definition had both social and theological dimensions. Physical proximity and residential relationships within the parish-church-school complex provided a social fulcrum for parishioners. Urban sociologists have noted that "the residential social organization is the locus within which the stages of the life cycle are given moral and symbolic meaning" (Janowitz and Street 1978, 93). Catholic theology taught that "The individual came to know God, and the community came to be church, within a particular, geographically defined space" (McGreevy 1996, 24). For Catholics, the passages of life are given spiritual meaning through sacramental rites: birth/baptism, age of reason/communion and reconciliation, adult responsibility/confirmation, partnership and reproduction/matrimony, and illness and end of life/anointing of the sick. The parish inculcates members into a ritual life that defines the person as sacred by connecting the theological with the communal. Catholic theologian Karl Rahner explained, "Communities became Church in the context of the liturgy, just as Christ became specific, and corporeal, in the celebration of the Eucharist" (quoted in McGreevy 1996, 24). Rahner (1958, 31) further argued that "the foundation of the parish community and its Eucharistic actualization [that is, the central sacrament] lie solely in that principle which forms the very basis of the placeness of the Eucharist; that is, the placeness of corporeal, place-time man himself." Thus, the church is the local community and the local community is united in the celebration of the Mass.

This social-theological understanding had particular consequences for Catholic urban neighborhoods in the industrial era. Both skilled and unskilled workers began as poor laborers in stockyards, steel mills, meatpacking, and transportation. Through trade unionism they became the working classes living within a nexus of work-school-church-community in neighborhoods adjacent to the industrial districts (Jablonsky 1993). These neighborhoods were never completely homogeneous, as they were often polarized by racial/ethnic, class, or religious (through the presence of non-Catholics) divisions (Pacyga 1995). Following World War II, expansion of the transportation infrastructure and low-interest federal mortgage opportunities facilitated the movement of the middle and working classes (mostly whites) to suburbs where light industry and corporate offices provided employment (Keating 2002). Industrial deconcentration began in earnest in the 1970s as heavy industry moved first to the Sunbelt and then to low-wage, low-regulatory Third World locations (Gottdiener 1983). The middle and upper classes were prepared for new opportunities in information technology and the finance, insurance, and real estate sectors that grew in suburban and central business district locations in the following decades. Few opportunities remained, however, for high school graduates that previously had been able to support a family on a single paycheck.

The social-theological interpretation of the parish-neighborhood linkage has undergone a transformation due to the demographic and geographic ramifications of urban restructuring and the cultural rethinking of the Second Vatican Council or Vatican II (1962–1965) (D'Agostino 2000). Parishes in the industrial era created neighborhoods that were community-minded ethnic enclaves in which parish-school-neighborhood units cultivated tight and often exclusionary bonds. Parishes today are developing flexible, collaborative structures that are geographically larger in scale and open to new forms of religious and racial/ethnic inclusion.

Vatican II raised the importance of, and expanded the theological development of, the social teachings of the Catholic Church. While the legacy of Vatican II is broad, it is also ambiguous and contested.[2] Yet two interpretations can be safely advanced. First, Vatican II provided new perspectives on the relationship of the Church to the modern world that affect how local churches and their members live day to day. Lay participation in running parishes is a direct legacy of the Council's notion of "people of God," however vaguely that idea is actually presented in the documents (O'Brien and Shannon 1992, 167; Burns 1992). For example, Joseph Cardinal Bernardin, who came to Chicago in 1982, decentralized the management of the archdiocese, developing a local focus and instituting financial and pastoral planning procedures that required active visioning and decision making by parishes. As a result, St. Jerome became an active participant in the formation of a new concept in Catholic education, the translocal and multi-parish school (see later in this chapter).

Second, social teaching is a continuing legacy of Vatican II. The American Catholic bishops distinctly advanced social teachings on the topics of capitalism, economic policy, just war, and nuclear deterrence

(US Catholic Bishops 1983; 1986). The bishops point out how economic restructuring, propelled by a laissez-faire market economy and the individualistic principles that underlie it, negatively affects community life. But Vatican II's statements on human dignity, human rights, work, peace, and justice expressed broad principles rather than official policy commitments. These principles took root among leftist Catholics more readily than among the members as a whole. Furthermore, the Council left implementation to local dioceses and parishes, whose members were given the responsibility to make practical applications that fit their needs (Hehir 1991, 66–68). In one such application, Cardinal Bernardin supported the community organizing response to urban problems by inviting the Industrial Areas Foundation to return to Chicago, which spurred the formation of the Southwest Organizing Project. This brings us to the first case study of the chapter.

St. Nicholas of Tolentine Catholic Church
Urban Context: The Southwest Side

St. Nick's parish is located within a cluster of working-class community areas on Chicago's Southwest Side (Figures 3.1, 3.2).[3] These areas remained largely undeveloped until after World War I, when workers living in and around the decaying Back of the Yards neighborhood could buy their own homes further south. The Southwest Side thus became an area of secondary settlement for many white ethnic groups, part of the "bungalow belt" that formed an outer ring around the industrial city during the booming 1920s. By the early 1930s, Chicago Lawn (commonly known as Marquette Park after the 300-acre greenspace in the southern section of the area) reached residential maturity, although it was not fully settled until after World War II (Pacyga and Skerrett 1986, 502–503).

Older residents in the area can recall family members working in the Union Stock Yard and living in Packingtown, one of the vilest slums in Chicago in the early years of industrialization (D. Miller 1996, 218), immortalized in Upton Sinclair's novel *The Jungle*. At the turn of the twentieth century, the massive yards, packinghouses, railroads, and auxiliary factories were the principal industrial engine of the city, providing underpaid employment to the many competing European immigrant groups that continued to arrive in Chicago until the restrictions imposed by the Johnson-Reed Act of 1924. As in Friedrich Engels's Manchester,

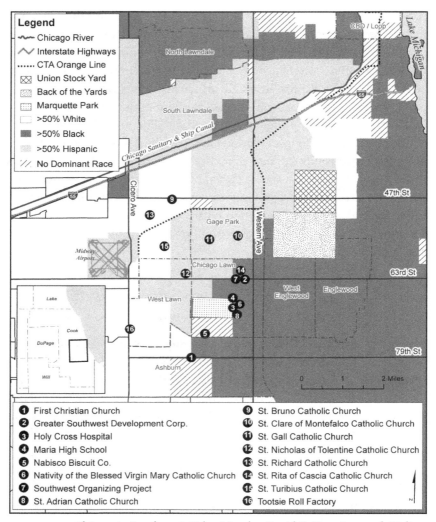

Legend
- 〰 Chicago River
- ∧ Interstate Highways
- ⋯⋯ CTA Orange Line
- ▨ Union Stock Yard
- ▦ Back of the Yards
- ▤ Marquette Park
- ☐ >50% White
- ■ >50% Black
- ▨ >50% Hispanic
- ⫻ No Dominant Race

❶ First Christian Church		❾ St. Bruno Catholic Church	
❷ Greater Southwest Development Corp.		❿ St. Clare of Montefalco Catholic Church	
❸ Holy Cross Hospital		⓫ St. Gall Catholic Church	
❹ Maria High School		⓬ St. Nicholas of Tolentine Catholic Church	
❺ Nabisco Biscuit Co.		⓭ St. Richard Catholic Church	
❻ Nativity of the Blessed Virgin Mary Catholic Church		⓮ St. Rita of Cascia Catholic Church	
❼ Southwest Organizing Project		⓯ St. Turibius Catholic Church	
❽ St. Adrian Catholic Church		⓰ Tootsie Roll Factory	

FIGURE 3.1. Chicago's Southwest Side. Map by David J. Treering and Melissa Gesbeck Howell, Loyola University Chicago.

the conditions of workers in machine-age Chicago were treated as an afterthought (Jablonsky 1993). Packinghouse employees lived in mudflats and tenements along open sewers in Packingtown. When first some of the skilled immigrants such as butchers and construction workers were able to afford their own houses, most moved south into the small, neat, brick bungalows and two- and three-flats typical of the period. But they brought their memories, along with an identity that was only partly in

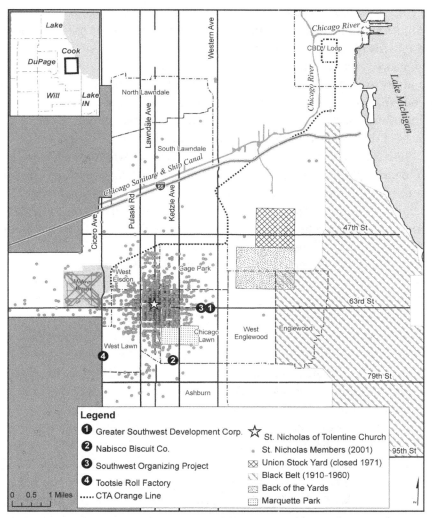

FIGURE 3.2. St. Nicholas Catholic Church and Members. Map by David J. Treering and Melissa Gesbeck Howell, Loyola University Chicago.

their control. "In combination with the massive packinghouses, the yards shaped the image of the entire South Side of Chicago: blue-collar, ethnic, and aesthetically unappealing" (Jablonsky 1993, 11).

During the middle decades of the twentieth century, the geographic isolation of the Southwest Side contributed to its working-class ethos of community and salt-of-the-earth character. Such tendencies developed partially as a result of being "boxed in" on all sides by both natural and symbolic boundaries (A. Hunter 1974, 67–71): the Chicago Sanitary and Ship Canal connecting to the Chicago River, and later the Stevenson Expressway (Interstate 55), sit on the north; Midway Airport and the southwest suburbs are to the west; middle and upper-middle-class community areas frame the south; and the Stock Yard industrial district and the expanding Black Belt face on the east. Limited transportation arteries, including a lack of rapid transit until 1994, contributed to the separateness of the Southwest Side from the larger city.

Furthermore, a shared history of immigration, working in the yards, and struggling to get a foothold in the harsh industrial landscape created a sense of identification with a place that denoted success and respectability. Irish, Germans, and Bohemians came first. The first Protestant and Catholic churches were established before the turn of the twentieth century, Elsdon United Methodist Church in 1892 and St. Gall Catholic Church in 1899. By the 1920s, Lithuanians, Slovaks, and Poles dominated, each having founded large Catholic parishes (Pacyga and Skerrett 1986). The Russian Orthodox established their church just north of Chicago Lawn in 1931. Congregation Lawn Manor, one of the few synagogues on the Southwest Side, was founded in 1925 and later merged with Congregation Beth Jacob. Religious homogeneity, although never absolute, added to neighborhood assumptions about what constituted right behavior. Class and racial homogeneity alongside the Catholic predominance developed a sense of commonality in the residents (Wedam 1996, 178–81).

These areas were heavily invested in the Fordist economy where skilled and unskilled labor did not require an advanced education. A single paycheck and a generally frugal lifestyle could support a large family. While small and generally unnoticed, the first manufacturing job losses began shortly after World War II—the purported golden age of urban and parish community—and were not replaced with alternative local employment opportunities (B. Bluestone and Harrison 1982; Abu-Lughod 1999). By the 1970s, the losses became inescapable and dramatic, and Southwest Siders felt an economic insecurity they did not have the resources to address. Economic uncertainty made residents less able to understand other changes facing the city, one being the intense overcrowding in the Black Belt that began to spill over after restricted real estate covenants were declared illegal in 1948. The second-largest black northward migration to fill defense and other manufacturing industry positions occurred during World War II. William Julius Wilson (1987) documented the ironic pattern of increasing black migration precisely as employment opportunities waned. Furthermore, Southwest Side residents observed with considerable anxiety the recurring patterns of racial integration and resegregation, and the economic divestment and impoverishment that followed in several neighborhoods to the east, especially in Englewood.

The ways in which industrial decline began to undermine white ethnic working-class investments in local community areas, including their parishes, are particularly important in understanding racial change and white flight in Chicago more broadly in the 1950s and not just on the Southwest Side. Catholics were historically less mobile than the Protestants and Jews they lived alongside because the archdiocese, as the *corporation sole*, owned the churches (Kantowicz 1983). For example, in 1950, 87,000 whites lived in the heavily Jewish North Lawndale community area on Chicago's West Side and forty-eight synagogues were active. By 1960 only eleven thousand whites lived there, while one hundred thousand blacks had moved in and all the synagogues had closed (McGreevy 1996, 102). In explaining Jewish mobility in this regard, Irving Cutler (1995, 159) states: "Relatively few members of the new generation of Jewish adults were interested in clinging to the great institutional structures that their parents and grandparents had built." Adjacent South Lawndale, the community area dominated by Poles, Bohemians, and Italians, remained virtually all white during this same period (McGreevy 1996, 102). Catholics were also less financially secure. The principal economic investment held by most of the blue-collar workers of the Southwest Side was the equity in their modest homes. The self-fulfilling prophecy of complete racial change that was set into motion mainly by unscrupulous real estate brokers—approximately sixty-five agencies operated in and around Marquette Park during the panic-peddling and block-busting years—and supported by discriminatory mortgage lending practices (sanctioned at the federal level) economically undermined both buyers and sellers during that era (Fish et al. 1968, 2–5). That black house buyers were equally affected by the steady closing of nearby factories was lost on insecure whites, but even more telling is that their common economic vulnerability was seldom recognized by political, academic, or media observers at the time.

Racial tipping is a self-fulfilling prophecy. Panicky neighbors among otherwise fair-minded people undermine the "rational" free market, as Fr. Francis X. Lawlor, the area's most notorious figure in the open housing battle during the 1960s and 1970s, told us in 1999. "Once a panic for home selling sets in, nobody can stop it. The communities were left helpless." Lawlor's community organization, the Southwest Neighborhood

Federation, tracked the complicity of federal home mortgage lending bodies who would have "no further role in the process once the houses were bought" by blacks, thus effectively "abandoning them" to the "high and rapid" mortgage defaults of the time.

While the church's commitment to an inclusive ethos was taught from pulpits and official pronouncements in the 1990s, a model for a racially inclusive working-class neighborhood was lacking in the 1960s and 1970s. "No one, including the Catholic Interracial Council, provided them with anything but moral platitudes as a solution during the early, critical years of social change" (Rosswurm 2004, 720). Indeed, North Side whites and so-called "lakefront liberals" cast aspersions at Southwest Side racist language and actions from a comfortable class and spatial distance. As historians Dominic Pacyga and Ellen Skerrett (1986, 505) point out, "with some justification, whites on the Southwest Side felt that they stood alone and were being sacrificed by powerful groups in other parts of the city. This feeling of abandonment was just as powerful a force as racism on the Southwest Side."

In 1960 in West Englewood, the population was 88 percent white. In 1970, after the 1966 open housing marches put a spotlight on smoldering racial tensions in the city's blue-collar communities, West Englewood's black population increased to 48 percent; by 1980, the transition to all-black was complete. As the pastor of St. Rita of Cascia in Chicago Lawn once described it, residents experienced change "like a wave coming off the lake." It was that sense of inevitability that informed the decisions of many whites on the Southwest Side. Continuing the pattern of ethnic succession chronicled by the early Chicago School urban sociologists, racial succession became a structural fact in Chicago, constituted by the actions of many individual homeowners but not in the control of any one.

The Southwest Side today features a residential mix of blue-collar workers, white-collar professionals, and small business owners. Heavy industry is no longer the basis of the local economy, having been replaced by small-scale factories, steel mills, and food processing plants such as Nabisco. Midway Airport has been revitalized as an employment anchor. Considerable economic investment in retail development and housing has occurred, led by the nonprofit Greater Southwest Development Corporation (DevCor), headed by longtime St. Nicholas parishioner James Capraro. Although travel time to work is higher on average from the Southwest Side than from any of the nearby suburbs, the Chicago Transit Authority's Orange Line rapid transit service was completed in 1994 and now provides the long-isolated Southwest Side with efficient transportation to the Loop, Chicago's central business district and the metropolitan region's largest employment center.

Immigrant Mexicans, Poles, and Arabs, as well as relocated blacks from elsewhere in Chicago, have diversified sections of the Southwest Side in recent decades. In 1990 Chicago Lawn was 43 percent white; in 2000 it was 10 percent white and 52 percent black. In 1990 West Lawn was 88 percent white; in 2000, 43 percent white and 51 percent Hispanic. Notably, these two community areas are among only a handful in the city that contain integrated neighborhoods. Arab women wearing *hijab*s (headscarves) can be seen pushing strollers along sidewalks, while Middle Eastern and Hispanic businesses stand side by side.

Religious change has also been evident. Congregation Lawn Manor Beth Jacob on Kedzie Avenue, the last remaining white synagogue on the Southwest Side, sold its property to Congregation B'nai Zaken, an Ethiopian Jewish synagogue, in 2003. Mosques can be found along 63rd Street, the principal commercial street, while Hispanic Pentecostals and other Protestants worship in storefronts and freestanding buildings. In Chicago Lawn, black storefront churches line Western Avenue.

Yet the Southwest Side lacks many of the cultural amenities often sought by young professional families today. While the park in Marquette Park/Chicago Lawn is an oasis, there are no movie theaters, museums, music venues, or high-end retail shopping. There is no Starbuck's on 63rd Street. It is not yet clear whether these community areas will remain stably integrated or are near the tipping point of significant racial change (Lewis et al. 2002; Maly and Leachman 1998, 149–50).

A Classic Catholic Parish

St. Nicholas of Tolentine is in many ways a "classic" Chicago Catholic parish. The church sits on the boundary between Chicago Lawn and West Lawn. It has been the home parish to a broad mix of Eastern European, Italian, Irish, and Mexican immigrants for most of its century-long history (it was established as a mission in 1909). St. Nick's stood in contrast to several mono-ethnic parishes in the local Catholic cluster (the smallest subdivision of a large diocese), such as St. Bruno, St. Richard, and St. Turibius, all of which continue to serve Polish-speaking members, and Nativity of the Blessed Virgin Mary, originally a Lithuanian parish. The historically progressive role played by St. Nick's—it was the first Southwest Side parish to institute the liturgical reforms of Vatican II, for example—positioned it to help Catholic parishioners face later urban restructuring in positive ways.

As for Catholics universally, the uniting ritual of the Mass ties the parishioners of St. Nick's to their parish and is the basis for their common beliefs. However, as they were confronted with demographic and social class shifts around and within their parish, they struggled to develop new shared norms of beliefs and behavior that eventually helped to embolden them to see beyond their parochial boundaries and engage in advocacy for their neighborhood.

Figure 3.2 above displays the dense, block-by-block distribution of member families, more than 77 percent of whom live within a one-mile radius of the church, making it a neighborhood congregation in our typology. The imposing but architecturally modest red brick neo-Renaissance church was built in the 1930s and is surrounded by neat bungalows just off 63rd Street, the main commercial thoroughfare through the parish. The school remains active, although without the high enrollment typical of the "golden age" just after the school was built in 1960. The parish today supports forty-five lay organizations and is served by two immigrant Latin American priests.

In the mid-1990s, membership at St. Nick's was in the first phase of a transition from predominantly European ethnicity to predominantly Mexican. Attendance at weekend masses averaged around two thousand individuals throughout the 1990s and in 2001, the pastor, Fr. Stanley Rataj, estimated membership enrollment at about 2,700 families, 30 percent white and 70 percent Hispanic. While many of these families have young children, they often cannot afford Catholic school tuition that is no longer subsidized by the sacrificial wages of nuns who taught during the classical period of ethnic Catholicism. Instead, these children attend the overcrowded public school across the street. The parish school enrolled about six hundred children in the mid-1990s, but in the early decades of this century enrollment declined to about three hundred. Today most of the children are Catholic, an unusual situation given that many non-Catholic black families seek alternative educational options in parochial schools. Weekly offerings are down about one-third from the mid-1990s. A survey conducted in 1991 showed that about two-thirds of the residents in the vicinity surrounding St. Nick's parish were Catholic; that figure has likely declined since then with the arrival of blacks and Arabs, as well as a few immigrants from Southeast Asia.

At the eightieth anniversary celebration Mass in the mid-1990s, Fr. Rataj, who is of Polish descent, asked the congregation, "Is this the last song for St. Nick's? Are the glory days behind us?" This was the unspoken fear felt not only among the remaining older ethnic European parishioners but particularly by their children, who had been steadily leaving the church for homes in the suburbs and elsewhere. The mostly Mexican and Mexican American parishioners often see St. Nick's as a stopping point along the road to outlying suburbs rather than the parish destination it once was for immigrant Europeans. While attendance has remained high, Fr. Rataj reported that in recent years about one-third of the membership has turned over each year. The groundedness of parish identity and life is as much a resource as a liability in the context of contemporary urban mobility, raising questions about the parish's ability to re-root its most recent ethnic groups. While Fr. Rataj gave a resounding "no" to his own questions above, adding that he would not have returned as pastor had he felt that way, a new St. Nicholas Church is taking shape in a new and uncertain urban context characterized by demographic shifts and employment losses.

Congregational Community Traits: Finding Common Ground

Constructing a post-Vatican II multiracial/ethnic parish identity at St. Nicholas of Tolentine Church required developing a new taken-for-granted moral reality. The question was, How can different groups of parishioners come to share values that they can use to develop mutually understood standards of conduct and decisions about right and wrong (Katznelson 1997, 48)? This is difficult relational work. The assumptions about ethnic homogeneity in urban neighborhoods have always been overdrawn. Nonetheless, language and historic (even if imagined) ties have brought an often defensive coherence to ethnic parishes, particularly in the face of long-standing nativist anti-Catholicism. Intergroup rivalry and conflict are also well-documented in Chicago history. It is the latter pattern, facilitated by the emergent "white" status of European ethnics, that continued in black-white residential divisions. The racial and economic hierarchy that permitted European ethnic groups to "become white" during the 1930s, 1940s, and 1950s hardened relationships against blacks (Barrett and Roediger 1997). A deacon at St. Nick's explained how the meeting of a newly forming parish council brought out unacknowledged suspicions by older white members against recent Hispanic immigrants, highlighting just how difficult the norm-building process is. When asked what their vision of parish was, older parishioners told stories about their past in ways that communicated a sense of "we built up something good here" and, detected the deacon, an implicit message to the newcomers of "don't tear it down." Subtle and usually unconscious attitudes such as these have imposed barriers between otherwise well-meaning parishioners in many churches. Some members sought instead to identify common ground.

They found an opportunity in the events that led to the institution of the Spanish liturgy. At a parish meeting in the early 1990s, an elderly Latina said through a translator that she didn't want to come to the United States but that she had to "follow her children." And now that she was here and too old to learn English, she asked that a Mass in Spanish be held "so I can talk to God—because I *must* talk to God." One participant in the meeting recalled the "magical feeling" that swept through the room because, he thought, despite their focus on ethnic and cultural differences, they were able to identify common religious needs. Gerardo Marti (2009, 59) calls this "ethnic transcendence," in which a shared religious identity "overrides potentially divisive aspects of ethnic affiliations in considerations of social interaction." This setting provides a face-to-face opportunity among already motivated parishioners. Indeed, many parishes experience the opposite, where economic and racial differences often trump a common religious identity when members are confronted by challenges in the abstract: "*they* are moving in," "did you see how *they* are starting to take over *our* parish?"

Motivated members of St. Nick's continued to seek other commonalities. For many, the church's first Cinco de Mayo festival aided the search because it required negotiated arrangements between Anglo culture and Mexican culture, between English speakers and Spanish speakers, and between lower-income and better-off parishioners. Because the pastor had a priest friend who ran an orphanage in Mexico, the festival committee agreed to make a folkloric performance by the orphans the centerpiece of a major parish event and run it as a fundraiser for the orphanage. In the process, the committee argued about whether to include American food in a Mexican celebration (American food was included), how to manage the money they would collect (they stationed both a Mexican and an Anglo at the door to collect tickets, making sure that everyone paid), and, some observed quietly to one another, whether faraway Mexicans or local deserving Americans should be the beneficiaries of the church's efforts.

Despite arguments, the joint effort paid material and symbolic dividends. Anglos learned that Mexicans were willing to support the parish financially regardless of repeated complaints by Anglos that Mexicans did not do so (echoing Irish complaints about Italians on the West Side during the deacon's youth in the 1930s and 1940s). The two groups demonstrated to themselves their newfound ability to work across cultural and language divides, at least in this instance.

The search for common ground has deep practical implications. One parish council member articulated issues of commonality differently from those who concentrate on cultural events. Not being Polish, she "felt like an outsider" at her former parish that had a large Polish constituency. "Polish language and culture is unifying for families," she observed, "but it is not for communities where other groups exist." She applied the same reasoning to Hispanics. "On the community level, the emphasis has to be on the common elements," she asserted, like the parish school, getting a job, and other basic necessities of life. "Focusing on them and the values attached to achieving them helps unite a group. Emphasizing differences creates stereotypes which then form blockades to realizing the same values. People think there are differences in morality when stereotypes are brought up." "Ultimately," she insisted, "the focus has to be on God." In this way, she was enjoining her fellow parishioners to "co-construct a shared religious identity as Christians," which requires that both Hispanics and Anglos occupy a subculture that transcends ethnic differences (Marti 2009, 62–63). Clearly there are alternative ways to solve fundamental problems of social order. Achieving consensus on complex strategies to address these problems is no small matter.

Congregational Action: Participating in an Area-Wide Strategy

Despite the cultural dominance of mass society and the effacing of spatial differences in today's restructured urban landscapes, urban sociologists have demonstrated that local sentiments persist (A. Hunter 1978). Yet these sentiments are strained under current urban conditions, and local institutions must identify new strategies for reclaiming them. In the mid-1990s, the parish council at St. Nick's sought new strategies for addressing the congregation's concerns about the neighborhood. Crime rates were still low and graffiti was a relatively new problem, but a large number of once-immaculate bungalow properties now stood foreclosed.

Several council members resisted strategies that involved knocking on parishioner doors or calling them on the phone. Like many residents, council members tell stories about no longer knowing people living on their blocks, feeling fearful when seeing abandoned houses, and becoming anxious when rumors of increased crime rates (often exaggerated) circulate. What lies underneath that insecurity is, of course, the fear of racial/ethnic, economic, and cultural differences. Anthony Giddens (1990) writes that traditional (or premodern) communities are characterized by the interwoven nature of social relationships, their stability across time, and the ontological security they imbue in (or transmit to) members, all of which has changed for Southwestsiders. The council members once recognized their neighborhood and now they do not. The work of retaining local forms of genuine particularity that resist global sweeps comes down to, in one dimension, overcoming the fear of a place that has been wrenched from the social relationships that once gave it identity and trust.

In the mid-1990s, Fr. Rataj searched for positive signs for the future of St. Nick's parish. For ten years, the signs had been less than encouraging. While St. Nick's continued to be one of the principal anchors of the neighborhood, he discovered that, unlike the independent fiefdoms cultivated by pastors of an earlier era, parishes can no longer act independently in the face of massive changes. As they viewed changes they were ill-prepared to absorb, St. Nick's and other parishes in their cluster were attracted to the Southwest Catholic Cluster Project, which soon became the Southwest Organizing Project (SWOP), a multireligious, multiracial/ethnic but Catholic-dominated community organization.

St. Nicholas responded to the demographic, racial/ethnic, and economic changes in two stages. The church drew on internal clergy-lay cooperative parish leadership in the first stage. In the second stage, SWOP directed parishes in the Southwest Side toward a broader area strategy that permitted St. Nick's to become a member of a larger pool of institutional actors attempting to respond to and simultaneously reshape urban structures.

The priest-sociologist Philip Murnion (2000, 6) argued that parishes take "people beyond the privacy of family into relationships not of one's choosing." Because the classic parish church has obligations to all who live within its parish boundaries, including non-Catholic residents, as well as to Catholics who live beyond the parish boundaries, "participation in parish life is then participation in public life." Rather than eschew the parish model in favor of the voluntary model, Murnion argued that parochial structures should remain the foundation for Catholic participation not only in ordinary church life but also in a great variety of civic activities. "It is the whole culture of the parish, more than its programs, that relates parishioners to the wider world" (2). Furthermore, "movements, organizations, and regional efforts have always been a necessary complement to parishes." This understanding anticipated the relationship that developed between St. Nick's and SWOP during the 1990s.

SWOP's significance is threefold. First, it originated in a Catholic base and mobilized the parishes in its cluster. The stimulus for the project can be traced largely to the willingness of several pastors and laypeople to address the economic and moral challenges of racial integration and resegregation. Second, SWOP's precursor organization established a translocal rather than a parish strategy, thus lowering the boundaries to the outside, just as Cardinal Bernardin had established a pan-parochial Catholic school strategy to continue providing Catholic options in education (see below). Third, while founded with a Catholic base, Catholic leaders of SWOP reconfigured the organization into an interreligious and interracial/ethnic membership that brought them together with newer immigrants to the area, modeling and becoming agents for the permanent integration they sought.

SWOP had its origins in Project ACTS (Area Christians Together in the Spirit), established in 1987 by three local activists. Two were priests, Fr. James Fridel of St. Clare of Montefalco and Fr. Michael Adams of St. Gall; the third was James Capraro from St. Nick's, the founder in 1974 of the nonprofit economic development organization DevCor. These three responded to what they saw as a deliberate refusal on the part of the Catholic community to acknowledge the city-wide economic and racial/ethnic changes then taking place. And, Capraro said, "no one was paying attention" to potential consequences for the Southwest Side. The late 1970s and early 1980s were relatively calm, after which local leaders perceived the start of another wave of white out-migration and economic divestment. In what was then an unusual move, Project ACTS succeeded in bringing together several parishes for dialogue and joint action. A realistic plan required that they combine an analysis of economic factors that addressed residents' anxieties through specifically Christian understandings of racial/ethnic harmony.

Project ACTS distributed comparative economic and demographic data for the section of the Southwest Side between 47th and 79th Streets and Western and Cicero Avenues to the parishes, real estate agents, retail businesses, government agencies, and others identified as potential investors in the neighborhoods. Contrary to rumors, these data indicated that housing values were projected to rise based on the scheduled 1992 opening of the Orange Line rapid transit service to Midway Airport (which was delayed until 1994). Project ACTS urged local Catholics "to do good *and* do well," reported Capraro, by "embracing the larger demand pool of new and diverse residents," thus assuring higher market value for their properties.

This early collaborative effort led to the creation of the Southwest Catholic Cluster Project, financially supported by all but one of the parishes in the cluster and by the archdiocesan Office of Peace and Justice. The Cluster Project offered a theological alternative to defensive self-understandings of neighborhood, such as those promoted by the Southwest Parish and Neighborhood Federation, a 1960s-era group that modified but did not eliminate its racist overtones. In 1991 the Cluster Project published a widely distributed pamphlet written by Fr. Michael Slattery and lay parishioner William Droel of St. Clare of Montefalco Church in Gage Park, Chicago Lawn's northern neighbor, titled "Christians in their Neighborhood," which provided a theological rationale of place that could supplant the ethnic model of ownership and turf. The authors wrote (Slattery and Droel n.d., 3), "For a Christian (and for others), a neighborhood is not merely a social phenomenon or shared geography, but a community. And the particular God that Christians worship and love is revealed in communities." The authors argued that this theology of neighborhood links individuals to the wider society as an expression of subsidiarity, the Catholic principle of governance in which higher levels of state power should not control the activities of local or voluntary civic leaders if those activities result in best practical outcomes for residents (Wolfe 1995). Acting on the subsidiarity principle helps to humanize the city by endowing local participants, rather than the "hierarchy," with moral responsibility and giving them both freedom and power to act.

The practical consequences of reconceptualizing the neighborhood in this way, argued Slattery and Droel, include, first of all, a focus on fully incorporating newcomers rather than on preventing people from leaving. Secondly, it means acknowledging legitimate and serious neighborhood fears such as economic insecurity, gangs, drugs, crime, and graffiti, while eschewing prejudicial hatreds and fears that dogged residents in past racial conflicts and have arisen anew in today's urban context. Finally, they argued, "self-interest in the context of the interests of others," a central theme in Catholic social teaching, more fully ensures both a moral and a practical foundation for viable community life (Slattery and Droel n.d., 10; cf. Curran 1991, 76).

This kind of cultural work addressed the local construction of community in a new way. Residents of Chicago Lawn and surrounding community areas invested emotion as well as money in their neighborhoods.[4] Their bonds with one another were captured in shared memories of a style of life that, however partial and filtered, supported an upwardly mobile, prudent, and communally Catholic identity rooted in individual parishes (McMahon 1995). "I love my parish," stated an older parishioner whose home overlooked Marquette Park, her "country club," and recalled how she raised her children in St. Nick's during the 1950s and 1960s. "The school, the sports program, the priests and nuns—it was a great place to be." But the cultural work of the Cluster Project required that the churches and the residents incorporate a new community discourse into their Catholic imaginary, to develop a perspective in which the accustomed features of "neighborhoodness" could expand beyond the safe circles of the parish-school complex. The closing of St. Rita of Cascia's parish school in 1993, the first in the cluster to do so, sent another signal that traditional parochial boundaries were crumbling and that earlier institutional strengths were no longer reliable guides to future development.

In 1995 the Metropolitan Sponsors, an Industrial Areas Foundation affiliate, returned to Chicago. They were persuaded to do so after Cardinal Bernardin raised $1 million toward a goal of $2.6 million and together with Bishop Arthur Brazier of the Apostolic Church of God convinced several Protestant denominations to contribute funds. The previous cardinal, John Cody, had banished the once-powerful community organizing movement founded by Saul Alinsky in the 1940s and based in churches in distressed neighborhoods. When Metropolitan Sponsors became a real possibility, the Cluster Project leaders chose to pursue a professional community organizing affiliation rather than remain a "church" project. The organizer hired by the Project succeeded in breaking the Cluster Project's institutional tie with the archdiocese, while retaining the Catholic parishes as the core constituency under the umbrella of Metropolitan Sponsor's new entity, United Power for Action and Justice. It was necessary to break that tie in order for SWOP to strengthen the political validity of the cluster and gain credibility with other urban actors, particularly secular organizations and non-Christian religious groups.

An area-wide strategy required participation that could both represent and mobilize the diverse population of the Southwest Side. For example, after the tragic events of September 11, 2001, SWOP organized a public demonstration against vandals that damaged a mosque on 63rd Street. For several consecutive Fridays, between fifty and one hundred SWOP members kept vigil by surrounding the building shoulder-to-shoulder in a public show of solidarity. Subsequently, the mosque's imam joined SWOP, although previously SWOP leaders had been unable to recruit him. It was the organization's religious base that helped to create a moral, not just a social, community among its increasingly diverse constituents.

Following traditional community organizing principles, SWOP focused on building relationships among constituent members around selected themes of education, security, and housing with organized political efforts. "Can you feel the power of relating to one another?" asked Jim Capraro, the chair of the organizational assembly held less than a year after the organizer was hired in 1995. Hundreds of "one-on-ones" had been held to recruit participation in SWOP by emphasizing the public force of neighborhood relationships newly built on "trust among all residents, *not* loyalty" to in-group categories. A father of five from St. Nick's spoke about the emotionally wrenching decision his family made to stay after a shooting occurred in their neighborhood. A Muslim woman reported how Muslims are beginning to recognize that their children are also at risk "of the problems of American youth—drugs, gangs, and violence." Teens from three racially diverse Catholic high schools formed a youth service organization to aid local seniors and clean up Marquette Park. The pastor of St. Adrian, the most racially mixed parish in the cluster, inspired the assembly with his "call to action," emphasizing again the need to amass local political power but also acknowledging its spiritual base, reminding the assembled that "God is power." Community organizing is programmatically oriented to drawing the needs of participants into the broader needs of the community, thereby reducing the tension between an internal versus external congregational focus.

The Sisters of St. Casimir, who run Holy Cross Hospital and Maria High School on the edge of St. Nick's parish, were asked by SWOP to participate in a protest of predatory lending practices. Spoke one of the sisters, "We've lived in this neighborhood for a long time [since 1911], and we've seen the abandoned houses, just like everyone else. Our community has never become involved in politics or issues like this. We were focused on religion and our own institutions. When the Southwest Organizing

Project came to us, there was some resistance. The sisters have seen other religious communities that are very actively involved in political work. They get arrested and things. Are we going to get in trouble? What's going to happen?" Nevertheless, seventeen sisters in their religious habits led a prayer vigil outside the office of one of the lenders.

The sisters decided that if they simply "let the market prevail" with regard to housing losses, "we will not have a neighborhood left." "We were afraid," one sister remembered. "But we did it and we were amazed at what could happen when you unite." Even the pastor at St. Nick's admitted to being surprised at the creeping housing blight affecting his parish. "I had no idea there were so many abandoned houses right around the parish," particularly in the eastern portion that is heavily black, which motivated him to join the SWOP steering committee.

Because of their size and resources, parishes continue to be among the principal anchors of the neighborhood and their members do the micro-level work crucial to SWOP. However, Jim Capraro suggests that their ability to confront the effect of suburbanization on city parishes is limited. He claims that this is partly due to the fact that Catholic churches are always reacting to "the feisty Catholic marketplace" and employ business entrepreneurialism to the detriment of the metropolitan region as a whole. This happens despite the US Bishops' pastoral letter on the economy, which severely criticizes strong free-market individualism (US Catholic Bishops 1986; Burns 1992, 109). "The church is different but we don't react differently than anyone else in this metropolitan juggernaut," Capraro offered, acknowledging both the diminished agency of individuals in an era of urban restructuring and the difficulty of making a moral argument that effectively challenges economic liberalism.

Deconcentration and deindustrialization have decimated many working-class neighborhoods in American cities. Yet resistance has occurred in Chicago through political negotiation among local interests, manufacturers, unions, and government in the form of enterprise zones (Rast 1999). Joel Rast (1999, 164) argues that urban growth strategies can be effectively shaped into local development opportunities by neighborhood coalitions. DevCor was created out of such a strategy. Reflecting on its work, Jim Capraro (2004, 153) argued for the interlacing of organizing and development:

> Organizing has been critical to the success of community development. Would we have powerful intermediaries like LISC [Local

Initiatives Support Corporation][5] and the Enterprise Foundation or national and local actors like Neighborhood Reinvestment Corporation/NHS if, in the early 1970s, there had not been an anti-redlining campaign that led to the Home Mortgage Disclosure Act (HMDA), which in turn led to the passage of the Community Reinvestment Act (CRA)? Similarly, community development work often reflects the fruits of organizing in the form of concrete physical development and other tangible activities.

Those tangibles included keeping the Nabisco and Tootsie Roll factories open on the Southwest Side. DevCor also developed Churchview Manor, a senior citizen housing complex on 63rd Street for local residents who could no longer care for their homes but preferred to remain in the "old neighborhood." In recent years, DevCor worked with SWOP to secure zoning and city TIF (tax increment financing) funding to build a black-owned plastics-molding factory in Chicago Lawn on the site of a former hazardous waste dump. The Illinois legislature passed anti-predatory lending legislation in 2001, after two years of SWOP advocacy. Retail outlets appeared along Pulaski Road and Cicero Avenue after the Orange Line opened stations on those streets, just as the early economic assessments produced by Project ACTS, SWOP's predecessor, had predicted.

Urban Impact: The Power of Relating to One Another

"Can you feel the power of relating to one another?" asked Jim Capraro. Two sets of relationships enhanced the urban impact of this neighborhood congregation. Internally, St. Nick's accomplished the ethnic transition from a predominantly European to a predominantly Mexican membership. It took diligent effort under wise leadership to find the common ground that all shared as Catholics. This positioned St. Nick's to join SWOP and DevCor in their efforts to enhance life on the Southwest Side. Jim Capraro may have been the point person in brokering these external relationships, but it is unlikely that his heroic efforts alone would have sufficed to sustain them. The underpinning of Catholic social teachings was a necessary condition. St. Nick's enhanced its ability to act through these strategic partnerships. It could not have exerted such strong influence without them, and it would not have joined them without Catholic justification.

St. Jerome Catholic Church
Urban Context: Rogers Park

Whereas both Rogers Park and the Southwest Side were initially settled by European immigrants, Rogers Park became racially and ethnically stable in the 1980s, sooner than the Southwest Side. Historically, Rogers Park was one-third Protestant, one-third Catholic, and one-third Jewish. Most of the synagogues have left; many have been replaced by non-Christian congregations. Indeed, the far northeast corner of Chicago became the most religiously, racially/ethnically, and economically diverse section of the city in the 1990s (Numrich and Peterman 1996, 19–21, 33–34).

Rogers Park is about ten miles directly north of the Loop.[6] It is named after the first white settler in the area, Irish immigrant Phillip Rogers, who built his cabin in 1839. Many of the local streets are named after other nineteenth-century settlers, such as Touhy, Pratt, Lunt, Morse, Farwell, Greenleaf, and Estes. The area was a farming community until Chicago annexed it in 1893. Rogers Park is bounded by the suburb of Evanston to the north, the West Ridge community area to the west, the Edgewater community area to the south, and Lake Michigan to the east. The Chicago Transit Authority's elevated Red Line and the Union Pacific North Line railway traverse the community from north to south, providing good public transportation linkages to a variety of job opportunities in the Loop and technology-based jobs in suburbs such as Northbrook and Schaumburg. Two major north-south thoroughfares cradle the area, Western Avenue on the west and Sheridan Road on the east.

The predominant ethnic groups of Rogers Park until about 1930 were Germans, Irish, and English, but Russian Jews became the single largest ethnic group by 1970. The demographics have shifted dramatically since then. The 1960 census showed Rogers Park to be 99 percent white; in 2000 the white population had dropped to 32 percent, while blacks (30 percent), Hispanics (28 percent), and Asians (4 percent) comprised nearly two-thirds of the population. Since 1990 Rogers Park has maintained a balance among the major groups, with only Asians declining by about 3 percent. Among the 832 neighborhoods of Chicago, about 6 percent are identified as "integrated" in the study of race and residential patterns conducted by James Lewis and colleagues. Rogers Park is one of four community areas identified in the study as having "numerous integrated [census] tracts that remained stable during the 1990s" (Lewis et al. 2002, 84). Much of this diversity is visible in the membership of St. Jerome Catholic Church, especially the variety of Hispanic groups.

The religious diversity of contemporary Rogers Park recalls its diverse racial and ethnic history. After the Jews of North Lawndale fled the West Side during the racial changes of the 1950s, many settled in Rogers Park and opened synagogues. Only four remain today, the rest having either closed or relocated to adjacent West Ridge, which still dominates Jewish life in Chicago with its more than twenty synagogues, or joined the growing Jewish presence in the northern suburbs. An International Society of Krishna Consciousness ("Hare Krishna") temple opened in 1979 in a former Masonic temple in Rogers Park and began to serve the increasing numbers of Hindu immigrants in the vicinity. A neighborhood mosque, Wallen Community Center, serves a predominantly South Asian constituency, while a variety of new religious movements are also represented in Rogers Park. There are two Catholic parishes and approximately thirty mainline Protestant, Pentecostal, and evangelical churches that serve white, black, and Hispanic constituencies (Numrich and Peterman 1996, 19).

Rogers Park has several features that promote its diverse composition and stabilize its socioeconomic base. Loyola University Chicago occupies the southeast corner of Rogers Park and in 2008 instituted a housing support program to stimulate home-buying by faculty and staff in the surrounding community areas. Rogers Park's housing composition simultaneously promotes diversity and mobility: about 85 percent is rental housing, most of it in handsome, brick courtyard buildings largely occupied by minority groups (Maly and Leachman 1998, 135). In the mid-1990s, the rents and housing prices were modest. Since then, Rogers Park participated in the housing market inflation that was led by the huge demand for lakefront residences, although its single-family houses and condos remained more modestly priced than those in lakefront areas to the south (Rodkin 2004). Multi-family dwellings can accommodate a wide variety of groups, from upwardly mobile singles to large, densely packed families of new immigrants. As a result, Rogers Park has a high mobility rate. Based on 2000 census figures, nearly two-thirds (64 percent) of the residents have moved within the last ten years. Increasing gentrification and condo conversions are adding middle-class stability but also anxiety about retaining Rogers Park's diversity.

The overall population of Rogers Park declined between 1970 and 1980 but rose in the next decade due to an inflow of minority and low-income residents. In 2000 the population reached its highest level up to that time, though the total number of housing units decreased, thus creating more per-room density. The public schools instituted a year-round schedule of classes to accommodate the growing number of children. Many residents endured substantial poverty and stress, whereas about 29 percent of job-holders worked in professional and managerial positions, much higher than the 13 percent in Chicago Lawn and 17 percent in West Lawn on the Southwest Side.

Broadly speaking, Rogers Park can be divided into three socioeconomic sections: the lakefront (affluent white), the western two-thirds (poorer non-white), and the northern edge, often referred to as "north of Howard (Street)" (very poor non-white). In recent years, gentrification has transformed rental properties into moderate-income condominiums in pockets throughout Rogers Park, including in the "north of Howard" section. The largest commercial district is along Devon Avenue, Rogers Park's southern border with the slightly more middle-class and white Edgewater community area. As condo development increased, other commercial strips improved (Davis 2008, 36). Loyola University participated in economic development projects alongside a dozen community non-profit groups that sprang up in the 1980s to address declining government support for housing and immigrant community needs.

Rogers Park and the Southwest Side represent largely different labor markets and socioeconomic statuses in the new Chicago. With its lakefront location, Rogers Park is economically more diverse and residentially more desirable than the Southwest Side (Maly and Leachman 1998, 150). Urban restructuring in Rogers Park has become an upscale project. While Rogers Park is poorer than its surrounding areas due to its large number of rental housing units, its accessibility by car and public transit, institutional stability, and residential flexibility attract people seeking an urban lifestyle. Even if Rogers Park lacks some of the cultural amenities a young urbanite might want, they are available nearby.

Given different locations in the city and the spatial limitations and advantages of each, the two areas unsurprisingly developed different kinds of neighborhoods. While similar parish-school-neighborhood units evolved according to Chicago-style Catholicism in each area, the Southwest Side became more spatially isolated, whereas both the location of Rogers Park and its more diverse opportunities kept it open to a broader movement of residents. These contexts permitted different emphases on local community life. As a result, Rogers Park became religiously and racially/ethnically diverse much before the Southwest Side; yet today both areas are among the few with diverse neighborhoods in Chicago. The historic social-geographic nexus of Chicago Catholicism has given way in part to other bases of solidarity, such as interests, occupations, education, social class, and military veteran status, which compete with residential ties for creating meaningful social groupings in the metropolis (Greer 1962; A. Hunter 1974; Fischer 1982; Perella 1996). Importantly, we argue that each form exists alongside the others, responding to particular needs as well as exemplifying new choices in the continual redefining of meaning and place in the new urban era.

A Diverse Catholic Parish

While St. Jerome is a neighborhood congregation in our typology, since the majority of its member families (more than 88 percent) live within a one-mile radius of the church (Figure 3.3), it also serves a significant number of Hispanic members residing outside of the neighborhood with Spanish-language baptisms, weddings, quinceañeras, religious education, charismatic and other prayer groups, youth groups, activities for the elderly, social services, and counseling. Today, more than four thousand worshippers attend three Spanish liturgies and three English masses each weekend in a basilica-style Italian Renaissance edifice framed by two imposing towers. The parish, founded in 1894, is about 85 percent Spanish-speaking (it is known locally as "the Mexican parish"), the rest a broad mixture of European ethnicities, blacks, Africans, Filipinos, and Haitians. Until 2003, a couple of dozen people attended the twice-monthly French Mass, down from about one hundred in the mid-1990s due to the loss of a number of Haitians to Pentecostal churches and out-migration from Rogers Park for economic reasons. St. Jerome has been slowly losing white members as well, even though Rogers Park as a whole has maintained stable population diversity since 1990. The current pastor, Fr. Jeremy Thomas, a transplanted Welshman who specializes in Hispanic ministry, maintains one Saturday and two Sunday English masses as a way to attract middle-class families with complicated schedules.[7]

Cuban refugees, the parish's first non-English-speakers, created the Spanish liturgy in 1975 with support from the pastor at the time. Unlike the experience at St. Nicholas on the Southwest Side twenty years later, incorporation of the new liturgy at St. Jerome did not create controversy or require negotiation within the parish. The difference rested partly in

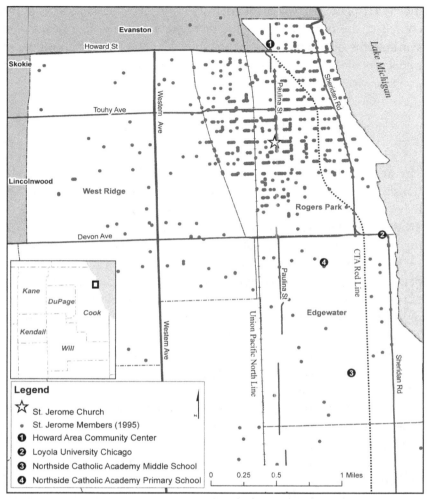

FIGURE 3.3. St. Jerome Catholic Church and Members. Map by David J. Treering and Melissa Gesbeck Howell, Loyola University Chicago.

acceptance of the pastor's traditional authority and partly in the relative openness to urban diversity on the North Side of the city in contrast to the more insular atmosphere that prevailed on the Southwest Side.

St. Jerome's multilingual staff is not large for the number and diversity of people they serve. With two full-time priests in addition to Rev. Harold Bonin, pastor emeritus, they rely heavily on their four deacons, religious education staff, and lay volunteers. The Jesuits at nearby Loyola University have been known to help out, especially for certain liturgies. We observed an Ash Wednesday service in which an estimated ten thousand people, mostly Hispanics, slowly made their way from the sidewalks around the church to the front of the sanctuary where eight priests, deacons, and seminarians distributed ashes throughout the day. The large number of undocumented immigrants with low literacy rates and high needs for social services stretches the staff's capacity.

Congregational Community Traits: Acknowledging Cultural Differences

The diversity of St. Jerome's membership invites questions about relationships among the groups. Are they cooperative or antagonistic? Do they submerge their differences or do language, class, and race/ethnicity divide them? These questions need to be answered in two parts, addressing relationships both across all groups and among Hispanic subgroups.

Like St. Nicholas, St. Jerome's parishioners were united in common beliefs through the Eucharistic liturgy that reinforced their shared norms, but unlike St. Nicholas, they were less able to draw on their past commonalities to create new relationships needed to face future challenges. The dispute over the restructuring of the parish schools in their cluster, on the one hand, moderated their external community orientation. Their continuing ties with several advocacy groups in Rogers Park, on the other hand, strengthened it.

During our primary research period in the mid-1990s, several parish leaders admitted that the Spanish, English, and French language groups at St. Jerome do not prefer to worship together. Instead, they have created their own ethnic sub-parishes. To counter these boundary-making preferences, then-pastor Fr. Bonin insisted on holding several trilingual masses annually. At the church's hundredth anniversary Mass in 1994, Cardinal Bernardin read his homily in English and Spanish, followed by a French version read by the Haitian deacon. The deacon commented to our researcher during the reception afterward that "the cooperation which was needed to put on this event should take place all the time, but it doesn't." Every Lenten season the Via Crucis, in which parishioners symbolically trace Jesus's walk to Calvary through the neighborhood, is conducted in the three languages. The stops for the Stations of the Cross are locations where violence had occurred in the neighborhood.

However, as the leaders acknowledged, these efforts are "not very successful" in building multiracial/ethnic and multi-language participation in other aspects of church life. Fr. Bonin conceded that, other than major celebrations such as the centennial, "no one has a good time" and little interaction occurs. One deacon was particularly reflective in his views when he said that "we're all scared to go out from the upper room," a reference to the reticence of Jesus' disciples to leave their secure surroundings (see John 20, Acts 1 and 2). He noted that in general as Catholics, "we're not doing our job, and we're not doing the evangelizing we should be doing. We're not reaching out." Other divisions based on social class or race/ethnicity have had an uneven record at St. Jerome. For example, African immigrants distinguish themselves from American blacks but Bosnians and Somalis mix easily with English speakers. The deacon concluded that St. Jerome needs to "get some chemistry going" in order to make the parish work. As late as 2007, Fr. Thomas remarked that St. Jerome "is a wonderful parish with a rich history and great people. But to a certain degree, it has to rediscover itself" (Coburn and Zivan 2007).

The *gemeinschaftlich* quality of Catholic parishes has been exaggerated, to be sure. A more complicated set of relationships forms the typical urban parish. Jesuit sociologist Joseph Fichter (1954) identified four types of parish members and the variety of relationships they have with one another. He argued that secondary associations are more typical than primary ones, and this is the case at St. Jerome, except for pockets of social intimacy like the Haitian prayer group. For example, Hispanic families inculcate Catholic teachings and faith practices into their children through extensive family-centered feast day celebrations rather than sending their children to parochial schools. Some of the most popular feasts include the adolescent rite of passage for fifteen-year-old girls called the quinceañera, the Mananita (serenade) for Our Lady of Guadalupe, the Via Crucis, and Dia de las Muertos (Day of the Dead). While well-attended, such activities reinforce ethnic identity but not social intimacy.

On the other hand, the Spanish-speaking youth group at St. Jerome (called Esperanza Latina) and the cell-based groups adapted from Latin American rural communities influenced by liberation theology are the most likely to form *gemeinschaftlich* communities. These groups attract adolescents and young adults. Esperanza Latina, one of the church's most active groups, is run by a half-dozen volunteer coordinators who oversee several programs to develop the spiritual/religious, social, intellectual, leadership, and cultural aspects of young people's lives. About fifty youth meet on Sundays to discuss diverse topics like learning how to pray and the difficulties of married life. Some discussions expand to challenging contemporary issues such as living together, contraception, and gender roles. One leader exhorted the youth to consider the negative effects of Latin American patriarchal attitudes by declaring that "*machista* is anti-biblical.*" Esperanza Latina succeeds in addressing some of the pressing concerns of first- and second-generation Hispanic youth caught in the crossfire between parental standards and tradition and the streets. It does not, however, seek to cross boundaries of race/ethnicity, language, or interests (Numrich and Peterman 1996, 27).

As to relationships among the Hispanic subgroups at St. Jerome, the assumption that groups with similar cultural characteristics are likely to exhibit ethnic solidarity does not hold. Mexican immigrants are the predominant Spanish-speaking group, with substantial numbers of El Salvadorans, a smaller number of other Central Americans, and a long-time Cuban group. One year the feast of Our Lady of Guadalupe provoked nationalistic tensions between Mexicans and other Hispanics that trumped their shared status as immigrants. Fr. Bonin had prohibited the display of the Mexican flag in the church during the feast. When the new pastor, Fr. Thomas Bradley, arrived in the early 2000s, some Mexicans sneaked it in. This so angered non-Mexicans, that the following year the flag was not displayed. The year after that, the groups organized a meeting with the pastor for a full airing of the matter. After two emotion-filled hours of debate—"the Virgin appeared in Mexico, so we must have a Mexican flag" countered by "the Virgin represents all the Americas, so one flag is not appropriate"—the groups agreed to incorporate the Mexican colors into the church's decoration but not to display the flag. As a result, they deemphasized the spirit of Mexican nationalism that often breaks through in other Hispanic parishes and achieved a small measure of the Catholic universalism expressed in Vatican II.

Throughout this debate, Fr. Bradley assumed a collaborative posture instead of the authoritarian style of his predecessors. "There were two trains running through that room," he later recalled, "so I would have been run over if I tried to dictate something." He waited until all the emotion had been spilled and then the solution presented itself. The groups remained together but had their separate cultural positions acknowledged. In assuming a more democratic pastoral style, Fr. Bradley acknowledged the legitimacy of cultural preferences, thus avoiding a potentially divisive standoff in the parish. In parishes built by industrial-era immigrants, cultural conflict often resulted in one group, for example, the Highlander Poles, leaving other Poles to form their own parish. One North Side

Chicago neighborhood in the early decades of the twentieth century had five Polish parishes in about a half-square-mile radius.

Congregational Action: A Catholic Voice in the Neighborhood, a Catholic Education on the North Side

A parishioner of St. Jerome started the Howard Area Community Center (HACC) in 1967, which initially worked out of the church but eventually relocated "North of Howard." HACC remains among the most active service agencies in Rogers Park today, working closely with all minority groups in the neighborhood and in six additional sites serving poor families on Chicago's North Side. St. Jerome supports HACC financially, participates in activities such as food and clothing drives, and supplies parishioners to serve on its board.

One type of conflict long monitored by HACC is that between residential property owners and renters. Single-family dwellings tend to attract stable middle-class families (many are white), while large tracts of small apartments attract transient singles and poor families (of all races). For more than ten years, most of the local community groups have resisted the condominiumizing of the larger apartments, which forces poorer families to double up with relatives while looking elsewhere for cheaper apartments of sufficient size. One apartment complex included public housing inhabited almost entirely by poor black residents. When the Hispanic Housing Coalition purchased it in order to provide low-interest condominium mortgages for working-poor families, one of the local community groups organized shrill emotional resistance. "Oppose the ethnic cleansing in Rogers Park!" read one of their flyers, setting up a black-Hispanic conflict that some of St. Jerome's members attempted to mediate. As happens in many publicly subsidized housing projects, a deteriorated site of concentrated poverty and social need offers no easy solutions. Race relations have a more open quality in Rogers Park compared to the Southwest Side, where, for example, there are still large pockets of white neighborhoods and where street life, especially on residential blocks, is quiet and controlled. A more explicit ethos of racial/ethnic inclusivity and tolerance for different ways of doing things is valorized at St. Jerome despite cultural obstacles.

In order to successfully mediate racial and ethnic tensions, former pastor Fr. Bradley claimed that the "Catholic voice needs to be heard in Rogers Park." This was based on his further claim that the Catholic

voice is the "voice of reason" and that the "reasonable voice will prevail." He asked, "If the Catholics were not involved, who else would
be doing the talking for the neighborhood?" He only laughed at our
researcher's suggestion of the alderman or secular organizations,
unconvinced that these others could or would adequately bridge the
interests of the diverse, sometimes divided, constituents of the neighborhood. Catholics bring "an interest that is higher than the person,"
he declared. While Fr. Bradley did not agree with the pastor of nearby
St. Ignatius parish on all things, he did acknowledge that they both
belong to the "Catholic party." The strength of this party is, following Cardinal Bernardin, the "search for common ground" among all.
Despite its limits in practice, the common ground position is explicit
in the broadness of the net it casts. As Fr. Bradley explained, changing
somebody else's views comes only with the willingness to "listen to others" and to "sacrifice for others," which he claimed the Catholic Church
can do, unlike secular institutions.

Perhaps it is exaggerated on the part of this pastor to make religious
claims on one of the most contested areas of the city. On the other hand,
it is possible that the neighborhood's religious, racial/ethnic, and class
diversity exposes vulnerabilities in secular leadership. Under these conditions, certain kinds of traditional resources become revalued: organizational depth, local knowledge, institutional resources, and the value of
place-dependent communities. These factors came into play with regard
to St. Jerome's parish school and the larger issue of Catholic parochial
education on Chicago's North Side.

As at St. Nicholas on the Southwest Side, transiency among new
immigrants at St. Jerome is high, both among poorer families seeking
affordable housing and better-off families who wish to purchase their
suburban dream home. While Rogers Park was a preferred settlement
area for earlier European immigrants, it has become increasingly, like the
Southwest Side, a transitional staging point for many new immigrants.
During the previous era, the parish school created an anchor for the parish, despite parochial school attendance in the United States never reaching, on average, even half of the church membership. Yet in Chicago in
1965, 95 percent of the parishes had a school (Rosswurm 2004, 718). The
parish-school-neighborhood unit was central to the identity of Chicago
Catholics, as we have seen. The Archdiocese of Chicago still has the largest Catholic school system in the United States. But by the time Cardinal
Bernardin began organizational and financial restructuring in the 1990s,

the parish school was up against demographic and financial realities that many local Catholics had difficulty accepting.

In this new context, rational financial planning was supported by a theologically reflective focus on the mission of the church initiated by the reforms of Vatican II, but it was also motivated by urban restructuring and the need to remake urban Catholicism into a force for the twenty-first century. Cardinal Bernardin's management changes decentralized and localized the decision-making process. Each parish was required to assess its mission and its parishioners' needs and, more importantly, its relationship to other parishes, the broader church, and the secular realities in which they lived. As the cardinal observed, when the archdiocese was predominantly immigrant, national separations were an effective approach to pastoral needs even though they engendered a "certain degree of parochialism or congregationalism" (quoted in D'Agostino 2000, 275). But in light of current demographic shifts, managing church resources requires a reallocation by which decisions are based on "just stewardship" of the body of the church over any particular local expression (that is, the parish). The cardinal applied this theological notion of stewardship to a call for a Catholic identity beyond the boundaries of one's own parish, reminding his parishioners that "we belong to a universal . . . not a congregational church." He wrote, "Planning for the future requires a greater degree of collaboration and sharing than has been our custom in the past" (quoted in D'Agostino 2000, 277). This required collaboration across social-geographic and racial/ethnic boundaries. As historian Peter D'Agostino has demonstrated, however, this process was often not understood by laity, and sometimes even by clergy, primarily because it challenged the ethnic "church and turf" model of historic Chicago Catholicism. What many Chicago Catholics heard was that the archdiocese was closing "their" parish or "their" school, and "simply" for financial reasons (D'Agostino 2000, 275–77).

As related above, Catholic school enrollment in the archdiocese declined sharply from 1965 to 1995 and continues to decline today. In 1994 St. Jerome's elementary school was consolidated with seven other parishes in its cluster due to declining enrollments and the cumulating inability to financially support their schools.[8] As of 1993, six of the seven parishes, including St. Jerome, owed the archdiocese a combined debt of more than $2 million. St. Jerome today feeds Northside Catholic Academy, with sites in nearby Edgewater but not Rogers Park (see Figure 3.3, above). One parish that could afford to support its own school independently withdrew from the planning process. Another school was at first retained despite archdiocesan resistance but closed after three years due to declining enrollments.

The consolidation process took two years to complete, stimulated much resistance from the parishes, and resulted in some alienation from the archdiocese. Yet the process of deciding how to address the parochial school matter in three North Side community areas was not authoritarian nor decided simply on the basis of financial calculations. Furthermore, there was no fixed model that schools were expected to follow in their restructuring efforts. The seven parishes were provided a variety of consultative and financial resources and the determining body had broad representation from each parish. Each pastor had veto power over collective decisions. The process was initially deemed voluntary, although the cardinal stepped in at a certain point, as we explain below. Finally, the process was religious, that is, the planning function was not merely rational but also applied "living faith, Scripture, Church teaching and the resources of tradition" to the experiences of the communities undergoing change (D'Agostino 1996, 254, quoting John A. Grindel). The planning group took the name SUCCESS—Schools United to Continue Catholic Educational Strength and Stability.

The early planning meetings revealed the extent of parishioners' anxiety about closing their parish school and their depth of loyalty to it. Such feelings were major obstacles to acknowledging the financial vulnerabilities of individual schools and the impending alternative of closing the weakest schools to the benefit of others. One deacon, whose five children attended St. Jerome School, attributed the school's population loss to a lack of "visible and involved leadership" from the school. Other parents we spoke with confessed that "there was no welcoming sense to the Hispanic population, no outreach," as one put it. It is impossible to speculate whether a sufficient number of Hispanic families could have been recruited, but the prevailing feeling among some of the parents was the perceived failure of effort.

Yet the resistance to institutional restructuring was religiously and sociologically complex. Some participants saw the change as fundamentally undermining parish life. Parochial schools are distinctive American structures that form the next generation of Catholics. They are part of a parish ecclesiology embedded in a complex set of institutional structures (D'Agostino 1997–98, 100). These relationships are the means by which most Catholics connect to the larger Catholic system. By becoming pan-parochial, schools become less tied to the "placeness" of the parish community.

Other resisters were persuaded that the church was mainly a business and so the weak links needed to be removed. Still others were keen to point out the power dynamics between "downtown" (the archdiocesan chancery office) and the "community," framing the discussion wholly in conflictive terms. Some suggested that bias was involved in the final selection of school sites since the most racially/ethnically and economically diverse community area, Rogers Park, was not included.

The formation of Northside Catholic Academy further revealed the tension within Catholicism between the power of the hierarchy and the consultative decision-making model promulgated by the reforms of Vatican II. Cardinal Bernardin's consultative management style was not always apparent to participants in SUCCESS. In point of fact, when early resistance by parishes with weak schools threatened to derail the consolidation process, he took steps to prevent its collapse.

The new school provided innovative administrative procedures and new educational resources. The Academy principals run the school in a collaborative fashion and the various sites follow a uniform curriculum. The Academy built a new science lab, an impossibility for a single parish school, and added previously unavailable extracurricular activities. The consolidated school is less expensive to run than the separate schools had been. The students and parents have gotten to know their counterparts from other parishes. Opinions about the process ranged widely, including some who expressed more trust in the new context and others who felt disgruntled about changes they experienced as a profound loss (D'Agostino 1996, 265–68).

Northside Catholic Academy demonstrates how Catholic schools that were once "owned" by their parishes can be reconfigured in broader geographic terms so that their strengths are maximized in a challenging financial and demographic context. Many new immigrants in older city neighborhoods are not able to afford Catholic school tuitions that were subsidized by the sacrificial wages of nuns and religious brothers in the industrial era. Many suburban Catholics prefer to send their children to the generally high-quality public schools for which they moved out of the city in the first place. In fact, the steepest rate of enrollment decline occurred between 1965 and 1975, when it dropped from 286,129 students to 160,129. Thirty years later, the enrollment stood at 60,891. Climbing costs and recessions in the American economy also help to account for the decline (D'Agostino 1997–98, 95). The new urban context requires not only that parish churches and schools collaborate and share resources in order to sustain services, but that they also develop a new, more inclusive Catholic identity that acknowledges a broader social horizon. New pan-parish entities such as Northside Academy can thrive if they absorb and maintain some of the material and symbolic resources of the parish, innovate administratively to sustain models such as these, and attract new adherents from among higher income professional classes seeking a positive urban lifestyle (D'Agostino 1997–98).

Urban Impact on Neighborhood and Area

St. Jerome exerts a more moderate urban impact than St. Nick's. Cultural differences across member groups are acknowledged at St. Jerome but with less overall cohesiveness than at St. Nick's. Fr. Bradley's metaphor of "two trains running through that room" is revealing in this regard. As we have hypothesized, congregations with a strong focus on internal needs, such as managing intra-congregational tensions, will tend to exert relatively weaker urban influence. In St. Jerome's case, it lacks powerful local actors such as SWOP and DevCor to institutionalize its external focus. Nonetheless, its participation in the Northside Catholic Academy gives St. Jerome some role in affecting life on the North Side. And that St. Jerome wields even a moderate impact on its neighborhood through the Howard Area Community Center and provides a Catholic voice on local social issues demonstrates the continuing power of place. As with St. Nick's, this impact is underpinned by Catholic social teachings; unlike St. Nick's, it is not enhanced through strategic partnerships.

First Christian Church
A Changing Protestant Church in a Changing Neighborhood

In 1957 the historic First Christian Church of Chicago, an independent and moderate evangelical Protestant congregation, was among those fleeing the racially and economically changing community area of Englewood for white middle-class Ashburn, adjacent to West Lawn and Chicago Lawn on the city's Southwest Side. Since then, the church has steadily lost members, from a high of about seven hundred to 120 today. Beginning with Filipino members in the late 1980s, it gained a multiracial/ethnic constituency that, like The Moody Church (see chapter 7), challenges the typical homogeneous pattern of evangelical churches in the United States (Emerson and Smith 2000). At the time of our primary research, First Christian's senior pastor was white, the board of elders included blacks, whites, and Filipinos, and the associate pastor was Puerto Rican. First Christian mirrored the Catholic pattern of changing with the neighborhood rather than moving to a different one.

First Christian was founded in 1884 in Englewood and during the 1930s and 1940s was a leading upper-middle-class white congregation. In the 1950s, as Englewood's population began to shift to majority black and "a couple of our people got roughed up," according to former pastor Alan White, the congregation "panicked" and moved to a large plot on 79th Street near Kedzie Avenue. They built a multipurpose facility that includes a gymnasium, offices, parking lot, greenspace, classrooms and meeting rooms, and a mid-sized sanctuary. Figure 3.4 shows the dramatic shift of First Christian's site and membership residential distribution away from predominantly black areas since 1950.

In the late 1990s, the pastor observed, "the neighborhood was changing again," but this time the congregation's response was different. First Christian underwent a self-examination in order to "reestablish purpose, vision, mission, and goals, primarily through the leadership," according to Pastor White. The leadership supported a transition in three areas, from a traditional to a contemporary form of worship, from a homogeneous to a multiracial/ethnic membership, and from an enclave congregational community to one that includes members from the neighborhood. Of the three, the last transition has taken the longest. The first two are interrelated and occurred somewhat contemporaneously. They provide an important glimpse into the mechanisms of change in this particular urban congregation. As Pastor White stated, "We've been given a living, learning laboratory at 79th and Lawndale."

Becoming multiracial/ethnic was initially a consequence of the church's missionary history. In 1984 two Filipino families found First Christian through a tie with missionaries in the Philippines. As Pastor White tells it, "I give them the most credit for breaking down racial walls. We had no preconceived notions about Filipinos, but they were different from us. So these people come in, and they cook, and they work hard, they go all out. And they are so loving—we go, 'Hey, this is great.' That crosses over the racial barriers to accepting others." Those "others" came a few years later when two Jamaican women crossed the church's threshold.

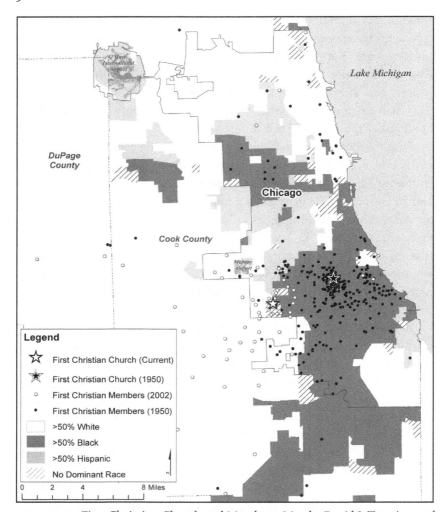

FIGURE 3.4. First Christian Church and Members. Map by David J. Treering and Melissa Gesbeck Howell, Loyola University Chicago.

As one of the women tells the story, she had become displeased with her former church and wanted to attend somewhere closer to her home in Ashburn. The first event the church held after she started coming was a baby shower for a fifteen-year-old from the South Side Pregnancy Center. "I was impressed," the woman said.

"Creating a multiracial church is not just a matter of deciding or wanting it to happen," asserted former Pastor White. "It will happen only if the church sets up the right atmosphere for it, . . . creating a climate [so] that people of different cultures would bring those cultures into expression in the church." He continued, "The term 'social gospel' is not comfortable for evangelicals but that is what First Christian is doing. Evangelicals are wrong if they perpetuate segregation by race and class. It's not biblical." Pastor White credits his ability to "read the Bible through multiethnic eyes" to Raymond Bakke's work on the meaning of the "urban church" (Bakke 1997; cf. Byassee 2009).

Like initially at St. Nick's, "culture" at First Christian acted as a riving force. For a multicultural community to work, as one member remarked to us, people "have to give things up." Said the Jamaican woman quoted above, joining First Christian "meant leaving everything I knew—the sanctified church, the Baptist tradition." An American black member said, "Everything changed": communion is now offered every week, the music is not just black gospel, Sunday services end at noon instead of later, stewardship is controlled by members rather than the pastor. Similar acknowledgments were heard among white members. Stated one, "We—some of us—are trying very hard to welcome all visitors and incorporate these into the church family and make them feel comfortable." This person's qualification—"some of us"—is noteworthy. Nonetheless, the current pastor, Steven Chapman, said he is sometimes told by white elders that the service is not what it used to be, or not something they are comfortable with, but they know they have to "respect others' styles who are in the congregation." Stated another member, sticking with one's "cultural preferences" is not "an adequate way to have church."

Ethnic culture was recognized as a barrier to unity at First Christian, similar to the view of one of the parish council members at St. Nick's. One difference we saw in the previous paragraph, however, was the view of some members of First Christian that their religious identities also acted as cultural barriers. The American black member quoted above offered her complex cultural perspective when she said "it's not 'race' as such, but how we do things." Another black member related how she was disappointed by the "cold atmosphere" she experienced in her local Catholic church, despite having grown up Catholic, and decided to seek out a "family-centered" church. A Filipino lay leader suggested an emotional dimension of community when she commented that "we love people into the church." Another Filipino member suggested how culture and race could work congruently to provide a new structural opportunity through which congregational members reorient their identities. He recounted his experience as a high school student in Chicago as relatively benign regarding racial issues. He felt no different from the white students; while Filipino, he did not see himself as a "minority," which conforms to a larger national pattern of white-Asian racialization (Zhou 2008). However, he continued, at First Christian he feels like an "in-between" person, less white than in high school since it matters now that he is Filipino and not European. Now, and perhaps by virtue of his "in-between-ness," he feels confident he can contribute toward racial reconciliation between whites and blacks. In fact, he expressed not a little pride in this form of cultural power. One can be a minority in one context, yet not in another—a kind of cultural "code-switching"—that can mediate in some circumstances but is unnecessary in others.

Nonetheless, the most frequent theme expressed by white, black, and Hispanic members alike is "having to go outside your comfort zone." Race was acknowledged as decisive. When Pastor Chapman was hired as an associate pastor in 1996, he was told by the board of elders that "the past action of the church regarding their 'white flight' from Englewood in 1957 was 'sinful.' We will not move again and are committed to building our church with whoever is here." "I wouldn't have come here without that admission," he told us, "because it wasn't just a mistake, it was a sin." Theological resources are mobilized to support the church's new identity, as one member reminded us: "The challenge the church faces today would be to remain true to God's teaching through His word." A new corporate identity was established at First Christian that channeled different forms of interpersonal relating (Marti 2009, 56). A multiracial/ethnic contingent of eight men and two boys addressed the congregation in a worship service about the power of Christian unity and racial reconciliation they experienced at a Promise Keepers convention in Washington, DC. These members expressed the variety of strategies the church developed to create the racial inclusion that their theological interpretations of racism as "sin" demanded (Becker 1998). Like St. Nick's, First Christian has achieved "ethnic transcendence" (Marti 2009).

The church has moved from majority white to majority black and Hispanic since Pastor Chapman's arrival in 1996. Like St. Jerome in Rogers Park, the percentage of white members at First Christian (about 20 percent) is smaller than the white percentage of Ashburn's population (34 percent). Blacks comprise 44 percent, Hispanics 20 percent, and Asians less than 1 percent of Ashburn's total population. Pastor Chapman estimated that about three-fourths of the church's members commuted from outside Ashburn in 1996; today, about 90 percent live within a mile-and-a-half radius of the church, thus making First Christian a neighborhood congregation.

Reshaping the Neighborhood

First Christian's self-conscious multiracial/ethnic identity is one vehicle for creating a larger concept of community, one that not merely embraces the world's cultures at their doorstep but also expresses their theology. As Pastor Chapman reasoned, "We have to check [differences of] culture against Scripture . . . because we need to create community with all." A second vehicle for creating a larger concept of community is First Christian's establishment of the Greater Ashburn Community Development Center (CDC) in 2005. The church attempted some social service programs in the 1990s, such as financial counseling, but they were unsuccessful. For a while the church was involved with the Ashburn Community Project and the Greater Ashburn Planning Association, local secular initiatives. In the end, the congregation preferred an independent route through CDC, although some of the older "establishment" members resisted investing in such an organization altogether. Through CDC, First Christian sponsors ESL classes, year-round youth sports and arts camps and leagues, an annual Halloween alternative for local families, an after-school tutoring and enrichment program for elementary grades, an angel tree at Christmas for children of incarcerated parents, and a volunteer income tax assistance program. Two of the nine board members of the CDC are from outside First Christian. Pastor Chapman is president of the school council at the all-minority local public elementary school. While First Christian does not belong to SWOP, Pastor Chapman acknowledged that they know of it and "are open to it."

The Urban Impact of Neighborhood Congregations

The urban impact of the congregational cases in this chapter ranges from strong to moderate. At the strong end of the continuum, St. Nicholas of Tolentine enhanced its ability to affect the larger Southwest Side by aligning with the public advocacy power of the Southwest Organizing Project and DevCor, and by modeling a racially/ethnically inclusive community in a contested social context with a history of exclusion. St. Jerome's influence has been moderate by comparison, its public advocacy more limited and its racial/ethnic congregational inclusiveness less countercultural in the Rogers Park social context. Both congregations responded to threats to their respective neighborhoods with translocal action, expanding the social-geographic boundaries of the classical Catholic notion of parish obligation and thus further lowering boundaries to the outside world. Other specifically Catholic parish traits that have augmented the urban impact of both Catholic churches include common beliefs (especially Catholic social teachings), uniting rituals, enforcement of internal norms, hierarchical though not autocratic clergy leadership, and the ability to manage disputes and tensions among diverse subgroups (with St. Nick's more successful than St. Jerome). One clear lesson from this chapter is that while Catholic parishes continue to anchor neighborhoods, they cannot act independently in the face of massive urban changes.

First Christian Church has also exercised moderate influence in its neighborhood. Like St. Jerome, its public advocacy efforts are modest because they do not benefit from a broad-based coalition like SWOP or DevCor or an area-wide initiative like Northside Catholic Academy. That said, First Christian's racial/ethnic inclusiveness may have a greater impact than the Catholic cases because it stands in judgment against the white flight syndrome common among urban Protestant churches. First Christian's "racial work" is more individually deliberate and demanding. Several black members explained that they had to go outside their comfort zone and give up "everything they knew." Some whites who stayed had to acknowledge past sins (at least by the leadership); others had to "learn to reach out to all groups." This requires significant personal effort to achieve a societal goal that transcends one's own needs. Theologically informed anti-racist norms and a new uniting ritual have lowered the social boundaries to new and different members and spurred community development activities. First Christian now attracts members to live nearby, thereby helping to create a multiracial/ethnic neighborhood.

Local re-embedding of social relationships into new contexts is enabled by a theologizing process based on the particular experiences of congregational constituents in their particular contexts and limited by their particular constraints. This theologizing process shapes the moral consciences of the participants, enabling them to do the cultural work that creates a new sacred place for themselves and others, as John McGreevy (1996) documented regarding an earlier era. The theology of parish/congregation and neighborhood confronts urban restructuring and reveals both cultural and material challenges faced by cities. The centrifugal nature of these challenges is especially clear. The social-geographic contexts of this chapter's three cases are powerful but insufficient to predict congregational composition for the long term since that also depends on individual choices informed by religious norms in a continuing context of economic and social globalization. An effective theology needs to provide a framework of action through which congregations offer meaning for their constituents as they individually and collectively rebuild a political economy within a redefined neighborhood and do cultural work that connects religious and social action.

4

Area Mosques and Diverse Corridors

"CULTURES MELDING IN Albany Park" (Worland 2003). "Port of Entry, Point of Interest: Albany Park Draws Immigrants, Housing Bargain Hunters" (Palmer 2003).

These newspaper headlines extol the demographic diversity of the Albany Park community area on Chicago's North Side. "It's a fascinating area to represent," Alderman Richard Mell explains in one of the articles (Worland 2003), "because it's so multilanguage, multireligion, and everybody gets along." A photo shows a female public school teacher wearing a traditional Muslim head covering or *hijab*.

Albany Park is one of several community areas of significant demographic diversity in the northern portion of metropolitan Chicago. Germans, Swedes, and Russian Jews predominated in Albany Park through the first half of the twentieth century. Many of them eventually moved north and northwest, making room for the next groups, including immigrant Muslims. Between the 1960 and 2000 censuses, Albany Park's non-white population increased dramatically, from virtually nil to more than 50 percent. By the early 2000s, Albany Park became the second largest entry point for immigrants to the city (Paral and Norkewicz 2003, 12, 86).

Muslim Community Center (MCC), one of Chicago's oldest mosques, sits along the southern boundary of Albany Park. MCC and its suburban satellite facility, Muslim Education Center, have contributed to the latest diversification in and around two major transit and development corridors on the north and northwest sides of metropolitan Chicago. The same can be said for the other case study in this chapter, Mosque Foundation, located in the increasingly diverse southwest corridor of metropolitan Chicago. This chapter examines the congregational communities created

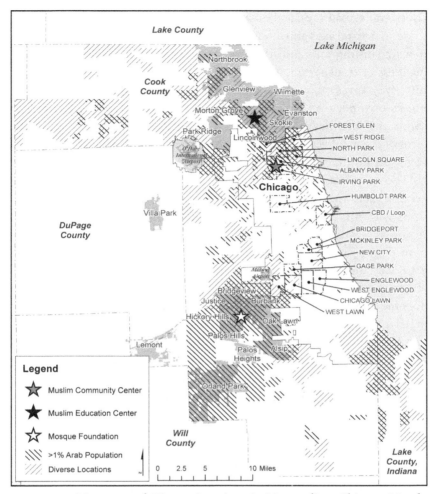

FIGURE 4.1. Mosques and Diverse Locations in Metropolitan Chicago. Map by David J. Treering and Melissa Gesbeck Howell, Loyola University Chicago.

by these mosques and the impact these mosques have had on their respective urban corridors (Figure 4.1).

Metropolitan Transit and Development Corridors

In his classic essay "The Ecological Approach to the Study of the Human Community," Chicago School urban sociologist Roderick McKenzie (1925, 73) noted that "The axial or skeletal structure of a community is determined by the course of the first routes of travel and traffic," such as rivers, trails, roadways, and railways. Subsequent urban development hugs these structural axes and often conforms to an invasion/succession pattern in which immigrants and other groups "gradually push their way out along business or transportation thoroughfares to the periphery of the community" (76). Invasion/succession cycles create "well-defined areas, each having its own peculiar selective and cultural characteristics. Such units of communal life may be termed 'natural areas,' or formations, to use the term of the plant ecologist" (77). The Chicago School soon substituted the term "community areas" for "natural areas" (A. Hunter 1974, 9, 25).

The community area became central to Chicago School urban analysis as a more meaningful social-geographic unit than either the smaller units within it (such as blocks and neighborhoods) or the metropolitan region as a whole. Nevertheless, expanses larger than community areas have played an important role in creating today's urban configuration, especially the transit and development corridors that command so much attention from urban planners. In metropolitan Chicago, five major corridors radiate out from the central business district (the Loop) in a "finger" pattern (see "Alternatives Analysis," I-2; cf. Cutler 2006, 381–82; "Sector of a Metropolis"). Three of these corridors are pertinent to the congregational case studies in this chapter: to the northwest and north (Muslim Community Center and its suburban satellite Muslim Education Center) and to the southwest (Mosque Foundation).

Muslim Community Center
Urban Context: The Northwest and North Corridors

The direction of the northwest transit and development corridor was set by the north branch of the Chicago River before it takes a more northerly course around Addison Street (3600 North). The Union Pacific District Northwest Line, which also carries Metra commuter trains today, and the Chicago Transit Authority's Blue Line both follow the northwest corridor (the Blue Line was extended west to O'Hare International Airport in the early 1980s), as does the Kennedy Expressway/Interstate 90 (opened in 1960). The Edens Expressway/Interstate 94 (opened in 1951) splits off from the Kennedy at about 4600 North and 4800 West in the city, following the north corridor (Bruegmann 1993, 170).

Economically, the northwest corridor has held its own during recent urban restructuring, thus serving as a consistent "pull" factor for new settlement. Janet Abu-Lughod (1999, 330) points out that the northwest (as well as southwest) portion of suburban Cook County fared best among all portions of the county in both population and per capita income growth from the 1970s to the 1990s. Aggressive municipal protection of the manufacturing base in the city segment of the northwest corridor played a significant role in the economic strength of the entire Chicago region. For instance, the battle in the 1980s over potential industrial displacement by mixed-use real estate development in the Clybourn Avenue Corridor was crucial to Chicago's successful economic restructuring of the city. Joel Rast (1999, 129) calls the passage of the Clybourn Corridor Planned Manufacturing District (PMD) ordinance in 1988, toward the end of Mayor Harold Washington's administration, "a key legislative milestone" in Chicago history: "Never before had city officials acted so aggressively to protect central area manufacturers threatened by the pressures of nearby commercial and residential redevelopment." Washington's mayoral successor, Richard M. Daley (the son of Mayor Richard J. Daley), supported the passage of similar PMD ordinances and in 1994 expanded his support for local manufacturers with the Model Industrial Corridors Initiative. Such aggressive policies have paid off, giving Chicago's PMDs a distinct edge in difficult economic times (Rast 1999, chap. 6).

The northwest corridor and its environs exhibit remarkable demographic diversity. The Milwaukee Avenue Corridor, near the southern end of the larger northwest corridor, typifies classic Chicago School invasion/ succession cycles. Milwaukee Avenue began as a Native American trail that intersected the southern end of the Chicago River's north branch and was later converted by white settlers into a wood plank road, a common pre-railway transportation mode. "Milwaukee Avenue has indeed been a transportation and residential corridor for generations of Chicagoans," write Pacyga and Skerrett (1986, 165).

> Like other neighborhoods that bordered the elevated lines or those that adjoined commuter railroads or streetcar lines, the communities along Milwaukee Avenue acted as corridor communities. People came and went. Ethnicity shifted, but the role of Milwaukee Avenue itself did not. Although the names of the people changed from German and Scandinavian to Polish and Jewish, and then to Hispanic, Milwaukee Avenue continued to play its role as a pathway in and out of the inner city. Its role in the economic and demographic life of Chicago remains much the same today as it always was . . . . The Milwaukee Avenue corridor began as ethnic groups

marched northwest to new neighborhoods further away from the central business district. It has always acted as a human express-way from the Loop outward (181).

"By 1900," Pacyga and Skerrett summarize (175), "the Milwaukee Avenue corridor had become a microcosm of Chicago's ethnic history."

Demographic diversification continued to characterize the larger north-west corridor throughout the twentieth century. Jews, for instance, left community areas like Albany Park and North Park in the 1960s and 1970s to settle in several northern suburbs, including Skokie and Lincolnwood in the north corridor (Cutler 2004). By 2000, we find a diverse northwest-erly swath that traverses the North Side of Chicago and certain suburbs. In its southern half, from the Loop to Albany Park, Hispanics comprise the largest new group; in the northern half, from Albany Park into the near north suburbs, Asians comprise the largest new group. In Figure 4.2, note how the northern half of this swath wends its way between less diverse areas like the predominantly white communities of Forest Glen in the city (87 percent) and suburban Park Ridge (95 percent), Niles (83 percent), Glenview (86 percent), and Wilmette (90 percent), as well as parts of Evanston with its large black population (22.5 percent).[1] In our usage, a census tract or other social-geographic unit is "diverse" when the com-bination of Arab, Asian, and Hispanic residents is between 15 and 50 per-cent of the total population and no one racial or ethnic group exceeds 35 percent of the total population. Figure 4.2 shows a significant overlap between the diverse locations of northern metropolitan Chicago and the constituent residential distributions of both Muslim Community Center and Muslim Education Center.

Six communities in the diverse northwesterly swath are of particular interest since they have the highest concentrations of Muslim Community Center constituents. All six experienced major racial/ethnic diversifica-tion over the last several decades, shifting from virtually all-white popu-lations in 1960 to the following percentages of non-whites in 2000: in the city, West Ridge 43 percent, North Park 36 percent, and Albany Park 50 percent; in the suburbs, Lincolnwood 25.5 percent, Skokie 31 percent, and Morton Grove 26 percent. In five of these six communities, Asians are now the largest non-white group, ranging from 21 to 24 percent of the population, one of the highest Asian concentrations in the region. Moreover, the Albany Park and West Ridge community areas now contain

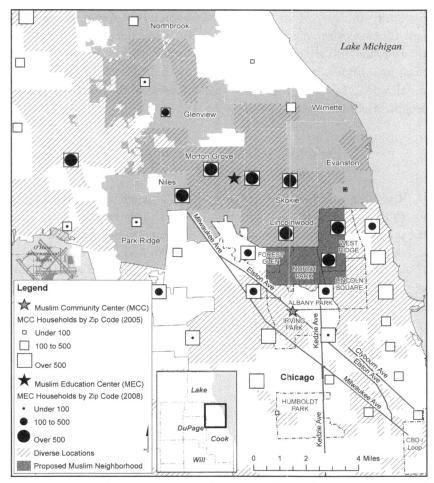

FIGURE 4.2. Muslim Community Center, Muslim Education Center, and Constituents. Map by David J. Treering and Melissa Gesbeck Howell, Loyola University Chicago.

the highest concentrations of Arab residents in the city outside of Chicago Lawn on the Southwest Side (the US census classifies Arabs as white).

The median family income for these six communities averaged more than $62,000 in 1999, close to the figure for the entire metropolitan region ($69,000). There was variation among these communities, with Albany Park and West Ridge at the lower end of the income and occupation range, Lincolnwood and Skokie at the higher end, but all benefited from the economic health of the northwest corridor, providing affordable housing for a variety of class groupings, local job opportunities, proximity and easy access to other employment hubs, and strong retail outlets. Moreover, an important new immigrant port-of-entry emerged with a robust infrastructure of South Asian and Arab businesses and cultural institutions, including the well-known multiracial/ethnic business district along Devon Avenue in West Ridge. Several mosques and Islamic organizations sprang up as well.

Establishing a Muslim Community in Northern Metropolitan Chicago

Muslim Community Center has been a major actor in the ensemble of forces that created the demographically diverse locations in and around the northwest and north transit and development corridors. MCC's story is told in general terms elsewhere (Raymond Williams 1988, 242–43; Husain and Vogelaar 1994, 237–38; Rangaswamy 2000, 263–64), including our own previous work (Numrich 1996, 236–37; 1997, 68–72; 2000b, 246–50). The relative economic stability of northern metropolitan Chicago made it an attractive option as MCC leaders contemplated potential locations for their mosque in the 1970s and 1980s, but other important factors influenced their decisions as well.

MCC's story begins with a dream of establishing a Muslim neighborhood in the city of Chicago. The immigrant leaders who founded the mosque in 1969 were motivated largely by two Islamic concepts, *hijrah* and *ummah*. Literally "to abandon or migrate," the Arabic word *hijrah* took on Islamic connotations in reference to two historic migrations, that of a group of Muslims from Mecca to Christian Abyssinia (Ethiopia) ca. 615 CE and the Prophet Muhammad's move from Mecca to Yathrib (later called Medina) in 622 CE. In the Qur'an, *hijrah* carries a meaning of "distancing—physical or otherwise—usually from evil and disbelief" (Masud 1990, 32). Over the centuries, Islamic scholars have attempted to sort out the conditions and contexts under which *hijrah* might be obligatory for Muslims, particularly with regard to the notion of *dar al-Islam*, that is, territory governed by Shariah (Islamic law). Much debate has centered on such questions as whether Muslims living outside of *dar al-Islam* must migrate thereto and whether they are obligated to migrate away from nominally *dar al-Islam* territories where Shariah no longer obtains.

A new debate over the meaning of *hijrah* has emerged since the nineteenth century, when many Muslims began migrating to non-Muslim countries primarily for socioeconomic improvement. Is this an acceptable *hijrah*? A growing consensus among Islamic scholars maintains its acceptability, some arguing that this type of *hijrah* may even be obligatory in certain cases, for instance when the freedom to practice and propagate Islam is more secure in a non-Muslim country than in a nominally Muslim country (Masud 1990, 42–43; Eickelman and Piscatori 1996, 144–45).

As M. Ali Kettani (1986, 5–6) observes, in whatever circumstances, "When Muslims find themselves outside *dar-al-Islam*, it becomes their duty to organize themselves in order to be able to safeguard as much as possible of this [Islamic] way of life." Their "organizational set-up should be aimed at establishing a viable Muslim community" and it "should be open to all those who are Muslims" (6, 7). No divisive subgroupings, such as those based on pious elitism, sectarian theology, race/ethnicity, or occupation, are acceptable within a local Muslim community, in keeping with the theological ideal that Muslims form a single *ummah* or religious people. This universalistic notion of community stands in contradistinction to a particularistic or delimited one and is shared with Christian thought as well (cf. Delanty 2010). Ideally, "all the Muslims of a town, or part of a town, or a county would form one *jamaat* (association)" (Kettani 1986, 7), within which it is acceptable to organize language subgroupings as long as these do not become divisive.

With this theological and historical background, we can better understand the early dream of Muslim Community Center leaders. In the 1960s, they made a *hijrah* to Chicago from India and Pakistan—countries with histories of internal debates over whether they truly represented *dar al-Islam* (Masud 1990)—largely for educational and occupational reasons. Once here, they took seriously their Islamic obligation to establish a viable Muslim community in order to safeguard an authentically Islamic way of life as Muslim minorities outside of *dar al-Islam*. In their judgment, the few mosques in the Chicago region at that time "had a prominent ethnic orientation, conducting certain activities that compromised Islamic value[s]." Instead, they wanted MCC to serve all Muslims, following the *ummah* ideal, and to "promote the Islamic way of living, strictly in conformance to the Shariah" ("History [of Muslim Community Center]").

The congregation initially met in ad hoc locations. In 1972 MCC purchased a former Danish community center on North Kedzie Avenue, just north of Humboldt Park in the Milwaukee Avenue Corridor (recall the early Scandinavian settlement there; see Pacyga and Skerrett 1986, 175). As one source explained to us, at that time MCC leaders did not care about the location as much as the availability and affordability of the property.

However, the unsuitability of both facility and location soon became apparent. The building was inadequate for MCC's programming needs, the neighborhood crime rate was high, and vandalism against the mosque and constituents' cars became routine.

By 1975, MCC formed a Masjid [Mosque] Planning Committee to study the prospects of relocation. This committee's 1977 report, titled "The Masjid and Community Development Project," advocated that MCC do much more than merely relocate—it should establish a Muslim neighborhood on Chicago's North Side. The report identified several problems with the Kedzie Avenue site, including this telling statement (13): "Due to its unsuitable location, few Muslims live in the area." The committee proposed seven criteria "for the selection of an area for the proposed Masjid and development of a neighborhood," as follows (14):

A. Good neighborhood; that is low crime rate, cleanliness, good public schools.
B. Present Muslim population density and trends.
C. Non-Muslim population mobility trends.
D. Availability of single and multiple housing units.
E. Availability of land.
F. Proximity of job opportunities.
G. Availability of public transportation and proximity of main roads and expressways.

Point C implies a wish to empty the non-Muslim population from the envisioned Muslim neighborhood, confirmed to us by an MCC leader. Points D through G pick up on the key characteristics of many metropolitan transit and development corridors that attract successive waves of immigrant groups: suitable housing, available property, employment opportunities, and adequate transportation.

Based on these criteria, the committee designated a potential Muslim neighborhood on Chicago's North Side, bounded by Howard and Devon Avenues on the north, Foster Avenue on the south, Cicero Avenue and the Chicago city limits on the west, and Western Avenue on the east. This tract of about six square miles lies near the split between the northwest and north corridors and includes portions of the West Ridge, Lincoln Square, North Park, and Forest Glen community areas. The committee's report visually represented this tract on a Chicago city map, labeling it "Proposed Muslim Neighborhood" (see Figure 4.2). This tract is larger than an urban neighborhood according to our definition, though it is smaller than any of the official community areas it overlapped. In effect, it would have carved out a Muslim "community area."

The committee described the motivations behind its proposal in some detail, emphasizing the importance of creating a localized tract of concentrated residential and institutional life that could serve as both a model and a resource for the larger Muslim community throughout metropolitan Chicago, as seen in the following excerpts from their report ("The Masjid and Community Development Project," 3, 10):

- The project is designed to provide a masjid, school, and facilities for assembly and meetings, health care, nursery, dorm, and cooperative investment projects in a selective neighborhood to be populated heavily by Muslims. The proposed complex is planned to serve as a nucleus for development of a strong Muslim Community in the Chicago area.
- One single point about the project is that it is designed to answer the challenge faced by the Muslim community in its efforts to lead a truly Islamic life in a non-Muslim environment. This is the focal point of planning, and the project should be judged on that basis.
- A recommendation was made [by the committee] to establish a *Muslim neighborhood, [and to] construct a masjid and a new center* within the Muslim neighborhood which would become a model community and a nucleus for the Islamic Da'wah [propagation of the faith] in the Chicago area [emphasis in original].

Here is a blueprint for a predominantly—if not exclusively—Muslim territory under some level of control by a local mosque and its attendant institutions that would nurture a comprehensive, coherent, and relatively small-scale Islamic urban community. Note how this resembles the construction of the classic Catholic parish in which a substantial territorial presence, interconnecting Catholic institutions under religious control, and residential density of parishioners created a Catholic neighborhood (see chapter 3).

But this was not to be, largely because MCC's multiple Muslim constituencies settled across a much larger geographic expanse. In Figure 4.2, note the residential clustering of MCC's constituents in the diverse locations along and near the northwest and north metropolitan corridors. The two largest groups of constituents, South Asians (captured under the census label "Asians") and Arab Muslims, who followed earlier co-ethnic

Christians to Chicago's North Side (Zaghel 1976; Cainkar 1988; [1997]), are represented in the diverse locations in Figure 4.2. Bosnian Muslims, a constituent group not represented due to their relatively small numbers, settled in the vicinity during the 1990s after fleeing ethnic turmoil in the former Yugoslavia (Husain 2004).

MCC sought a sufficiently large parcel of land on which to build a grand new mosque to anchor its dream of a Muslim community area. The 1977 report had proposed three possible architectural models for such a mosque, replete with a dome and/or minaret, saying, "The design of the Masjid will conform to the traditional Islamic architectural style, in keeping with our heritage. This will make the building a landmark in the American environment" ("The Masjid and Community Development Project," 13). Mosque leaders identified several promising parcels, but, as one source told us, in each case the realtor informed them that they were just a little late and that the property had already been sold. This was interpreted by our source as a cover-up for anti-Muslim bias; MCC's "History" reports it matter-of-factly: "Having difficulty in finding suitable land, the focus of the search was later shifted to looking for a building." In 1982 MCC purchased a former movie theater at 4380 North Elston Avenue, along the boundary between the Albany Park and Irving Park community areas of Chicago, about one mile south of the proposed Muslim community area.

Although the Elston Avenue site fulfilled most of the criteria for the proposed Muslim community area listed above, it could not support the construction of a grand new mosque. Of course, the mere presence of such a landmark does not guarantee a demographic shift in the immediate vicinity—this has occurred in the case of Mosque Foundation in southwest suburban Bridgeview, where a newly built mosque has attracted significant Arab Muslim settlement around it (see below). According to our source, this magnet dynamic has begun to occur around MCC's full-time school in suburban Morton Grove, which in 2009 opened a grand new mosque in traditional Islamic architectural style.

Several other mosques on the North Side of the city of Chicago function as neighborhood congregations (L. W. Livezey 2000a). Although it has no official institutional relationship with these smaller mosques, the latter consider MCC the "Mother Masjid" of the vicinity, according to our source, and look to its leaders for advice in interacting with the larger society. Local Muslims, even those who regularly attend one of the other mosques, recognize MCC's primacy. One important role MCC plays concerns end-of-life issues. In the early 1990s, MCC purchased 1,500 lots in Rosehill Cemetery, in the north corridor, alleviating the previous inconvenience of traveling to west and south suburban cemeteries for Muslim burials. MCC also provides funeral services that the smaller mosques cannot typically furnish.

A significant milestone in MCC's history came in the late 1980s, extending the mosque's territory into the near suburbs of the north metropolitan corridor. By then, MCC once again felt the need to expand its programming and facilities. Leaders hoped to find seven to ten acres adjacent to or close by the Elston Avenue site on which to erect a new mosque, harking back to the earlier dream of building a landmark *masjid* from the ground up. However, once again no viable property could be found in the city. Debate arose when leaders began considering sites in the near north suburbs as some constituents feared a schism between MCC's better-off suburban and less-well-off city dwellers. After much discussion, MCC decided to subsume both the Elston Avenue site and any eventual suburban site under one organizational polity.

In 1989 MCC purchased a former public school facility at 8601 Menard Avenue in near north suburban Morton Grove, prevailing over the local resistance described in an MCC source as follows ("Islam in North America," [12]): "Some citizens of the Village of Morton Grove had launched a campaign to deny sale of the building to the Muslims. MCC counteracted by launching its own public relations campaign and succeeded in reversing their opposition in favor of the Muslims." The establishment of a full-time day school at this site, known as Muslim Education Center (MEC), confirmed the higher socioeconomic status of MCC's suburban constituents, for they could better afford the tuition than those living in the city. But this territorial expansion also solidified MCC's position as the premier Islamic institution in the demographically diverse northern metropolitan Chicago. MEC's statement of philosophy echoes the motivations behind the original Muslim neighborhood project, namely, "to provide an Islamic environment for the education of young Muslims" as an alternative to the "un-Islamic" public school system (Numrich 2000b, 247–48). For years, MEC was the only full-time Islamic school in the vicinity.

MCC and MEC today serve as twin institutional anchors for Muslims living in a large swath of northern metropolitan Chicago. Had it desired to do so, MCC could not have created an exclusively Muslim community area on Chicago's North Side in the way that it originally envisioned. Such a scenario was not possible given the realities of urban restructuring in Chicago in the 1980s and 1990s, which included immigrant settlement patterns and institutionalized discrimination.

Congregational Community Traits: Facilitating Muslim Life in Northern Metropolitan Chicago

MCC's Elston Avenue site offers all five daily Muslim prayers, a service many Chicago mosques cannot provide. The congregational Friday (*jum'ah*) prayer typically draws a large (about 1,500) and racially/ethnically mixed gathering. During the annual sacred month of Ramadan, many Muslims attend the evening prayers and ritual breaking of the daily fast at the mosque. MCC has many committees, including several that oversee religious activities and educational programs. Moreover, MCC accommodates religious, family, and social events for its constituents.

MCC pays particular attention to programming for its American-born children. In addition to its full-time Islamic school in Morton Grove, MCC offers an extensive weekend school at the Elston Avenue site, covering such topics as Arabic, Qur'an, Hadith (the record of the Prophet Muhammad's words and deeds), and *haram/halal* (prohibited/permitted) behaviors. MCC also offers male and female youth groups.

MCC has successfully negotiated the distinctive cultural needs of its two largest ethnic constituencies, South Asians (the majority) and Arabs. We observed the wedding of an Arab man and an Indian woman, which serves to illustrate both MCC's commitment to the Islamic ideal of the *ummah* and its role in facilitating an Islamic lifestyle for Muslims living in a non-Muslim society, such as commemorating major life passages for individuals and families.

Upon arrival, our researcher, a woman, was escorted to a room where approximately 130 women and fifty children awaited the festivities. American-style paper wedding decorations graced the perimeter of the room, while a table near the door featured a punch bowl, bottles of soda pop, and plastic cups. The majority of the Arab women wore tightly fitting *hijab*s (head coverings), many decorated with gold or silver threads. About a dozen Indian women wore colorful saris with more loosely draped *hijab*s. It was difficult to strike up conversations with some of the women since they did not know English well. One, accompanied by her three-year-old child, told our researcher that she had been in the United States less than three years. An elderly woman, sitting with her fifteen-year-old granddaughter, spoke virtually no English but was quite friendly in her manner. The girl could tell us only that her grandmother had arrived from Saudi Arabia about six months earlier.

Word came that the men were bringing food. Several women began serving the guests, apparently by families. The food was a simple but flavorful dish of rice and meat—nothing more, including no "wedding cake," a rather spare meal compared to the typical American-style wedding reception. But this communal feast was important in that it consolidated the marriage, following the couple's signing of a marriage agreement and a specified period of engagement.

Excitement filled the air as the guests anticipated the entrance of the bride and groom. Each was accompanied separately by his/her parents, who walked them arm-in-arm to the front of the room and seated them on the dais while the Arab women gave out a high-pitched trill. After the couple took their seats, many pictures were taken as family members bustled around them, especially the bride. Then the women began to dance, led by the mother of the groom. The groom stayed only briefly after the dancing began, leaving to join the festivities in the men's room where an all-male singing group performed (the music was piped into the women's room).

MCC's religious affairs committee oversees the ritual observances of weddings and funerals. With regard to Islamic marriages, whether arranged or self-selected, the chair of the committee explained that "for a successful life, constant teaching by the family, the community, and the mosque is required." Our researchers spoke a little more with the chair about problems in marriages. He explained that the Muslim approach to marital problems differs from the American approach. There is another committee within MCC to help people with marital problems. "However, the MCC does not agree with the American notions of freedom, rights, and women's shelters." His concern revolved especially around the role of shelters, which he asserted seem to "antagonize the husband rather than help the situation." For instance, the counseling received in the shelter is not directed toward reconstructing the marriage, but rather toward the wife becoming self-sufficient. The chair gave an example of a woman whose husband was prohibited from contacting her at a shelter. The chair stated, "There is no way to save the marriage when people are not allowed to talk to each other." In the Muslim way, he explained, if the couple cannot resolve their problems on their own, a member of each partner's family is asked to participate in a discussion with the couple in an effort to mediate the dispute by supporting and presenting each partner's side. All efforts are made to preserve the marriage, but if there is no alternative, he acknowledged, divorce is permitted, although "it is the worst among *halal* [permitted] things to do."

MCC's important role in facilitating a Muslim life for its immigrant constituents became apparent to us during MCC's annual congregational dinner in 1993. It was held in the prayer hall with rugs removed. Vestiges of a once ornate movie theater remained in the presence of five large cut glass chandeliers and sconces along the walls. Over the stage was a sign in Arabic and English quoting from the Qur'an: "Thus we [Allah] have made you a model community that you may be witnesses over the nations." About four hundred women and men were seated at separate tables with the many children treated to pizza and movies in an adjacent room, although many nonetheless buzzed around the tables in the prayer hall. Our female researcher noticed that while most of the women wore the *hijab*, some did not. Our female informant (herself a Muslim convert married to a Muslim man) explained that there are "different cultural traditions regarding wearing the veil," and therefore, "no assumptions about piety can be made." Furthermore, she claimed, "it takes courage to wear the veil, in spite of jeers and comments like 'raghead' to which Muslim women are subject."

The dinner began with an opening prayer, followed by children ages six through ten years from the MEC school reciting Arabic prayers, songs, and poems that they had learned for the occasion. The opening prayer was led by the vice president, who included heartfelt thanks to the congregation for their support during his six-month detainment in Israel. The president's report began with further prayer requests for a second MCC member who was currently being held in an Israeli jail. The financial report contained the disbursement of the mosque's $60,000 *zakat* (charitable donations) fund to three hundred families this year. Regarding the mosque's religious education program, the president reported that a thousand children were served each weekend and that the MEC school enrolled 150 children in grades K–6 with the aim of expanding to the upper grades. He concluded with other congregational housekeeping matters such as the $150,000 remaining on the $1.8 million cost of their property. He reminded the attendees that "This is owed to brothers and sisters who loaned the money at no interest, and is two years overdue."

The evening concluded with a speaker from New Jersey, Safet Abid Catovic, an executive board member of the Bosnian Task Force of the

United States. His talk focused on a commitment to "excellence in character" rooted in religious faith as expressed in family and community. He advocated the kind of character that would inhibit belief in the media message that "Muslims would blow up the World Trade Center" (the 1993 bombing had recently occurred). He continued that such beliefs cannot be based on superstition or "cultural Islam," that is, on the "beliefs of our parents." Rather, it must be "informed belief." And it must involve "all our human resources without restricting *anyone*." Our researcher noted that Mr. Catovic engaged in "an eloquent discourse on the unfortunate restrictions placed on women, historically and today." He argued that "We have denied ourselves the insights and knowledge of half our people. We must build character based on everyone's knowledge." To conclude, the speaker called on his listeners to build unity, an *ummah* based on the mix of ethnic populations uniquely found in the United States. The audience signaled their approval with several shouts of "Alahu Akbar" (literally "God is great," a mixture of applause and "amen") during the speech and at the conclusion.

In these and many other ways, MCC facilitates a Muslim lifestyle for its members living as minorities outside of *dar al-Islam*, consistent with the Islamic ideal of creating a unified *ummah* that transcends distinctions and divisions among its constituents. Through daily prayers and life cycle rituals as well as active engagement with the problems and needs of its constituents, MCC strengthens the shared norms needed for a "successful" Islamic life in a non-Islamic country. MCC's choice not to identify with any particular Islamic school of thought (*fiqh*) or sectarian Islamic tradition and its hesitance to appoint a permanent imam likewise embody the *ummah* ideal.

Congregational Action: Civic Involvement, Territory, and Muslim Voice

MCC's civic involvement with the larger society has increased over time. Two interviews a decade apart with MCC president Mohammed Kaiseruddin touched on the shift. In 1994 he told us that "up until now, the [Muslim] community has been focused on itself. However, people have been starting to raise questions about that: 'Should we not be participating in civic projects?'" This led to a small but significant project in which the mosque's *zakat* (charitable donations) were taken to local homeless shelters during the month of Ramadan. Each day of that month a different shelter received a contribution that fed 150 to two hundred people. MCC also sent several volunteers to work at the shelters. Kaiseruddin spoke of a good feeling within the Muslim community about this project and he hoped it would continue "now that there is an awareness" of this kind of need.

In a 2004 interview, Kaiseruddin described many new civic initiatives at MCC, including working with United Power for Action and Justice, a social advocacy group that provides services around low-income housing, health insurance, and the state's Kid Care Program. MCC also joined the Albany Park Neighborhood Council, made up of religious organizations, schools, unions, and other groups, which focuses on voter registration, immigrant rights, and state driver's license services. By its own account, MCC has excellent relationships with local government, especially the police department (MCC is a corporate donor to the Chicago Police Memorial Foundation) and the alderman's office. MCC also opens its facility for use by community groups and has expanded its health programs (CPR training and cholesterol, blood pressure, and diabetes screening), originally limited to Muslims, to Albany Park residents at large.

Kaiseruddin characterized this evolution of MCC's civic involvement as steadily increasing, especially due to the influence of young adult members. These are now in the workforce and coming back to lead MCC after leaving in their late teens and early twenties. They recognize the importance of being contributing members of the larger society, Kaiseruddin explained. He also emphasized the impact of the September 11, 2001, attacks on New York City and Washington, DC. When members of local Christian churches formed a human chain around MCC in order to protect it from possible 9/11 reprisals, MCC realized that it must reciprocate such support.

Kaiseruddin was rather apologetic when describing MCC's record of civic involvement to us, pointing out that MCC is so dependent on volunteers that such activities are hard to sustain. He felt that insufficient numbers of volunteers and the lack of paid staff have undercut such involvement. But the will was there, as well as the direction. This is borne out by initiatives of MCC's Outreach and Interfaith Committee. In 2008 the committee hosted a Ramadan Iftar dinner for approximately forty community activists associated with the Faith Leaders Committee of the local Chicago Alternative Policing Strategy (CAPS) program that included brainstorming ideas to improve the larger community ("40th Annual

Report," 4). In 2009 the number increased to approximately seventy-five community activists ("41st Annual Report," 4).

With regard to the full-time school in Morton Grove, Kaiseruddin explained that MCC "dropped the ball" by not capitalizing on the local support they did have when they bought the property in 1989. That might have minimized later resistance to their plans to build a new mosque on the school's property (Mendieta 2004). This time around, MCC leaders sought to nurture relationships with local supporters and stepped up its civic profile by providing health programs to the general public at the school, sponsoring an annual food and fun fair (distributing fliers to neighbors and offering discounts), participating in the community Thanksgiving interfaith service (proceeds going to a local charity), and joining in Fourth of July festivities.

The English-language newspaper *Indian Reporter and World News* covered MEC's participation in the 2004 Fourth of July parade ("MEC Celebrates 4th of July"). MEC's principal remarked about the significance of this event, which came fifteen years after the school opened and symbolized the growing civic consciousness of the school: "We're happy to celebrate our nation's independence with Morton Grove today. Today is the first year of our school's participation in the 4th of July parade. We enjoyed walking down Dempster [Street] and interacting with parade bystanders. We look forward to participating more in the future." Students and school supporters waved American flags, distributed free bottles of water to spectators, and carried posters saying "Happy 4th of July" and "MG [Morton Grove] Pride." The last sentiment is all the more noteworthy given both the history of tensions between the school and some of its non-Muslim neighbors and the chilling effect of 9/11 nationwide. In a study released by the Pew Research Center around this time, more than half of the Muslims surveyed felt that "since the 9/11 attacks, it has become more difficult to be a Muslim in the United States" ("Muslim Americans," 35). Over many years—predating 9/11—MEC and Morton Grove have been about the mutual hard work of civic neighborliness.

In 2005 Muslim Community Center's website stated the following hope under a list of institutional challenges for the future: "return to our original plan, of erecting a grand Masjid on the North side of Chicago, where most of [the] Muslim population resides." The recently constructed mosque at Muslim Education Center in suburban Morton Grove features Islamic architectural elements—a dome and a minaret—that fulfill this hope of a grand territorial presence on the urbanscape. As some anticipated, a Muslim neighborhood may be growing up around this mosque (a significant 12.5 percent of households with students enrolled in the school live within a one-mile radius of MEC). Ironically, the neighborhood group that opposed the new mosque was correct in its geographic analysis: they feared that the site would become a "regional ["area" in our terminology] Mega-Mosque" (Leinwand 2004).

Urban Impact: A New Muslim Presence

Shifting from its initial dream of creating a Muslim community area in the city, Muslim Community Center eventually became the leading Muslim institution in an evolving diverse portion of metropolitan Chicago with significant Muslim presence. Instead of creating a geographically limited Muslim territory, MCC provided the means for Muslims to live a comprehensive and fulfilling Islamic life among a diverse, non-Muslim majority population. As its own written "History" explains, "MCC has also given the Muslim community of Chicago a distinctive identity among the various ethnic communities that comprise Chicago's cosmopolitan diversity. Moreover, we have created a voice for ourselves in the media and political circles. More and more, one can observe a growing awareness and recognition of the Muslim way of life." For these reasons, we assess MCC's urban impact as high moderate. We will elaborate on the urban impact of the mosques in this chapter in the concluding section.

MCC is widely regarded as one of the most influential mosques in metropolitan Chicago. An MCC source identified the four premier mosques in metropolitan Chicago as MCC, Islamic Foundation in west suburban Villa Park, Islamic Cultural Center of Greater Chicago in north suburban Northbrook, and Mosque Foundation southwest suburban Bridgeview (Hack and Hantschel 2003). Kniss and Numrich (2007) feature Islamic Foundation and Islamic Cultural Center in their study. We turn our attention here to Mosque Foundation.

Mosque Foundation
Urban Context: The Southwest Corridor

The southwest metropolitan transit and development corridor, like its northwest counterpart, begins at the Chicago River in the Loop. The river's south branch connects to a continental watershed that forms a geological corridor between Lake Michigan and the Illinois River. As Michael

Conzen (1988, 22) puts it, this geological corridor has been "making history" since the beginning of human occupation, serving the transit and development needs of Native Americans, early French explorers and traders, later permanent settlers, and today's multiple municipalities and governmental bodies.

The first major transportation mode constructed in the southwest corridor, the Illinois and Michigan Canal (completed in 1848), was soon eclipsed by railways (M. Conzen 1988, 12–14). Today, commuter rail traffic is carried by two Metra lines, the Heritage Corridor to Joliet and the SouthWest Service to Orland Park, plus the Chicago Transit Authority's Orange Line to Midway Airport (opened in 1994). The Chicago Sanitary and Ship Canal (completed in 1900) replaced a portion of the I&M Canal and famously reversed the flow of the Chicago River in order to take sewage away from Lake Michigan, Chicago's drinking water source. The leg of Interstate 55 known as the Stevenson Expressway (opened in 1964) paved over some portions of the old I&M Canal.

The I&M Canal project was serviced by a former Native American trail that eventually became Archer Avenue, named after the principal project engineer. As Pacyga and Skerrett (1986, 512, 513) explain, "the Archer Avenue corridor has long served Chicagoans as a gateway to the southwest . . . . Many of the ethnic groups of the South and Southwest Sides used Archer Avenue as an escape route from the inner-city." The major exception to this rule has been the Chinese who remain concentrated near the Loop.

A cluster of community areas along and near the Archer Avenue Corridor have come to be known as Chicago's Southwest Side.[2] Gage Park, Chicago Lawn, and West Lawn have particular pertinence to our story due to a significant Arab Muslim presence there. These are all historically diverse community areas that served as places of secondary settlement for European ethnic groups moving out from the inner city along the southwest corridor during the early decades of the twentieth century. Gage Park was heavily settled by Roman Catholics, many coming from McKinley Park, Bridgeport, and New City. Chicago Lawn, also known as Marquette Park after its major public greenspace, attracted many secondary settlers from New City, Englewood, and West Englewood, including several Protestant and Catholic groups. Lithuanian Catholics formed a particularly noteworthy presence in both Gage Park and Chicago Lawn, establishing the largest Lithuanian parish outside of their homeland, Nativity of the Blessed Virgin Mary Parish (established 1927), and developing a vibrant residential and institutional section of Chicago Lawn known as the Lithuanian Gold Coast. In West Lawn, Poles became the predominant ethnic group after World War II, many moving in from Bridgeport, Englewood, and around the Union Stock Yard.

The Southwest Side has faced significant social challenges since the 1960s. Demographic shifts there and in adjacent community areas generated serious conflict in the 1960s and 1970s, epitomizing Chicago School sociologist Gerald Suttles's notion of "the defended neighborhood" (Suttles 1972, 21–43; Wedam 2000b, 108), and continue to challenge the stability of the Southwest Side. In Chicago Lawn, where Martin Luther King's 1966 open housing march met a violent reaction, the non-white population increased from nil in 1960, to 17 percent in 1980, to 76 percent in 2000. The two largest non-white groups in Chicago Lawn today are blacks and Hispanics. In Gage Park, where many white parents resisted the integration of the public high school in 1972, the non-white population increased slowly from 1960 (nil) to 1980 (7 percent), but then reached more than half (53 percent) in 2000, with Hispanics the largest new group. West Lawn remained more than 90 percent white through the 1990 census but dropped below two-thirds in 2000, the largest new group again being Hispanics. Much of the white out-migration from these community areas has traveled along the southwest corridor to the near southwest suburbs, though Lithuanians have moved even farther out to Lemont.

Local efforts to address these demographic shifts in a positive way have been spearheaded by religious groups. Most importantly, the Southwest Organizing Project (SWOP, established 1995), an interfaith outgrowth of the Southwest Catholic Cluster Project (established 1988), "has given a voice to community residents who are committed to a religiously based understanding of community in a pluralistic society" (Wedam 2000b, 128). SWOP and other religious initiatives have brokered a constructive approach of reformulating the local moral community in more inclusive terms than the defended neighborhood approach.

Economically, these community areas have generally held their own in the last few decades, anchored by such viable enterprises as Ford City Shopping Center in West Lawn, several commercial strips (including the important one along 63rd Street), a variety of light industries, and nearby Midway Airport. Local community development groups like the Greater Southwest Development Corporation (DevCor) have played a significant stabilizing role. Joel Rast (1999, 147–48) notes that DevCor was one of the first organizations to receive funding from the Model Industrial Corridors

Initiative in the 1990s and lifts up DevCor's 1995 strategic plan for the Southwest Side as representative of the kinds of comprehensive plans generated throughout the city by grantees of the Initiative. The Southwest Side includes a 900-acre industrial corridor with several food manufacturers vital to the local economy.

The story of the diversification of the southwest corridor cannot be told without including the story of the Arab Muslim population (cf. Wedam and Livezey 2004).[3] The first Arab Muslims arrived in Chicago around 1910. Mostly Palestinian peddlers and shopkeepers, they took up a "middleman" economic niche in predominantly black areas, initially living along the eastern edge of the Black Belt between 18th and 63rd Streets (Oschinsky 1947; al-Tahir 1950). In the decades following World War II, Arab Muslim residential concentration shifted to the western edge of the expanding Black Belt, forming a racial/ethnic buffer with white neighborhoods to the west. By the 1990s, Arab Muslims were concentrated largely in Chicago Lawn, Gage Park, and West Lawn. The economic hub of Arab Muslim settlement during its heyday was 63rd Street between Western Avenue and Pulaski Road in Chicago Lawn. As Louise Cainkar ([1997], 6) reports, "The successes of Arab immigrants in small business and in securing factory work, and the growth in the size of the Arab community through immigration and childbirth, led to the development of an expanding ethnic business market on the southwest side in the 1970's and 80's. Grocery stores, bakeries, restaurants, insurance agents, realtors, barbers, beauticians, doctors, dentists and lawyers catering to Arab clients emerged . . . . Most of these [enterprises] were owned by well-educated or well-established members of the community, not new immigrants."

But even in its heyday there were signs of problems. Ali Zaghel (1976) described a process of de-assimilation or ethnic enclavism within the local Arab population in the 1970s, the result of the Arab-Israeli conflicts of 1967 and 1973 and subsequent negative reactions against Arabs in the United States. In the late 1980s, Cainkar (1988, 106, 133) reported severe social and political alienation among local Palestinians, which spiraled down into communal insularity and socioeconomic deterioration in the Southwest Side Arab population by the mid-1990s, as the following portrait shows (Cainkar [1997], 8):

Forty five per cent of our Needs Assessment respondents living in Gage Park and West Lawn reported receiving some type of Public Aid. Seventy percent of them disliked their neighborhood. They cited problems with crime, drugs, gangs, and shootings as the main reasons they felt unsafe. Of these, 70% say they cannot move for economic reasons, because of unemployment or underemployment. Sixty per cent of respondents from these and neighboring areas reported having domestic problems they need help with and having no where to turn for assistance. Alcohol and drug abuse, as well as cases of domestic violence, are now readily apparent in the community. Broken families are no longer unusual, nor are Arab youth at the police station or in juvenile court, as measured by calls for intervention at the Arab-American Community Center. Arab street gangs are part of the local scene, and Arab theft rings, who largely victimize other Arabs, have instilled fear and distrust among community members. Many Arab parents feel they have lost control of their children and, as immigrants, do not know how to handle parenting in urban America. There is no longer a strong, insular Arab community to provide them with help.

Cainkar dates the onset of this decline to the late 1980s. A new influx of Arabs from Palestine and elsewhere in the Middle East could not be absorbed into the two traditional employment sectors that had supported previous immigrants, small businesses and unskilled factory labor. A middle-class "Arab flight" to the suburbs began at this same time. "Co-ethnic support and community cohesion were shattered by this loss as the poor and newcomers were left to care for themselves," writes Cainkar ([1997], 12; cf. Cainkar 2005). "This departure of middle class immigrants and their children left Arab immigrants and Arab Americans living in the 'old neighborhood' to fend for themselves in a context characterized by a service and support vacuum." This process is similar to the out-migration of the black middle class from the Black Belt after World War II.

In her earlier work, Cainkar (1988, 116–17) placed these latest developments within the overall history of Arab Muslim out-migration via the southwest corridor:

[M]ost of the chain immigrants—the original immigrants and their relatives—have moved to the suburbs. While many of their newest members cannot afford independent life in the suburbs, within five years or so, they move there. Suburban Palestinians are clustered in the suburbs of the city immediately adjacent to the urban southwest side community. This group of Palestinians moved southwest in a kind of natural progression from their first settlement, low-rent, innercity locations of the 1900's to 1940's, to their second settlement, mid-city, urban apartments of the 1950's and 60's, and then to their third settlement middle-class suburbs of Oak Lawn, Burbank, Palos Hills and Alsip.

Establishing a Muslim Community in Southwest Metropolitan Chicago

Like Muslim Community Center in northern metropolitan Chicago, Mosque Foundation became the leading Muslim institution in the increasingly diverse southwest portion of metropolitan Chicago. A major difference between the two cases is that the Muslim population in the southwest is predominantly Arab, today comprising several Middle Eastern groups in addition to the Palestinian majority, while the Muslim population in the north is more racially/ethnically diverse. Another major difference is that Mosque Foundation left its original location in the city, whereas MCC did not. Sheikh Kifah Mustapha, Mosque Foundation's associate director, explained that the original Arab population that lived around 63rd Street was attracted to "a nice neighborhood" that was also white. As we would put it, they were not immune to the racialization of the Southwest Side. His view was that when blacks began to move into the Southwest Side, the Arabs began to move out. "They [Arabs] relate to Europeans," he claimed. As Arabs became more settled, they became upwardly mobile, preferring houses over apartments. In fact, a case can be made that Mosque Foundation anticipated and even facilitated Arab migration to the southwest suburbs.

Mosque Foundation was the first Arab mosque in Chicago, established in 1954.[4] This date seems surprisingly late (local Arab Christians established their first church in 1905), but it can be explained by the general absence of complete families and a largely nominal religious identity among the early Arab Muslim immigrants. Abdul Jalil al-Tahir (1950, 124) reported soon after World War II that Chicago Arabs had no mosque of their own, but also that several leaders advocated expanding the religious programming of a recently formed Arab Club in response to the establishment of the state of Israel and the resulting influx of Muslims from Palestine: "The Arab community feels today in need of an organization which will be able to teach their children the Arabic language and the Islamic values; to make the new generation conscious of their Arab inheritance and to harmonize their activities in regard to the Palestinian question." These leaders agreed that the Arab Club should include "a particular place for praying," which they referred to as a "mosque" (57–58).

Mosque Foundation's dual focus of preserving Arab ethnic identity and Islamic religious identity in a non-Muslim society is reflected in the following 1978 statement ("The Mosque Foundation Project," [i]): "The Mosque Foundation represents aspirations and efforts of the Muslem [sic] Arabs, living in this country, to preserve the Islamic Faith and Arabic language among the community members and their new generations. The main objectives reflect the belief that Islam is the eternal message of peace, love, contentment and well-being for all mankind, and that Islam should be preserved among its followers then spread to the world." Like the founders of Muslim Community Center to the north, leaders of Mosque Foundation took seriously their Islamic obligation to establish a viable Muslim community in order to safeguard an authentically Islamic way of life as Muslim minorities outside of *dar al-Islam*. However, we have no evidence of a territorial vision as focused and comprehensive as MCC's. Moreover, the multiracial/ethnic *ummah* ideal seems not as strong in this case as at MCC, although al-Tahir (1950, 104, 125) reports amiable relations between the Arab Club and "the Negro Muslim Temple" on 43rd Street, a Nation of Islam center.

Before relocating, Mosque Foundation had two locations on the Southwest Side of the city of Chicago: 65th Street and Stewart Avenue from the 1950s to 1964 (Hanania 2005, 39), then 63rd Street and Western Avenue. In 1978 Mosque Foundation began constructing a new facility on 93rd Street near Harlem Avenue in southwest suburban Bridgeview. This opened in 1982, making it the first mosque in metropolitan Chicago to be newly built with traditional Islamic architectural features (a dome, though no minaret). In 1986 Mosque Foundation opened a state-accredited girls school called Aqsa School (grades 4–12), and another for both girls and boys called Universal School (grades K–12) in 1990.

In a 1993 interview, the mosque's president told us that few Arabs lived or worked in Bridgeview before Mosque Foundation relocated there in 1982. Since then, Arab settlement has increased significantly in Bridgeview and nearby suburbs. Maureen McKinney (2001) reported that nearly one-third of the estimated 150,000 Arabs of metropolitan Chicago lived in the near southwest suburbs in 2001. Economics certainly played a major role in this migration, as these suburbs boast robust economies and convenient access to employment in other parts of metropolitan Chicago (cf. Abu-Lughod 1999, 330). Bridgeview, for instance, has a diversified economic base across the industrial, retail, and service sectors, and receives more than $13 million in annual tax revenues.

But Mosque Foundation also played a significant role as a magnet for Arab residential, commercial, and institutional development in the southwest suburbs. The census tract of the mosque is 11 percent Arab, higher than the 7 percent of Bridgeview as a whole. Our sources estimated that the eleven square blocks of residential properties surrounding the mosque are 95 percent Arab Muslim. (We were able to verify that twenty-nine of the thirty-three addresses on one street—88 percent—appear on Mosque Foundation's constituent list.) Moreover, our "windshield survey" of businesses near the mosque revealed many Arabic names and signage. Thus, Mosque Foundation has created a Muslim neighborhood around itself, although it is not a neighborhood mosque in our typology (less than 12 percent of its total constituency lives within a one-mile radius of its site).

In Figure 4.3, note the diversity south of Interstate 55 (the Stevenson Expressway) and west of the predominantly black south metropolitan corridor. Suburbs with significant Arab settlement include Bridgeview, Justice, Burbank, Hickory Hills, Oak Lawn, Palos Hills, Palos Heights, Alsip, and Orland Park. The non-white population of these suburbs has grown in recent years: Justice now has the largest percentage of non-white residents in this group of suburbs (29 percent), followed by Alsip (18 percent), Bridgeview and Palos Hills (both 13 percent), and Palos Heights, Oak Lawn, Hickory Hills, Burbank, and Orland Park (4 to 9 percent). Figure 4.3 also shows a significant overlap between Mosque Foundation's constituent residential distribution and the diverse communities in and around the southwest corridor.

Congregational Community Traits: Facilitating Muslim Life in the Southwest Suburbs

Whereas Mosque Foundation was established primarily by Palestinian immigrants, it today fosters pan-Arab Islamic solidarity across a constituency from sixteen Arab countries of origin (with the majority coming from Syria, Lebanon, Jordan, and Palestine) while also reaching out to non-Arab Muslims ("Mosque Foundation Strategic Plan 2008–2012," 60, 64, 66). As a brochure for non-Muslim visitors puts it, "Worshippers come from diverse origins and backgrounds. Many were born into Muslim families,

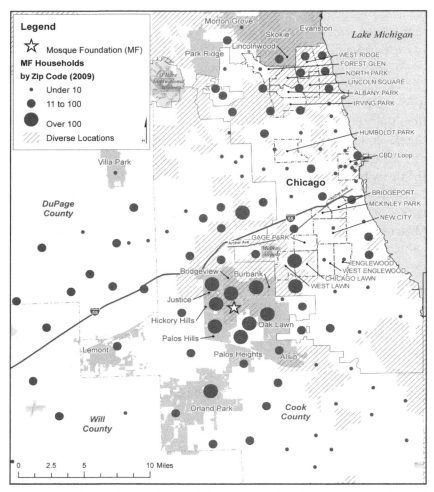

FIGURE 4.3. Mosque Foundation and Constituents. Map by David J. Treering and Melissa Gesbeck Howell, Loyola University Chicago.

while others are converts to Islam. Immigrants come from Arab, Asian, Latino, African, Turkish, and Bosnian origins."

Mosque Foundation's programming addresses the gamut of Islamic community life and needs, such as religious education, youth activities, women's issues, almsgiving (*zakat*), publishing, counseling, dispute mediation, immigrant services, marriages, and funerals. Several leaders of the mosque disclosed to us the challenges they face with youth issues such as dating and, in their terms, "uncontrolled sexual behavior" in American society. To provide an alternative, the mosque built a social center on its campus offering sports and educational activities in a "clean environment" that is also open to non-Muslims. Another area that is challenging to Muslims is the economic system that depends on usury or the charging of interest in banking transactions. Some senior leaders noted that most Muslims do not have enough cash to buy houses, cars, and businesses as they become more integrated into American society. The mosque has encouraged members to establish businesses that follow Islamic law as well as attempting to convince some American companies and banks to offer these services for Muslims.

Sheikh Jamal Said, Mosque Foundation's senior imam, confided to us that most of his time was taken up with family counseling. On the day of our interview, for example, he was asked by a Muslim family to judge a dispute over an inheritance from their father. The father left an "un-Islamic" will that the children were challenging. Sheikh Jamal reported that, as imam, he will not intervene in any dispute unless he is asked to do so and only after being assured that the petitioners will accept his decision. He acknowledged that he has "no official legal power" to enforce his rulings, but, as a religious authority, he warns people that "Allah will punish them if they chose an un-Islamic solution." Furthermore, he reminds them that "at the time of death, when all wealth and power will not help, they will be judged by their deeds." One of the mosque's women leaders, who was training for a degree in social work, often counsels women on sex-related issues, such as problems about which they are more comfortable speaking to another woman. Sheikh Jamal noted that he does not hesitate to recommend professional psychological counseling. In a separate interview, Sheikh Kifah, the associate director of the mosque, noted that in order to meet the needs of the growing Muslim community, "Muslims need to get training in the humanities and social areas," not just in medicine and technology.

Large numbers attend the two Friday (*jum'ah*) prayers (to accommodate Arabic and English speakers), the evening prayers and ritual breaking of the fast during the month of Ramadan, and the two annual Eid celebrations. One Eid al-Fitr provided us a glimpse into Arab Muslim life as facilitated by Mosque Foundation. The crowd, estimated at between five and six thousand by a Bridgeview traffic officer we talked to, included all age groups and appeared to be predominantly Arab. Males and females kept largely separate; the majority of the women wore some type of head covering, although a notable number did not (usually younger and well-dressed). When the call to prayer came over the public address system, many in the crowd outside the mosque queued up and performed the rituals. However, the great majority continued to mill around the grounds, talking to each other or patronizing one of several stalls selling toys, trinkets, literature, even American "junk food." The atmosphere reminded us of a Middle Eastern bazaar, with a good deal of noise, including recorded jingles from the ice cream vendors.

Congregational Action: Confronting Cultural Friction

As McKinney (2001) notes, "The suburbs to the southwest of Chicago have never been known for eagerness to embrace diversity. Nevertheless, diversity is beginning to embrace them." The resulting "cultural friction," to use McKinney's phrase, is a major part of the story of Muslim life in the southwest suburbs, such as tensions between white and Arab youths and Arab complaints about discrimination at public pools. Although the US census places Arabs in the white category, we separate the two groups for analytical purposes. The distinction is also real on the ground, as expressed by the president of a local girls' softball league, a forty-year resident of suburban Burbank: "[F]rom talking to the kids in the high schools, there is a tension we never had before—a tension between the regular white kids and the Arab kids" (McKinney 2001).

This cultural friction was placed in high relief in 2000 by the unsuccessful attempt of a second Arab mosque, Al Salam Mosque Foundation, to relocate from the Southwest Side of the city of Chicago to a former church facility in suburban Palos Heights. Although a federal jury eventually rejected the mosque's charge of discrimination against the town, the case was widely interpreted as an example of anti-Arab/Muslim bias on the part of residents and some town officials, which even the mayor admitted and decried ("Federal Jury Sides with Chicago Suburb in Mosque Dispute"; Stevens 2000).

Mosque Foundation has confronted this cultural strife in many ways over the years. In 1995, for instance, a few months after the Oklahoma City bombing (for which Muslim terrorists were initially but erroneously blamed), Mosque Foundation invited the local US congressman to a question-and-answer session following Friday prayers. Responding to questions about what could be done to combat negative stereotyping of Muslims, the congressman said, "You're not going to like what I have to say. You have chosen, to a great degree, to stay among yourselves. You have to make yourself known to the news media . . . . No one is going to do it for you." "We do this already," responded one member of the audience, miffed at what he perceived to be the congressman's unfair criticism ("Congressman Blunt during Muslim Visit"). In a 2003 interview, however, Sheikh Kifah echoed the congressman's view by stating that Muslims need to be part of the process of "fixing the problems" and not "be a victim." "We tell people: go to meetings in the city, volunteer your time." He reported that before 9/11, he was asked to speak to non-Muslim groups about two to three times a month, whereas after 9/11, this increased to two to three times per week. At the same time, Mosque Foundation's persistent civic engagement belies the congressman's view. Moreover, the Council of Islamic Organizations of Greater Chicago has been a member of United Power for Action and Justice since that community organization's founding in 1997, which, Sheikh Kifah asserted, had the effect of bringing mosques, including this one, into much greater contact with churches.

Mosque Foundation's striking territorial presence makes it a lightning rod for this cultural friction. It attracted national headlines when a large crowd gathered in Oak Lawn in the late evening of September 12, 2001, and then made their way to the mosque, where the Illinois State Police blocked the entrance to the property. During the ordeal, Arab residents of Oak Lawn and Bridgeview were advised to stay inside their homes ("Anniversary Update on Commission Activities Related to September 11"). Continuing debates about fundamentalist elements in the mosque contribute to suspicions among local residents (Hack and Hantschel 2003; Ahmed-Ullah et al. 2004; cf. Cainkar 1988, 212).

Even before 9/11, McKinney (2001) reported rising "Muslim political clout" in the southwest suburbs. McKinney's article featured photos of Mosque Foundation and its Aqsa School, and quoted Louise Cainkar, the main chronicler of the steady decline in local Arab fortunes, as saying that Muslims are "starting to get politically involved, to run for office. There's been *some* progress" (emphasis in original). McKinney cites a prime example of political clout in the passage of the Halal Food Act by the Illinois state legislature in August of 2001. The bill was proposed by the senator who represented Bridgeview and other southwest suburbs "at the request of well-organized Muslims in her district." It is also important that, according to Sheikh Kifah, area schools have learned to call the mosque about problems with Muslim families "before they call DCFS [the state's Department of Children and Family Services]." Since 9/11, Mosque Foundation leaders have increasingly met with southwest suburban officials in order to maintain good relations and anticipate friction points with non-Muslims.

Urban Impact: Helping to Create
the New Southwest Suburbs

The principal of one of Mosque Foundation's Islamic schools, also a member of the Bridgeview public library board, once summarized the primary urban factors that brought Mosque Foundation to the southwest suburbs (McKinney 2001): "The decision in the early 1980s to locate the mosque in Bridgeview was based mainly on the site's affordability and its proximity to Chicago's Southwest Side." He went on to make an astute observation about Mosque Foundation's urban impact on the southwest suburbs: "But it now looks as though [the move] was part of a strategic plan . . . . The area surrounding the mosque has become a core, a center for south-west suburban Arabs." This may not rise to the status of a strategic plan but it pinpoints the main reason why we see Mosque Foundation's urban impact as strong—remove Mosque Foundation from Bridgeview and the demography of the southwest suburbs would look very different.

The Urban Impact of Area Mosques

The mosques of this chapter qualify as area congregations in our typology. Slightly more than 50 percent of Muslim Community Center's constituent households live within seven miles of its facility, 57 percent of Muslim Education Center's constituent households live within five miles of its facility, and more than 52 percent of Mosque Foundation's constituents live in Bridgeview and eight nearby southwest suburbs (Figures 4.2 and 4.3 above). This is not surprising considering the requirements of Islamic practice that mitigate against the likelihood of a mosque attaining metro status, such as the Friday *jum'ah* prayers and the daily fast-breaking during Ramadan that pose serious inconveniences to participants who commute any distance. Strong incentives are necessary to make such an urban trek, as in the Arab ethnic solidarity afforded by Mosque Foundation. The primarily area (rather than metro) geographic orientation of Muslim Chicago as a whole becomes evident during the Eids, when celebrations are organized at strategic locations throughout the metropolitan region. Houston's Sunni "zonal mosque system" seems to indicate a primarily area geographic orientation there as well (Ebaugh, O'Brien, and Chafetz 2000, 110).

We have hypothesized that area congregations tend to exert relatively weaker urban influence, as do congregations with a strong focus on the needs of their own constituents. The area mosques in this chapter provide counterexamples to both tendencies, rising instead to the stronger end of the urban impact continuum, with MCC/MEC high moderate and Mosque Foundation strong.

These mosques are quite similar in several respects. They have created congregational communities united by shared Islamic beliefs, rituals, and norms, and by the need for mutual support and solidarity as a beleaguered ethno-religious minority group in American society. All of this helps to temper internal social differences. Paradoxically, these mosques maintain high boundaries with the outside world while engaging it for self-protection. Thus, although ethno-religious minority status can be a powerful limiting factor on congregational urban impact, it can also impel a congregation to function as both safe harbor and public advocate. These mosques have advocated for civic rights and privileges, steadily increasing their engagement with municipal governments, neighborhood groups, and other local entities. And they have created racially/ethnically heterogeneous congregational communities that have contributed to the diversification of their respective urban corridors.

This last point deserves thorough consideration. Whereas MCC prized heterogeneity from its inception, Mosque Foundation slowly evolved from a primarily Palestinian to a pan-Arab constituency, no small accomplishment despite shared aspects of Arabic culture. Mosque Foundation has lately begun to attract Muslims from other backgrounds, both for mosque activities and in the makeup of its Universal School (37 percent non-Arab; http://www.universalschool.org/school_profile.htm, accessed January 10, 2011).

This heterogeneity is only partly attributable to these mosques' status as area congregations. It is true that their respective social-geographic contexts provide a pool of potential constituents in a kind of supportive loop—the mosques helped to create the diverse local Muslim population that supports the mosques. But other mosques in the same (and other) diverse contexts have not attracted a heterogeneous constituency. The social-geographic context offered the potential for congregational heterogeneity but these mosques turned that potential into reality by appeal to the Islamic theological ideal of a single *ummah* in MCC's case and pan-Arab solidarity in Mosque Foundation's case.

Although other mosques may hold to these values, not all realize them to a significant extent despite generalized claims to that effect. For instance, in what was called "the first major survey of organized Islam on the continent," the Islamic Resource Institute reported that seven of ten North American mosques are "multicultural." However, no definition of "multicultural" was given and the survey relied on anecdotal and observational data supplied by the mosques themselves, as confirmed to us by a contact at the Islamic Resource Institute (see "Directory of Masjids and Muslim Organizations of North America"; Dart 1995). Likewise, the report of the comprehensive Mosque Study Project claimed that "Mosques are ethnically diverse. Ninety percent of mosques have at least some Arab members. And 87 percent of mosques have at least some South Asian and African American members." However, "some" is defined as "one percent or more" representation of a racial/ethnic group, a very low threshold of heterogeneity. Moreover, the report acknowledged that "Sixty-four percent of mosques have one dominant ethnic group," although the definition of "dominant" is unclear (Bagby, Perl, and Froehle 2001, 17, 19).

In an attempt to quantify this issue at least preliminarily, we visited thirty-six immigrant mosques of metropolitan Chicago over a period of several months between 1996 and 1997, recording the racial/ethnic composition of regular Friday *jum'ah* prayers. Of the thirty-six mosques, thirteen (slightly more than one-third) drew an attendance of what we and others consider substantial congregational racial/ethnic heterogeneity, that is, 20 percent or more of the worshipping body had an identity different from the majority group in attendance (cf. Emerson and Woo 2006, 35). We tested our observations against the self-perceptions of our subjects, asking Muslim contacts whenever possible for their own appraisals of the racial/ethnic diversity within their local mosques, which consistently matched our own. From information provided by local informants about the mosques we did not observe directly (namely, immigrant mosques that do not offer *jum'ah* prayers and black mosques), we estimate that about 30 percent of all mosques in metropolitan Chicago qualify as substantially heterogeneous in racial/ethnic composition.

Thus, the actual racial/ethnic heterogeneity at the mosque level in Chicago does not rise to common Muslim claims. Muslim diversity does appear to exceed that found in the other major pan-racial/ethnic religions of the region, namely, Buddhism and Christianity, though Catholic parishes most closely approximate the Muslim case (see Emerson and Woo 2006, 38–39, 86–87 on the diversity within Catholic parishes nationwide).

According to a spokesperson from its Office of Research and Planning, the parishes of the Archdiocese of Chicago (Cook and Lake Counties) show at least as much substantial racial/ethnic heterogeneity (as defined above) as the Muslim mosques of metropolitan Chicago.[5] In any case, congregational heterogeneity is not the norm across American religions. Thus, the urban impact of the mosques in this chapter is strengthened by their implicit criticism of the racial/ethnic homogeneity of religion in the larger society.

The growing residential presence of constituents of MCC and Mosque Foundation has diversified their respective urban corridors. Such corridors link a number of community areas, both city and suburban, creating what Albert Hunter calls a "region," his largest and most diffuse level of "symbolic community." "However," as Hunter (1974, 113) clarifies, "such a level is so broad and includes such heterogeneity that it cannot convey social distinctions with which residents may symbolically identify. It is the least likely to involve primary relationships among its members, and except through federation of smaller units is unlikely to be a basis of collective social action . . . . [S]uch areas are too broad to capture finer social distinctions and too inclusive to provide any but the most minimal local identifications, sentiments, and attachments" (cf. 192).

The demographic diversity we have identified in and around the north, northwest, and southwest metropolitan Chicago corridors betrays no coherent sense of social-geographic community in the Chicago School sense—at least not yet. However, Muslims recognize a measure of their own social-geographic community coherence in these locations. This certainly stems from a relatively long-standing Muslim presence, as scholars have documented (Zaghel 1976; Cainkar 1988; [1997]), but we argue that the mosques in this chapter have facilitated and enhanced this awareness. Recall MCC's desire to "return to our original plan, of erecting a grand Masjid on the North side of Chicago, where most of [the] Muslim population resides" and also the fear of the neighborhood group that the new mosque in Morton Grove that it would become a "regional [that is, area] Mega-Mosque." "The Mosque Foundation Project" document from 1978 indicates an incipient Muslim social-geographic community coherence going back several decades: the document's subtitle is "The Islamic Center for the Muslim Arabic Community in Southern Chicago" and its opening sentence reads [i], "The 'Mosque Foundation of Chicago' was established in 1954 by the Muslem [*sic*] Arab community residing mainly in the south west neighborhoods and suburbs of Chicago, Illinois."

Significant territorial claims through mosque facilities and Islamic day schools, the role played in diversifying their respective corridors, and increasing civic involvement and advocacy place MCC/MEC and Mosque Foundation at the stronger end of the urban impact continuum. We assess Mosque Foundation's impact as stronger due to the greater social and political significance of the new Arab presence in the southwest suburbs plus the commercial and institutional density around Mosque Foundation's facility. This density would not exist without Mosque Foundation's physical presence and functions as a kind of "sacred space" that is redolent of Catholic parishes during the classical period of American immigration (McGreevy 1996). While Mosque Foundation's constituents may not think of the immediate vicinity in this sense, this space nevertheless reflects their vision and sense of belonging. It is less like the Catholic model in that the mosque lacks the theological requisite to be responsible for all persons living within the parish boundaries.

Finally, we note that Mosque Foundation's success has contributed to the establishment of another large mosque in nearby suburban Orland Park, newly built on the model of the Dome of the Rock in Jerusalem. According to our source, a majority of the new mosque's initial constituents came from Mosque Foundation. Much had changed since 2000, when an Arab mosque's plan to locate in nearby Palos Heights was thwarted.

Area Congregations in the City

IN THE MIDDLE of Chicago's predominantly black South Side, New Covenant Missionary Baptist Church creates a vibrant black Baptist community that holds forth against encroaching blight. On Chicago's Near North Side, Fourth Presbyterian Church serves both the privileged who shop on the glitzy Magnificent Mile and the poor who can barely afford to live in nearby public housing. On the far North Side of the city, Congregation Ezra-Habonim struggles against the challenge of membership out-migration to the increasingly Jewish northern suburbs.

These are area congregations—that is, a majority of their members live within areas mid-range in size between a neighborhood and the metropolis as a whole. Each congregation has been affected differently by racial and socioeconomic restructuring in their respective urban contexts, but all three have created congregational communities in the face of those changes. Fourth Church has a strong urban impact, New Covenant Church has a moderate impact, while Congregation Ezra-Habonim is shaped primarily by the forces of the new metropolitan conditions, exerting relatively little reciprocal influence.

New Covenant Missionary Baptist Church
Urban Context: Greater Grand Crossing and Chatham

Greater Grand Crossing begins about eight miles directly south of Chicago's Loop.[1] Its earliest residents represented a variety of European ethnicities drawn primarily by employment opportunities in farming, railroads, factories, and building trades. By 1920, Greater Grand Crossing was mostly residential and virtually all white. Blacks began to move in during the 1920s, occupying a small section north of 67th Street. Larger numbers arrived during World War II as whites began moving out and the Second Ghetto on the South Side took shape. Blacks comprised 86 percent of Greater Grand Crossing's population in 1960, 98 percent in 1970, and 99 percent in 2000. The overall population declined steadily and significantly between 1960 and 1990 but only slightly between 1990 and 2000. Median family income for Greater Grand Crossing as a whole increased steadily since 1970 to nearly $32,000 in 2000, as did median home value (to nearly $84,000 in 2000). The census tract (6914) where New Covenant Church is located, however, was slightly better off and more comparable to the status of Chatham. The *Local Community Fact Book, 1990* (196) characterized Greater Grand Crossing as a mix of "solidly working class and poverty-ridden neighborhoods." The number of families living below the poverty level increased slightly between 1990 and 2000, from 23.3 percent to 25.5 percent.

Chatham lies immediately to the south of Greater Grand Crossing.[2] A few homes were built in Chatham in the late 1800s but residential development began in earnest only after 1910. By 1920, nearly ten thousand people lived here, many of them immigrants, especially Hungarians. The population swelled to more than thirty-six thousand by 1930, with Irish and Swedes then the largest immigrant groups, and continued to increase during the Great Depression, the 1940s, and into the 1950s. The Chatham Park housing complex, built in 1941, was occupied mostly by Jews and helped to support businesses along Cottage Grove Avenue. The racial transition of Chatham began in the 1950s, a bit later and slower than in Greater Grand Crossing, though both community areas became predominantly black by 1970. Blacks comprised 64 percent of Chatham's population in 1960, 97.5 percent in 1970, and 98 percent or more in every decennial census since then. After an increase in the 1960s, the overall population declined steadily and significantly between 1970 and 1990 and remained stable between 1990 and 2000. Median family income in Chatham increased steadily since 1970 to slightly more than $38,000 in 2000; the same steady increase in median home value occurred over that period, to more than $99,000 in 2000. These figures are significantly higher than Greater Grand Crossing as a whole, though closer to the figures for New Covenant's census tract. The number of families living below the poverty level increased to nearly 15 percent in the 2000 census, though lower than the 25.5 percent in Greater Grand Crossing.

Chatham may be the only community area in Chicago that transitioned from middle-class white to middle-class black status, due in large measure to successful black enterprises like Johnson Products Company and local banks. The *Local Community Fact Book, 1990* (142) reported that "Chatham is still an attractive residential community, despite increasing problems with crime and generally deteriorated and unattractive business strips, particularly 79th Street." The Greater Grand Crossing Organizing Committee, which includes Chatham in its purview and represents about twenty member congregations, claimed several modest victories in the mid-1990s. The largest was a part in reopening Provident Hospital, the only trauma center on the South Side. Nonetheless, Wallace Best (2004a, 129) reported a continuing downturn: "Toward the end of the 1990s Chatham seemed on the brink of another transition as reports of crime, property neglect, and economic instability were on the rise." Still, Best pointed to continuing hope that Chatham would not slide further toward the status of Greater Grand Crossing and other depressed black community areas on Chicago's South Side: "Community leaders and residents, however, devoted their energies to a number of revitalization projects designed to assure that Chatham would remain, in the words of real-estate developer Dempsey Travis, 'the jewel of the Southeast Side of Chicago.'"

Being Black and Baptist on the South Side

New Covenant Missionary Baptist Church, located two blocks north of Chatham at East 77th Street and South Cottage Grove Avenue, is among the largest congregations of Greater Grand Crossing.[3] In the 1990s New Covenant boasted more than six hundred member households, a Sunday morning attendance averaging one thousand persons across two worship services, and an annual vacation Bible school serving more than two hundred children. More than half of the congregation's members lived in eight contiguous community areas with black populations of 93 percent or higher, including Greater Grand Crossing/Chatham (nearly one-fourth of the members), thus making New Covenant an area congregation in our spatial typology. Note the dramatic coincidence of the member scatter dots and the predominantly black residential area in Figure 5.1.

Throughout much of its history, New Covenant has been pastored by the overlapping tenures of four generations of Thurstons.[4] In the tradition of family churches, patriarch Elijah Thurston (d. 1968) co-pastored New Covenant with his son, John Lee Thurston (d. 1979), from 1956 to

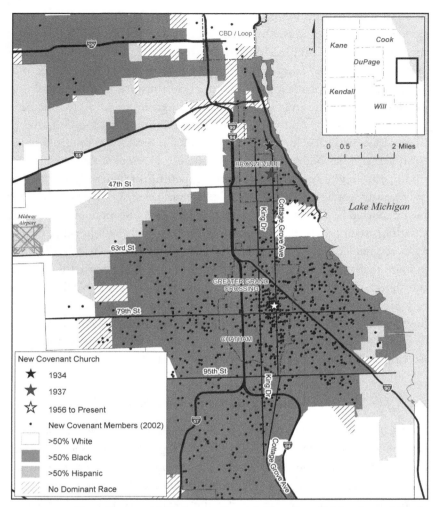

FIGURE 5.1. New Covenant Missionary Baptist Church and Members. Map by David J. Treering and Melissa Gesbeck Howell, Loyola University Chicago.

1968. Stephen John Thurston (b. 1952) served with his father, John Lee, as co-pastor from 1975 to 1979, and with his own son, Stephen John II (b. 1978), since 2004.

New Covenant's history, marked by three locations along the Cottage Grove Avenue corridor, is part of the southward expansion of Chicago's black population. In 1934 the congregation (then named Salem Baptist Church) was located at 37th Street and Langley Avenue in Bronzeville, a recently reclaimed designation for the "cultural mecca" of the black South

Side since the 1930s (Drake and Cayton 1945). When Salem's pastor died, Elijah Thurston, who had been the chair of the deacon board, was elected pastor. In 1937 the congregation moved to 735 East 44th Street (taking the name 44th Street Baptist Church) after the federal government purchased the Salem property in order to build the Ida B. Wells Housing Project.

The congregation relocated from the predominantly black Bronzeville farther north to its current location in the then-transitioning Greater Grand Crossing in 1956, taking the name New Covenant. At that time, some nearby white congregations like Chatham Fields Evangelical Lutheran Church and Crerar Memorial Presbyterian Church welcomed black members (Gregory 1989, 72–73). The move was advocated by John Lee Thurston, who sought to attract the progressive, upwardly mobile, and educated members of the black middle class who were also moving to Greater Grand Crossing/Chatham. New Covenant joined other black groups and institutions in constructing an interracial Greater Grand Crossing with vital economic, commercial, and civic resources, such as nearby industrial jobs in the steel, shipping, and manufacturing sectors; small- to medium-sized businesses on Cottage Grove from 70th to 87th Streets, as well as along 75th and 79th Streets; and block clubs, social clubs, and congregations scattered throughout the neighborhoods. While the area was interracial, it was clearly not residentially integrated because the color line continued to be redrawn block by block as commercial interests renegotiated the segregation patterns. Black-owned institutions like New Covenant Church could have attracted white members. However, the accelerating exodus of whites from Greater Grand Crossing diminished the chances that the color line would be redrawn within New Covenant Church (Brazier 1969).

During the first half of the twentieth century, Chicago's South Side was racialized in a way that created a "black metropolis" with its own banks, department stores, theaters, restaurants, schools, and religious institutions (cf. Drake and Cayton 1945). Whereas the white elite dominated the central business district and citywide political structures, blacks dominated the social, cultural, and religious (though less the economic) territory of the South Side. The late twentieth century saw the reterritorialization of the residential urbanscape by pluralities of non-whites in many areas, the deindustrialization of the local economy, divestments leading to blight and white flight from many neighborhoods, and increasing spatial inequalities throughout the metropolitan region. The resegregation of Greater Grand Crossing/Chatham during the mid-twentieth century anticipated and reinforced the resegregation of metropolitan Chicago during the late twentieth century.

Congregational Community Traits: Norms, Boundaries, Offices, and Authority

New Covenant Church's members are largely successful blue-collar workers and professionals, comfortably well-off home owners, secure though not wealthy. The strength and stability of the church rests on long-standing members and families who have been involved for two, three, and four generations. A certain vitality and growth also comes from those who join each year through the evangelistic efforts of the church, especially its revival services and the personal witness of its members.

New Covenant has created an intense, elective community in which norms of belief and behavior are enforced by strong congregational, particularly pastoral, leadership and the boundaries to the outside world, political and cultural, are moderately high. New Covenant's members deeply identify with the church community and constrain the pursuit of individual interests. The congregation also evidences complex levels of stratification in which authority and gender norms firmly operate. These traits are illustrated in worship, the principal mechanism for integrating the congregation, and in prayer practices and missional expectations and execution.

The sign we observed inside the church's entrance on our first field visit indicated the operative norms of this congregational community: "Ladies: No pants allowed in the sanctuary." Although this specific prohibition was dropped after the pastor's wife wore slacks one Sunday morning, the high level of moral authority exerted by the church remained. Inside the sanctuary, the stained-glass windows held the likenesses of three generations of Thurston pastors and their wives. The walls featured a red, black, and green African liberation flag, a Bible verse and a phone number for a dial-a-prayer service (above the choir stand to the right of the pulpit), and a banner proclaiming the church's affiliation with the National Baptist Convention of America. The ushers moved with military precision as they directed the gathering worshippers. Rev. Thurston processed into the sanctuary with one deacon in front and two following. Representatives of the church's key ministries were prominently visible and seated in orderly fashion: the deacons, the nurses and church mothers dressed in white just behind the deacons, all seated in the first rows of the theater-style sanctuary. The choir and associate pastors, with Rev. Stephen John Thurston in the middle, sat on the dais. All of the main leaders of the service, ten deacons and six pastors, were male.

The three-and-a-half-hour service began with devotions led by the deacons, which included their testimonies and the song, "Spirit of the Living God, Fall Afresh on Me." As they and the congregation sang, one of the deacons knelt and the other deacons surrounded him as he led the church in prayer. One of the ministers read the call to worship, with the congregation responding using verses printed in the bulletin. At this point, the ushers limited the movement of the congregation by placing theater-style posts around the main part of the sanctuary. The message was clear: "Church is over when we're done." The congregation sang "My Faith Looks Up to Thee" and the "Gloria Patri." Visitors were then given a formal welcome accompanied by "Something Good (Is Going to Happen to You)," co-written by Isaac Hayes, and also received a hug or a handshake from members and a packet of materials about the church. After an extended and lively reading of announcements followed by the offering, the high point of the worship service, the pastor's sermon, began.

Rev. Thurston is a virtuoso preacher in the American black Baptist tradition, as adept in his command of alliteration and song as he is in interweaving biblical imagery with the history and collective experience of black people. The sermons we heard carried a strong theme of black Christian identity in an oppressive contemporary urban America. On this Sunday the topic was "How Pure Is African-American Religion?" based on James 1:27. Rev. Thurston began by explaining that black people need to take the lead in providing a better perspective of the African motherland because the dominant culture's school system does not teach children their African-American heritage. "We do not have control over the school system," Rev. Thurston asserted, "but we do have control in the church and in our homes. . . . We must teach them ourselves."

He continued by saying the "Eurocentric outlook" does not emphasize the generational relationships that made the black family and black church strong in the past. As a result, "African-American culture is at a crossroads and now we are enslaved again . . . by drugs, immoral behavior, thankless children, gangs, crime, more black men in jail than in college, destruction of the family unit, and a high dropout rate." He continued, "We come to the church to get away from the world around us," but, "if we come and cannot go out and affect the world," then we still "need to be [made] free," and "there is no freedom like the freedom Christ gives!"

At this point, the pastor began "whooping" and the congregation increased their "Amens!," clapping, "shouting," dancing, and waving of hands. One of our researchers wrote, "The audio system almost shot me out of my seat!" The choir and instrumentalists shared a musical call and response with the pastor throughout the sermon, adding to the increasingly intense and emotional atmosphere. Rev. Thurston emphasized how the black church grew out of "grassroots needs" as reflected in the slave songs. Today black churches need to recapture "the spirit of their history and instill within their children the spirit of struggle." "Pure religion," he exclaimed, "focuses on needs." "Is the church still seeking to meet needs today?" He concluded at an intense pitch by saying that as Jesus met the needs of people in his day, so must the black church today.

In the sermon, Rev. Thurston reflected an awareness of both structural and individual aspects to the "slavery" threatening contemporary black people. A sermon by one of New Covenant's associate pastors elaborated on the racialized structures of American society. Titled "The Illusion of Freedom," this sermon was preached on a Fourth of July Sunday and took its key text from John 8:32: "and the truth shall make you free." The preacher challenged the notion that the nation's "freedom posture" included black Americans. This nation's true posture, he asserted, instead "keeps us from becoming all that we could become." There is no doubt that we live in a racist society, he continued, and that this racism is born out of a "systemic design" in which sin and inequality have become institutionalized. He decried the "evil trinity" of racism, capitalism, and militarism and its adverse effects on black men especially.

What should black Americans do in the face of this structural evil? The preacher gave both sociological and theological advice: resist the "structural sin of oppression" by developing "our own economic power and strength"—consistent with Rev. Thurston's view, he clarified that this is a separatist approach, not segregationist—but remember that Jesus holds the ultimate power. As Rev. Thurston pointed out on a succeeding Sunday, "God hates race prejudice but loves race pride." Rev. Thurston justified the separate black church because integrated churches do not give positions of power to black people and the society as a whole is not prepared to offer full equality to blacks. Rev. Thurston enjoined his flock to "support black businesses" and "write our own books."

Rev. Thurston articulates a conservative moral ethic and a way of life for the people of New Covenant that differs significantly from the dominant culture, one that requires Christians to take care of each other and of people in need and to observe the conventions associated with biblical communities that have proven valid for generations of black Christians. Traditional gender and family roles, conservative behavioral norms, disciplinary vigilance, and intergenerational respect are not only found in scripture but have been found worthy in providing moral bearings for black churches in a permissive and destructive society.

In one of the women's mission meetings, our researcher noted that the (female) leader "chastised those who were not doing their share of the work." Another researcher reported that "obedience" regarding their financial obligations was required of the women attending another mission meeting. An assistant pastor reprimanded some of the deacons from the pulpit during a period when the pastor was out of the country. Rev. Thurston and other congregational leaders, both male and female, illustrate what Robert M. Franklin calls "signifying language," a "folk rhetorical style of calling people out and shaming them to improve" (2007, 51). Franklin notes that such language in public forums may be counterproductive today (he cites Bill Cosby's criticism of poor parenting practices in the black community), but it was used in previous eras when bonds of social attachment and trust were stronger. It may be argued that New Covenant contains exactly those elements of attachment and trust that support the leadership's broad authority and chastising language.

Another dimension of this conservative cultural pattern illustrates some tension between women's anchoring work in the congregation as a whole and the requirement that their status be subservient to male leaders. The orientation of new church members includes joining mission groups organized by age and gender and focused on Christian education and evangelism. Most of the dozen or so mission groups are headed by women. On the one hand, women are encouraged to be involved and take leadership positions; on the other, they are socialized into an appropriate role in the gender and authority hierarchy of the congregation. None of the worship services or prayer meetings is led by women. None of the deacons is a woman. Young boys and teenaged males are systematically mentored for the diaconate that consisted of fifty men at the time of our observations. All of the worship and prayer services we attended were led entirely by men.

One prayer service particularly captured men's centrality at New Covenant. Several men gave introductions, preached, played the organ, and offered the altar call and personal testimonies, but the women only participated when singing or reading from the Bible in unison. "Gossiping" or "talking" about others was added to the list of requests the leader was "putting before Jesus." On another occasion, an associate pastor chided the "seasoned" women of the church from the pulpit for reportedly speaking "harsh words" to younger women. These incidents suggest how the talk of women and men is differently labeled. Chastising from the pulpit validates men's, particularly clergy's, public leadership role, while "gossiping" is done in private, and requires monitoring by men.[5] Worship services at New Covenant are predominantly male venues in which men's individual autonomy is publicly ratified yet women's communal role is merely expected, despite the fact that the collective life of the community depends on women's high participation levels and restorative service.

Related to this point is the unapologetic patriarchy practiced by Rev. Thurston—"Church is not a democracy," he has said. The separate roles he espouses for women and men are grounded in the scriptures, interpreted literally. During the Women's Day worship service, while praising the women of the church for their service—"the women have learned it pays to work for Jesus"—he continued with the text from Matthew 27 that describes how only women followed Christ to his crucifixion. Yet he continued by reminding the congregation that "man must be committed to God first" and that woman (according to the Genesis creation story) was "made for man." Therefore, "woman needed to submit to man, but only if man was committed to God first. If a man is not godly, woman should be submitted to God directly." Note that men were directed to "commit to God" but women were to "submit to man" or "submit to God." Rev. Thurston justified this traditional position through his belief that today's permissive society is the direct cause of the pathologies afflicting black family life, using religion as a countercultural power defining his objective and rationale for the use of separate gender roles to restore moral order.

Congregational Action: Claims for Race and Space, Mission Ministries, and Public Policy Advocacy

Over the decades, New Covenant has purchased or received bequeaths of several properties, significantly expanding its territorial footprint in the area. The edifice at 740 East 77th Street, now called the John L. Thurston Chapel Building, is joined by a $13 million worship center next door at 754 East 77th Street, completed in 2008. The honorary name of this portion of East 77th Street is Rev. Stephen John Thurston Street, a designation granted by the Chicago City Council in 1993. Rev. Thurston decries the loss of control by the local black community when the properties of deceased residents are sold by their heirs to outside interests. He worries about the implications of non-blacks, especially "Arabic persons," opening businesses without a sense of responsibility to the people living in the area. In this way, the church is reinforcing a residentially segregated enclave and addressing issues of black empowerment through separation, a strategy with its roots in the works of Booker T. Washington and Malcolm X, among others. Detractors to this strategy who espoused empowerment and justice through integration included W. E. B. DuBois, Martin Luther King, Jr., John Perkins, and possibly Barack Obama in current times.[6] Promoting a racial enclave as the only path to black self-determination, as Rev. Thurston does, creates a tension between the "imagined community" of African Americans and the reality of most New Covenant members, who work, if not mainly live, in a pluralistic urban world.

On its properties, the congregation has operated a series of outreach activities attempting to meet people's material needs. During our research period these included New Covenant Day Care Center, Community Savings Federal Credit Union, Jesus Helping Hand (a clothing and food benevolence ministry), a community development agency, and a community relations committee that served as a liaison between the congregation and representatives of the larger community. One member founded a spiritual and psychological support center for women without partners who choose to carry their pregnancies to term.

New Covenant uses the phrase "mission ministries" to describe both these community service activities and its specifically evangelistic activities, including street worship services, door-to-door witnessing, and visitations. Almost every mission group in the church engages in bimonthly visits to nursing homes, hospitals, and correctional facilities, such as Drexel Avenue Nursing Home, Alden Nursing Home, Cook County Jail, and the Juvenile Detention Center. On these visits, New Covenant members claim spiritual jurisdiction over the spaces, permitting the incarcerated to experience a moral authority that subsumes and delimits the juridical relationships operating otherwise. On one occasion during a visit to a women's prison, there was no clergy present for the service. Instead, all the women gave testimonies, creating a sacred space in which the inmates were "children of God" rather than people "caught in a system."

A similar time of testimony occurred at a workshop for representatives from a battered women's shelter held at New Covenant. While the discussion centered on how women could get out and stay out of abusive relationships, the women of New Covenant exercised their missionary spirit. One member spoke of her abusive husband who followed her to the courthouse and threatened to "blow her brains out" if she divorced him. Finally, she "got saved." It was then that she was "set free" from her "spirit of fear and rejection." She explained, "This was crucial because even though he left, I would have still been bound and would have ended up back in the same situation." Often, teachings about divorce and women's submission limit a conservative church's response to these kinds of situations or introduce ambiguities about the issues involving the abuser and the abused. In this case, the exchange focused not on submission but on healing and coping strategies and, importantly, on the power of prayer and how salvation meant being freed from the fear and low self-esteem that keep women bound.

New Covenant's public policy advocacy has diminished over the years. During the civil rights era, some of the most prestigious local congregations affiliated with the National Baptist Convention of America, Inc. (NBCA) were active in Martin Luther King, Jr.'s Southern Christian Leadership Conference (SCLC) campaign in Chicago. New Covenant's Rev. John Lee Thurston served as a national board member and president of SCLC's Chicago chapter. He was also an early supporter of Operation Breadbasket, the predecessor of Operation PUSH, in which his son, Stephen John Thurston, has also been active.

In the 1980s, several local NBCA pastors participated in the campaign to elect Chicago's first black mayor, Harold Washington, including New Covenant's Stephen John Thurston. Key to the campaign was a massive voter registration drive in 1982. Operation PUSH convened a meeting of more than one hundred black clergy to encourage voter registration drives among their parishioners, which helped to add 230,000 new registrants to the voting rolls (Travis 1989, 150; Cotton 1988, 68). In the struggle to solidify support for the Washington mayoral bid, the Task Force for Black Political Empowerment compiled a "political target list" of black pastors and aldermen who supported incumbent Mayor Jane Byrne and Cook County State's Attorney Richard M. Daley in the Democratic primary race. Thurston led a group of ministers who vowed to publicize the names of all black pastors who invited Byrne or Daley to speak at their churches. Harold Washington went on to win the Democratic primary as well as the general election ("Coalition Tells 'Political Targets'"; "Washington Announces 'Blue Ribbon' Team").

Today, New Covenant is not collectively engaged in social transformation through such obvious political involvement, in keeping with national trends of declining social activism, although Rev. Thurston is still connected to Operation PUSH. In response to economic issues, the church fosters mutual aid and charitable giving through its many ministries but rarely seeks to influence public policy directly. Except for an occasional critical reference to public officials and willingness for political organizations to use church facilities, the world of secular politics does not enter the discourse and symbolic world of New Covenant Church. Rev. Thurston's priorities have shifted to evangelization and pastoral leadership within the congregation and the wider black church.

Urban Impact: Culture and Structure in Challenging Racist Chicago

While attachment to place is often loosened in the restructured metropolis, "new forms and combinations of social spatiality and territorial identity" also emerge (Soja 2000, 152). The racial attachment of blacks to Chicago's South Side has continued throughout its reterritorialization over more than a half century. New Covenant Church has participated in reterritorializing its area as a middle-class black community that holds forth against creeping urban deterioration and moral threat. In a global metropolis where blacks rank low on the indices of wellness, educational achievement, and wealth but high on the indices of poverty, incarceration, homicide, and gang activity, New Covenant challenges Chicago's racist structures. They have redefined the meaning of social-geographic borders by reframing the notion of monoraciality as they strive for collective autonomy and control of their area through a process of self-racialization (Balibar and Wallerstein 1991).

New Covenant falls at the moderate point of our urban impact continuum because its cultural work on race does not alter the racial structures in which they are embedded. Instead, New Covenant has altered the meaning of those structures, providing strategies of individual and corporate identity-building. The church has created a congregational community sustained by the recollection and retelling of the stories of previous generations that resonate with present-day experiences. For many of its members, this congregation may be the only redemptive community on which they can rely. Nonetheless, New Covenant makes significant territorial and jurisdictional claims on its area. Radiating out from its territorial holdings to its mission ministries on the street, with families, and in local institutions, New Covenant brings a spiritual and moral message to various constituencies. Note that New Covenant is thus an exception to the hypothesized tendency of both area congregations and congregations with a strong focus on the needs of its own constituents (exhibited in its strict enforcement of internal norms, reinforcement of racialized boundaries with the outside world, and stratification of gender roles) to exert a relatively weak urban impact. New Covenant's beleaguered minority racial status provides the motivation for significant external exertion.

New Covenant's urban impact, however, does not rise to the strong end of our continuum due to its diminished public policy advocacy in recent years and its mix of both adaptation and agency in addressing racist structures. New Covenant has chosen both to adapt constructively to these structures and to confront its members by enforcing internal community norms in order to survive on the South Side of the new Chicago. In the long term, their form of monoraciality may be as powerful as multiraciality in altering the racist character of America, but the contemporary evidence is as yet decidedly ambivalent.

Fourth Presbyterian Church
Urban Context: The Gold Coast and the Slum

The Near North Side is bounded by Lake Michigan on the east, North Avenue on the north, and the Chicago River on the west and south.[7] According to the 2000 census, the Near North Side had the third highest median family income of all community areas in the city of Chicago (nearly $94,000, after Lincoln Park and the Loop) and the highest median home value (more than $625,000). But the Near North Side's deep socioeconomic fault lines were given classic description in Chicago School sociologist Harvey Zorbaugh's (1929) *The Gold Coast and the Slum*. The Magnificent Mile extends north from the river to Oak Street, which forms the southern boundary of the aptly named Gold Coast. In census tract 801 of the Gold Coast, for instance, the 2000 median family income was more than $144,000, whereas it was only about $5,300 in nearby census tract 808, which included some Cabrini-Green public housing units (see below). The number of families living below the poverty level was a mere 1 percent in tract 801, a staggering 68 percent in tract 808.

The Near North Side's socioeconomic fault lines were initially drawn by some of Chicago's most prominent citizens. William Butler Ogden, a realtor and the city's first mayor, orchestrated the siting of industrial and residential tracts in the area, for instance forcing Irish factory workers out of their neighborhood in order to bring in the city's first rail line in 1848. Cyrus McCormick built his first Reaper Works factory near the Chicago River, while members of his family "established an island of wealth when they built homes in the eastern quarter of the area" (Seligman 2004c, 562), an "island" quickly inhabited by Potter Palmer, the businessman known for his role in developing State Street in the Loop, and other wealthy Chicagoans. Meanwhile, the western portion of the Near North Side was allowed to deteriorate, a buffer strip of rooming houses separating it from the wealthy eastern portion.

The first immigrant settlers of the western portion of the area were Irish, Swedes, and Germans, followed in the early twentieth century by large numbers of Italians and smaller numbers of Greeks and Assyrians. Blacks arrived throughout the twentieth century, comprising more than 30 percent of the total population of the Near North Side in each decennial census from 1960 to 1980 but dropping significantly in 1990 (23 percent) and 2000 (19 percent).

The Cabrini-Green Homes public housing project became an iconic representation, not only of the Near North Side's socioeconomic fault lines, but also of the spatial inequalities of the new urban era.[8] The original facility, named the Frances Cabrini Row Houses after the first American Catholic saint, was built for war workers in 1942 and replaced a notorious Italian immigrant neighborhood called Little Sicily. The high-rise Cabrini Extension buildings were erected in 1958, the William Green Homes in 1962. By then, the Cabrini-Green complex had evolved from its initial mixed racial/ethnic composition to predominantly black. At its height, it accommodated some fifteen thousand residents.

By the 1990s, federal and city authorities agreed that such high-density public housing projects had failed and set in motion plans for replacing them with mixed-development housing for mixed-income residents. The neighborhood around Cabrini-Green changed dramatically as a result of the Chicago Housing Authority's Plan for Transformation, initiated in 2000. According to a study conducted by *The Chicago Reporter* (Rainey and Woodward n.d.), the largest increase in home mortgage values in the city of Chicago during the period of 2000 to 2003 occurred in one of the census tracts of Cabrini-Green. "However," the study noted, "the

Cabrini-Green area continues to grapple with safety concerns. Many new residents, most of whom are white and middle-class, remain leery of their public housing neighbors, most of whom are black." "It doesn't really feel like a neighborhood at all," a resident of the Old Town Village West development explained. "As long as there is a very condensed source of crime and poverty next door, there will never be a true neighborhood here." The study pointed out the continuing spatial inequalities: "as a community, Old Town Village West and Cabrini-Green have not mixed very well. The racial and economic differences are hard to miss when looking down Division Street."

The city demolished the last of the Cabrini-Green high-rises in 2011. At this writing, only the row houses remain, about one-third of which are remodeled, while the rest sit vacant and shuttered behind a chain-link fence. Many residents remain in temporary housing or are homeless, awaiting the CHA's promise to return them to their former neighborhood (Corley 2013).

Being Responsible White Protestants on the Magnificent Mile

Fourth Presbyterian Church occupies the block of North Michigan Avenue between Chestnut Street and Delaware Place along a stretch of prime real estate known as the Magnificent Mile.[9] Fourth Church stands as a religious symbol among some of the most visible symbols of capitalism, wealth, and consumerism. (Figures 5.2 and 5.3 locate the church's membership in metropolitan Chicago's income and racial/ethnic contexts.) The spatial inequalities of the Near North Side have been both replicated by and ameliorated by Fourth Church. The church exemplifies the best circumstances of the new metropolis and stands as a critic of the worst consequences of those circumstances for its well-off constituents and poor clients.

Fourth Church began with a merger of two Presbyterian congregations in February of 1871. A few months later, the Great Fire destroyed its facility at the corner of Grand and Wabash Avenues, prompting relocation to the corner of Rush and Superior Streets in 1874. Forty years later, in 1914, the congregation moved to its present location on what would become North Michigan Avenue. The famous Water Tower that survived the Great Fire is the only structure older than Fourth Church on North Michigan Avenue.

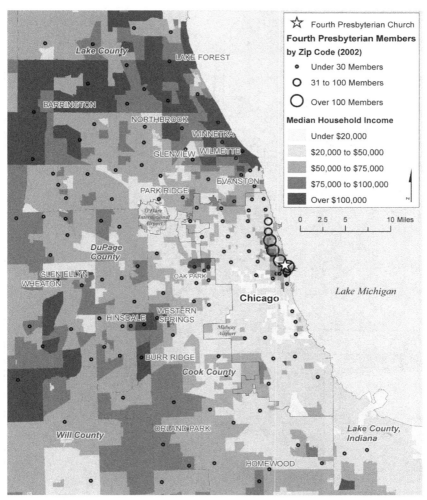

FIGURE 5.2. Fourth Presbyterian Church and Members, with Census Income Data. Map by David J. Treering and Melissa Gesbeck Howell, Loyola University Chicago.

The church's blend of French and English Gothic architecture contrasts starkly to the surrounding modernist urbanscape. Its properties comprise a main worship edifice and a set of connected buildings that include a chapel, a parsonage, church offices, and a courtyard along Michigan Avenue. Ralph Adams Cram, the renowned architect and leading proponent of the Gothic Revival School, designed the edifice, Howard Van Doren Shaw the parish buildings and fountain in the courtyard. James K. Wellman (1999, 161) notes that the courtyard "attracts many into the gardens and

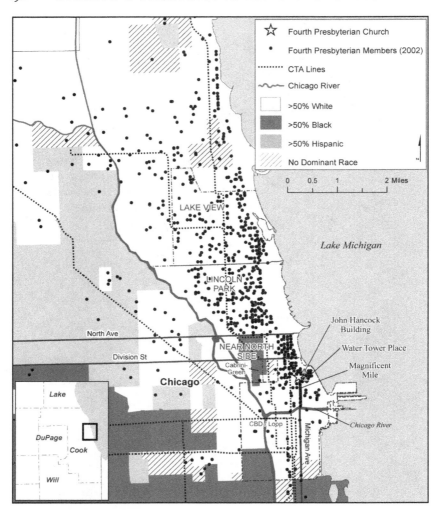

FIGURE 5.3. Fourth Presbyterian Church and Members, with Census Race and Ethnicity Data. Map by David J. Treering and Melissa Gesbeck Howell, Loyola University Chicago.

to the beauty of the building and fountain." The sanctuary holds the second largest organ in Chicago (after the University of Chicago's Rockefeller Chapel) and one of the largest in the Midwest. Stone pillars support an arched wood-paneled ceiling with tall, narrow, leaded windows and brass chandeliers providing light to an otherwise dim interior. Thus, Fourth Church not only demarcates a distinctly recognizable religious territory, it projects itself as a welcoming place and a sanctuary in one of the glamour zones of the new metropolis. When the congregation completed a major renovation of its facilities in the mid-1990s, it reaffirmed its commitment to this location.

Fourth Church is an area congregation in terms of the residential distribution of its constituency but also in its own self-perception of its relationship to the Near North Side. In the 1990s Fourth Church had approximately 3,800 official members, 52 percent of whom lived in the Near North Side and the two community areas immediately to the north, Lincoln Park and Lake View (Figure 5.3). The church grew to 4,900 by 2000 and stood at 6,200 in 2010, according to the most recent annual report. James Wellman (1999, 163) observed that Fourth Church "reflected the income status, education, and ethnicity of the Gold Coast's upper-middle-class population." This continued its legacy as an elite church, which Zorbaugh reported had earned it the early nickname "The Millionaires' Club" among locals. Wrote Zorbaugh (1929, 184, n. 2), "This church is a 'community' institution only in its own eyes. The 'community' feels keenly the barrier between itself and the world of fashion of which the church is a part." Yet this tells only half the story of Fourth Church's participation in creating the Near North Side. The other half is "its history of philanthropic generosity and 'hands on' social service" (Price 1996, 93). This encompassed programs for single adults in local boarding houses and tutoring for immigrant men in the 1890s, the latter including Cyrus McCormick, Jr., who was a member and contributed heavily to the building of the current edifice, as one of the tutors. As a Chicago journal noted in 1914, "The great mission of Fourth Church will be to grapple with the conditions by which it is surrounded" (cited in Price 1996, 92).

Over the span of a century, Fourth Presbyterian has been served by four pastors whose tenures extended twenty years or more each: John Timothy Stone (1908–1928), Harrison Ray Anderson (1928–1961), Elam Davies (1961–1984), and John Buchanan (1985–2012). (The church is undergoing a pastoral search at the time of this writing.) Rev. Buchanan's (1996) book, *Being Church, Becoming Community*, provides theological grounding for Fourth Church's continuing efforts to contend with the conditions surrounding it. "So Where Exactly Is the Church?" asks Buchanan (19). He begins his answer: "The church, I believe, is a respite of silence from the noise of the city; a cloistered, reflective place where mystery and transcendence may be pondered, where prayers are lifted in solitude." He cannot leave it at that, however: "But if that is all church is, an escape, a retreat from the world, it has made a critical mistake. The church is called to be in the world, in the city, and that means intentionally, imaginatively, creatively, and aggressively in the city, living in and for the human community in order to be faithful to God."

What better place to do this than on the city's most secular avenue in the city's most spatially inequitable area? This theology of incarnational grace in and through the church, which expanded the church's historic commitment to lowering the boundaries with the outside world, continued that of Buchanan's immediate predecessor, Elam Davies, who wrote that attending a church "is a deliberate setting of oneself side by side with people who spiritually are poor, maimed, blind and halt, and confessing by our presence that we are one of them, one of the least, last, lost, met by God in the company of our fellow needy" (cited in J. Wellman 1999, 145).

Congregational Community Traits: Communal Bonds and Public Ties

We found worship at Fourth Church to be inclusive and participatory yet orderly and formal, with an elegance befitting its Gothic sanctuary. We illustrate with the following service. It began with an organ prelude by Bach as the ushers assiduously directed worshippers to cushioned wooden pews. The majority of the congregation was white, with about 15 percent African Americans and Hispanics, plus a sprinkling of Asians. Age and gender were fairly evenly represented, including couples and singles. A serious but not particularly devotional atmosphere typified the service.

Promptly at 11:00 am, the professional-sounding choir processed into the sanctuary in full voice, followed by the pastor (male) and two associate pastors (one male and one female) in Geneva gowns with "preaching tabs" in the manner of John Calvin. The clergy and the choir sat in the ornately carved chancel facing the congregation. One associate pastor gave a formal welcome, asking newcomers to fill out an information sheet in the pew (they were not asked to stand) and announcing that tours of the building would be available after the service. The choir sang the seventeen-century anthem "Also hat Gott die Welt geliebt" by Heinrich Schuetz. Another pastor read from scripture, after which the congregation recited a responsive prayer followed by the general prayer of confession and declaration of pardon. Announcements included a number of ways people could serve the church and the community. Scarlotti's "Alleluia" introduced the Gospel reading by the pastor.

The church lights then dimmed as Rev. Buchanan mounted the imposing pulpit to preach on "Faith and Your Demons." He began lightly by pointing out the "demons" that inhabit our answering machines and computers, seemingly removing our control. Perhaps these are the demons of our age. He continued by telling the Gospel story of how Jesus encountered demons, acknowledged them, and cast them out. Demons are threats to the integrity and well-being of the whole person, Rev. Buchanan explained. "The demonic is powerful. Just think about how crowds can take over a person's moral judgment": fans at the opening of a Bulls game, the *volk* at a Nazi rally, the Los Angeles rioters, the massacres in Rwanda. Political oppression stimulates the demonic. But it can also be personal, as when codependency impairs our judgment. Invoking the theologian Paul Tillich, Rev. Buchanan asserted that faith, "the state of being grasped by a power greater than ourselves," was the response to the demons that can save us from them. Furthermore, "naming the demons is the beginning of healing, not only for you but for the community." The service ended with a hymn during which the choir and clergy recessed from the sanctuary to greet worshippers as they left.

Worship is a window into congregational community identity. Fourth Church is a leader congregation, one that endeavors to "live our values" by attempting to "change the world" (Becker 1999, 15). Furthermore, while this church may be a network of friendships for many, it is not constituted as a village or a family. It is more like the ideal norm of city life described by Iris Marion Young (1990, 240): "the being together of strangers." "In the city persons and groups interact within spaces and institutions they all experience themselves as belonging to, but without those interactions dissolving into unity or commonness" (237). The formality of the worship service represents this notion but is simultaneously participatory. The congregation knows its part: hymn-singing, responsive Bible reading, confession of sin, affirmation of faith. There are no spontaneous "joys and concerns," no enthusiastic "Amens!" Children are not a regular part of Sunday morning services; they have Church School and Children's Chapel. The sanctuary is for the spiritual and moral formation of adults.

Nonetheless, family-themed sermons are significant elements of Fourth Church preaching, with a focus on theological principles of grace and responsibility. Sermons bring out the Bible's realism about disastrous family dynamics or cite current biblical scholarship against patriarchal interpretations of the Christian tradition. The question of patriarchy is particularly notable in that in both sermon content and the STEP (Systematic Training for Effective Parenting) class for members, the family is characterized as a democratic institution. Democratic citizenship skills are seen as transferable from family to public life on the cornerstone value of responsibility.

"The Fourth Presbyterian Church of Chicago is a *public* church by virtue of its sense of place," writes Lois Gehr Livezey (1998, 120, emphasis in original). "It is graced—and challenged—by the significance of its location and the sort of centrality, visibility, and accessibility such a location affords" (135–36). Fourth Church is comfortable with its location in the center of the dominant culture. The pastor directs his cultural criticism to specifics within the congregation's experience rather than a systemic critical analysis of that dominant culture. Even the changes stemming from the restructuring of family, home, and work are addressed with a problem-solving approach rather than a focus on "crisis." Middle-class professional lives are faced with benefits and costs in which problematic changes and a host of choices must be taken up as a challenge. In a similar way, Fourth Church is comfortable with contemporary poetic, practical, and scientific literature, combining biblical and modern wisdom.

This ethos connects members to each other through the church's extensive programming and the civil discourse that occurs there. More than a dozen activities are scheduled at Fourth Church on any given day, ranging from AA meetings to men's breakfasts to noon concerts. There are groups for runners, young adults, single parents, seniors, and those interested in the arts or theological study—needless to say, something will suit every taste and interest. We observed a panel on "Family Values: A Global Perspective" in which representatives of diverse religious groups spoke from their traditions with the aim of initiating relationships with neighbors, a talk on obsessive-compulsive disorders in a young adult group that led to a discussion of whether the city of Chicago should permit casino gambling, and Employment Support Group meetings that were not restricted to church members. These events were characterized by Fourth Church's norms of respect for alternative viewpoints, self-discovery, and responsibility.

Yet despite this richness, members expressed concerns about their relationships to the staff and each other during our research period. A 2008 congregational survey indicated that "creating a sense of community" was an ongoing concern. The size of the membership and the scale of its activity require a large professional staff. This tends to channel discussions and decision making to administration rather than convoking discussion among members. The church's own success seems to be an obstacle, since size is a significant factor in the ability to create communal intimacy (Simmel [1908] 1971). It is also worth noting that the survey captured a desire for spirituality at Fourth Church: "One need expressed was for evening opportunities for adult small groups that focus on spiritual matters, as opposed to socializing." The low boundary between Fourth Church's cultural identity and that of mainstream society may be an additional obstacle to achieving the spiritual climate some of its members seek.

Congregational Action: Social Service, Public Witness, and Public Policy Advocacy

Fourth Church embodies its theology of incarnational grace through three main forms of congregational action: social service programs, public witness through its territorial and jurisdictional claims, and, to a lesser extent, public policy advocacy.

Over the years, the church has operated or cosponsored an extensive array of social service programs in the Near North Side and other locations around the city, including North Side Housing and Supportive Services, Career Transitions Network, the PACE Institute (educational services for Cook County Jail inmates), The Door (assistance with food, clothing, and other necessities), the Center for Older Adults, Deborah's Place (services for homeless women), and the Greater Chicago Food Depository. Fourth Church has been a conduit for volunteers from other churches as well as some without a church affiliation. One measure of the church's commitment to these activities is that one-third of its current professional staff positions is dedicated to social services.

Fourth Church's involvement with the Cabrini-Green public housing project became emblematic of its social service profile. As Rev. Buchanan (1996, 28) once put it, "Cabrini-Green represents the most dramatic contrast to the affluence of the near north side and is therefore God's clearest call to mission for the church." The church's first venture into Cabrini-Green, in 1964, involved tutoring public school children. This was followed by the City Lights Summer Day program for school children (1966) and a comprehensive nonprofit organization called Partners in Education (1991) that extended educational services beyond Cabrini-Green. In 2004 Chicago Lights succeeded Partners in Education, tracing its origin to the 1964 Cabrini-Green tutoring program and continuing the Cabrini-Green legacy in four of its six signature programs: Tutoring, Urban Farm, Summer Day, and Chicago Lights Academic Success in Schools (CLASS) (http://

www.chicagolights.org/cgi-bin/WebObjects/cl.woa/wa/b?t=About+Us, accessed September 9, 2013).

The motto of Chicago Lights is "Changing Lives One at a Time." According to its 2012 annual report, Chicago Lights served nearly 4,500 people through the efforts of more than 1,800 volunteers, nineteen full-time and twenty part-time staff, and more than 120 partner organizations. In our previous discussions of Fourth Church we wondered whether the anticipated demolition of Cabrini-Green would fundamentally change the congregation's identity and purpose (Price 1996, 100; 2000, 77). Chicago Lights provides the answer: Fourth Church continues its social service programs to the least, the last, and the lost in the Near North Side and throughout the city.

Through some of its social service programs, Fourth Church gives public witness against the injustices of the new urban era by making jurisdictional claims beyond its privileged location in the Near North Side, for instance in public housing complexes, public schools, and correctional facilities. The church also gives public witness by its considerable physical presence on the Magnificent Mile. As membership and programming continued to grow in the 2000s, the church considered expanding its territorial footprint. The first plan was a sixty-three-story high-rise with condominiums on the upper floors, the second a hotel. Selling the air rights would have realized significant funds for programming and congregational needs. Both plans met with intense opposition from neighbors and two city aldermen.

The eventual five-story Genevieve and Wayne Gratz Center, opened in 2013, illustrates the limits of the church's ability to alter its territorial holdings. Height, density, and traffic impacts were cited in the local opposition but some speculated that the "real" reason centered on how the church's high-rise would have obstructed the view of affluent neighbors (Galef 2010; Kamin 2010; Slosar 2010). Fourth Church's public witness requires financing and, apparently, "clout." The church was forced to forego considerable future revenue despite its moral authority and the general goodwill its programs have generated with many groups in the city.

Public policy advocacy can take various forms. In the 1990s, Fourth Church eschewed community organizing efforts through the Industrial Areas Foundation, a model of public action that employs conflict as a strategy for social change, due to reported disagreements within the Presbytery of Chicago on that issue, according to an associate pastor. In 2013, however, the new associate pastor for ministry began community organizing training. Nonetheless, Fourth Church was involved in a local affordable housing effort in the mid-1990s called Central City Housing Ventures, in partnership with Chicago Temple-First United Methodist Church and Holy Name Cathedral. This partnership was formed in an attempt to reopen the former Lawson YMCA as a mission. Although that effort failed, the historic facility eventually became the Lawson House, still part of the YMCA system, the largest single-room occupancy supportive housing facility in the Midwest providing housing and wraparound social services for extremely low-income or formerly homeless men and women. Central City Housing Ventures later built the first single-room occupancy residence in fifty years in Chicago and in 2012 involved more than a dozen downtown Protestant, Catholic, and Jewish congregations (http://www.cchvchicago.org, accessed July 24, 2012).

Fourth Church carefully considers its involvement in the political arena. In an interview with the associate pastor, we learned of the church's politically diverse membership and thus its preference for non-partisan advocacy. Political education within the church is the prelude to informing politicians about problems the church takes up. In the 1990s, the church sponsored a four-week educational series on the Middle East. More typical activities included letter-writing campaigns by the peacemaking, hunger, and housing committees.

To clarify the legal status of church-based advocacy and address the "appropriate" uses of the church's institutional as well as individual members' power, the church issued a protocol for public policy advocacy that included two key directives: first, advocacy must emerge directly from the outreach activities of the church or positions of the General Assembly of the denomination; second, courses of action can include building relationships with officials whose policies affect people served by the church, educating members about public policy issues, and encouraging members to communicate with public officials as "individual Christians, not as representatives of Fourth Church." This implies that political influence is most effective when it is personal. Nonetheless, the associate pastor confided to us that he "would like to see the church develop use of its corporate and business capacities as a resource for job-training, for example, with Cabrini-Green youth and adults, and toward systemic advocacy on economic development issues." Views such as this vary with the individuals holding those positions and in recent years the church's activities have moved away from political involvements.

The Urban Impact of a Liberal Protestant Church

Drawing upon the work of Robert B. Reich, Edward Soja (2000, 267) discusses the role of the so-called "fortunate fifth" in the new metropolis, that is, those in the top 20 percent of American incomes: "in terms of taxes paid, proportion of income given to charity, local political participation rates, and choices of residential environments, larger numbers of the 'fortunate fifth' seem to be seceding from civic life and its public responsibilities, creating new kinds of privatized postmetropolitan enclaves and new ways of reinforcing and securing their isolation." Fourth Church counters such social and civic trends through its congregational action, particularly its extensive social service programs through which it addresses the growing "spatial mismatch" in the new metropolis, the "hyperghettoization" that "marginalizes and isolates the underclass in concentrated enclaves of poverty" (271). The irony of the Near North Side is that the hyperghetto is merely blocks away from the hyperglitz of the Magnificent Mile.

In an era when liberal Protestantism is on the decline, Fourth Church has thrived. Its members are among the business and cultural elite of Chicago and it attracts young families to a downtown church when the suburbs continue to be the location of choice for raising children. Fourth Church has not been successful in all its pursuits, particularly in its plan to build an income-generating high-rise. And it faces the dilemmas of all large successful churches in meeting the personal needs of members who seek sustaining social and emotional bonds. Nonetheless, Fourth Church's moderate focus on internal community needs has translated into a strong urban impact.

Congregation Ezra-Habonim
Urban Context: The Far North Side and the North Shore

Rogers Park and West Ridge are contiguous community areas in the northeast corner of the city of Chicago.[10] Beginning with a small population of German and Irish farmers during the decade of Chicago's incorporation (1830s), Rogers Park became a village in 1878 and was annexed to the city in 1893. Until the 1970s, Rogers Park was overwhelmingly white, though with great European-American ethnic diversity. This diversity established a foundation for what would become a stable, racially/ethnically and religiously integrated area after the 1980s (Maly and Leachman 1998).

The Rogers Park population began to grow significantly after the Chicago Fire of 1871 and the expansion of the railroad from Chicago's Loop northward to Evanston. Up to the turn of the twentieth century, Rogers Park contained mainly single-family frame houses. New residential construction began after Jesuit-run Loyola University moved in 1908 from Chicago's Near West Side to the largely unsettled marshland in the southeastern corner of Rogers Park. More construction came with the addition of the Howard Street public transit station, the last stop going north in the city. After World War I, the pressure of incoming populations forced the construction of large, sturdy, pre-Depression era flats that filled in much of eastern Rogers Park, giving it its distinctive rental character.

Churches and synagogues followed their members to Rogers Park beginning in the 1870s. Historians Dominic Pacyga and Ellen Skerrett (1986, 133) note that the period between 1915 and 1930 was Rogers Park's "golden age of building." St. Jerome Catholic Church rebuilt a grander church in 1916. Other large structures included St. Ignatius Catholic Church (1917), St. Paul's By the Lake Episcopal Church (1926), Temple Mizpah synagogue (1924), B'nai Zion synagogue (1928), and Sixteenth Church of Christ Scientist (1929).

The earliest Jews moved to Rogers Park after 1910, numbering about ten thousand by 1930 and more than twenty thousand by 1950, nearly one-third of Rogers Park's total population. The Jewish population declined thereafter, to about thirteen thousand in 1980. An even larger intra-city movement of Jews to West Ridge from the South Side, North Lawndale, and Albany Park from the original settlement in the Maxwell Street ghetto occurred after World War II, culminating in a 1960 Jewish population of forty-eight thousand, or about three-fourths of West Ridge's total population. West Ridge remained the largest Jewish community in the city into the early 2000s, comprising nearly 50 percent of West Ridge's total population and featuring ten (mostly Orthodox) synagogues.

Many of the West Ridge synagogues are located along California Avenue between Peterson and Touhy Avenues. Orthodox men can be seen walking to their daily prayer services. Jewish shops operate along Devon and Touhy Avenues, along with kosher establishments, *mikvah*s (ritual baths), religious schools for children and adults, the Jewish social service agency known as The Ark, a large community center and housing for elderly Jews, and the central agencies for Orthodox Jewish law and custom, such as the Associated Talmud Torah and the Chicago Rabbinical Council. This population is securing, with some tenacity, a Jewish presence within the city, anchored by the larger families of Orthodox Jews (compared to other Jewish groups). In contrast to the city's population as a whole, the Jewish population of West Ridge is older and has higher median income and educational levels, indicating their importance in the restructuring economy.

In 1950 only about 5 percent of metropolitan Chicago's Jewish population lived in the suburbs; by the 2000s, about 70 percent were suburban, living mostly north of the city. New Jewish epicenters with the necessary infrastructure of synagogues, religious schools, kosher shops, rabbinical associations, and denominational offices were forming in the North Shore suburbs of Northbrook, Buffalo Grove, and Long Grove. In 1930 the Jewish population of the city of Chicago was an estimated 275,000, more than 80 percent being of Eastern European descent. By the 2000s Jews numbered about 270,500 throughout the entire metropolitan region and the ethnic distinctions had largely disappeared. Cutler (1995, 94, 169) listed a variety of reasons for the local Jewish population decline: low birth rates, migration to the Sunbelt, intermarriage, decreased immigration, and "lack of identity among some youth."

The suburbanization of Chicago's Jewish population was consistent with the out-migration of Protestants and other white groups beginning in the 1950s. The reasons are structural and cultural, including racially based "white flight" after the removal of restrictive housing covenants, increases in the number and size of young families, federal mortgage loan guarantees for mainly white buyers, the desire for better schools and newer homes on generously sized lots, and federal investment in highway transportation out of the city. Suburbanization and early globalization of manufacturing were fully visible by the mid-1970s, yet urban manufacturing job losses and the shift to a service economy began shortly after World War II, stimulating some of the earliest mobility (B. Bluestone and Harrison 1982; Abu-Lughod 1999).

Being Conservative Jews on the Far North Side

In the mid-1990s, Congregation Ezra-Habonim was located at 2620 West Touhy Avenue in West Ridge, in the heart of the remaining Jewish infrastructure within the city of Chicago.[11] This location falls within the physical boundary markers of the West Rogers Park Community Eruv, one of six *eruvs* in the city of Chicago and northern suburbs maintained by Chicago Eruv Inc. in accordance with Orthodox Jewish legal requirements for Shabbat activities (http://chicagoeruv.tripod.com/, accessed October 3, 2014). Thirty-one percent of Ezra-Habonim's member households lived within a one-mile radius of the synagogue, a significant number, though not enough to qualify as a neighborhood congregation in our typology. Sixty-nine percent lived in West Ridge and the nearby suburbs of Skokie and Evanston, thus making Ezra-Habonim an area congregation (Figure 5.4). As a Conservative synagogue, Ezra-Habonim did not require

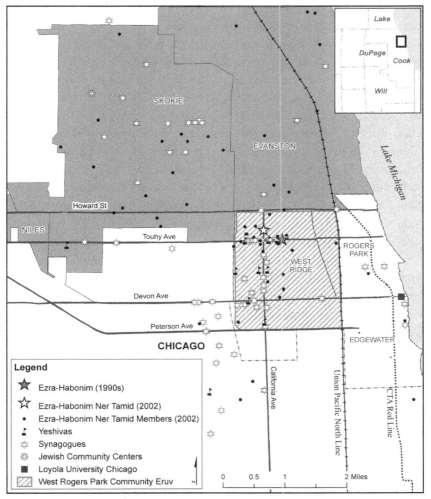

FIGURE 5.4. Congregation Ezra-Habonim and Members. Source for Jewish institutions: *The Jewish Chicago Synagogue and Worship Directory*, 2010. Map by David J. Treering and Melissa Gesbeck Howell, Loyola University Chicago.

its members to walk to Shabbat services, although many members explicitly valued that as an ideal and some regularly made the walk.

The first organizational precursor to Congregation Ezra-Habonim began in the Jewish "golden ghetto" on the South Side in 1935. As related in the congregation's fifty-fifth anniversary commemorative booklet, the founders were German immigrants who had fled Nazism. They were invited to Reform services conducted in German by Rabbi Herman Schaalman at Temple Sinai, located at 46th Street and South Park Way (later Martin Luther King, Jr. Drive), but, as the booklet [3] reports, "These Reform services did not appeal to most of the worshippers, especially the older people." They subsequently organized themselves as the Jewish Center and worshipped separately in Temple Sinai's facility until merging with a nearby Conservative synagogue in 1946. Their first Kristallnacht Memorial Service was held in 1949. By then the congregation had relocated to Hyde Park, as had several other major German synagogues. The well-known liturgical composer Max Janowski served as the Center's choir director for several years. When members began moving to South Shore in the 1950s, the congregation sold their Hyde Park building and built a new one at 76th Street and Phillips Avenue, changing their name to Congregation Habonim. In 1973, in the face of racial change in South Shore and subsequent loss of members, Habonim merged with a North Side Conservative congregation, Temple Ezra, which shared a similar immigration history.

By 1977 younger Ezra-Habonim families had moved farther north and the congregation made a provision for their future by establishing a branch synagogue in suburban Northbrook. The frugal émigrés, however, chafed at investing money in a second permanent building, resulting in a formal separation from the suburban group. "A lost opportunity," said a former president of the synagogue; "a big mistake." By the late 1990s, Congregation Ezra-Habonim had lost too many of its members to suburbanization and death to sustain a worship and social center. In contrast to the usual pattern of younger families trekking to the suburbs and leaving older members in the city neighborhood, a contingent of younger members at Ezra-Habonim preferred the city location, against the desires of older members who wanted to merge with a suburban synagogue.

In its successive mergers, splits, and geographic relocations, Congregation Ezra-Habonim offers a glimpse into larger patterns of change in Chicago Jewish life. At the same time, this synagogue resisted the demographic push to the North Shore suburbs typical of other

Conservative congregations and retained its commitment to a city model for contemporary Jewish life, though not without great internal struggle and eventual schism, as we shall see.

Boundary Lines across Congregational Community Traits

A constellation of congregational community traits stand out in Ezra-Habonim's case: ritual, mutual support, social ties, social similarities, and dispute resolution. The common feature across these traits is the serious fault lines caused by generational, economic, gender, and theological differences among its members. It requires an enormous amount of energy to maintain congregational cohesion in the face of persistent differences.

The community of memory that sustained Ezra-Habonim for more than sixty years was ritually commemorated in its annual and emotionally moving Kristallnacht (Night of Broken Glass) service that attracted Jews from across the metropolitan region. A Kristallnacht "music drama" with candlelight ceremony was originally commissioned in 1988, the fiftieth anniversary of the Nazi-organized violence against Jewish-owned businesses and synagogues in Germany, Austria, and other Nazi-controlled lands. One speaker proclaimed, "As an American-born rabbi, I cannot fully appreciate the horror of what occurred as those who lived through the event. Therefore, I ask those present to tell their story, to remember, and to make the world remember the horrific results of racism and indifference."

As Durkheim (1965) showed, ritual occasions often reinforce social ties and identity by symbolically recreating a group's perceived origins. Yet new contexts can challenge this ritual function. Despite the poignancy and dignity of the occasion and the personal testimonies to the original event, the power of Kristallnacht commemorations affected mostly those who themselves experienced the Holocaust, rather than younger Jews whose life experiences were shaped in urban America in a time of material prosperity and cultural assimilation. The German and Austrian Jewish identity of Ezra-Habonim declined as the founding émigré core shrank. While Holocaust remembrance formed a post–World War II Jewish "imagined community" (Anderson1991), younger Jews have a more complex understanding of their religious, national, and cultural identity (Dashefsky, Lazerwitz, and Tabory 2003). Ezra-Habonim members, for example, held differing views on the meaning of Israel.

A community of memory is not just expressed in ritual or transformative experiences like the Holocaust but also in shared lifecycle events and cohort contexts. Ezra-Habonim's founding generation, coming from a history of flight and refuge, identified strongly with one another and created a synagogue that supported them both socially and religiously. Conservative Judaism developed in response to the more liberal Reform practices in the United States, offering immigrants and their descendants a more traditional Jewish lifestyle without Orthodox gender restrictions that violate American cultural norms and with a looser adherence to halachic (Jewish legal) requirements. Conservative Judaism also took a more "synagogue-centered" institutional approach to Jewish life than the family-centered approach of Orthodoxy (Sklare 1974, 179). It was to this institution that Ezra-Habonim's founding members dedicated themselves financially, socially, and religiously. Indeed, we were told that the commitment of that generation "cannot be duplicated—they gave their lives to it."

One form of this commitment was the congregation's *Gemuleth Chesed*, a perpetual fund supported wholly by the founding generation, established initially to help refugees but later applied to any form of financial hardships, to the dismay of some founders. As one former president explained, "When [they] see younger families struggling to buy a house and moving to a nice suburb at the first opportunity, they do not see them giving a priority to Ezra-Habonim." To be sure, the older generation produced entrepreneurs and businessmen who succeeded during the period of post–World War II economic expansion. They tended to have both time and treasure to invest in congregational life. Another former president from the founding generation acknowledged that he could devote thirty hours a week to the synagogue because he owned his own business. With decline in manufacturing and the rise of the "knowledge economy" (Drucker 1969), younger Jews became salaried professionals with fewer resources and less flexibility. Thus, career options and economic contexts are indirect but important structural constraints on commitments to congregational community.

Ezra-Habonim's internal community cohesion was challenged by generational fault lines among the women as well. Virtually none of the younger women showed any interest in the traditional Sisterhood, a social organization that contributed substantial annual financial support for the synagogue. Fashion shows and entertainment like Eddie Cantor's "My Yiddishe Mama" and the Viennese operetta pop hit "Wien, Wien, Nur Du Allein" came from another era. Furthermore, the Sisterhood generally met in the afternoon when most of the younger women worked. For the older generation, however, the Sisterhood's strong supportive network was vital to the life of the congregation. These women provided much of the social glue in the congregation as mothers do in families, offering succor in times of illness and death or when a person or family becomes needy. So, when the younger women declined to participate, the older women saw them as "separating themselves" in a way they could not understand. Lest Ezra-Habonim be seen as exceptional in this regard, the rabbi at the time reported that in his experience the regional sisterhood association conventions also attract mainly women over the age of sixty.

What did attract some of the younger women was Jewish feminist spirituality. A women's spirituality group devoted to searching for the missing pieces of their history and redefining their role as modern Jewish women was in its formative stages during our research period. Some members of the congregation were clearly mystified by the group's purpose and suggested that since the feminist group did not raise funds to support the synagogue, they were only interested in themselves. The group grew out of a feminist Jewish conference held at a nearby university several years before. These women began meeting monthly to "discuss the male-identified language of the liturgy which various branches of Judaism deal with differently" and "whether Ezra-Habonim should include the matriarchs more significantly in the study of Judaism" or "wait until the Rabbinical Assembly [the governing body of the Conservative movement] has made a ruling." At least one of the congregation's male leaders considered people "who want to change the patriarchal nature of the biblical text" to be "extremists" who should not be tolerated within the Conservative movement. While an interest in study clearly falls within the Jewish tradition, a feminist interpretation of Jewish study was struggling to take hold in this historically patriarchal congregation.

When some of the feminist spirituality group members and their families joined Ezra-Habonim in the late 1980s, it was, in their words, a "dynamic, vibrant" synagogue with a "progressive" Hebrew school and charismatic rabbi, Shlomo Levine. Rabbi Levine had been hired at the time of the 1973 merger and brought innovation and energy that attracted many young families. "The place was jumping," recalled a former president. The congregation was scandalized, however, when the rabbi and his wife divorced. Although the congregation was able to work through that situation, the rabbi's clashes with two successive presidents created organizational difficulties that were compounded by the rabbi's demand for a lifetime contract. After Rabbi Levine's departure, the congregation spent a couple of years carefully considering his replacement and settled on a young rabbi with Orthodox training who appreciated their egalitarian policy and would strive for the inclusion of women.

Rabbi Robert Rhodes came to Ezra-Habonim in 1991 with a progressive view of interfaith relations and gender roles yet a traditional understanding of Jewish religious practices and the education of children. Shortly after his arrival, he suggested in an interview that Ezra-Habonim was too "synagogue-centered" and insufficiently "family-centered," thus challenging a central emphasis of the Conservative movement (as noted earlier). The rabbi related that his efforts to reshape worship, education, and social life into an observance that he considered adequately "literate" in the tradition was resisted in content and tone by most of the members. Yet one officer asserted that the rabbi "made no serious attempt" at providing opportunities for the congregation to participate in these reshaping efforts.

Ritual services in particular exposed both theological and generational fault lines within the congregation. The older German and Austrian members were raised in the assimilative, "Lutheran" ritual style developed by upper-middle-class Reform Jews in nineteenth-century Europe. Thus, Ezra-Habonim's sanctuary looked church-like with forward-facing theater-style chairs rather than in-the-round seating with the *bimah* (dais) in the center as favored by the Orthodox.

However, in the 1970s and 1980s, younger and professionally educated American Jews began turning in a more "traditionally Jewish" direction, as the American Conservative movement tipped toward Orthodoxy and away from Reform. Conservative Jews began practicing an informal and participatory style of worship and chanting, as well as following a stricter observance of kosher laws and other Talmudic practices, reflecting a cultural turn toward what some call religious authenticity in American Judaism (Davidman 1994). We saw this among a number of Ezra-Habonim's younger families and youth. One youth leader gave a thoughtful critique of his contemporaries' social focus in celebrating the bar or bat mitzvah: "If the kids were more mature at an earlier age than they are today, then there would be more of a religious atmosphere at the bar mitzvah." Reflecting on his own, he said, "If I could do it again, I would have learned more prayers to say during the service, and I would have a traditional dinner with only close family, not a big party. And there would be traditional Jewish dancing—religious dancing—not modern dancing." Similarly, another youth leader celebrated her bat mitzvah with greater focus on family and synagogue and less on partying.

Ezra-Habonim hired Rabbi Rhodes in part to help the congregation make this cultural turn in ritual. Rabbi Rhodes reported that a condition of his acceptance was the phasing out of the nontraditional orchestral music and choir for the Friday night services, which he considered "highly inappropriate." That this did not occur indicated the level of resistance to the rabbi's traditionally "authentic" understandings among the older members.

Yet Ezra-Habonim's generational differences did not predict the levels of support for Rabbi Rhodes. While the older congregational leaders appeared keen to "work with him" and "develop his potential," as one of the leaders noted, the younger members could not acquire the rapport essential for a long-term relationship. The rabbi's redirection of the Hebrew school into a more family-inclusive educational process rather than a child-focused pedagogy, for example, led to the departure of the well-liked principal and a subsequent loss of children from the program. The new principal maintained that, while very attractive to parents, the highly individualized program grew too large to be sustainable. Indeed, one youth reported to us that while the one-on-one tutoring was very beneficial, the tutor "couldn't give enough time to each of us." Furthermore, it developed very high expectations, so that when the program was changed, parents felt their "special needs were not being met."

Rabbi Rhodes left Congregation Ezra-Habonim in 1994. Concern over the long-term stability of the congregation simmered quietly. "Ezra-Habonim used to be perceived as a very energetic and innovative place," said one member, "but no longer." Said another, "I think the future of the congregation is precarious."

It was a noncontroversial point that the future of the congregation rested on the younger families, despite the larger financial contribution of the older members. The Holocaust identity continued to be celebrated, though less compellingly as the years passed. "It was not central to my thinking," one of the leaders confided to us. The older members were "history," declared a former president, himself an older member. While the rabbi's personal style was not unimportant in his departure, the congregation's declining fortunes rested at least as much on uncertainty within the congregation about their direction and identity.

At a Yom Kippur service in 1994, the president of the synagogue announced that a long-range planning committee had been formed to evaluate their locational choices. He authorized it to undertake an "honest self-examination" in order to address how best to care for all the members of the congregation and beyond, in his words, "to foster a good life for all." The committee recommended staying on Touhy Avenue and strengthening the congregation at that location. To that end, they offered an ambitious plan to hire a new rabbi, *hazzan* (cantor), and executive director. Yet by 1996, the congregation could no longer afford to maintain the building. The choices came down to renting another facility until something permanent could be found in West Ridge or merging with a suburban Niles Township synagogue with which they had some historic ties. In the words of one of the leaders who chose to stay, the ensuing conflict was "bitter, acrimonious, and accusatory." After a year-long court battle, the congregation formally split in 1997. The Touhy Avenue property was sold. The settlement required that if the city congregation should later move to the northern suburbs, the remaining assets would revert to the side that had already established itself there. A smaller group of mostly older members joined the renamed Ezra-Habonim Niles Township Jewish Congregation and the larger, mostly younger group rented space at Temple Menorah, a Reform synagogue in West Ridge. In 2002 the latter group merged with the last remaining Conservative synagogue in West Ridge to form Congregation Ezra-Habonim Ner Tamid. As of this writing, that synagogue, too, has closed and some of the original Ezra-Habonim members joined the Niles Township congregation. In the words of one of these members, "we made our peace with them."

The Urban Impact of a City Synagogue

Congregation Ezra-Habonim's corporate memory originated in the social-geographic context of Nazi-controlled Europe. Although an urban American context did not require Jews to live in a ghetto, Ezra-Habonim nevertheless located their congregational community in an area of the city with a dense Jewish infrastructure, thus combining both of Steven Brint's types of community, elective (voluntary) and geographic (place-dependent). The importance of a Jewish place in the new metropolis can be seen in the fact that both factions of the 1997 schism located within the orbit of the Jewish infrastructure of the far North Side and North Shore.

In this sense, Ezra-Habonim in its various institutional iterations has contributed to the evolution of Jewish places throughout the history of metropolitan Chicago. That granted, we assess its independent urban impact as weak. The reader will have noticed a missing section on congregational action for this case. Only one action indicator is salient, namely Ezra-Habonim's territorial claims, and those have been meager. An argument can be made that Ezra-Habonim did not need to apply much urban effort since it benefited from the strong impact of the Jewish infrastructure around it.

But there is more to this case. Two other factors help to explain Ezra-Habonim's weak urban impact. First, we have seen the fault lines across several congregational traits: ritual, mutual support, social ties, social similarities, and dispute resolution. Community can be powerfully emotive, deep, and intense, so much so that members are often willing to draw battle lines in response to both internal and external threats. In some cases, like Ezra-Habonim's, the internal battles consume nearly all of the collective energy.

Second, Ezra-Habonim faced the same external structural threats to Jewish community cohesion as have all synagogues (except generally the Orthodox) in the new metropolitan Chicago, particularly with regard to the powerful trend of Jewish out-migration from the city. Ezra-Habonim's commitment to an urban location was a Conservative redoubt against this de-urbanization and decentralization process. Nonetheless, it failed. Being a city congregation was an ambiguous reality for many of Ezra-Habonim's members despite its location in a Jewish *eruv*. As early as the first wave of suburbanization of Jews in the 1970s, it became clear to some that "life on Touhy [Avenue] surely meant stagnation and eventual death," in the words of a former president of the congregation.

The Variety of Area Congregations

The congregations in this chapter have created different kinds of communities in different urban contexts in the new Chicago, from conservative black Baptists in the South Side's racial enclave, to liberal white Protestants in the socioeconomically polarized Near North Side, to Conservative Jews in the demographically transitioning far North Side. For each congregation, a different set of community traits characterizes its identity.

We have argued that area congregations tend to exert a relatively weak urban impact. The congregations in this chapter illustrate both that tendency (Ezra-Habonim) and its exceptions: New Covenant has a moderate impact through territorial and jurisdictional claims motivated by its beleaguered minority status while Fourth Presbyterian exerts strong impact particularly through its extensive social service programs and visible public orientation.

We have also hypothesized that a strong focus on a congregation's internal needs tends to leave less energy for shaping its environment. Ezra-Habonim exhibits this tendency but New Covenant does not, devoting considerable energy beyond itself and toward the needs of others within the embayed minority spaces of the South Side. Fourth Presbyterian has chosen to focus relatively moderate energy on congregational internal needs as it devotes considerable energy to the social needs of the least, the last, and the lost.

As we saw in the previous chapter and will see again in the next, area congregations vary more widely in their urban impact than either neighborhood or metro congregations.

6

Area Congregations in a Suburban Boom Town

SOME OF THE most dramatic indicators of recent urban restructuring can be seen on the western edges of metropolitan Chicago in DuPage County and its largest city, Naperville. By the 1990s, DuPage County had become one of the region's premier economic engines, with Naperville as the poster child for successful transition from small town to booming technoburb (Ebner 1993), one of the most desirable locations in the new metropolitan Chicago.

This chapter features two area congregations in Naperville: Calvary Church, a Pentecostal megachurch, and Congregation Beth Shalom, a nonaffiliated synagogue. We describe their ways of creating congregational communities in new growth suburbia and explain why they exert relatively little impact on Naperville (Beth Shalom's impact being slightly greater). We also discuss Wheatland Salem United Methodist Church as an example of congregational adaptation to changing urban structures and selected Catholic parishes to illustrate the roles played by religious identity, choice, and mobility in the creation of congregational communities. We begin by setting the urban context for all the congregations in this chapter (Figure 6.1).

Urban Context: Living the Good Life in Naperville

The city of Naperville sprawls across the southwest corner of DuPage County, one of the nation's "boom" counties, and edges into neighboring Will County to the south.[1] Between 1965 and 1989, DuPage County

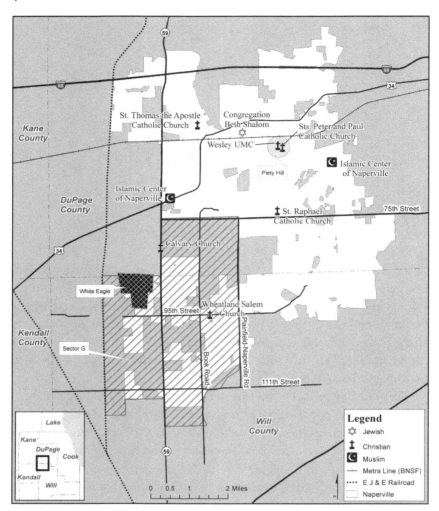

FIGURE 6.1. Naperville Congregations. Map by David J. Treering and Melissa Gesbeck Howell, Loyola University Chicago.

generated nearly 40 percent of all new jobs in the Chicago metropolitan region. During that same period, the Illinois Research and Development Corridor running through the county became a high-tech industry center, and the East-West office market, roughly following county boundaries, accounted for the highest suburban office building inventory and new office space. In the 1990s DuPage County generated more than seven hundred thousand jobs and was a daily net exporter of jobs, meaning that more residents of other counties commuted into DuPage County to work than DuPage residents commuted out to other counties. The county's largest employers at this writing include Alcatel-Lucent, Argonne National Laboratory, BP America, Fermi Lab, Northern Illinois Gas, and McDonald's Corporation. One sector of DuPage County's economy has suffered as a result of the growth in these other sectors: between 1950 and 1992, 93 percent of the county's farms disappeared, the highest percentage decrease of all counties in the region.

Named after Great Lakes steamship captain Joseph Naper, Naperville was founded in 1831 and developed into a small, economically stable town over the next century. Rail service to downtown Chicago, about forty miles directly east of Naperville, was established in the 1860s. What would eventually become the nation's largest furniture supplier, Kroehler Manufacturing Company, had its start in the 1880s and was the largest local employer for most of the twentieth century. By its centennial in 1931, Naperville's population slightly exceeded five thousand.

Following World War II, Naperville began to position itself for its later role as a major outlying node in the postindustrial metropolitan system. The opening of the East-West Tollway (Interstate 88) in 1958 connected Naperville to the interstate highway system. Argonne National Laboratory, built in nearby Lemont in 1947, became the "high-technology seed" for Naperville's growth into "the geographic center of Chicago's version of California's Silicon Valley" (Ebner 1993, 59). "As America underwent the electronic and biotech revolution at the end of the twentieth century," writes Mark Abbott (2007, 1180), "the places of innovation were located at the [metropolitan] periphery to take advantage of the new amenities of the edge cities, as well as their ease of access. In metropolitan Chicago, Naperville was transformed into a cluster of research campuses."

Naperville's "boom" growth began in the 1970s as manufacturing entered its period of sharpest decline in metropolitan Chicago. The city expanded its municipal boundaries from twelve square miles in 1970 to fifty in the early 1990s. By 2002, the Naperville city council was discussing how to use the last remaining 1,400 acres of open land in Sector G, the highest growth area (Mellen 2002). Also known as the Southwest Community Area, Sector G extends roughly from 75th to 111th Streets north to south and from Plainfield-Naperville Road on the east to beyond Route 59 on the west ("Commercial Design Guidelines").

Naperville's population increased from just below 23,000 in 1970 to more than one hundred thousand by 1994, making Naperville the tenth-fastest growing municipality of its size in the country at the time.

By 2010, Naperville had nearly 142,000 residents. The city's racial/ethnic composition has diversified in the last two decades, although whites still comprise more than 75 percent of its population, with Asians at 15 percent, Hispanics and blacks at around 5 percent each. Naperville's demographic diversity includes new religious groups. Exclusively northern European and Christian at the end of World War I, Naperville's religious landscape today includes Korean and Chinese Christians, Baha'is, Vietnamese Buddhists, and a multiracial/ethnic Muslim population. The Islamic Center of Naperville has grown steadily since its origins in the late 1970s and now occupies two sites, a former Jehovah's Witnesses Kingdom Hall and a former Lutheran church. The Jewish presence in Naperville has grown from almost none in the 1970s to supporting two synagogues today.

By most measures, Naperville life is good. Median family income in 2006 was $117,110, just over twice the national median, while the median home value was $416,400, well over the national median of $185,200. Less than 2 percent of Naperville's families live below the poverty line, whereas the national average is nearly 10 percent.

"Naperville has a good reputation," in the words of one real estate agent. "It's got a family atmosphere and a nice downtown. People just want to live here." A marketing analysis by Virginia-based Claritas Inc. characterized Naperville as an Elite Suburb with predominant "lifestyle clusters" featuring children and business executives. Naperville regularly makes *Money Magazine*'s annual list of America's best small cities. In 2008 it ranked third overall due especially to its downtown attractions, job opportunities, schools, and public library, ranked the best small city library in the nation.

Naperville's public schools are considered some of the best in the state. At the time of our primary research, Indian Prairie School District 204, which serves parts of Naperville (including Sector G) and racially diverse Aurora, was the fastest growing school district in the state and trailed only the Chicago public school system in student racial/ethnic diversity. The district has continued to grow and diversify since then—its student body is more than 40 percent non-white today—necessitating the opening of a third high school in 2009. Its second high school, Neuqua Valley, was the costliest public school in state history when it opened in 1997. Rev. Jesse Jackson visited it soon afterward, opining that all high schools in Illinois should be so remarkable.

But Naperville's downsides are also evident. Like elsewhere across the country, the dynamics that create attractive new growth suburbs like

Naperville include potential points of diminishing return in the quality of life. An *Atlantic Monthly* feature story about life in Naperville in the late 1980s captured an important aspect of this in its title, "Stressed Out in Suburbia." "In Naperville," wrote Nicholas Lemann (1989, 42), "the word 'stress' came up constantly in conversations." Much of this is work-related, exacerbated by long hours that can drain energy from employees and impinge on their free time. Writing in the late 1990s, Sally Helgesen (1998, 51–53) reported that working Naperville women felt they did not have enough time to do all they had to do. Moreover, even Naperville's relatively strong economic position is subject to unpredictable market trends and corporate shakeups that can pull the rug of job security out from under its anxious residents. Naperville's home foreclosure rate paints an ambivalent picture vis-à-vis nearby suburbs: At just over 9 percent in 2012, it is much lower than that of Aurora (34.77 percent) and Bolingbrook (43.46 percent) but slightly higher than in Lisle (8.68 percent) and Woodridge (8.67 percent) and much higher than in Wheaton (4.63 percent) and Glen Ellyn (2.05 percent) (Marketwatch 2012). For Naperville homeowners who overextend their finances in order to live in this desirable city, the good life is guaranteed by only a few paychecks.

Naperville's increasing traffic congestion poses an irony not lost on residents who had hoped to escape the gridlock of other urban locations. Route 59, for instance, the primary north-south artery in Sector G, can be slow going at any time of the day but especially during morning and evening rush hours. When, in 2007, the Canadian National Railroad announced plans to acquire the EJ&E rail line that closely parallels Route 59 to increase the freight volume on the line, Naperville joined a coalition of more than forty government bodies to protest anticipated negative impacts along the line, including increased noise, hazardous cargo, and street traffic congestion ("Naperville Notice").

Our survey of congregational leaders in Naperville confirmed concerns about everyday life in new growth suburbia and several responses carried a critical tone. "Reality therapy!"—that's what residents need, according to one respondent. "The suburban dream is less than expected. They are easily traumatized by 'life's experiences.'" "They are pretty well provided for materially," said another, "but have tremendous voids/vacuums in home/ marriage/family relationships—high housing costs keep both spouses working long hours outside homes, hindering family intimacy, powerful materialistic forces robbing many of joy in relationships, moral onslaught through media and pornography making solid role models rare."

Of course, such vocational and personal stressors are not confined to upper middle-class professionals in suburbia. Yet the congregational leaders we surveyed are highly sensitized to these matters. How do they respond to their constituents? By providing "[p]astoral care, support and religious meaning and values as they cope with the stresses of suburban life," penned a Lutheran respondent. A Catholic wrote, "A feeling of rootedness and belonging due to the transiency of the area." "Stability," noted a respondent from Calvary Church.

Calvary Church
Born and Raised in the New Naperville

Calvary Church was born and raised during Naperville's boom era.[2] Originally named Calvary Temple Church, this Assemblies of God (Pentecostal) congregation began in July of 1967 at 129 West Benton Avenue, a few blocks west of downtown Naperville, under the pastoral leadership of Rev. Robert Schmidgall and the lay leadership of his wife Karen Schmidgall. The church's opening fell between the establishment of the corporate precursors of Alcatel-Lucent (in 1966) and BP America (in 1969), vanguards of Naperville's technologically driven growth and two of its largest employers today.

As Naperville grew and expanded southward, so did Calvary Church. In 1978 it erected a new facility at 1155 Aurora Avenue, adding an educational wing in 1984 for a combined floor space of more than 80,000 square feet on a forty-acre parcel. In 1993 the congregation opened a massive facility on a 116-acre campus along the western border of Naperville with Aurora, on Route 59 just south of 75th Street along the edge of Sector G. The prestigious White Eagle subdivision, built around a signature Arnold Palmer golf course, sprawls nearby to the south. Calvary dropped the word "Temple" from its name in 1994 to avoid possible misunderstandings about its identity.

In 2003 Calvary Church's Sunday morning worship services (excluding a separate children's service) drew an average attendance of some 2,900 people.[3] The great majority (78 percent) of these attendees were not officially members of the church. The 2003 attendance figure marked a 30 percent increase since 1995, the first year of our research at the site, and a 27 percent increase since 1999, the first full year following the death of founding pastor Schmidgall. The latter increase indicated that Calvary Church made a successful transition to the second generation of pastoral leadership, a major test for churches like Calvary that were established by gifted and beloved individuals.

In 2003, 48 percent of Calvary's worshippers fell in the thirty to forty-nine age range, 52 percent were in their first marriage, one-fourth were single, and nearly 90 percent had lived in the "Chicagoland/Naperville area" for three or more years. (Unfortunately, this phrasing from church sources does not allow us to disaggregate Naperville from the rest of metropolitan Chicago.) The racial/ethnic breakdown was as follows: 72 percent white, 11 percent black, 8 percent Hispanic, 4 percent Asian, and 5 percent others. This differed from Naperville's overall demographics in that Calvary drew fewer Asians and more blacks and Hispanics than live in Naperville. One of the church's staff pastors suggested that the large number of Hispanic attendees was attributable in part to Calvary's location along the border with Aurora, which has a sizable Hispanic population. Likely most of Calvary's black and Hispanic attendees reside outside of Naperville and are attracted to the congregation's Pentecostalism.

The residential distribution of Calvary Church's constituents can be determined from three sources. First, 73 percent of attendees report traveling ten miles or less one way to Calvary. Second, 78 percent of the entries in Calvary's mailing list come from cities within this ten-mile radius of the church, with Naperville and Aurora together representing half of the total. If we add towns contiguous to the ten-mile radius, we can account for 93 percent of Calvary's mailing list (the towns are shown in Figure 6.2). Third, Calvary's Small Groups Ministry program covers a comparable geographic area (Figure 6.2 shows the geographic distribution of the small groups).

Calvary Church can thus be categorized as an area congregation in our typology. Its constituents comprise a congregational community within the greater Naperville/Aurora area, roughly the shaded portion of Figure 6.2. In 2006 the congregation opened Calvary West Campus in Sugar Grove. The website describes Calvary as "one church with multiple locations." Given its size and constituency, Calvary can be called an "area megachurch."

Congregational Community Traits: Social Intimacy, Megachurch Options, and Pentecostal Identity

Why have Calvary's constituents chosen to attend this church? After all, the booming area around it offers a great variety of church choices. Calvary's 2002 "Baseline Survey" helps to explain its appeal.

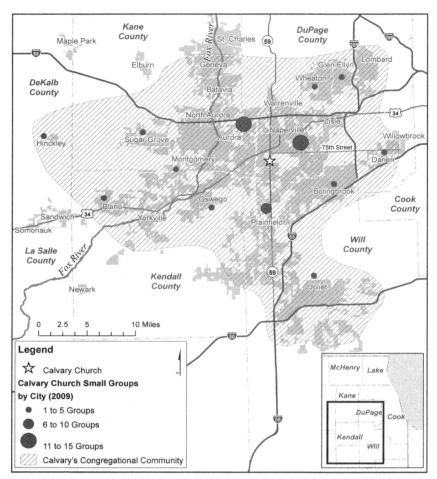

FIGURE 6.2. Geographic Distribution of Calvary Church's Small Groups Ministry Program. Source: www.calvarynaperville.org/templates/cuscalvary06/ details.asp?id=22090&PID=610640, accessed August 19, 2009. Map by David J. Treering and Melissa Gesbeck Howell, Loyola University Chicago.

More than half of its worshippers (54 percent) have attended Calvary for four or more years, including more than 30 percent who have attended for more than ten years. This is noteworthy long-term loyalty considering both the available church choices and the residential mobility rates in the area. It may also indicate that some portion of Calvary's attendees do not come from the new and transient cohort of the population, but rather from older and more stable cohorts in the area. In any case, a connection through friends or relatives was listed as the predominant motivation for attending a worship service at Calvary Church for the first time (58 percent), far outdistancing the second leading motivation of driving by the church (10.5 percent), indicating a substantial network of relationships among residents. Before attending Calvary Church, 79 percent were regularly involved in another church—thus Calvary is mostly attracting the "churched" of the area, both longtime and new residents. Nearly 80 percent know at least a few people well at Calvary Church, defined as "having significant relationship both inside & outside of church activities," and nearly two-thirds (64 percent) indicated that they know at least two non-relatives at the church upon whom they could call in a crisis.

Thus, despite Calvary's megachurch proportions, many attendees have established intimate social ties through the church. The social theorist Georg Simmel, in his 1908 essay, "Group Expansion and the Development of Individuality" ([1908] 1971), offers insight into how the growing size of a congregation affects the types of social ties that constituents develop. He observed that smaller milieux produce less individuated but more autonomous members; as the group grows larger, individual freedom expands as people are more influenced by outsiders. Consequently, in modernity (which was Simmel's concern), social groups such as megachurches begin to look more alike because they develop similar roles and positions, hence limiting the types of social ties their members create. Furthermore, as the urban context produces increasingly individuated personalities, individuals seek refuge from increasingly impersonalized experiences, and also from problems of fragmentation and identity construction. Several of Calvary's congregational community traits—the uniting function of ritual, enforcement of strong internal norms, mutual support, dense and demanding social ties, internal social similarities, and maintenance of high boundaries with the outside world—confirm Simmel's observation and are illustrated in Calvary's Small Group Ministries program.

Seven couples, all white and ranging in age from late twenties to forties, together with seven children, gathered on a Friday evening for their bimonthly fellowship meeting. The hosts live a few miles south of Calvary Church in an attractive home with a large yard and a pond in one of Sector G's many new subdivisions. This group has been meeting for at least five years and can number as many as sixty people.

The adults engaged in familiar small talk as they gathered—children, golf, summer activities, the backyard—but not work-related topics. The children seemed to know each other and played together in the basement most of the evening. The meeting opened with sharing "praise reports and prayer requests," as the leader called them. Many prayed for health and impending surgeries among family and friends: a couple had just learned they were expecting a baby; a woman's brother was enmeshed in sexual sin and her mother condoned it; two men were stressed over layoffs at their workplaces. One explained later that his boss has been terminating managers without any explanation and he was afraid of being next. He was also troubled by the fact that state law does not protect employees from this kind of thing. We noted that his prayer focused only on the individual who was fired—no petition was offered about establishing more ethical business practices or for legislators to intervene in an unjust situation.

After this sharing time, the group entered into ten minutes of formal prayer, opened and closed by the host but with free petitions raised by individuals in between, to which the whole group responded robustly, "Yes, Lord," "Thank you, Jesus," "Praise God." Following this, the group sang contemporary Christian songs, including "I Love You Lord." The lyrics emphasized a personal relationship with the Lord and many sang with their eyes closed.

On this particular evening, a Chicago Bulls playoff game was broadcast, so the group skipped its usual Bible study session. Most of the men watched the game, joined by the children, while most of the women sat in the kitchen. The men talked about the game and no one brought up a religious topic or even used religious language. Some in the group seemed unfamiliar with the TV commercials; our researcher wondered if they were seeing them for the first time.

Some notable trends showed up in the prayers that evening, demonstrating how this ritual reinforces the group's identity and conformity while maintaining high boundaries to the outside. One was the desire to share the Gospel with others through the difficulties they were facing. For instance, one person prayed that he might witness to hospital staff during his hospitalization. Another trend was to point out how wonderfully and complexly God works in people's lives. Several told complicated tales about meeting someone somewhere who later turned up somewhere else in their lives, which served as proof of God's mysterious workings.

A second small group meeting we observed took place in a home on the other side of Naperville in a subdivision built during an early expansion of the city. This meeting included four couples in the same age range as the other group, along with two children belonging to the host couple. One individual was Hispanic, the rest white. These couples had been meeting together for several years. One of the regulars told us that she and her husband started attending Calvary when it was a small church and developed a close network of young couples in the early years. Now many of those friends had moved away, so this fellowship group served as their circle of friends. She and her husband did other activities at Calvary that forged relationships as well, but this fellowship group provided their primary support through hardships and pain.

People engaged in initial small talk as did the other group, but this time the topics included work and religion. The spiritual fellowship time began with a prayer and two songs, "This Is the Day That the Lord Has Made" and "I've Got a River of Life Flowing Out of Me." The Bible study addressed the topic of Calvary's pastor's sermon from the previous Sunday. The group leader worked from a sheet titled "Suggested Topics" written for all the small group meetings that week. The main question for consideration concerned times in our lives when we wonder where God is. Several people pointed to the deaths of loved ones of group members over the years. The group looked at New Testament passages showing how God can be found in Christ. A key point that emerged was how Christ's experiences were like ours but his responses differed from ours.

Next came a time for more prayer and singing. Individuals spoke randomly while others whispered earnestly, all in a subdued Pentecostal manner. The prayer focus was the "needs" in people's lives, especially illnesses of family and friends. At one point, the group split into two according to gender. One woman gave a long report about the teenager who lives next door to her, who was severely depressed but last week gave a testimony at Calvary of being saved. The upshot was that God works wonders.

The group then moved to the kitchen for snacks and more small talk. One of the men ran his own home repair business, half of his customers coming from Calvary Church. Another man was a teacher at Naperville North High School. He noted that the students were great for the most part, although some lacked respect for authority due to their superior attitude. They are likely to say, as he put it, "My parents make more money than you do so why should I respect you?"

Through its Small Groups Ministry program, Calvary Church has seeded its new growth suburban area with fellowships that offer an alternative communal experience to the centrifugal forces around them, thereby contributing to the stability some members seek in the new urban era. But this church offers much more than small groups: "as at other megachurches [as Simmel might have predicted], Calvary Church's full-service programming offers mega-options to a consumer-oriented potential clientele. Virtually every need can be met and every talent accommodated" (Numrich 1998, 82). Groups are organized by gender, age, and family status (men, women, singles, couples, kid-friendly, young adults, senior adults, and empty nesters), special interests (including the Men's Gun Group and the Calvary Saints Motorcycle Riding Group), and Spanish language usage. Calvary's staff dwarfs those of many churches in the area, including twenty-one staff pastors (http://www.calvarynaper-ville.org/, accessed December 1, 2013).

Although Calvary has many of the typical megachurch trappings, it has also maintained a distinctly Pentecostal identity. Its massive facility includes some of the architectural features of a traditional church build-ing, like a peaked roof and prominent crosses, thus distinguishing it from seeker-type megachurches that eschew such symbolism (Thumma and Travis 2007, 93). Significant efforts are made to appeal to the typi-cal baby boomer spiritual seeker, such as through the Alpha Ministry, a ten-week course offered twice annually that draws in skeptics, cynics, and disaffected people to discuss Christianity in a nonconfrontational con-text. Yet, as the assistant pastor explained to us, in many ways Calvary's Pentecostalism is "seeker hostile" in that "the message of the cross runs counter to the secular humanism and self-centered values of the typical baby boomer" (Numrich 2000a, 198; on "seeker sensitive" churches, see Sargeant 2000). Calvary's countercultural message is most evident in the issues of marriage, divorce, and sexuality. Calvary is uncompromising in its stance against sex outside of marriage and holds to the New Testament passages that allow fornication and a non-Christian spouse as the only legitimate biblical grounds for divorce (and thus also for legitimate remar-riage). "As the assistant pastor noted, matter-of-factly, Calvary loses mem-bers over this stance. He went on, however, to say that Calvary is not just about doing what is scripturally lawful, but also what is good for the per-son. Many divorced people today remarry without having worked through the problems that led to the divorce in the first place. Such cases simply become 'same problem, different address'" (Numrich 1998, 93).

In an earlier report (Numrich 1998, 93–94), we described how Calvary responds to out-of-wedlock pregnancies, illustrating both the church's countercultural morality and its pastoral ministry:

> Not long ago, a single woman at Calvary became pregnant. The counseling staff advised her to go to Pastor Schmidgall. She

repented of her sin in his presence, and he forgave her. But then she asked to confess her sin before the congregation, which the church does not require. At a Wednesday Family Night service she stood before the assembly and asked forgiveness. The congregation wept with her, Pastor Schmidgall publicly affirmed his support for her, people came forward and prayed over her. The church supported her throughout the pregnancy, after which she decided to give the child up to adoption to a Christian family. (Other women in similar circumstances have kept their babies, even dedicating them in services at Calvary Church. No stigma attaches to such women if they repent of their sin, though the church makes every attempt to establish a loving, Christian, nuclear family around these children.)

The stresses of new growth suburban life surface poignantly in Calvary's singles ministry. Job dissatisfaction, conflict in the workplace, the threat of layoffs—these and other vocational concerns show up regularly in the prayers during singles get-togethers. Some are single parents struggling to raise children and work long hours at the same time. Others, recovering from divorce, are attracted to Calvary's twelve-week program that emphasizes "common sense, good counseling techniques, and general Christian principles of forgiveness and freedom from bitterness and anger" (Numrich 1998, 93). The explicit conversion message is saved for the last week. We were told that the majority attending this workshop are non-Calvary people. The singles pastor averred that many seek meaning in their lives through jobs, friends, workouts at the health club, and the like, yet a spiritual void remains. Calvary seeks to fill that void in their lives by turning "their undivided attention to service for the Lord" (Numrich 1998, 92; cf. Numrich 2000a, 199).

Calvary Church exhibits some aspects of Donald Miller's (1997) new paradigm churches, although it has crafted an interesting blend of the old and the new, for instance in its architecture and performance arts. Calvary's music is a mix of contemporary Christian praise songs and traditional hymns. As at the typical seeker megachurch, dramatic performances are regularly staged, but some carry a message that would shock the typical spiritual seeker. We observed one such play, titled "Heaven's Gate and Hell's Flames," produced by an outside group but highly promoted by Calvary Church. The play packed Calvary's approximately 2,500-seat auditorium for four showings. Following a literalist biblical interpretation, the director set up the drama by ridiculing the evolutionary theory of human origins, stating his conviction that we came from God and will stand before God on Judgment Day. The play consisted of several scenes following the same plot line. Actors portraying real-life situations die and are transported to heaven's gate. If the angel finds their names in the Book of Life, they run ecstatically up the stairway into heaven; if not, Satan and his demonic hordes drag them to an offstage hell of eternal torment. The scenarios included two teenaged girls who overdosed on drugs (to Hell), a corporate vice president and church board member (yet uncommitted to Christ, thus to Hell), and several families separated for eternity since they were not united in their commitments to Christ. An altar call followed the play, to which about a third of the audience responded. The director concluded the evening by encouraging everyone to attend church, their own or Calvary.

As in other new paradigm churches, we saw how community life at Calvary Church is structured around small fellowships and cohort groups defined by age and life circumstances. According to Donald Miller (1997, 155), new paradigm churches have "created a form of human community that addresses many of the crises of our late-twentieth-century postmodern culture." In these churches, the victims of contemporary isolation and alienation "can experience a sense of community" and find "a safe haven for taking care of their social as well as spiritual needs" (184). Here suburban people can learn coping skills as well as thriving skills for the new urban era. Calvary Church has created a congregational community of moderate Pentecostals whose worldview and lifestyle stand at some odds with the larger suburban culture. Ironically, a church that helped to create new growth suburbia nevertheless sits uneasily with its lifestyle.

Congregational Action: Facilities, Local Outreach, and Global Missions

Calvary Church makes a noticeable territorial claim on the suburban landscape. Its massive campus is prominently visible to thousands of weekday commuters while Sunday morning traffic is controlled by police at both public entrances. In 2013 Calvary constructed its own exit road to alleviate the congestion.

The church's facilities are heavily scheduled. In addition to the usual religious programming, a coffee shop is open daily and Bistro 59 provides gourmet dining on Sundays and Wednesday evenings when church traffic is highest. Calvary Christian School offers an accredited K-8th grade education, employing four administrative staff and two dozen teachers. The school describes itself as "a ministry to parents to help them with their God-given task of educating their children as a ministry arm of Calvary Church" (http://school.calvarynaperville.org/school/, accessed October 2, 2013). Calvary occasionally offers its facilities for civic purposes, for instance as a polling place, for orientation and testing of police recruits for the city of Naperville, and for staff meetings of one of the local public school districts. Calvary's daylong Anniversary Festival held in conjunction with the Fourth of July includes activities for children and adults, a classic car show, an arts and crafts show, food concessions, live Christian music performances, and a fireworks display that rivals any city in the vicinity. This festival epitomizes Calvary's goal of offering a Christian alternative to the larger culture, in effect saying, "Spend the Fourth with us."

Calvary's Outreach and Evangelism Ministry seeks to follow the example of Christ: "The very heartbeat of Jesus is to serve our local community by reaching out to those who are hurting, alone, in need, struggling or oppressed." Most of this involves partnering with local or national initiatives, including Safe Families for Children, Feed My Starving Children, homeless ministries in Aurora and Chicago, and a prison ministry at the DuPage County Jail. Calvary runs two programs of its own: Helping Hands, which provides practical services for widows, single parents, the elderly, and the disabled, and a food and clothing pantry at the church's original Benton Avenue site (http://www.calvarynaperville.org/ministries/adults/outreach, accessed October 2, 2013). Calvary makes spiritual and moral jurisdictional claims on its area through some of these activities. It also does so in a less obvious way when it maps out its Small Groups Ministry (see Figure 6.2 above). By meeting in homes (always potentially temporary), Calvary's small groups give subtle witness to an alternative lifestyle and set of values.

As its name implies, the Outreach and Evangelism Ministry is motivated primarily by the church's evangelical concern to save souls. That concern has created a much more substantial emphasis on global missions in the church. Calvary today supports more than two hundred missionaries and mission organizations around the world, thus continuing the legacy of founding pastor Robert Schmidgall, who was "consumed with world missions" (Batterson 2011).

Urban Impact on a Recruitment Ground

We have assessed Calvary Church's urban impact as weak. This is not surprising for two reasons. First, like most area congregations, Calvary Church is more likely to exert a relatively low impact on its locale. Second, like most congregations with a strong focus on consummatory, that is, self-needs, less effort is channeled outside, in this case much of it toward global missions. Calvary Church creates a strong, supportive community environment with high moral and spiritual boundaries to the larger society. As one staff pastor explained, social service to non-constituents is secondary to the focus on conversions. The church's territorial and jurisdictional claims seek to bring people into a moderate Pentecostal lifestyle.

Omar McRoberts's study of Boston congregations is helpful in understanding Calvary Church's relationship to its suburban environment, which it envisions as a "recruitment ground to be trod and sacralized" (2003, 82), though with some degree of avoidance. Calvary's impact on the lives of its constituents is strong; its impact on the surrounding suburban context is weak. But because Calvary Church is a good cultural fit with the structural changes that created the new Naperville, it will continue to prosper and grow.

Congregation Beth Shalom
Creating a Jewish Community "Out Here"

Until recently, Congregation Beth Shalom was the only synagogue in Naperville and one of only two synagogues in western DuPage County.[4] Beth Shalom is similar to Calvary Church in that both congregations stand at some odds with the larger culture in terms of spiritual and moral perspectives. The major difference is Beth Shalom's minority religious group asserting an equal status with dominant Christianity in a city where diversity has been slow in coming.

Congregation Beth Shalom had its origins in the Naperville Jewish Community Organization (NJCO).[5] NJCO was founded in 1972 after a small group of Jewish families from Naperville and western DuPage County gathered together for social and religious events with a special focus on "Jewish educational and cultural activities for their children." To this end, NJCO's education board "hired an educational coordinator and teachers; started a religious school; and celebrated its first bar and bat mitzvahs." In 1978 NJCO expanded its focus to include adult education and religious services, hiring a part-time rabbi "to direct religious, educational and cultural activities for the adult membership" and renting a facility for the services. NJCO's mission statement redefined the organization as a synagogue under the name Congregation Beth Shalom.

During its early years, Beth Shalom's membership comprised young families with children and represented a variety of Jewish backgrounds. For its first five years, the congregation remained unaffiliated with any of the institutional branches of American Judaism, seeking to create an egalitarian and inclusive environment, as some members explained to us. Gender equality was a valued goal, which encouraged discussions of the language of the prayer book, women's role in the rituals, the possibility of including women in the *minyan* (the traditional requirement of a minimum of ten Jewish men for worship), and women in governance positions within the synagogue. Religious inclusiveness was also valued. The congregation sought to be a place where Jews from the various branches of Judaism would "feel comfortable," as would Gentiles (including the congregation's many non-Jewish spouses).

For some years, Beth Shalom used the facilities of Wesley United Methodist Church in downtown Naperville (see Figure 6.1 above). By 1983, the Jewish congregation had grown to one hundred families. That year, they hired a full-time rabbi, Michael Remson, who had been ordained at the Rabbinic School of Hebrew Union College/Jewish Institute of Religion in New York City in 1973. Just prior to his hiring, the congregation had chosen to affiliate with the Federation of Reconstructionist Congregations and Havurot, later called the Jewish Reconstructionist Federation.

In 1985 Beth Shalom purchased the former Evangelical Free Church in a residential neighborhood just north of downtown Naperville. The congregation converted the former Christian edifice without major architectural remodeling. The exterior was devoid of prominent Jewish symbols. The sanctuary retained its Christian design, with long, rectangular nave, regimented pews, and raised chancel, but now featured Jewish ritual objects and furniture: two electric menorahs, a large *bima* (pulpit), the Ark of the Torah, and a memorial wall with plaques commemorating the anniversaries (*yahrzeit*) of departed loved ones. In the hall outside the sanctuary, members placed inscriptions marking important personal events on a Tree of Life.

By 1995 membership had grown to more than two hundred families and the professional staff comprised the rabbi, an education and program director, an early learning center director, and a cantor. In 1997 Beth

Shalom broke ground for a new synagogue facility in a commercial setting a mile and a half away from the neighborhood to which it had had few ties. A clear majority (69 percent) of Beth Shalom's member households lived in the city of Naperville. Most of the remaining households lived in the nearby cities of Lisle, Aurora, Wheaton, Downers Grove, and Bolingbrook, qualifying it as an area congregation in our typology, what a former president of the congregation called a "geographic synagogue" (see Figure 6.3). He emphasized Beth Shalom's openness to all Jews regardless of their theological perspective.

In our interview with three members, the phrase "out here" was used five times in contrasting Jewish life in Naperville to that in Chicago's North Side and North Shore suburbs. One interviewee remarked that in West Ridge, for instance, you simply breathe in being Jewish, but not

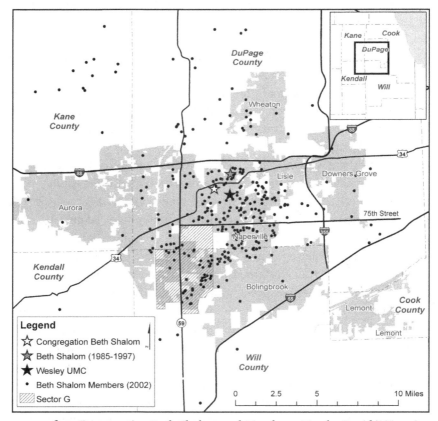

FIGURE 6.3. Congregation Beth Shalom and Members. Map by David J. Treering and Melissa Gesbeck Howell, Loyola University Chicago.

so in Naperville. Moreover, if you're dissatisfied with a synagogue in West Ridge, there are several others to choose from, especially if you are Orthodox. In Naperville, Beth Shalom was "the only show in town."

Since our primary research period, a small Orthodox Lubavitch Chabad has emerged in Naperville and another Jewish organization, called Fox Valley Jewish Neighbors, was established just northwest of Naperville, serving some 150 Jewish families. The latter encourages inquirers to contact the group if they "just want some confirmation that Jewish people DO live in the far-west suburbs of Chicago" (http://www.fvjn.org/?page_id=2, accessed July 17, 2009; also see Girardi 2004). These developments indicate that creating a Jewish community "out here" in the predominantly Gentile suburbs continues to be a priority for some Jews.

Congregational Community Traits: Mutual Support Through Diverse Jewish Identity

In a newsletter message during Sukkot, the traditional Jewish festival of temporary shelters (*sukkahs*), Rabbi Remson addressed his congregation's experience in the new growth suburbs (October 1995 newsletter, 1):

> We live with insecurity. Some of us worry about losing our jobs. Some about money. Some about family problems. Almost all of us are worried. We look at our nice homes and tell ourselves that we have nothing to worry about. But *gornisht helfn* [a Yiddish phrase, literally "beyond help"], it doesn't help. It even makes us feel worse.
>
> So the sukkah reminds us that life is not secure; that worrying is part of the human condition . . . . So at least we aren't crazy for being afraid. Come; eat in the sukkah. If life is insecure at least it can be fun.

Congregation Beth Shalom seeks to nurture a Jewish communal identity as a buffer against the insecurities of suburban life. As one lay leader told us, Naperville is more like California than Chicago's Jewish North Side when it comes to a sense of community identity. Naperville is not a very social place, but rather a "distant" place where "you have your car and you do your thing." As Rabbi Remson explained to us, life in the new urban era tends "to make people feel anonymous and isolated . . . [with] no sense of community. For Jews this provides an added incentive to come to the synagogue since it is the place people come to find community." This includes "increased responsibility for strengthening the Jewish family."

Many of Beth Shalom's programs during Rabbi Remson's tenure were organized according to age and lifestyle cohort groups. The adult education program offered courses on various topics, including learning to read Hebrew, the European heritage of Judaism, spiritual approaches to Torah, Soviet Jewry, and Jewish mysticism. Adult auxiliaries called the Sisterhood and the Brotherhood emphasized fellowship, topical discussions, and fundraising.

The Havurah or small fellowship group program at Beth Shalom was organized in 1990 by a member who had participated in such a group at his previous synagogue. He saw *havurot* (the plural of the Hebrew word *havurah*) as the solution to his own family's feelings of isolation in moving to Naperville and also as providing opportunities for Jewish children to get to know other Jewish children, a more difficult task in Naperville than in areas with dense Jewish infrastructures like Chicago's North Side and North Shore suburbs. After distributing a questionnaire seeking input from congregational members, he set up three groups according to shared interests and affinities: childless couples, Jewish couples interested in religious topics, and couples (both Jewish and mixed-faith) who wished to socialize together. His previous experience showed that the common identity of being Jewish or members of the same synagogue did not suffice to make a *havurah* successful. Moreover, he rejected the option of organizing the groups geographically since he believed that friendships do not form that way. Note the contrast with the geographic basis of the small groups at Calvary Church or the growing trend among Naperville Catholics to select their geographic parish (see below). Seeking "placeness" may be a more tendentious matter for the Jewish cases in our research. As Irving Cutler (1995) pointed out, Jews left North Lawndale when it began experiencing early indications of racial change during the 1960s and 1970s because they did not keep ties to the religious institutions their parents had built. The North Lawndale Jews eventually built new institutions on the city's North Side and, as they moved up the social class ladder, in the north and northwest suburbs. While Jews create new relationships to place when they move, their ties to locality (except for the Orthodox) are generally in the service of other needs.

The *havurot* were intended to be "self-directed and independent, although it is understood that each havurah group would work to enrich congregational life as well as the [group] members' lives" ("Havurot at

Congregation Beth Shalom"), acknowledging both a consummatory and an instrumental purpose in their community life—that is, creating a satisfying set of relationships for themselves and using those to benefit the congregation as a whole. The groups came to shoulder a significant amount of responsibility in the congregation, such as organizing Sabbath Onegs (post-worship social gatherings) several times a year, sponsoring family-oriented activities around the Jewish festival calendar (at Rosh Hashanah, Sukkot, Hanukkah, Pesach, and Purim), and actively participating in the political discussions within the congregation. One *havurah* group comprised four married couples without children, another seventeen mixed-faith families.

As relatively small as Beth Shalom is, it is still too big and impersonal for many members; small fellowship groups make membership a more personal experience. As a congregational newsletter put it, "In a havurah, being together is an end in itself," with a focus on sociality and sharing food, not on religion or ritual. For one couple, the open and democratic style was "comforting" and the group met their need for social belonging that exceeded what the larger congregation could provide.

One of the goals of Congregation Beth Shalom's religious school is "to make our kids proud of their Judaism" (1994–1995 Parents Manual, [2]). This sounds straightforward enough, yet attaining such a goal is complicated by the congregation's variegated Jewish identity, the large number of mixed-faith marriages (approximately 40 percent of the congregation's married couples), and the predominantly non-Jewish social context in which the children move during most of their week. At the time of our research, Beth Shalom's education program served more than two hundred children ranging from pre-kindergarten to tenth grade. Most students attended only Sunday school, while those preparing for bar/bat mitzvah also attended Tuesday afternoons. The curriculum included music, art, and religious activities. Graduates were expected to have obtained a competency in the Hebrew language, an introduction to the Hebrew scriptures, knowledge of Judaism, and awareness of the politics of Israel and the Middle East.

In our interview, the chair of the religious school board, who had taught at an area public high school for nearly thirty years, shared his concerns about Beth Shalom's children. Noting that he attended religious school nearly every day as a child, he bemoaned the many interests that lure today's children away from the synagogue. If sports have come to overshadow the educational process in the public schools, he pointed out, how much more so will a synagogue's educational program be overshadowed in the lives of these young people? When we asked whether teenagers feel a conflict of interest between attending the synagogue or the high school game on a Friday night, he was unequivocal: they choose the game.

As students in the public school system, these Jewish children feel their minority status in palpable ways. A past president of the congregation noted that they live within the "Bible Belt" orbit of nearby Wheaton, a global center of evangelical Protestantism. Every year at Christmastime, being Jewish becomes particularly challenging as the public schools offer their Christmas programs. "Several times a week, from Thanksgiving on, people will wish me a Merry Christmas," Rabbi Remson was quoted as saying in a local newspaper (Cary 1996). "It can make [Jewish] people feel as though they are somehow outside of the American society. It can be harder on kids. It's a real powerful presence." The rabbi's concern about peer pressure on Jewish children to convert to Christianity prompted him to include in his annual confirmation class a focus on the various branches of Christianity, especially the proselytizing ones.

One of Beth Shalom's most interesting education programs at the time of our research was called Jr. K'tonton, the name derived from a Jewish Tom Thumb character created by writer Sadie Rose Weilerstein. Parents brought their preschoolers for unstructured play at the synagogue once a week, during which time the adults shared in informal conversation. One woman described her experience upon moving to Naperville from New York City. People here had never met either a Jew or a New Yorker before, so she was doubly "strange" to them. She began looking for "pockets of acceptance" wherever they could be found. She said she cringes when the Christmas season starts, since Jews must always explain "why we are Jewish."

The challenges of forging a congregational community out of a theologically and ideologically diverse constituency came to the fore in the question of institutional affiliation. As noted, Beth Shalom affiliated with the Reconstructionist movement in the early 1980s, mostly as a practical compromise between the Conservative and Reform backgrounds of most members. The smallest of the four main branches of American Judaism, Reconstructionism emphasizes the creative application of Jewish tradition to the context of modern society (Alpert and Staub 1986). As time went on, some members questioned whether Reconstructionism accurately reflected the identity of the current congregation. Responses to a 1993 congregational survey revealed the great variety of preferences and opinions within the membership ("Congregational Assessment Task Force Survey Data Pertaining to Affiliation and Choice of Prayerbook"). The issue may have become whether a different affiliation or non-affiliation would better accommodate the congregation's diversity.

Our interviews revealed several factors underlying members' decision to join Beth Shalom, including geographic location, programming, and the rabbi, as well as affiliation. Reconstructionism was valued by a significant portion of the membership—at least a fourth, if the pertinent survey question was accurate—because it reflected their understanding of Judaism. Another portion of the membership—how large is difficult to determine—appeared to see a Reconstructionist affiliation as the best alternative for a diverse congregation. A vocal but influential minority found Reconstructionism unsatisfactory.

The process of selecting a prayer book for worship services brought the issue of affiliation—and, thereby, congregational identity—into high relief. A prayer book committee began meeting in June of 1994 to consider recommendation of a prayer book for use in both Friday night and Saturday morning Shabbat services. The committee evaluated six prayer books: two Reform, one Conservative, one ecumenical, and the two already in use at Beth Shalom (the Reconstructionist *Kol Haneshamah Shabbat Vehagim* on Friday nights, the Orthodox *Birnbaum Prayerbook* on Saturday mornings). The committee's criteria for evaluating each prayer book included whether it "relate[s] to most members of the Congregation," "address[es] values of a Reconstructionist Congregation," reflects "[g]ender neutrality," and preserves "traditional elements" of Judaism ("Prayer Book Committee Report," 2–3). The committee's report identifies the congregation's diversity as an important consideration (4) and several times mentions the issue of gender-specific language, including this statement: "Most members prefer a prayerbook that has gender-neutral language" (4). The gender-neutrality and Reconstructionist perspective of *Kol Haneshamah* seem to have been the key factors behind the committee's recommendation of this prayer book over the others.

The prayer book committee's recommendation was put to a congregational vote at the annual congregational meeting in April of 1996. The congregation rejected the committee's recommendation to adopt the Reconstructionist prayer book for both Friday night and Saturday morning services, which would have discontinued the use of the Orthodox prayer book for Saturday. Many felt that such a change would divide the congregation at the very time it needed unity for a new building campaign.

Disagreement focused on liturgical style and gender-specific language, some members expressing preference for the more traditional style of the Conservative prayer book that had been considered by the prayer book committee.

During our interview of some of Beth Shalom's self-identified feminist members, the crux of the congregational debate was explained as a matter of "comfort" during worship. Following Durkheim, we expect ritual to produce an integrated outcome, yet this account reminds us that a certain threshold of agreement, if not already some integration, is needed to benefit from a ritual's lasting effect. Some men in the congregation vehemently opposed any non-masculine reference to God, and thus the language of the Reconstructionist prayer book made them uncomfortable during Friday night services. One of those men we interviewed called the substitution of gender-neutral or feminine names in the ancient, admittedly patriarchal liturgy an unacceptable form of political correctness comparable to editing historical American documents, such as "Fourscore and seven years ago, our forefathers and foremothers . . . ." At those places in the liturgy where the divine name is invoked, the congregation had compromised by saying "Adonai," but that made feminist members uncomfortable since its literal meaning is masculine ("Lord"). To be "comfortable" in worship is important to most members in any congregational community, but it is difficult to create a comfortable atmosphere in a congregation as diverse as Beth Shalom. As these interviewees noted about Beth Shalom, "comfort" is typically gauged by each individual according to the synagogue in which he or she was raised.

Thus, the congregation implicitly recognized the binding power of ritual where disagreement led to a dispute in need of resolution. Gender-neutral versus patriarchal language challenged the traditional norms of Judaism, which brought to the fore certain individual (in this case, feminist) interests. The resolution of the dispute—to keep the status quo of using the Reconstructionist prayer book on Friday nights and the Orthodox prayer book on Saturday mornings—was formal and preserved the unity of the congregation.

In the years since our primary research period, Congregation Beth Shalom decided to become an unaffiliated synagogue, building on the strength of their internal diversity. In this way, the congregation turned the fractured nature of Naperville's transient population to its advantage by celebrating its hybrid religious identity. "We value community," reads their website. "We seek to be: A place of participation and programming

for all segments of the Jewish community" (http://www.napershalom.
org/aboutcbs/whoweare.html, accessed October 3, 2013). While this type
of hybrid congregation provides a "looser connection" than a denominational affiliation, it also reduces religious inequalities by not privileging a
single denomination. In Edward Soja's (2000, 155) words, such an arrange-
ment "preserv[es] difference and foster[s] flexible 'transversal' identities."
Beth Shalom has created a diverse Jewish congregational community that
can both manage internal disputes about its most binding rituals and
offer a mutually supportive Jewish experience in an area that offers few
options for Jews.

Congregational Action: Challenging the Majority

Congregation Beth Shalom makes minimal territorial or jurisdictional
claims on Naperville. However, nearly daily reminders of their minority
religious status as Jews present opportunities for public policy advocacy
and positions that challenge insensitivity and discrimination from the
Christian majority.

Jewish children can find themselves on the frontlines of this culture/
religion clash in the public schools. One mother noted how little the
teachers know about any religion other than "mainstream Christianity,"
as she put it. For instance, the first PTA meeting at the newest elementary school in District 204 was scheduled on Yom Kippur, while its
first fundraiser was a "Hot Diggity Dog" lunch for the schoolchildren
that served non-kosher hot dogs. The mother complained to the school
about the Yom Kippur scheduling conflict and received a letter of apol-
ogy. Moreover, the school initiated a program in which children can share
their family's cultural (including religious) heritage. Another woman
suggested that District 204 will come around to the sensitivity shown by
Naperville's older District 203, which she attributed at least in part to the
advocacy efforts of Beth Shalom's Rabbi Remson. The rabbi told us that
he was called upon each Christmas season to speak at local schools about
sensitivity to Jewish traditions. He also commended the Naperville City
Council for rescheduling a meeting that was originally to be held on Yom
Kippur eve. Ironically, the city manager, himself a Jew, had decided not
to say anything and simply not attend, but a non-Jewish member brought
the issue to the Council's attention.

Members of the synagogue respond to these challenges in various
ways. One advocated compromise in a predominantly Christian society

since she had been taught as a Conservative Jew to remain separate from other groups. Another said she had been taught as a Reform Jew to value the kind of civic pluralism in which no group needs to compromise itself in the face of a majority. She pointed out that this issue no longer affects just Christians and Jews because other religious groups are now represented in Naperville as well.

Urban Impact: The Difference in Being Jewish

We have assessed Congregation Beth Shalom's urban impact as low moderate, that is, on the weaker end of our continuum. This is not surprising for the same two reasons that place Calvary Church on this end of the continuum. First, like most area congregations, Beth Shalom is predisposed to exert a relatively low impact on its locale, but this predisposition is exacerbated by the high mobility of its members. Rabbi Remson estimated Beth Shalom's membership turnover rate to be about 20 percent per year, more than the national Jewish turnover rate of 10 percent. Moreover, many, perhaps most, of its members do not consider Beth Shalom their home synagogue. This becomes clear at certain holy day services, when many leave town to celebrate with family at the synagogue of their upbringing. Drawing upon Nancy Eiesland's (2000, 125) insight, Naperville's Jews seek "social embeddedness" in their new urban context after being socially disembedded from previous locations and identities. Moving to Naperville represents a kind of freedom from the geographic constraints of modernity, yet significant life events continue to be geographically situated (Dear 2002b, 26). The irony of this synagogue is clear, as Rabbi Remson explained: "Only one adult in our Congregation was born and reared in Naperville, and almost everybody in the Congregation has, at one time or another, been 'the new kid on the block.' Were it not for this mobility our Congregation would not exist and yet it adds to the stress and the need for community."

This points to the second reason for Beth Shalom's relatively weak urban impact—its strong focus on meeting the congregation's internal needs. However—and this is where Beth Shalom differs from Calvary Church—this synagogue's minority religious status calls for vigilance in protecting Jewish rights and status in predominantly Christian Naperville. "Beleaguered" may be too strong a word for the Jewish minority in Naperville, especially when compared to the Muslim and black cases in chapters 4 and 5, but Jews "out here" feel their vulnerability as a religious minority. This is why the Jews of Beth Shalom are motivated to exercise greater influence on Naperville than the Pentecostals of Calvary Church, whose religious identity is less vulnerable.

But there is another reason for Beth Shalom's relatively weak impact on Naperville, namely, the nature of Naperville itself as it shapes Jewish identity and experience. We heard a good deal of ambivalence about being Jews in Naperville. In many ways, these Jewish suburbanites are much like their Gentile neighbors, as one member explained: "We're a *Naperville* congregation. Jew or not Jew, look who's living in Naperville. We're not all that different from the rest of the folks who live in Naperville." In one group interview, the women shared the importance of a Jewish educa-tion for their children, the value of adult fellowship with other Jews—and how wonderful life is in Naperville. The last comment demonstrates the potential Naperville has to compromise Beth Shalom's Jewish identity and dilute its ability to advocate for Naperville's Jews.

"We like it in Naperville," Rabbi Remson happily admitted at a forum held at the Bernard Horwich Jewish Community Center in Chicago's West Ridge community area, the heart of Chicago's Jewish North Side. "We west suburban Jews are a self-selected community." Beth Shalom has created a Jewish community in a Gentile suburb, and thus carries double religious outsider status. It both stands outside the dominant religion of its area and stands apart from the Jewish infrastructure on the North Side and North Shore suburbs. Beth Shalom's Jews connect to Naperville in terms of occupation and social class rather than religion, ethnicity, or historical experience. It seeks to be both "a Jewish voice in the secu-lar community" and "[a] Jewish community center for the western sub-urbs" (http://www.napershalom.org/aboutcbs/whoweare.html, accessed October 3, 2013). This can be difficult without the benefit of a thick Jewish infrastructure in an attractive non-Jewish suburb.

Wheatland Salem United Methodist Church
Transforming with the Area

Just off Route 59 south of Calvary Church sits Wheatland Salem United Methodist Church.[6] This congregation made strategic changes in its iden-tity, vision, and location in order to adapt to its new suburban context as the farmland around it transformed into new growth suburbia.

German farmers settled the area in the mid-nineteenth century, estab-lishing two churches in 1860: Copenhagen Church, whose name recalled an earlier Danish settlement in the vicinity, at the intersection of today's 83rd Street and Route 59, and Wheatland (or Emmanuel) Church several miles southwest of Copenhagen Church at the intersection of 119th Street and 248th Avenue. By 1908, the two congregations consolidated as Wheatland Salem Evangelical United Brethren Church (or simply Salem Church) and built a new facility at the intersection of 95th Street and Route 59. In 1928, one year after a fire destroyed that facility, the congregation erected the one that stood until the 1990s. Wheatland Salem Church became part of the United Methodist Church through a denominational merger in 1968.[7]

As one of the few remaining old timers reminisced to us, "everybody knew everybody" years ago. Many of the original farm families were related to each other, and folks rarely moved far from their ancestral home—he and his six siblings all lived within two miles of the church. Back then, when something needed doing at the church, the trustees simply did it, like building the parsonage. They could all take time off from their chores and donate their labor, in *gemeinschaftlich* manner.

The beginning of the congregation's shift in character occurred after World War II when many of the original farmers moved ten to fifteen miles farther west and no other farmers moved in to replace them. The church remained relatively stable until 1960, but decline set in over the next two decades. By 1979, membership had dropped from a high of 165 to eighty-seven, worship attendance to fifty-four, Sunday school attendance to eighteen, and the congregation yoked with a nearby church for clergy supply since it could not afford its own full-time pastor. The bishop appointed Pastor Scott Field to preside over Wheatland Salem's demise, conceding the irrelevance of this dying rural church to new growth suburban Naperville.

However, under Pastor Field's leadership, Wheatland Salem Church made several key decisions that not only insured the congregation's survival in the evolving configuration of Naperville's booming Sector G but in fact contributed significantly to the character of that configuration. The first decision concerned the identity and organization of the congregation. In 1987 the church's administrative council committed to a strategy of growth and development that emphasized moving the laity into ministry roles and making the pastor their ministry manager. Congregational leaders drew advice and inspiration from well-known church consultant Lyle Schaller, a member of the congregation; the Institute for American Church Growth; Frazer Memorial United Methodist Church in Montgomery,

Alabama, the fastest growing UMC congregation in the country; and the Charles E. Fuller Institute, particularly its seminar, "Breaking the 200 Barrier." Wheatland Salem broke the two hundred barrier in worship attendance in 1989, a decade after its lowest point (Field 1991).

Drawing from the church growth literature, Pastor Field explained in his Doctor of Ministry dissertation that a congregation becomes a new type altogether when it breaks the two hundred barrier. In other words, it is not just a small congregation writ larger. "In the case of a small church attempting to grow through the '200 Barrier,'" wrote Field (1991, 33–34), "we can see that secure, one-to-one relationships will be changed, fewer people will have an overall perspective on what is going on within the congregation, and the prime beneficiaries of the work on the church will no longer be the 'folks already here' but the largely unknown 'folks yet-to-come.'"

This conforms to Steven Brint's (2001) observation that size is a key variable in determining the nature of community relationships. Wheatland Salem also offers a closer look at Simmel's claim that certain invariable patterns occur as groups grow in size: when a group is small, the members are internally undifferentiated, but the group as a whole has a unique, individual character; when the group becomes larger and more differentiated or specialized in individual statuses, there is room for individuality of persons but only as parts of the whole. Persons have less uniqueness and look more like others in the same social positions. Indeed, as Field (1991, 102) noted, "several long-time members are no longer supportive of the continued change within Wheatland Salem. The increasing number of people whom they do not know well, the dramatically increased budget, the growing complexity of the organization, the difficulty in knowing everything that is going on and every decision that is being made are all elements which have made their church feel less and less like home." The change from a country church in which members embodied holistic rather than segmented roles sharply reduced the ability to "know everybody" and develop a unique identity for the congregation.

Field (10–11) described Wheatland Salem as "a church in transition," using phrases like "rural to suburban," "farmers to professionals," "pastor-centered to unifying goals," "behavioral to ideological," "small to large," and "simple to sophisticated." Employing concepts from a book by George Hunter (1987), Field (5–6) explained that Wheatland Salem had evolved from an "open country church" to a "metropolitan regional church," the latter defined by its location on a major artery or intersection

and a constituency of people who identify with the church's local vicinity—in our typology, an area congregation. Figure 6.4 shows the signature configuration of an area congregation, with 53 percent of Wheatland
Salem's members living within a four-mile radius of the church, many
within Naperville's Sector G. Pastor Field (5–6) described his new member demographics in the early 1990s: predominantly professionals/man-
agers, two or more preschool or grade school children per family, more

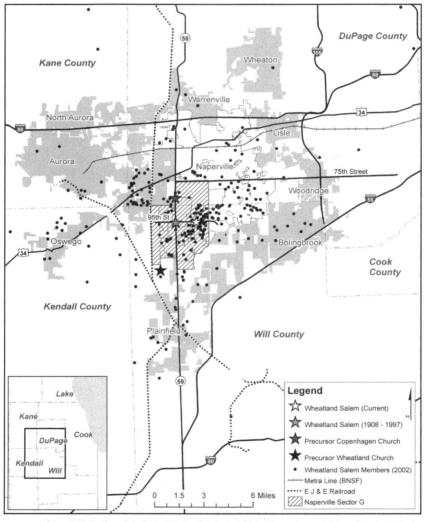

FIGURE 6.4. Wheatland Salem United Methodist Church and Members. Map by
David J. Treering and Melissa Gesbeck Howell, Loyola University Chicago.

than 70 percent college graduates, approximately 50 percent of households with both parents working, more than 85 percent recent arrivals to the area—an apt profile of Sector G residents.

In the early 1990s, Wheatland Salem Church began to consider relocating from the site it had occupied since the 1920s. The first impetus for the move came in 1990 when leaders decided that the growing Sunday school program needed more room and Pastor Field gave an ultimatum that the church purchase a new parsonage off-site since he refused to raise his children on the increasingly busy Route 59. The congregation voted on July 1, 1990, to buy a new parsonage with money to be raised in the following three weeks. The day before the deadline, the old-time member mentioned above came through with the necessary funds to seal the deal. A second impetus for relocating the church came from Pastor Field's personal prayer retreat in 1993, at which he decided that the church was being much too timid in its development plans. He felt that the "faithful thing to do" would be to move, to think bigger, and not simply to continue improving the current physical plant (which was expanded threefold in size in 1986). To his surprise—and delight—the congregational vote on selling the property was overwhelmingly positive, with less than a handful of No's.

As Pastor Field explained to us, the old farm church would have stuck out like a retrograde sore thumb in the proposed reconfiguration of its immediate surroundings at 95th Street and Route 59. Today, commercial developments occupy all four corners of the intersection while new subdivisions have sprung up to the south and west. Neuqua Valley High School is within view on 95th Street, which has become a major east-west artery for Sector G. A new pedestrian bridge over Route 59 was completed in 2008 to facilitate access to the high school, elementary and middle schools on both sides of the highway, a branch of the Naperville public library, and a YMCA facility. Several respondents to a city survey about the bridge voiced the following composite sentiment about life in this area: "With this project and many others in the south Naperville area I would like there to be focus on making it look more 'hometown' looking. There are too many strip malls and housing projects [that is, subdivisions] going in here that do not allow for access except for driving. This makes traffic a nightmare. It would be nice to be able to get to places without driving."[8] The "hometown" reference may be a mix of an idealized American past and nostalgia for what these residents actually left behind in moving to a new growth suburb.

Wheatland Salem Church's new location at 95th Street and Book Road is one mile east of the old site. The immediate vicinity looks very much like the one the church left behind, with comparable surrounding residential and business development. But, of course, Wheatland Salem's new physical plant fits well now—no retrograde farm church here. The congregation needed $6 million to construct the facility, which included a bank loan of $3.5 million. Boldly, they leveraged the move vis-à-vis their relationship to the Northern Illinois Conference of The United Methodist Church, which, according to denominational polity, owns all properties of its local churches (sometimes to the consternation of congregations). Should Wheatland Salem's venture fail, the Conference would assume its debt. Congregational leaders banked on the hunch that the bishop would not reassign Pastor Field under such circumstances. In 2012 Field ended his thirty-three year tenure as pastor of Wheatland Salem Church, far above the average for parish appointments within the Conference.

Offering Assurance to Suburbanites

Of course, by no longer sticking out like a sore thumb, Wheatland Salem has blended in, becoming one more large suburban church serving the needs and concerns of its young, middle-class, professional, and mobile constituents. Pastor Field shared with us something of the unfortunate lives of residents in prestigious White Eagle subdivision just north of the church's old site. They have no sense of community at all, he explained, living in sad, isolated pain. One had confided to him, "I can't tell anybody about my problems because I'll be the topic of conversation at the next cocktail party." Apparently, the staff at the local public elementary school felt relieved when White Eagle students took their family problems with them to the new school in their own subdivision.

To the families of the new suburbia, Wheatland Salem Church offers the hope of the Gospel in familiar idioms. A recent sermon series was titled "My Crazy, Mixed-Up Family," drawing lessons from dysfunctional family lives in the Bible. In the last Easter service before the congregation moved to its new location, Pastor Field's sermon drew upon newsworthy recent events: the University of North Carolina's loss in the NCAA basketball tournament; the mass suicide in the Heaven's Gate religious "cult," which Field attributed to the group's disconnectedness from other people, making them susceptible to believing anything; a racist beating in Chicago's Bridgeport community area; and tensions between Israelis and

Palestinians in the Middle East. He also described numerous experiences relevant to his hearers' everyday lives: loss of a newborn, Alzheimer's disease, occupational downsizing, teen sexual temptations, abusive family situations. For all such circumstances, he assured the gathering, faith in Jesus Christ provides the answer, a certain word, something real, hope and assurance, significance for life, love, and wisdom.

Pastor Field gave two particularly memorable illustrations of his main point. One came from a Michigan State and Wisconsin college football game some years back. Wisconsin was losing badly but their fans would cheer at odd times during the game. They were listening on handheld radios to a major league baseball game in Milwaukee where the Brewers were beating the St. Louis Cardinals. The point: no matter what the disaster in front of you, there is victory, in Christ, not far away. The second story came from a hospital visit that Pastor Field had made the previous evening. He told the patient's family that hope for victory, even on a deathbed, is the true Easter. If the Christian faith can stand up to that, it can uphold people in the face of any anxiety.

Wheatland Salem's services and program offerings suit its constituents well. Wheatland Salem Christian Academy offers preschool and kindergarten daycare, including provisions for early dropoff and late pickup of the children. Children and youth programming is offered on Sundays and during the week. Adults can choose from nearly fifty small groups that offer opportunities for fellowship, support, study, and service. On Serve the Community Days, groups of volunteers work at schools, senior living facilities, residences, and service providers.

Wheatland Salem Church downplays its denominational affiliation in seeking to serve its potential constituent pool. Its website answers the question, "What does it mean that you are Methodist?" in this way: "There are no exclusively United Methodist doctrines. Although we have distinctive emphasis we have no affirmations that are not also believed by other Christian groups. So it may not mean a whole lot to you, but you should check out John Wesley—he sort of founded the Methodist movement and was generally a cool guy" (http://wheatlandsalem.org/im-new-here/, accessed October 2, 2014).

Under strong pastoral leadership, Wheatland Salem Church remade its image to match the dramatic transformation of its locale. In a sense, Wheatland Salem has always been an area congregation, but when the character of its area shifted from rural to suburban, the church did the same. It continues to be focused on its area: a majority of its members during our primary research period lived in the relatively homogeneous subdivisions near the church (see Figure 6.4 above) and when the church looked to establish a satellite site in 2010, it chose another dying farm church only a few miles away (Vergara 2010). Its constituents identify more readily with the larger culture than either the Pentecostals of Calvary Church or the Jews of Congregation Beth Shalom. Wheatland Salem Church adapted to the structural changes of its area and thus its urban impact is the weakest of the three. Its religio-cultural impact, however, is every bit as significant as the other two in that it has also created a viable congregational community in new growth suburbia.

The Catholic Case: Religious Identity, Choice, and Mobility

The Catholic parishes of Naperville offer instructive comparisons to the three congregations considered thus far. In this section we offer a glimpse into the congregational community of the city's oldest parish, Sts. Peter and Paul, a Catholic variation on themes found in our other congregations, as all create viable communities for their constituents. The Catholic case also illuminates the interplay of urban structural dynamics and area congregations in places like the new Naperville. Religious identity, choice, and mobility factors influence the makeup of these congregations.

"The most distinctive feature of Naperville's skyline," wrote local historian Genevieve Towsley (1975, 62) just as the town entered its period of exponential growth, "is the graceful spire of SS. Peter and Paul church."[9] Known in Catholic circles as the "Cathedral of DuPage County" because of its striking architecture,[10] Sts. Peter and Paul has thrived while some of the other original downtown churches (collectively called Piety Hill) have closed or dwindled in membership. This church now stands at the epicenter of several parishes that have fanned out since the 1960s to serve the expanding Catholic population of the area.

Catholic immigrants hailing from German-speaking areas in southern Germany and Alsace began settling in the Naperville area around 1840, about a decade after the town's founding. Naperville's first Catholic Mass was held in a home in 1841; five years later the parish of St. Raphael was established with twenty-five families. A visiting bishop in 1849 noted in his diary that the church had about six hundred members, virtually all Germans, who settled mostly on Naperville's west side (Protestants tended to settle on the east side).

The cornerstone for a new church structure to replace the original modest wood frame building was set in 1864, the same year the Chicago, Burlington & Quincy rail line came through town. With completion of the structure two years later, the priest changed the name of the parish to Sts. Peter and Paul, and the parish school (est. 1850) took over the old frame church.

A fire of mysterious origins—some said it was set by the Ku Klux Klan—destroyed the church in 1922. The resplendent "cathedral" that took its place, dedicated in 1927 by George Cardinal Mundelein of Chicago, still dominates downtown Naperville. At least for a time, pilots used its 230-foot steeple to align their flight paths with Midway Airport on Chicago's Southwest Side.

Post–World War II demographic changes in Naperville affected Sts. Peter and Paul, which now had new members coming "from the four corners of the country," as the church's history puts it. In a perceptive comment about the effects on Catholic community, the history explains that "The sense of belonging would have to be rethought and nurtured" (*150 Years of Sharing the Word*, 29).

What does it means to be a member of Sts. Peter and Paul's congregational community? Part of the answer to this question can be found in the remarkable church facility. When a new rectory and parish center was being built in the 1990s, the congregation's planning committee made sure that the new would blend in with the old. "We didn't want a glass and steel monstrosity going up," said one committee member, while the pastor pointed to members' great affection for a classic structure that is certainly "not a '90s church" (Hostert-Cassidy 1996, 4). "Naperville is conditioned for change, but the stability of the parish is that little building that sits at the corner," explained Fr. James Burnett. "There has to be something that stays the same and acts as our anchor" (Slykas 1996, 20).

We were in attendance on two consecutive regular Sundays when Fr. Burnett presided over the 9:30 am Mass. As we arrived each time, large numbers of people from the 8:00 am Mass streamed into the street toward their cars. As the worshippers filled up the pews for the next service, most genuflected and then knelt in prayer. A long line formed at the front of the sanctuary on the first Sunday, writing the names of deceased loved ones in a book of remembrance for the upcoming All Saints Day commemoration. The interior of the church is massive and breathtaking. High vaulted ceilings, large stained-glass windows, numerous statues of saints, a substantial altar, paintings at each station of the cross—all befit the church's reputation as a de facto cathedral.

As late as a few minutes before 9:30 am, the sanctuary was only about half full each Sunday, but by start time it was standing room only as the ushers worked hard to fill in the last spaces for the thousand or more worshippers. They were virtually all white, with every age group represented, young families with small children comprising the largest group. The many children present made rather a lot of noise throughout the services, though no one complained that we noticed.

On the second Sunday, Fr. Burnett preached a brief homily (nine minutes) on the topic of community. He opened with a story from his childhood about Jehovah's Witnesses visiting his home and his mother defending the Catholic usage of the title "Father" for priests. This clearly set the context for a Catholic understanding of community in familial terms. The basis for Christian community, Fr. Burnett explained, is love and compassion; Christians are a "countercultural community" that needs the solidarity of each other. He commented on the state of community in today's society, with all the stresses on people who feel so "frayed at the ends" that they simply cannot afford to be pulled into any more relationships with other people. He pointed to the past, when a Catholic community of parish, neighborhood, or town gave people a strong sense of identity and meaning. Today, societal pressures work against creation of such communities.

It is instructive to compare this understanding of Christian community with Calvary Church's. Both congregations offer an alternative to the individualistic urban culture by invoking the powerful notion of "family," but that notion is nuanced differently: Calvary emphasizes moral norms, whereas Sts. Peter and Paul creates a Catholic sense of a familia or religious household.

Fr. Burnett dovetailed his homily into a ritual of renewing the vows of a couple celebrating forty-five years of marriage. Humorously, when the husband failed to respond quickly to his portion of the vows, the priest needled him: "You stumbled there, Tom!" At the end of the ritual, the priest proclaimed, "You may kiss the bride," after which the congregation applauded. During the petitionary prayer time, the lay leader could not find her notes, so the priest simply and kindly said, "I'll do the prayers." One could sense a friendly familiarity between priest and people in these interchanges.

Fr. Burnett presided over the Eucharist in a post–Vatican II posture, that is, from behind the communion table/altar and facing the congregation in a symbolic gesture of gathered community. The entire congregation was served in seven minutes. The benediction was combined with a blessing for the couple who had renewed their wedding vows. At 10:23, Fr. Burnett announced that the Mass had ended. Next a brief hymn was sung and the postlude began at 10:25.

On both occasions, the entire service was completed within one hour. We found the worship experience professional and efficient, yet elegant and theologically substantive. The Easter service we attended was more perfunctory. It was also a bit more diverse, with about a dozen blacks and Asians in attendance. But it retained its efficiency—despite the overflow attendance and the added Easter rituals, communion was distributed in seven minutes and the service lasted only a few minutes past an hour. In a sense, such efficiency mirrors life in technoburban Naperville. But there were signs that a community identity underlay the large numbers and the routinization of the service. The petitionary prayers included calling the names of about a dozen individuals who were ill that week. The presiding priest (not Fr. Burnett this service) sprinkled holy water over the congregation, ritually binding them together as a Catholic body whether or not they knew each other well.

To be Catholic is still important to many in an era of declining denominational loyalty. But how has the traditional Catholic understanding of a geographic parish fared in the fluid, fragmented, decentered, and rearranged geography of a new growth suburb like Naperville? And how does the Catholic case compare to our other Naperville congregations in this regard?

Five Catholic parishes have been established in Naperville since the 1960s, mirroring the growth of the area. Based on data we received from three parishes, a significant number of Catholics in the area go "out of their way" to attend the parish church of their choice. This varies from parish to parish, as Table 6.1 shows: one-fourth of Sts. Peter and Paul's membership commutes from outside of the parish boundaries, while nearly two-fifths of St. Thomas's membership does so. The mobility trends are more striking when Zip Codes are considered, ranging from two-fifths at Sts. Peter and Paul, to one-half at St. Thomas, to three-fourths at St. Raphael, the last well-known for its innovative programming.

Moreover, Naperville's three Catholic elementary schools accommodate family mobility and choice. Private elementary education—Catholic

and otherwise—is a more ambivalent commodity in new growth suburban Naperville than in its neighboring old city to the west, Aurora. With
approximately the same total populations and number of public elementary schools, Aurora has more than twice as many Catholic elementary
schools (seven) as Naperville (three). That Naperville has even three
Catholic elementary schools is significant given the excellence of the public schools. Catholic education is important to enough parents to be viable
in Naperville, and the Catholic schools accommodate them: Sts. Peter
and Paul and St. Raphael allow applications from outside their respective
parishes, while All Saints Academy, a joint venture of three parishes that
opened in 2005 as the Diocese of Joliet's first new school in more than four
decades, describes itself as a "regional" ("area" in our terminology) school.

These indicators suggest that the traditional Catholic understanding
of a geographic parish has eroded somewhat in Naperville. That said, the
residual strength of parish loyalty is remarkable—three-fourths of the
membership of Sts. Peter and Paul and three-fifths of St. Thomas stay
within their respective parish boundaries. As the comparative Zip Code
analysis in Table 6.1 indicates, Calvary Church and Congregation Beth
Shalom have higher mobility rates than even the most mobile Catholic
parish. Thus, choice and mobility are factors in the composition of area
congregations, but religious identity continues to play an important role.
Note that the congregation with the most generic identity (Wheatland

Table 6.1. Percentage of Membership Outside Zip Codes and
Parish Boundaries of Congregation's Location

Congregation	% outside Zip Code	% outside parish boundary
Calvary Church	Not available but high	Not applicable
Congregation Beth Shalom	83	Not applicable
St. Raphael Catholic Church	75	Not available
St. Thomas Catholic Church	51	37
Sts. Peter and Paul Catholic Church	43	23
Wheatland Salem Church	38	Not applicable

Salem Church) has the lowest mobility rate—not as many people seek it out from a distance compared to the other congregations.

Area Congregations in Suburban Boom Towns

There are many reasons why area congregations predominate in the new urban era. The social-geographic configuration of the new metropolis provides strong structural advantages for this type of congregation. Suburban boom towns like Naperville are preferred destinations and their residents both enjoy the benefits and face the challenges of life in such places. We have seen how the congregations in this chapter helped in different ways to create the new Naperville. The influence of Calvary and Wheatland Salem was, in our terminology, non-agentive. That is, they were responders to the pulls of suburban development rather than, as in the case of Mosque Foundation in the southwest suburbs, stamping the area with a new culture and challenging set of norms (see introduction and chapter 4). Using its minority Jewish voice, Beth Shalom exerted somewhat more influence, but on the whole, these congregations would not be what they are today without the influences of the new Naperville.

Area congregations can mitigate the "acute fragmentation of the urban landscape" (Dear and Flusty 2002, 68) and its deleterious effects on the formation of community through propinquity and connectivity (64–65, 67). Even though a substantial proportion of their constituencies may move in and out of the area, the congregations, especially the parishes, remain. And if a congregation happens to move, it likely will remain in the area. Here is place-dependent institutional stability in an era that invests diminishing value in places.

This loyalty to the area helps to explain why none of the congregations in this chapter became metro congregations. Both Calvary Church and Wheatland Salem Church offer something that could attract metro-wide commuters. Calvary's megachurch Pentecostalism might appeal to a "seeker hostile" niche market, while there was no necessary reason why Wheatland Salem could not "think bigger" by marketing its message of assurance to suburbanites beyond Naperville. Congregational decisions and the powerful influence of Naperville as an attractive place explain why these churches have not developed a metropolis-wide constituency.

These factors obtain in Beth Shalom's case as well, but an additional factor stems from its religious heritage that emphasizes a Jewish community's residential propinquity, as in a traditional *eruv*. Similar geographic emphases are found in the Roman Catholic and Islamic heritages. We know of only one Catholic church in the Chicago region that has attained metro status, Old St. Patrick's in the West Loop (Wedam 2000a), and we discuss the requirements of Islamic practice that mitigate against the likelihood of mosques attaining metro status in chapter 4 of the present book.

By most accounts, the new urban reality is not only decentralized but rife with socioeconomic inequities, fragmentation, and realignment of community identities, as well as threats to quality of life even at the outer fringes of the metropolitan system. "The fundamental reality," write Dreier, Mollenkopf, and Swanstrom (2004, 18), "is one of growing economic segregation in the context of rising overall inequality. People of different income classes are moving away from each other not just in how much income they have but also in where they live. America is breaking down into economically homogeneous enclaves." Automobility—or lack thereof—plays its part in this since the privileging of automobiles over other forms of urban transportation favors those able to afford and use them to access employment hubs in outlying areas (Jackson 1985; Hayden 2003).

The new Naperville provides advantages to residents that simultaneously undermine both the desire and the ability to challenge what troubles many—rampant consumerism, disrespect across generations, uncertainty, and mainstream cultural inducements. Challenges to massive societal changes are easier for people not deeply invested in the direction of these changes or who do not benefit materially or culturally from them. This is a very large reason why the congregations in this chapter exert relatively little impact on Naperville. The conundrum seems to be that those willing to defy the deleterious structural changes of the new urban era do not possess the resources needed to do so.

7

Metro Congregations

A WIDER VIEW OF
THE RESTRUCTURING METROPOLIS

THIS CHAPTER CONSIDERS the metropolitan or metro type of congregation—that is, a congregation with a simple majority of its constituents living throughout the metropolitan region rather than in its neighborhood
or in or around its community area. We feature The Hindu Temple of
Greater Chicago, describing the patterns of its congregational community
and explaining its relatively weak urban impact, the latter a tendency of
metro-type congregations. Within our discussion of this temple, which is
located near an expressway interchange, we offer an excursus on community near such places in the new American metropolis. We also present two
other metro congregations—The Moody Church and New Life Community
Church—describing the kinds of congregational community they have
nurtured in response to the contemporary urban experience and offering
them as counter cases to the metro-type congregation's tendency to exert a
relatively weak urban impact. New Life is a different kind of metro church
whose metropolitan-wide influence emanates from neighborhood loci.

The few observers who pay serious attention to the metropolitan-wide
role of religion typically emphasize political activism. Myron Orfield
(2002) and David Rusk (1999), for instance, call for a strong religious
presence in regional urban reform that would draw upon the civil rights
movement model. Rusk concludes his book *Inside Game/Outside Game*
with a section titled "Faith Can Move (Political) Mountains" (333–35),
illustrating his point with the Gamaliel Foundation and the Industrial
Areas Foundation. Such faith-based public policy advocacy in the Saul
Alinsky mold clearly has created urban change. This chapter will explore

some less conflictive means by which metro congregations contribute to the restructuring of urban America.

The Hindu Temple of Greater Chicago
Urban Context: Lemont: From Canal Town to Suburban Node

The sign along Interstate 55 southwest of Chicago lists three points of interest: Historic Lemont, the Lithuanian World Center, and The Hindu Temple of Greater Chicago. Passers-by might find this an odd combination, yet the historical and geographic confluences of an old canal town, classical European immigrant groups, new immigrant Hindus, and the interstate highway system exemplify contemporary urban restructuring.

Lemont is one of the "classic canal towns" of Illinois (M. Conzen 1994a). Preceded by the towns of Keepataw (established 1836) and Athens (established 1839), Lemont aligned its street grid vis-à-vis the Illinois and Michigan Canal that was constructed between 1836 and 1848 along the south bank of the Des Plaines River. This placed Lemont, incorporated as a village in 1873, in the southwest metropolitan transit and development corridor, one of five major radial corridors in the Chicago region. The impressive bluffs carved out of the valley floor by the Des Plaines River were recognized early as one of the village's most attractive natural features. Lemont's other early distinction came from the limestone deposits uncovered during the canal's construction. Lemont's quarries flourished in the latter half of the nineteenth century, providing jobs for European immigrants and materials for many high-profile buildings, including Chicago's Water Tower (1869) and Holy Name Cathedral (1875), the Illinois state penitentiary at Joliet (1858), and the state capitol buildings of Illinois and Michigan (Alberts 1994; Selman 1994).

According to the 1900 US census, two-thirds of Lemont's residents were American-born but fully 83 percent of their parents' generation were immigrants. The major ethnicities at the turn of the twentieth century were Germans and Poles, combining for more than 60 percent of the town's population, followed by Irish and Scandinavians (Robert Williams 1994). Their churches—Roman Catholic, Lutheran, and Methodist—played such an important historical role that Lemont adopted the motto "Village of Faith." The decline of the quarries by the end of the nineteenth century was more than compensated by stability and growth in other economic sectors, including local businesses, aluminum manufacturing (from 1892), and oil and petrochemical plants (from 1922) (see Klowden 1994).

Robert Buerglener (1994, 139) explains that Lemont was never extremely isolated in the metropolitan system: "Directly in the path taken by electric, telephone, and railway lines between the metropolitan center of Chicago and the larger hinterland outpost of Joliet, Lemont benefited from transportation, telephone, and electric services which it might otherwise not have received until much later, if at all. Lemont lay in Chicago's hinterland, but by the beginning of the twentieth century was intimately tied to the core through infrastructural improvements." The first three decades of the twentieth century brought the interurban electric train and the automobile. As Benjamin Lorch (1994, 137) notes, "At each evolutionary step changes in the methods of personal mobility in Lemont further increased people's ability to travel further, faster and with greater frequency and freedom." This mobility only increased as the twentieth century advanced.

Still, Lemont remained on Chicago's outer belt through much of the twentieth century, an attractive location for a notable combination of urban fringe land usages—Catholic religious facilities, private golf courses, public nature preserves, and Argonne National Laboratory (Hannaford 1994). The religious facilities found the tranquil rural setting conducive to both body and spirit. These included headquarters for three Franciscan orders, all established in the 1920s, and a series of institutions run by the Archdiocese of Chicago dating back to 1929. The golf courses also date to the 1920s as refuges for Chicago's social elite. Cog Hill, opened in 1927, has hosted many prestigious professional golf tournaments. Forest preserve land around Lemont has steadily increased since 1920, driven by the desire to protect natural habitats from ubiquitous metropolitan development. Argonne was created by the federal government in 1946 to continue the work of the Metallurgical Laboratory at the University of Chicago, the site of the first sustained nuclear reaction in 1942.

Geographer Michael Conzen (1994a) calls this period of Lemont's history, roughly the first half of the twentieth century, the first wave of metropolitan expansion. He suggests that land users were more oriented to Chicago than Lemont during this wave (6), but we would note two exceptions: the Slovenian Franciscan friars of St. Mary's Retreat House, who lent a hand in the local Catholic parishes, and the more than 250 Argonne employees who lived in and around Lemont by the early 1970s (Buschman [1973], 115, 85).

The impact of Lemont's second wave of metropolitan expansion, roughly throughout the second half of the twentieth century and into the twenty-first, has been more dramatic. Michael Conzen (1994a, 6) characterizes this wave as "the suburban housing tracts, freeway extensions, and shopping malls," saying it is "not to be ignored. It threatens to bury, if not erase, the town's historic character as a small, discrete, industrial canal town." A map titled "Growth of the Chicago Metropolitan Area" in the *Encyclopedia of Chicago* shows Lemont being swallowed up by urban expansion between 1955 and 1990. The map's caption explains the role of the automobile in this development (Grossman, Keating, and Reiff 2004, facing 543): "By 1955, . . . widespread automobile ownership had encouraged the extension of the continuously built-up zone around the urban core. After 1955, construction of the expressway system permitted a vast decentralization of population and activity, filling in many of the interstices between the railroad axes radiating from the central city and producing a more rounded overall geometry. By the end of the twentieth century, there was hardly a farmer's field to be seen within 40 miles of the city center in any direction."

Two expressways integrated Lemont into this new metropolitan system. Interstate 55, completed near Lemont by 1960 and extended as the Stevenson Expressway into Chicago in 1964, follows the southwest metropolitan transit and development corridor. The North-South Tollway (Interstate 355) opened in 1989 as one of the region's major interstitial connectors, linking I-55 with the far northwest suburbs. After a long delay due in part to local resistance, I-355 was extended south of I-55 to Interstate 80 in Will County in 2007 and renamed Veterans Memorial Tollway.

This, of course, is part of the larger story of urban development in the United States throughout the twentieth century. The "transportation revolution," as Kenneth Jackson (1985) dubs it, ensconced automobility as the primary mode of American urban transit and created the interstate highway system that facilitated urban decentralization and sprawl, economic segregation, and the fragmentation of individual lives and community identities in the new metropolis. How have these large urban dynamics affected Lemont?

Lemont was geographically stable from the 1930s through the 1960s, but since the 1980s, "Lemont has entered a major new geographical era: it has lost its status as an independent town surrounded by countryside, and become a service node within the advancing tide of metropolitan suburbs. Tract housing has arrived on Lemont's doorstep, and co-opted the town. The village now plays the metropolitan game of aggressive land annexation, zoning laws, expanded tax base, and utility provision . . . . Suddenly, Lemont is many more communities than it used to be" (M. Conzen 1994a, 5).

Michael Conzen (1994b, 229–35) lists "five features of the new Lemont," signs of its current "metropolitanism," as he dubs it: (1) new homes along its outskirts, driven more by metro-wide housing dynamics than local demand; (2) an outlying retail and service area that replaced the old downtown; (3) the transformation of the old downtown from its once dominant position to an historic attraction with tourist appeal; (4) the I-355 extension passing just west of town, whose interchanges, Conzen predicted, would enhance mobility throughout the metropolis and solidify the importance of Lemont's outlying retail and service area; and (5) new institutional centers with metro-wide constituencies—the Lithuanian World Center (which has its roots in earlier Lithuanian institutions dating to the 1940s; see Buschman [1973]; Hannaford 1994), The Hindu Temple of Greater Chicago, and the Rock Creek Center psychiatric facility—about which Conzen comments, "Lemont offers relatively inexpensive sites for such institutions, often scenically attractive, adjacent to a settled community, and close to connecting expressways" (234).

Conzen suggests that Lemont is transitioning reasonably well compared to nearby Bolingbrook and Romeoville, newer communities with less history to draw upon. "There is an old community here [in Lemont], with its own historically developed center of gravity, and with a collective memory that works in curious ways to put matters in a larger historical or geographical context than would be possible for bedroom suburbs not many seasons beyond the farmer's last harvest and full of people with no experience of working with each other" (236).

Creating a Hindu Enclave near Lemont

The *Encyclopedia of Chicago*'s entry for Lemont reads (Schroeder 2004, 475): "[T]he Lithuanian World Center and the Hindu Temple of Greater Chicago have added to the village's cosmopolitan flavor. Although they did not radically alter village life, these developments marked the start of a new era." We have seen how Lemont attained its new cosmopolitan status. What kind of congregation is The Hindu Temple of Greater Chicago (HTGC), why did it locate in Lemont, and how does HTGC relate both to Lemont and to metropolitan Chicago as a whole?

The new urban era has been shaped by global mass migrations, among other factors. The Los Angeles School of urbanism holds up Los Angeles as the archetype of the new metropolis, a "polyglot, polycentric, polycultural pastiche" (Dear 2000, 21), but every American metropolis has been significantly affected by recent immigration trends. "The immigrants to the United States since 1965 are overwhelmingly an urban population," wrote Roger Waldinger (1989, 211) at the threshold of the 1990s. The 1990s became the largest decade in American immigration history, and by 2000, 70 percent of foreign-born residents lived in six states, mostly in urban regions.

The Hindu Temple of Greater Chicago could not have existed prior to the federal immigration act passed in 1965. A critical mass of Asian Indian Hindus sufficient to establish a major temple did not coalesce until the effects of the immigration reform began to be felt in the 1970s. The 1965 immigration act reversed decades of restrictive US immigration policy, bringing large numbers of immigrants from Asia and other non-European lands during the next decades (Fawcett and Carino 1987; Portes and Rumbaut 1996; Riemers 1992; Kurien 2007). The act privileged highly skilled and educated professionals and technical workers, who predominated in the initial post-1965 wave of Indian immigrants. Later shifts in immigration policies and trends brought more socioeconomically diverse waves, including many relatives of the earlier immigrant cohort.

At the turn of the twenty-first century, metropolitan Chicago ranked third among US cities in the number of Asian Indians.[1] The 2000 census counted more than 125,000 Asian Indians in the region—probably a low estimate given the Census Bureau's admitted undercounting of minority groups (Hogan and Robinson [1994])—a nearly fourfold increase since the 1980 census. However, the 2000 census showed only eighty-six Asian Indians living in the Zip Code of HTGC. In the heavily populated Downers Grove Township, which includes the temple but extends far north into DuPage County, Asian Indians comprised only 3.4 percent of the total population.[2]

A socioeconomic gap exists between the city-dwelling and suburban Indian populations in metropolitan Chicago. Devon Avenue on Chicago's North Side functions like a traditional ethnic neighborhood and continues to serve as a port of entry for many new Indian immigrants. Several impressive temples have been built in the outlying suburbs, where land is more readily available (Holt 1998; Yates 2001a; 2001b; Kniss and Numrich

2007). The Hindu Temple of Greater Chicago was one of the first such Hindu architectural wonders in the suburbs (Figure 7.1).[3]

HTGC began in conversations among local Indian leaders in 1977. The group, facilitated by the president of the Telugu Association of Greater Chicago, a South Indian cultural organization, discussed "the possibility of founding a religious organization and building a temple" and soon formed an ad-hoc committee that convened weekly at a member's residence in the near west suburb of Oak Park (Jayaram 1997). Registered

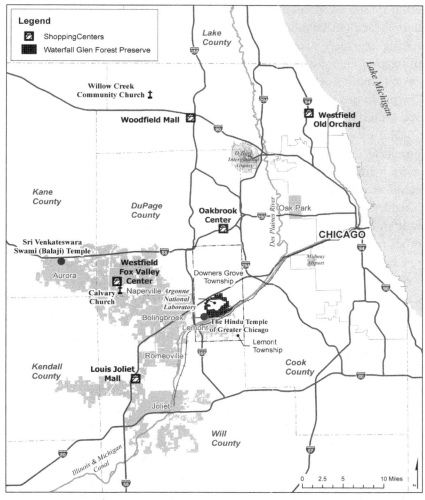

FIGURE 7.1. The Hindu Temple of Greater Chicago. Map by David J. Treering and Melissa Gesbeck Howell, Loyola University Chicago.

as a not-for-profit corporation with the State of Illinois in December of 1977, the temple name's inclusive phrasing—The *Hindu Temple* of Greater Chicago—carries no sectarian or India-region-specific connotations, bespeaking the founders' "ecumenical" strategy to accommodate the many subgroups within the local immigrant Hindu population (Raymond Williams 1992, 238–40). For pan-Hindu appeal, HTGC's founders selected Sri Rama, an *avatara* (literally "descent" or incarnation) of the great god Vishnu popular throughout India, as the temple's principal deity.

In the years following incorporation, the congregation consolidated its ethnic-based resources and developed architectural plans for a permanent temple facility (Raymond Williams 1988, 229; Rangaswamy 2000, 248). An eighteen-acre parcel of undeveloped bluff property near Lemont was purchased for $300,000 in 1981. The site is two miles south of Interstate 55 on Lemont Road, just north of the Des Plaines River in Downers Grove Township of DuPage County,[4] adjacent to Argonne National Laboratory and Waterfall Glen Forest Preserve.

The new urban geography was an important consideration in this purchase. Temple leaders considered more than thirty sites throughout metropolitan Chicago, the presupposition being that any number of sites could accommodate the temple's widely dispersed constituency. Three considerations sealed the choice, according to one of the temple's own written histories ("A Historical Review," 19): "[1] its proximity to I-55 and other major highways, [2] its quiet spot secluded from thickly populated residential and commercial areas, as well as [3] budgetary constraints." In a sense, the site offered an accessible suburban retreat similar to Lemont's Catholic centers, golf courses, and nature preserves, but now the location was far more integrated into the larger metropolitan system than a century earlier. The natural beauty of the bluff property may have helped tip the decision, but any naturally beautiful site in metropolitan Chicago could have sufficed. Accessibility often trumps aesthetics in the new metropolis, but HTGC achieved a fortunate convergence.

Although the property was purchased in 1981, construction of a permanent religious facility would take some time. After using a series of temporary suburban venues, by the end of 1983, "the patience of the devotees was getting exhausted" by construction delays at the Lemont site ("A Historical Review," 20). Raymond Williams (1988, 213) identifies the causes of the delays as "internal dissension over the location and plans for the temple combined with external problems related to governmental approval," the latter presumably referring to the township since the temple's property was not annexed into Lemont until 1991. In 1984 a group split off to establish Sri Venkateswara Swami (Balaji) Temple along Interstate 88 (the East-West Tollway) in the far west satellite city of Aurora.

In June of that year, the chief minister of the south Indian state of Andhra Pradesh laid the foundation stone for the main structure on the site, the Sri Rama facility, which was dedicated with a traditional *kumbhabhishekam* ceremony two years later, on July 4, 1986. The impressive white exterior of this structure follows a traditional south Indian temple architectural model, with a large *gopuram* or pyramidal entryway and cupolas over the cubicles of various deities. Altars to several deities line the main interior hall, including Ganesha, the remover of obstacles, Krishna and Radha, Venkateswara and his two goddess consorts, and Hanuman, the loyal servant of Rama. The worshipper's attention is directed to the images of Rama, his wife Sita, and his brother Lakshmana at the front of the hall, the ceiling dropping dramatically as one enters the *garbhagriha* or "womb chamber," the spiritual center of a Hindu temple (Eck 1985, 62–63).

True to its ecumenical strategy of appealing to all Indian Hindus, HTGC added a structure in 1994 dedicated to the deities Ganesha, Shiva, and Durga built in east central Indian architectural style, a dramatic visual complement to the adjacent south Indian style Rama structure. Between the two religious structures, HTGC also constructed a large community center with an auditorium, a multipurpose hall, and a full kitchen. In 1998 the Vivekananda Vedanta Center of Chicago, the oldest Hindu center in the region (originally serving a non-Indian American clientele), donated a life-sized statue of Swami Vivekananda, the well-known Hindu speaker at the 1893 World's Parliament of Religions, which now stands in an elaborate shrine at the entrance to the property.

Congregational Community Traits: Cultivating a Hindu Identity

The HTGC complex rises impressively above the Des Plaines River valley floor, attracting Hindus from all over metropolitan Chicago and well beyond, joining the growing number of temples across the United States that similarly attract Hindu pilgrims from wide distances in large part because of their traditional architecture (Clothey 1983; Fenton 1988; Narayanan 1992; Bhardwaj and Rao 1998). In India, Hindu temples are ubiquitous. "Religion is 'in the air' in India," writes Padma Rangaswamy (2000, 246), "a living, breathing tradition, which Indians do not have to make a conscious effort to imbibe." But in the United States, temples are few and far between, and they arise largely through the diligent efforts of immigrant laypeople. One interviewee told us that he took Hinduism for granted in India, but here his "thought process" has become far more conscious about cultivating his Hindu identity.

HTGC serves as an umbrella for several religious and cultural subgroups, including the Sat Kala Mandir (Tamil), the Hindu Satsang of Greater Chicago (north Indian), and a Bengali association. This kind of "ecumenism" is uncommon in India and differs from many Hindu temples in America that organize according to ethnic/regional and/or sectarian identity (such as the Aurora temple). At one point, HTGC offered instruction in seven Indian languages—Hindi, Marathi, Gujarati, Tamil, Malayalam, Kannada, and Telugu.

HTGC shapes its congregational community first through its religious practices and celebrations. "Religion" is not typically separated from other aspects of Indian culture, although in an American context the relationship between ethnic culture and religious identity can become a major topic of discussion and negotiation within a group. One posted calendar during our primary research period, for instance, distinguished "cultural" from "religious" events at HTGC by using different colored ink. Two committees, the religious committee and the committee on Hindu *dharma* (religious and moral teachings) and philosophy, bear primary responsibility for the explicitly "religious" emphases of the institution.

The temple is open every day from 9:00 am to 9:00 pm for devotees and visitors, averaging several hundred each week. The priests offer daily *puja*s (worship services) for individuals and families. After ringing an overhead bell, worshippers enter the inner sanctum of the Rama temple, where the priest chants in Sanskrit while waving an oil lamp before the images (*arati*). Incense and smoke fill the air. He then offers the lamp to the worshippers, who bless themselves by holding their hands over the fire and then stroking their face and head, connecting physically and symbolically with the deities. Worshippers place food, money, and other items before the deities. The priest sprinkles them with blessed water and gives them a spoonful of nut meats and raisins (*prasad*) blessed by the gods, thus completing the ritual. The temple also facilitates the practice of various Hindu *samskara*s or life-cycle rituals, such as at birth and marriage.

Major communal religious celebrations in Hinduism follow the lunar calendar and draw thousands of people to HTGC. Our researchers observed the following festivals: Holi (March), during which episodes from the life of the *avatara* Krishna are celebrated with the use of various colors; Janmashtami (August), commemorating Krishna's birth; Navaratra (September–October), a ten-day celebration of the triumph of good over evil through the efforts of Durga and Rama; and Diwali (October–November), a festival of light celebrated with sparklers and "Christmas" lights. Holi is especially popular with children and youth, who gleefully throw powders of various colors on one another, covering hair, head, and clothing with thick strokes, making it hard to identify the person beneath. Other major festivals at HTGC include Shivaratri (February), a vigil to the god Shiva, and Ramanavami (April), a nine-day celebration of the birth of Rama.

Two other committees deserve mention here for the "nonreligious" programming they facilitate at the temple. The cultural committee organizes programs of Indian performing arts, but also a Bhajan-a-thon (*bhajan* is a sacred devotional song) and a class on meditation, activities most Americans would consider "religious." Well-known artists, such as Hariprasad Chaurasia and Patric Marks, have performed at the temple regularly. Also, a popular summer festival called Greeshma Mela features entertainment, various cuisines of India, clothing and jewelry sales, and even free health screening.

The humanitarian committee has stepped up efforts to address the needs of the temple's elderly members. These seniors, who have joined their children and grandchildren in this country through the family reunification provisions of US immigration laws, often feel lonely and unproductive in their new surroundings. The president of the temple recounted how, after a luncheon organized for them, these senior citizens were "very active both physically and mentally." He noted that they "do not want any charity. They want to come to the temple and want to serve the organization in whatever way they can. They want to do something; they want to help in any way, such as stuffing the envelopes, cleaning the temple, cooking in the kitchen, etc."

An important programmatic emphasis at HTGC has to do with children and youth. Recall that serious discussions about building a Hindu temple in Chicago did not begin until a critical mass of immigrants had arrived by the late 1970s. Also by then, a second generation of Indian Americans had been born. "As the families grew and settled down," one of HTGC's histories observes, "it became apparent that there was a necessity to actively encourage to continue our traditional religious and cultural values" (Jayaram 1997). As Rangaswamy (1995, 449, emphasis in original) elaborates regarding local temple building generally, "So the temples of Chicago have become the focal point of culture propagation among second-generation Indians, something that the first generation sees as a very critical, if not *the* single most important issue at this stage in their development as an ethnic group."

Through the auspices of its education committee, and with the help of numerous volunteers, HTGC offers Sunday school classes every other week. The program began with four children in 1984 but grew to more than 130 within a decade. The curriculum includes Hindu scriptures, *bhajan*s, and Indian vernacular languages.

Two Sunday school teachers we interviewed emphasized the importance of language instruction in the overall objectives of the education program. It is much easier, they insisted, to teach traditional Indian values through the native languages of India than through English. The language curriculum is "scripture inspired," they stated. One teacher pointed out how her two children benefited from the temple's education program, which gave them "courage to speak up in school about their culture." Parents can use the temple library's English-language children's books published in India, since public libraries have little on Hinduism. This language instruction is particularly beneficial to families who visit India in enhancing their children's ability to communicate with relatives.

In 1991 temple youth started In the Wings, described in a flier in this way: " 'Waiting In the Wings' means waiting to take over; these youths are the future of our temple." In the Wings organizes many activities and programs, including a discussion series called Youth Speaks that sometimes tackles controversial issues such as substance abuse and AIDS. The group's vice president frankly stated that "many parents do not encourage such topics." In his opinion, they prefer to remain "totally aloof" and also are "naive when the issue of such talks comes up. They say 'Oh! Our child is not involved in any such thing' and don't like to send their kid. As a result the attendance becomes very thin."

Nevertheless, the Sunday school teachers recognized that parents are often in need of some help in dealing with their teenaged children in this immigrant context, offering the temple as a place to provide this support.

Marriage appears to be another sensitive topic for both parents and youth. Ironically, one youth leader told us that most of the youth supported marrying other Indians, whereas an adult leader predicted that they would likely marry non-Indians.

At one Youth Night program held at a public high school in nearby Naperville, In the Wings presented a skit called "Adventures in Matrimony" that offers insights into the relationship between youth and adults in the temple. The story portrayed a Devon Avenue restaurant owner who wants his son to become a physician and marry an Indian girl. Despite some hesitancy, the son pursues his medical studies in Hawaii, where he falls in love with a native Hawaiian. After a while, the two break up because the cultural gap between them is too wide. Returning to Chicago as a physician, the son again hesitates to accede to his father's wishes about marriage, and falls into a great depression. A deity intervenes, convincing the son to make his father happy by fulfilling his wishes. In the end, father, son, and the eventual bride and her parents all come to an agreement, though not without some humorous moments contrasting Indian and American expectations about marriage.

We were impressed by the warmth with which many youth greeted each other at this event. Few among the crowd of five hundred were non-Indians. All of the program's leaders and actors spoke in unaccented English. When we asked an officer of In the Wings on another occasion why the temple is important to him, he replied, "Relationship. I have made so many friends. It gives me a feeling of being a member of the group. The atmosphere is free, everyone is like you, you are not discriminated [against] or looked down upon." Two other youth leaders, young women, elaborated on the importance of Sunday school and In the Wings in their lives. "Self-confidence," they explained without hesitation: "We know who we are, we know about our culture and roots. If a question is being asked, we don't have to look down, we can answer the things. When we were small and did not know the meaning of *bindi* [the traditional dot on the foreheads of Hindu girls and women], people could make fun of us and we would start crying. Now we can tell them what does it mean. Similarly we can explain so many other things. We are proud of the fact that we inherit a rich culture." These young women characterized HTGC as a healthy and safe place where they can gather with peers and learn about their culture and religion.

Clearly, youth and parents in this temple wrestle with what it means to be Indian American Hindus. In an effort to give youth a voice in temple affairs, every committee had youth representation during our research period, although some complained that they were not always taken seriously. Youth also had an adult liaison who handled tensions with the board of trustees. "Most of the time he successfully resolves the conflict," one youth leader told us, "and almost always there is a compromise."

A group called Akshaya ("Perennial") comprises young adults in their twenties and thirties "who are seeking to explore, learn, and expand upon their knowledge of the Hindu religion," as the group's flier puts it. "We are affiliated with the Hindu Temple of Greater Chicago (HTGC) and our goals are to begin the transition to future leadership of the temple and increase public awareness of the HTGC and its goals."

Excursus on Community near the Expressway Interchange: Malls, Megachurches, and Megatemples

Immigrant congregations like The Hindu Temple of Greater Chicago create ethno-religious enclaves near the expressway interchanges of the new American metropolis. But much more is happening in these locations. Robert Lang (2003, 20–22) suggests that the classical Chicago School notion of concentric zone urban development may still hold in such a place. Be that as it may, there is no Chicago School understanding of social-geographic community here: it has no name, its institutions do not have a communal interrelationship, and, although it may have more-or-less definable boundaries, many of the people found within those boundaries on a daily or weekly basis do not live there. These interchanges may be a new "social constellation," to use Robert Park's (1925, 115) phrase, but it is no community (cf. A. Hunter 1974, 67).

Various entities comprise the social constellation near the expressway interchange, including corporate headquarters, warehousing and industrial parks, sports and entertainment complexes, research and high-tech facilities, and shopping malls. All have both arisen from and contributed to the dynamics of the new urban era: decentralization, socioeconomic inequities between the metropolitan core and periphery, and increased mobility and lifestyle privileges of better-off residents. But collectively they have failed to provide a social-geographic sense of community.

Many early shopping malls were conceived as community centers for new suburbs, "[b]ut when it became clear that malls were highly trafficked and that any space not being used for commercial purposes was not producing revenue, those 'community' spaces began to disappear" (Lombardi 2008). Mall proponents may see them as "the identifiable collecting points for the rootless families of the newer [suburban] areas" (K. Jackson 1985, 260), but shopper satisfaction has been declining according to an annual survey of consumer dissatisfaction ("Mall Pall," 1): "consumers are aggravated and uninspired by the sameness and predictability of shopping malls, which for decades epitomized America's consumer society." Cultural communities spring up in malls—walking groups (Lombardi 2008), teens ("Mall Pall"), churches that rent space—but malls are not part of a larger social-geographic community. Figure 7.1 above shows selected malls and their proximity to the expressways of metropolitan Chicago.

Megachurches also locate near expressway interchanges. It has been postulated that megachurches imitated the success and strategies of outlying shopping malls (e.g., Niebuhr 1995, 1; Trueheart 1996, 47). Moreover, a case can be made for a correlation between megachurches and metropolitan sprawl, an increasing cause for concern for local residents and governments (Weiss and Lowell 2002; Evans-Cowley and Pearlman 2008). Mark Chaves (2006, 339, emphasis in original) suggests that "suburbanization, the ubiquity of cars, and decreasing travel costs explains something about the *location* of megachurches—why the very largest churches used to be in central cities but are now mainly in suburbs." Applying the notion of "religious districts" from the work of Omar McRoberts on poor city neighborhoods, Chaves points out that "religious districts occur at the edge of suburban development zones because that is where land is cheapest." Chaves attributes the creation of religious districts "at both ends of the income distribution, and in both the inner city and the outer suburbs" to "[t]he forces of urban geography" and identifies 1970 as the pivotal date in the rise of the contemporary megachurch phenomenon. Clearly, such megachurches are implicated in the current urban restructuring. Their studious avoidance of poor urban locations contributes to the economic stratification of metropolitan regions. As Karnes and colleagues (2007, 267, n. 13, emphasis in original) note, "[I]t is not only that megachurches are, on average, not located in relatively poor areas; they are not located *near* relatively poor areas either."

Some megachurches turn into "the neighbor from hell," in the words of one newspaper editorial (cited in Weiss and Lowell 2002, 318), a "mega-headache" in terms of traffic congestion and other negative impacts on their locales (Evans-Cowley and Pearlman 2008, 231; also, see Weiss and Lowell 2002, 324–27). In effect, the megachurch is a "big-box approach" to religion (Greenblatt and Powell 2007, 781). Although megachurches have many positive effects on the lives of urban people, particularly their own constituents, they are also complicit in negative impact. Applying Dolores Hayden's (2003, 175–79) argument about malls and other commercial enterprises, we can say that all expressway inter-change entities, religious and nonreligious alike, depend heavily on vehic-ular traffic and impinge significantly upon local ambiance. Although we are not aware of any research to confirm this hunch, we suspect that both shopping malls and megachurches draw a relatively small percentage of their constituents from the immediate vicinity.[5] "It is hard to find a small town or older suburb that has not been disrupted," writes Hayden (178). This helps to explain the local resistance that often arises against large religious facilities, which can become mixed with local prejudices when the new presence is non-Christian and/or non-white.

Some megachurches qualify as "area congregations" in our typology, such as Hebron Baptist Church near Atlanta (Eiesland 2000, 196) and Calvary Church in suburban Chicago, but many if not most megachurches locate in easily accessible suburban areas in order to draw spiritual seekers from across an entire metropolis (Weiss and Lowell 2002, 327; Karnes et al. 2007; Evans-Cowley and Pearlman 2008, 205). The founding pastor of Willow Creek Community Church in suburban Chicago, for example, told a journal-ist who marveled at the church's weekly attendance of fifteen thousand in the mid-1990s (Trueheart 1996, 53), "There are two million people within a one-hour drive of this place. In business parlance, we've got two percent of market share. We've got a long way to go." One church's motto captures the sentiment: "The difference is worth the distance!" (Thumma 1996, 203).

We can note some instructive analogies between megachurches and immigrant temples like HTGC that locate near expressway interchanges. The most obvious is the size of the constituent base. These are large congregations serving thousands, and in this sense we can call HTGC a megatemple. Of course, the megachurch phenomenon is more than a matter of numbers, despite the attention often paid to this aspect (e.g., by Vaughan 1993). Large churches have been around in the United States for more than a century (Tomasi 1975, 138–40; Chaves 2006, 340; Thumma, Travis, and Bird 2005, 1). The ambiance and strategies of paradigmatic seeker megachurches like Willow Creek set them apart as a post–World War II trend (Sargeant 2000, 8; cf. Eiesland 2000, 224, n. 28). Thus, Willow Creek (begun 1975) and HTGC (incorporated 1977) are both prod-ucts of the new urban era.

Seeker megachurches and immigrant megatemples serve niche clienteles. Seeker megachurches have been phenomenally successful in addressing the spiritual and personal needs of mobile, middle-class suburbanites (Sargeant 2000). In their study of immigrant religious groups in metropolitan Houston, Ebaugh and Chafetz (2000, 25) found a preponderance of niche-type congregations "composed of members who live widely dispersed throughout a metropolitan area and are drawn to the institution because of some specialized identity in terms of ethnicity, style of worship, interests, or other tastes."

The nature of "membership" in both seeker megachurches and immigrant megatemples offers another useful analogy. Commitment to formal membership in the organization is fluid and participation in programming beyond large public activities is limited. Megachurches attempt to draw the anonymous crowds into core Christian commitment, especially through involvement in small groups that offer social intimacy. But as Kimon Sargeant notes, further research should "assess how good a job seeker churches actually do of moving people from the crowd to the core." Willow Creek staff members themselves have estimated that as many as two-thirds of the attendees at seeker services do not advance toward the level of commitment the church desires of them (Sargeant 2000, 221–22, n. 28). The majority of HTGC attendees likewise appear satisfied with less intimate participation in temple activities, due largely to the individual and family orientation of Hindu worship. In other words, neither HTGC nor the typical seeker megachurch provides *gemeinschaftlich* relationships for the majority of their large clienteles.

Yet in their small groups, megachurches offer "micro-intimacy" and take a "very thoughtful approach to building community," in the words of sociologist Robert Putnam (quoted in Hinkle 2006, 32). "The communities they create," observes sociologist Robert Wuthnow about the small group movement in churches, including megachurches, "are seldom frail. People feel cared for. They help one another" (quoted in Hinkle 2006, 32). The same can be said of megatemples, at least to a degree, as our evidence points to emerging small groups among some of the youth as well as elderly grandparents at HTGC. Whether congregations represent enclaves of spiritual seekers or immigrants, they create cultural communities amidst the social constellations near the expressway interchanges of the new metropolis.

Congregational Action: Territorial Presence,
Social Distance

The Hindu Temple of Greater Chicago chose to locate in the Lemont area, not because its constituents lived there but because they could drive there. Hindu temples like HTGC stand out on the cultural landscape as monuments of America's increasing religious diversity. But unlike the majority of immigrant religious centers in the classical period of American immigration, and unlike some other recent immigrant religious centers, these temples do not anchor neighborhood enclaves. Constituents cannot gaze upon a temple's *gopuram* from their homes as Catholics in an ethnic neighborhood once gazed upon the parish church steeple.

Given its striking territorial presence and its importance as a religious and cultural center, HTGC draws many curious visitors each week, including local high school and college students studying Hinduism. The public relations committee provides information and tours in order to "enhance the image of the temple" in the eyes of the larger community (Bylaw 9). This function as a metropolitan attraction for non-Hindus was anticipated from the beginning. In 1986, months before the dedication of the first structure on the site, the temple's president said that he expected 20 percent of the estimated fifty to a hundred thousand annual visitors to be non-Hindu tourists. That translates into between ten and twenty thousand tourists coming to Lemont from across the metropolitan region. A busload of senior citizens from the northwest side of Chicago had already been there (Johnson 1986). Whatever the actual numbers over the years, the tourist function remains an important consideration for both the temple and Lemont.

HTGC's organizational ecology—that is, its pattern of interaction with other groups and entities (Kniss and Numrich 2007, chap. 10; cf. Eiesland and Warner 1998)—typifies an enclave metro congregation that is socially distant and relatively uninvolved in its locale. A schematic representation of the temple's primary relationships would show linkages to Hindu individuals, families, and groups scattered throughout the metropolitan region, the United States, and the world, including the Indian homeland of its founding immigrant generation. For instance, the temple's humanitarian committee coordinates relief efforts for the needy in India and in metropolitan Chicago and other parts of the United States. This outward orientation is similar to the organizational ecology of nearby Argonne National Laboratory, whose primary relationships are with the national and international scientific community (see Buschman [1973], 80–85). The temple draws both Indian pilgrims and non-Indian tourists to Lemont who eventually all go home. Argonne may actually have more employees living in the immediate vicinity than HTGC's constituents.[6]

"When asked for any assistance with local needs, they [the temple] have been very generous and always seem eager to help," explained a spokesperson from the Village of Lemont (e-mail message to authors, January 7, 2009). The temple has sponsored a food drive in support of the Lemont pantry for the poor around Thanksgiving. HTGC cooperates with village authorities during major religious festivals that require overflow parking lots, shuttle service, and traffic control. But such minimal involvement reinforces HTGC's status as an enclave of relative strangers in the Lemont area. "As far as public holidays go, they have their own very well-attended religious celebrations throughout the year and do not really participate in [Lemont] community festivals, etc.," noted the village spokesperson. "They are always gracious about inviting the [Lemont] elected officials and staff to any celebration they are having. We consider them very good neighbors."

The temple's relationship with Lemont can be characterized as amicable but not particularly close. This has been the case from the beginning. In the same newspaper article that discussed the temple's tourist function (Johnson 1986), Lemont's village administrator reflected on the reaction to the new addition on a bluff outside of town: it "hasn't generated waves of excitement in Lemont," the reporter summarized his opinion. Quoting the village official directly: "It appears to me that most of their followers are pretty well-established, and, sure, there might be some spinoff where some of them might discover the town and build a house here or something like that. But I haven't heard people say, 'Oh, there's going to be a boom here.' People are aware what's there, and it doesn't seem to create real strong emotions in either direction." Even so, the village administrator thought the locals would mostly welcome the newcomers.

A few years later, when Lemont annexed the temple's property, he had more to say, again intimating some ambivalence about the relationship between the temple and the town. On the one hand, the temple would bring Lemont no tax revenues. On the other hand, he thought the addition gave the village "a little prestige," but not in and of itself. Rather, it could lead to annexation of commercial property next to the temple ("Temple Annexation Brings 'Prestige'").

HTGC's primary congregational action is its striking territorial claim on a bluff outside of Lemont. A Hindu temple complex proclaims a new ethno-religious presence on the suburban landscape, thus posing an implicit challenge to the racial/ethnic stratification of the new metropolis. We note the irony of both territorial presence in and social distance from its locale.

Urban Impact: The Effects of Internal Focus, Congregational Action, and Spatial Type

HTGC exerts weak urban influence due to three factors. First, the temple focuses most of its energy on its constituents' ethno-religious needs. It has succeeded in cultivating a pan-Indian Hindu communal identity by negotiating internal variations in beliefs, rituals, and social (that is, ethnic/regional) groups. It provides mutual support in the face of social boundaries between the Indian minority and the larger American society. This is all important work, and typical of the internal focus of all congregations (Ammerman n.d.). HTGC has chosen to expend less energy externally.

Second, HTGC's weak influence on its urban surroundings also stems from its minimal congregational action, primarily through its territorial presence. Here again the megachurch analogy is instructive. The physical size of many megachurches catches the eye (Goldberger 1995). Both megachurches and megatemples can function as architectural magnets for their respective niche clienteles and thus both can be labeled "modern American cathedrals."[7] Both may thereby seem "out of place" as residents, passersby, and perhaps even attendees sense that cathedrals do not "belong" here in the way they did in urban neighborhoods of a previous era (cf. Cresswell 1999). As one of our interviewees put it, the trend toward big churches in cornfields is disturbing. Indeed, "cornfield" imagery has become emblematic of suburban and exurban religious transformation in the Midwest, as megachurches, mosques, and temples spring up in previously rural settings (e.g., Ostling 1993; Muck 1988). Something new—and unsettling to some—has staked a territorial claim on the local landscape. When that territorial claim represents an enclave relationship with its locale, it can further unsettle the local population.

The question of territorial longevity deserves comment here. The significant cultural and capital investments of a temple like HTGC bode better for long-term occupancy than for-profit enterprises that benefit from government subsidies and accelerated depreciation (Hayden 2003,

162–64) or nondescript megachurches that may more readily abandon their sites and move to other locations. "If megachurches fail to achieve a level of sustainability," states a study of megachurches and urban sprawl, "they will leave behind abandoned complexes where green space once stood" (Weiss and Lowell 2002, 325). Immigrant religious facilities with minimal cultural and capital investments in a particular site can more readily relocate to suit their needs. But HTGC has made a long-term territorial commitment to Lemont that could evolve into a closer relationship in the future.

The third factor that contributes to HTGC's weak urban influence is its status as a metro congregation. Due at least in part to the metro-wide residential dispersion of its constituents, the urban impact of this type of congregation is structurally limited. These are not neighborhood congregations. Trueheart's (1996, 47) observation about megachurches holds in many ways for megatemples as well: "People may drive forty-five minutes to an hour to get to a church like this—but then, as normal Americans, they're in the habit. [Quoting from an interviewee:] 'People don't work in their neighborhoods. People don't shop in their neighborhoods. People don't go to the movies in their neighborhoods. So why should anyone expect them to go to church in their neighborhoods? They'll drive right by small churches in their neighborhood to get to attend a larger one that offers more in the way of services or programs.'"

"Because members do not share a common residential neighborhood," write Ebaugh and Chafetz (2000, 25), "niche congregations tend not to be involved in local neighborhood affairs" (cf. Ebaugh, O'Brien, and Chafetz 2000). The organizational ecology of niche congregations can easily "jump over" their locale in order to connect with other places and groups, such as through inner-city ministries, global missions, or transnational networks. Megachurches seem to engage in relatively more local service programs than The Hindu Temple of Greater Chicago (Sargeant 2000, 125, 174, 200; Thumma 1996, 211–12; Thumma, Travis, and Bird 2005, 9; Hinkle 2006, 30–31), but the tendency toward incidental rather than integral social and civic relationships to the immediate vicinity seems analogous.

Immigrant metro congregations like The Hindu Temple of Greater Chicago create cultural enclaves that serve their constituents well, but at the same time they contribute to the diminishing sense of social-geographic community identity. This does not have to be the case. An enclave metro congregation can choose to become more locally involved. Bhardwaj and Rao (1998, 141) reported in the late 1990s that Hindu temples in the United States "have started to participate in a broader spectrum of community activities such as humanitarian service, even promoting Habitat for Humanity." "In this respect," the authors continue, "the Hindu temple has become more like a Christian church rather than remaining only a center of worship." Of course, the implication here that Christian churches are integrally involved in their locales needs nuance—as we know, the extent of local involvement varies among congregations no matter what the religious identity.

Some observers unequivocally tout the positive contributions of recent immigrants to American society. The presence of Hindu temples and more immigrant suburbanites than ever before are good things, editorialized the *Chicago Sun-Times* ("A Positive Outgrowth"). "That this is good for the immigrants, good for the suburbs, and good for the country cannot be emphasized too much, since there is a small, vocal and mistaken element of nativists who argue that immigration is a bad thing, citing various economic theories to disguise what is, at heart, xenophobia." The real story of the immigrant congregation's role in the new metropolis is more complicated than this, as we have seen.

The Moody Church and New Life Community Church: Metro Congregation Counter Cases
The Moody Church: Evangelical Mission to the Metropolis

The Moody Church and its related organizations, such as Moody Bible Institute and the radio station WMBI, are world-renowned evangelical Protestant institutions born out of the missionary energy of Dwight L. Moody (1837–1899).[8] Since 1915 the church has been located at 1635 North LaSalle Street, along the border between the Near North Side and Lincoln Park, two of Chicago's wealthiest community areas. In the 1990s less than 15 percent of the congregation's official members lived in these two community areas, less than 10 percent lived within a one-mile radius of the church, and nearly 50 percent lived more than ten miles away and throughout the Chicago metropolitan region (Figure 7.2). The present commanding edifice, which melds Romanesque and Byzantine styles, was built in 1925 and seats 3,800. Its non-pillared auditorium and curved balcony were constructed to direct all worshippers' eyes toward the

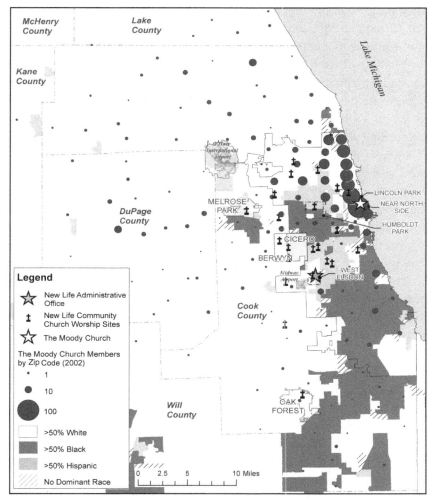

FIGURE 7.2. The Moody Church Members and New Life Community Church Locations. Map by David J. Treering and Melissa Gesbeck Howell, Loyola University Chicago.

central pulpit and the cantilevered construction contains almost perfect acoustics. The upholstered theater seats and red-carpeted aisles add to the elegant ambiance.

A typical worship service begins with the fifty-voice choir filing into the choir stalls high above and behind the pulpit platform. The small orchestra on the platform accompanied them on a recent Sunday as they sang traditional hymns, "Take My Life and Let It Be" and "Come, All Christians, Be Committed." The congregation is about 20 percent non-white, with a notable presence of Asians and somewhat fewer blacks and Latinos. In the tradition of American evangelical worship culture, formalized ritual is minimized in favor of testimonies, preaching, and congregational singing. On this day, the jumbotron screens flanking the choir stalls presented a young, white, apparently middle-class couple recounting their friendship with a church member who was homeless. They were particularly clear about how their relationship with someone who was not "like them" led to deeper reflection about their Christian stance in the world. The service continued with the congregation singing "We Are God's People" and a reading from Matthew 25:31-40 that included the familiar text, "Lord, when did we see you hungry and fed you, or thirsty and gave you to drink? And when did we see you a stranger and welcomed you, or naked and clothed you? And when did we see you sick or in prison and visited you?" Singing was vigorous, as usual, but our researcher took note of how many more hands were raised and bodies swayed when the music leader, on his guitar, began a Christian-rock-style praise song, "Everlasting God."

Rev. Dr. Erwin Lutzer, who has led the church for thirty-three years, preached on the theme of "The Compassionate Community: The Touch of Jesus," drawing on the story in Mark 5 about the woman who touched the hem of Jesus's garment in the effort to be healed of a twelve-year affliction. Dr. Lutzer began by asserting that "Jesus loved outcasts and marginalized people," such as this woman who was considered "unclean," and that "he broke with [Jewish] protocol by touching her" so that she would be healed. Pastor Lutzer invited the congregation to connect with marginalized and poor members of society today "in the streets of Chicago, in banks and hospitals or wherever You [God] put us." He acknowledged the ministry program by Moody women who rescue young girls from sex trafficking in Chicago. He then reminded his listeners that "Jesus will do the final miracle" and "to thank God for a savior who actually saves." The congregation was mostly quiet as they listened, but clapped when they appreciated a particular point, notably when the pastor referred to the saving power of Jesus. The service concluded with an "old song" requested by Pastor Lutzer, "There Is a Fountain Filled with Blood, Drawn from Emmanuel's Vein" by nineteenth-century hymnist William Cowper, and an altar call that the church refers to as "Prayer Partners." Over the span of our observations beginning in the mid-1990s, Moody has continued to provide a formal and not particularly emotional service, but, in the words of one researcher, "very classy."

The Moody Church is led by a large, multiracial, and mixed-gender staff of thirty-seven that includes eleven pastors (all of the latter males). Several small-group activities provide the intimacy that the Sunday worship lacks, including twenty age-graded and status groups that meet before and after the Sunday morning service, engaging in Bible study targeted to their interests. The college and university group meets additionally on Thursday evenings for dinner, Bible study, and worship. Each Wednesday evening, the church holds an open prayer and Bible study that mixes song, preaching, and prayers for needs brought to the attention of the church's staff. Pastor Charles Butler typically opens the session at the piano, playing and singing familiar hymns. Prayer for global conversions is often raised, as Dr. Lutzer has embraced a particular concern for the conversion of Muslims through his preaching and publications. Among the eleven "ministries" active at Moody is The Artists Circle that meets on Sunday evenings. They describe themselves as "a network of artists who are eager to connect with other artists in the church, learn to think biblically about the arts, and engage and shape culture through compelling art that is borne out of a biblical worldview" (http://www.moodychurch.org/artist-circle/, accessed November 19, 2013). The group recently produced "Reflections," an eighty-five-page literary journal of work by members of the church.

Moody Church has made strategic decisions to remain in the city and has periodically revisited its original mandate to make the city a better place for its residents. That mandate originated with Dwight L. Moody, who came to Chicago in 1856 to work as a shoe salesman but instead met the urban poor. Moody established a Sunday school and a mission church for the slum residents living along the north branch of the Chicago River and worked through the YMCA, serving as its president from 1865 to 1871. He co-founded Moody Bible Institute in 1889 to train Christian workers for the "neglected masses of Chicago" (Gilbert 2004), mainly impoverished European immigrants.

A potential turning point came in the 1960s as many of the church's white members began moving to the suburbs. Senior pastor Alan Redpath laid out a theological rationale for staying in the city at the 1960 annual meeting of the National Association of Evangelicals held in Chicago. Redpath also accomplished the integration of Moody's membership in 1962, reversing a whites-only trend initiated by a previous pastor in 1915.

We observed the legacy of this shift during our primary research period, as the non-white attendance at Sunday worship services, Wednesday Bible studies, and other regular programmatic activities exceeded 20 percent of the total number. As Figure 7.2 implies, Moody's evangelical theology attracts constituents across the racial/ethnic boundaries of metropolitan Chicago.

Under senior pastor George Sweeting's leadership in the late 1960s, the congregation conducted a survey of its members and made a study of its locale, concluding in a report that the church should serve three local groups: well-off families moving into Lincoln Park, students and young singles living in the Near North Side, and poor black residents of the Cabrini-Green Homes public housing project. The congregation appealed to the first two groups through changes in its Sunday evening adult education program. The report proposed that Moody Bible Institute students should tutor Cabrini-Green children and that The Moody Church should tap its network of Christian businessmen to find employment for black males. The report put the motivation in this way ("Report to the Board of Moody Church"): "We would strongly recommend that Moody Church make plans to minister to the nearly 20,000 Negroes, half of whom are children under 18 who live within the shadow of the church. We are well aware of the attitudes on the part of some toward involving oneself in the racial issue. It seems inconceivable to us that a church that sends $1,000,000.00 a year to evangelize people of another color miles across the sea can ignore them on their back porch."

In the 1990s The Moody Church offered several programs that modified local urban life. Two that continue today are of particular interest. A preschool called the Children's Learning Center has grown steadily. The Center offers poor working mothers both practical assistance in watching their children and spiritual support in their own lives. Single Focus has ministered to adult singles especially on the North Side of Chicago, seeking to provide points of connection for those without family ties and/or sources of spiritual support.

In addition to these programs, Moody also provided opportunities to serve the needy across the city through its Branch Ministries partnerships with major Christian social outreach organizations. Today these number thirteen, including Gospel Outreach, an after-school club for inner-city children; Inner City Impact, which provides after-school activities as an alternative to gang life; and Love and Action Midwest, an outreach program to HIV/AIDS victims ("Missionary Preparation Program Handbook,"

56–57). The Branch Ministries flier we saw contrasted Moody's approach to the perceived indifference of many evangelical Protestants toward the needs of the city. "Here at Moody," the flier stated, "as we seek to 'become known in Chicago as a caring culturally diverse community,' we must recognize a God given call to be sacrificially involved in helping to meet these needs."

Despite these significant programmatic efforts, we earlier judged Moody's work in the city as neither central to the congregation's identity nor up to the standards set by its founder (Price 1996, 81–82). We felt that the congregation's commitment to the urban poor was overshadowed by Dwight L. Moody's other emphasis, global evangelism. But we discovered during a follow-up visit that the church had reevaluated its work in the city and instituted significant changes. A new Children's Ministry served Cabrini-Green children identified by the public schools as having the "greatest need" for extra help with their schoolwork. The Chicago Housing Authority gave over two floors of a Cabrini high-rise on the condition that the church remodel them. The Children's Ministry served fifty elementary school students three days a week, with home visits on Fridays. As many as fifty volunteers participated in the ministry, including recruits from other local churches, while the six-person multiracial staff included three black Cabrini-Green residents. Today, the Children's Ministry initiative has expanded into a tutoring and mentoring program called By the Hand Club for Kids that serves four impoverished locations around the city, reaching more than eight hundred children by their account (http://www.bythehand.org, accessed June 19, 2009). The founder of the club, Donnita Travis (who is white), was named a 2012 Chicagoan of the Year by *Chicago* magazine. In a YouTube interview, Travis asserted that the program addresses the children's "mind, body, and soul" (http://www.youtube.com/watch?v=t_0BEGRNCbU, accessed November 19, 2013). Another program that continues today, the Sidewalk Sunday School, began as a pilot project in the summer of 2000 under the direction of a black Moody staff person and was held in Stuart Park near Cabrini-Green. The program grew dramatically the following summer to serve an average of between 200 and 250 children every Saturday for twelve weeks. It has also included home visits by teams of Moody volunteers from the beginning.

It is possible that these new ministries aimed at Cabrini-Green residents were influenced by similar programs conducted by other local churches, including Fourth Presbyterian Church. In fact, we suspect that Moody's leaders were motivated by our research to take stock of their local mission (Price 1996; 2000). Even so, the motivation for these changes was complex and certainly included a desire to recapture the spirit of Dwight L. Moody. This was not just about providing social services, but also about outreach rooted in an understanding of community. Pastor Erwin Lutzer explained to us that he designated 2002 as the year of community, focusing his sermons on "the variety of ways community is formed, for example in small groups, in service, in suffering." "The success of a church," he continued, "depends on the ability of members to bind to one another," emphasizing that this is more important than "the architecture, the music, and the preaching." The church encourages a variety of small groups, some focused on Bible study and others around different interests. Their purpose, however, in the words of Pastor Lutzer, is to be "vehicles for sociability."

The investment that Moody has made, particularly its increased commitment to reaching impoverished people, and increasingly non-white people, is driven significantly by the church's historic understandings of evangelism and service mission. But in the new urban era, this understanding is interlaced with particular leadership decisions that have varied in their emphases on outreach. It is fair to say that in the 1990s, this aspect of mission waned in favor of global evangelization, that is, an emphasis on the exotic "other." In the 2000s the "other" next door became a reality in a new way, benefiting from leadership decisions of a more entrepreneurial kind. The result is a strong impact on the church's urban environment.

New Life Community Church: Connected to Multiple Places

On a cold Sunday morning in April 2012, New Life Community Church's Rogers Park campus (as they refer to their church sites) held an immersion baptism in the parking lot of the neighborhood YMCA, where they had begun offering services the month prior. Two young men and a young woman, barefoot and wearing casual clothes covered by a New Life tee shirt, took turns being baptized by their lay mentors. Wrapped in a towel, each gave a heartfelt testimony despite the chilly air that made our researcher shiver inside her jacket. The older of the two men narrated his spiritual journey through a troubled life. He concluded that "nothing else worked for me. This worked for me." The young woman spoke about her uninspired Catholic upbringing. "I stopped going to church in high school but then one of my friends at work asked if I would come to church with her. I started to like going to church again." All the newly baptized spoke emotionally about their mentors. "I wouldn't have been able to come this far without her," said the young woman. "[Mentor] gave me what I needed. She worked with me in understanding how Christ could be a part of my life. She brought me through every step."

New Life Community Church offers an intriguing institutional model for a metro congregation. Through ministries offered at several dispersed sites but under a central administration, the nondenominational New Life Church is experimental, youthful, and quick to address the needs of residents in its multiple locations in the city and suburbs.

New Life began as a children's ministry in the Back of the Yards neighborhood in the 1940s, funded by a south suburban businessman. The ministry grew into a congregation that in 1970 bought a former Russian Orthodox Church at 44th Street and Paulina Avenue on the Southwest Side of the city. In 1986 Mark Jobe, who grew up in Spain, became pastor to the congregation that had shrunk to only twenty members by that time. Within two years, however, the congregation was growing again and took the name New Life Community Church.

In 1991 New Life adopted a home-based small-group strategy to expand its reach. In 1996 the church established a second site called Nueva Vida, a Spanish-speaking congregation in the Humboldt Park community area of Chicago. At this writing, New Life has twenty worship sites in the city of Chicago and the suburbs, each with its own pastor (see Figure 7.2 above). Eight of the sites are Spanish speaking. The average weekly attendance at thirty-three Sunday worship services across all sites is a reported 4,500, which qualifies New Life as a kind of aggregate megachurch. The pastoral and administrative staffs are multiracial. The church's administrative office is a converted factory in the West Elsdon community area on Chicago's Southwest Side. As printed in the church's brochure, New Life's vision statement explicitly claims its metro-wide religious jurisdiction: "to change the spiritual landscape of Chicagoland by reaching and teaching 30,000 people with the gospel of Jesus Christ." The church hopes to open forty new campuses by the year 2020. It is worth noting that by centralizing the administrative and pastoral functions, New Life wards off the fissiparous nature of independent Protestant churches without building a single-site megachurch.

Early on, New Life considered planting a new church to accommodate its growth but decided that Chicago "didn't need another storefront church," as Lead Pastor Jobe recounted. What Chicago really needed, New Life decided, was a way to counteract the impersonal, anonymous, and alienating contexts that weigh down on urban residents by facilitating face-to-face, personal contact. They hit upon the idea of dividing the congregation into home-based cell groups led by facilitators and mentors. After experimenting with different leadership styles and reorganizing traditional forms of church programming into home-based activities, they began to craft a "fluid model of church" suited to the mobility and uncertainty of contemporary urban life. Part of that model included incorporating older congregations with declining memberships and "re-birthing" them by building on their histories as local churches while adding contemporary elements of style, music, and preaching.

On Sunday mornings at the High Ridge YMCA, a rock beat greets visitors at the entrance, whether one is there to exercise or to worship. For those indicating they come for church, two enthusiastic greeters will shake their hands. If one follows the sound of the music, s/he will move down the hallway and pass a table where volunteers escort children for child care into four separate rooms. Turning the corner one will see the entrance to the gym where chairs are set up over plastic tarps protecting the wooden floor. Two more friendly greeters pass out church bulletins and offer to find people seats. A nine-piece band plays and sings contemporary praise songs for a half hour with words projected on the wall of the gym next to the basketball backboard. The band members are black, white, and Hispanic, young and middle aged, men and women. The keyboard player is a middle-aged white woman. A twenty-something athletically built white man gives the announcements, followed by the pastor, thirty-something, white, also athletic, with a stylish haircut and goatee. The congregation reflects the population of Rogers Park with regard to age and with approximately equal numbers of blacks, whites, and Hispanics, plus a smaller number of Asians.

New Life's approach is highly personal, tailored for the needs of a physically or emotionally uprooted population. Testimonies are offered every Sunday before the pastor preaches. Ernest related that he grew up Catholic but "was separated from God." He witnessed angry violence by his father against his mother as well as his father's substance abuse. He thought himself a failure in school when, in the second grade, the teacher exclaimed, "Can't you do anything right?" Children taunted him on the playground when his mother came to pick him up. Before long, "I learned that my problems should be dealt with by anger, just as my father had and my grandfather had."

He stopped going to church, but, nonetheless, asserted that "God had a plan for me" when he met his wife (who was sitting in the front row) at a New Year's Eve party. Even though they were happy together, "something was missing." Ernest's anger management problems spun out of control when one day he broke his wife's arm during an argument. "To this day I still apologize to her for that." (At that point Ernest shot her a rueful look.) His wife suggested they go to church and while he reluctantly agreed, he found he couldn't answer the question, "If you died today, do you know if you're going to heaven?" This led to a conversion experience in which he could announce, "The old me was gone. None of us are [sic] worthy but God's grace is offered us every day. I love my wife and my kids as God loves the church." Applause and vocal affirmations greeted his testimony at various points.

With about 150 New Life home groups throughout metropolitan Chicago today, people can find one close to wherever they might move, providing a stable congregational community. "Urban people live with a lot of change and the cell groups can provide a sense of continuity, a sense of stability in their lives," Pastor Jobe says. Our researcher attended an evening cell group meeting of nine parents ranging in age from twenties to forties and whose children were cared for in another room by one of the fathers. After the opening prayer, the group leader passed around an "attendance" list that asked how many people they had invited to the meeting, if they had read their scripture, and who their mentor was. Sharing began with one member who closed on a house that day, located a block away from another family in the group. He planned to start moving on the following Saturday, so anyone who wanted to help was asked to come at 9:00 am. This member talked about reaching out in his new neighborhood, where he and his wife had prayed about being witnesses and had already invited one family to church. Another member announced an upcoming fellowship meal at her house. A third shared what God had been teaching him about using discernment when he wants to be critical of other people. A fourth shared that she went to a bar this past week as a favor to her husband. She said she sat all night drinking water—an amazing thing for her since she used to be a smoker and almost an alcoholic.

Another cell group met at 10:00 am for women working second or third shifts. In this meeting our researcher heard how one of the women begins her job at 8:00 pm and had to work a double shift last week and will do so again next week. As a result she had only been able to get two hours of sleep that day. During prayer time, this woman prayed and cried as she asked for strength to stop getting angry at her husband because she is tired. She prayed for energy to work and take care of her family.

Such small, intimate, lay-led faith groups can be found in many Protestant and Catholic churches as well as the Jewish *havurot*, particularly in large congregations attempting to overcome the experience of urban strangeness among their constituents. Each of New Life's worship sites has its own home groups, but they all fall under a central pastoral leadership team that shares ideas, crafts the general outline of the weekly sermons, and "builds synergy." This last point suggests New Life's urban strategy. As Pastor Jobe explained to us, if churches in one area developed "synergy," they could have more impact on the whole city. As he explained to his staff, his vision included a conviction that they "are a church like no other before in the urban area. A church that needs to be different to reach others."

New Life's emphasis on intentional conversions is a means of "growing" the church in a way that potentially addresses urban structures. "If the church is going to make an impact and grow in the city, it has to focus on [such conversions]," Pastor Jobe explains. He views suburbs as places where young churched families are moving, and thus suburban churches can grow due to transfers. But he claims this does not happen in the city. As a result, New Life teaches its members to develop relationships by "getting out of their shell and finding the many needy people in the city." While we might question the assumption that residents moving into the city are less churched than those moving into suburbs, the material challenges of city life are arguably higher and thus provide a gainful opportunity for a conversion-based ministry.

What specific needs has New Life identified with this model of church? Youth problems are high on the list and New Life hosts a number of youth-led home groups, some with youth who do not belong to the church but are looking for a setting in which they can be "spiritually fed." That may not necessarily mean a Sunday morning worship service. Pastor Asa App pointed out in a mentoring session with youth leaders that bringing youth to worship services is not "touching the youth where they are." Instead, the group worked on developing activities that would build relationships among youth while engaging them in various service projects. One time they handed out food to the homeless on Chicago's Lower Wacker Drive. Pastor App noted that "youth are selfish, but when they serve, they can get very excited about it." A co-leader of another youth group related to our researcher that he works with "guys in gangs," reporting that "the work is really hard." He stated that the "guys try to justify using and selling drugs and are rough, but they keep coming." Another leader quit his engineering job to begin working at a youth center in the Canaryville neighborhood "and do mission work from there." Discussion at the mentoring session expanded to activities the church leaders might do there: "invade the neighborhood, go on a prayer walk, confront people, whatever it took." Related problems identified by Pastor Jobe include the lack of intact families and families without sufficient parental involvement. "Youth workers find themselves doing parental things, asking about school and things. Youth need a place to belong. Sometimes they end up in gangs to belong. This is a trend the church is working on," he told us in the mid-1990s. In the early 2000s New Life Church formed New Life Urban Impact, a nonprofit organization that offers family support services, GED classes, and the Urban Life Skills Program. This last program includes an initiative on youth gangs called Stop the Violence that was featured on the local ABC TV affiliate news in 2009.

Racial/ethnic diversity is another focus of New Life's urban ministries. In a staff meeting we attended, Pastor Jobe stated that the church should contain people "from every background, every walk of life, every race, every socioeconomic class." He argues that the home-based cell model combined with Sunday worship celebration helps to bridge differences. "Two different races may not be going to the same cell group during the week, but they celebrate together on Sunday. A professional with a college degree working downtown does not have much in common with the new immigrant with broken English, so being in the same cell group is difficult, but they can worship together on Sunday, can meet each other and connect in that way." Pastor Jobe related this to us in the mid-1990s. Recently, he asserted that economic barriers are even harder to bridge, what he calls a "financial cultural divide" ("A Culture of Generosity"). Based on our observations at worship services and home groups, the majority of New Life's members are Hispanic, followed by about 20 percent white and 10 percent black members. Based on our observations as well as the locations of the church sites, most members are blue-collar, though a significant number appear to be middle class, especially in the recently opened sites on Chicago's North Side.

New Life espouses a conservative, patriarchal theology but does not have an authoritarian, pastor-driven church hierarchy. The decentralized organization emphasizes lay leadership development as well as personal mentoring by lay members. Each campus has a board of elders that is responsible for that church. A gendered division of labor has become an acceptable structure in which men preach but both women and men undertake social, spiritual, and personal guidance for prospective members. Moving members toward baptism is a mark of mature Christian discipleship. As a result, and despite institutional limitations, women share in a visible mentoring role without challenging male leadership, which helps to explain New Life's rapid growth. As mentioned above, full immersion baptisms are performed by the mentors and leaders rather than the pastors. Worship celebrations are led by the pastors and focus on teaching and preaching. Indeed, strong emotional attachments are often formed with home-group mentors and leaders, more so than with the pastors, nurturing personal loyalty and commitment.

New Life Community Church combines the intimacy of a *gemeinschaftlich* community with a flexible organizational structure. Its conservative but non-authoritarian theology aims to provide both stability and hospitality for urbanites facing economic displacement, immigration issues, and other challenges. Urban historian Lewis Mumford (1938) characterized the city as a place of diversity, complexity, and spontaneity. A church that has the flexibility and willingness to experiment with what it offers urbanites is likely to survive, and even thrive, in the new urban era. Such a church can also develop a high moderate urban impact.

The Urban Impact of Metro Congregations

Metro-type congregations tend to have a weaker impact on the urban environment than the neighborhood and area types. This stems primarily from the broad spatial distribution of a metro congregation's constituency, which makes it difficult to focus on a particular locale, such as the neighborhood or community area in which the congregation's site is located. New Life Community Church offers a different model from what we hypothesized regarding spatial types: it is both metro and neighborhood in that centripetal administrative energies combine with centrifugal services that address local needs. That said, the metro congregations featured in this chapter vary in their urban impact, from weak (The Hindu Temple of Greater Chicago) to high moderate (New Life) to strong (The Moody Church). They also vary with regard to the hypothesized tendency that a strong internal focus produces a relatively weak urban impact: this holds for HTGC but not for New Life. These variations can be explained by differences in location, congregational traits, and congregational action across the two groupings.

HTGC is located in an isolated suburban place, on bluff property outside of town, whereas Moody and New Life are located in dense urban places, multiple locations in New Life's case. Social-geographic isolation combines with a particular set of congregational traits to diminish the urban impact of HTGC. Its ethno-religious minority status is a powerful limiting factor. Congregational bonding around mutual support, internal social similarities, and high boundary maintenance to the larger society creates an ethno-religious safe harbor for both immigrant and American-born generations. The temple may be an enclave of strangers in its locale, but its constituents are not strangers amongst themselves. The need for solidarity overcomes internal congregational differences in beliefs and rituals, as well as the modest level of internal social ties that stems from megatemple size, an episodic ritual schedule, and individual and family-based worship style.

The locations of Moody and New Life combine with a different set of congregational traits to enhance their urban impact. Moody's hierarchical pastoral leadership invoked the congregation's heritage of socially engaged evangelicalism to capitalize on the church's central location, launching a series of new service projects to the city's poor. A high level of internal solidarity around evangelical beliefs, worship, and norms, along with an increasingly diverse racial/ethnic constituency, lowered the congregation's boundaries to the city's needy residents. New Life shares several congregational traits with Moody—a high level of internal solidarity around beliefs, worship, and norms, racial/ethnic diversity, and low boundaries to the city—differing from Moody in its geographically decentralized organizational model and semi-democratized leadership, which also enhance New Life's urban impact.

Particular kinds of congregational action also help to explain the differential urban impacts of the metro congregations in this chapter. Moody and New Life make wider jurisdictional claims than HTGC, asserting spiritual and social responsibility for the entire populace and initiating programs that challenge urban inequality across the metropolitan region. Moreover, their diverse racial/ethnic constituencies stand over against both the demographic polarization of the new metropolis and the typical homogeneity of American Christian congregations, and their service programs and mission activities target a wide audience. New Life stakes the greatest territorial claim on the metropolis of all these cases with its dispersed network of congregational "campuses."

As noted earlier with regard to Hindu temples across the country, weak urban impact is not a necessary outcome for ethno-religious minority congregations. Neither is weak urban impact inevitable for the metro-type congregation nor for a congregation with a strong focus on the needs of its own constituents. Congregational traits and action can, in different ways, enhance a congregation's effect on the urban environment, as The Moody Church and New Life Community Church illustrate.

PART III

Religion's Urban Significance: Chicago and Beyond

8

Congregations and Change

INTERPRETING RELIGION'S SIGNIFICANCE
IN THE NEW METROPOLIS

IN THIS BOOK we have argued that to grasp how Chicago metropolitan life has changed over the last several decades, religion must be part of the story. Through our examination of fifteen Chicago congregations—Catholic parishes, Protestant churches, Jewish synagogues, Muslim mosques, and a Hindu temple, city and suburban, neighborhood-based and commuter—we described congregational life and measured congregational influences on the urban environment from the mid-1990s to the present. We examined the economic, political, and social changes of this new environment and how they affect the kinds of community life these congregations have created and maintain. In doing so, we employed a multidimensional analysis that did not privilege structural factors over cultural influences or underestimate the meaning of individual and group action.

We created three analytical categories by which we assessed the role of each congregation in shaping its urban surroundings: the spatial residential distribution of its constituents, its internal congregational traits, and external actions directed beyond its constituency. We developed a summary measure of impact along a continuum of weak to moderate to strong, thus providing a new understanding of the significance of the religion factor in the contemporary American urban context. We also gained important insights into the nature of each congregation's community life. The present chapter pulls together the key findings about congregational community life and congregational urban impact from the chapters of Part II. It also brings forward several implications of our research into broader questions, namely, the effects of late modernity on the ability of religious communities to create lasting social and moral bonds and the nature and degree of the influence religion has on matters of social change.

Congregational Community in the New Metropolis

Chapter 2 described the powerful urban dynamics that challenge the creation and maintenance of a place-based cultural community—that is, a local collection of people who engage in common activities and share an identity based on beliefs, values, social intimacy, and personal concern and loyalty. Chapter 2 also noted that congregations continue to account for a ubiquitous form of urban community, while chapters 3 through 7 provided ethnographic accounts of the unsentimentalized religious communities created and maintained by selected congregations in metropolitan Chicago in response to—perhaps in spite of—the constraints of the contemporary urban context.

Two topics deserve further consideration at this point in our analysis of religion and community in the new urban era: the need for community and the distinctively religious form of community.

The Need for Community in the New Urban America

Our analysis has been helpfully informed by the Los Angeles School of urbanism's description of the "postmetropolis" (Edward Soja's term), which portrays the contemporary urban experience as increasingly polarized, decentered, fragmented, and anxious. In the new metropolis, "the real and imagined problems" of urban life can be found anywhere (Soja 2000, 260). At the same time, the new metropolis removes or inhibits constitutive places for community to grow in response to the problems of urban life. The LA School has been criticized for its "relentlessly noir interpretation of the urban condition" (Judd 2011, 7; cf. Bridges 2011, 79), yet judicious use of its insights can be fruitful. Soja points out that "new forms and combinations of social spatiality and territorial identity" (152) can be found in the new metropolis and that notions of identity, community, and association are being re-formed amidst a "scene of creative new 'hybridities' and a cultural politics aimed not just at reducing inequalities but also at preserving difference and fostering flexible 'transversal' identities" (155). Such developments cast light on the shadows of the noir metropolis, and congregations have been involved in them.

The LA School is fond of characterizing the new urban era as "post-modern" (e.g., Soja 1989; 2000, 111; Dear 2000; Dear and Flusty 2002; Dear and Dahmann 2011, 66–71). We find the notion of "late modern" more compelling, particularly with regard to the need for community in the new metropolis. Sociologist Zygmunt Bauman (2001) has argued that late modernity's emphasis on individual freedom and autonomy undermines the fundamental attribute of community belonging—possessing a secure identity. Bauman (2013, 5) writes: "In multiple ways the word 'solidarity' is patiently looking for flesh which it could become. And it won't stop seeking eagerly and passionately until it succeeds." This is the perduring human desire for community in late modern mode.

Social philosopher Marshall Berman (1988, 345) has described modernity as the experience of living in a "maelstrom" in which our social and personal worlds are in "perpetual disintegration and renewal, trouble and anguish, ambiguity and contradiction . . . ." In offering a critical view of modernity that focuses on the changing intersection of time and space, sociologists Roger Friedland and Deirdre Boden (1994: 42) state that "[i]dentities and narratives have historically been grounded in place, revolving around powerful and sacred centers. Now the cultural calculus of self, time, and space—that collective 'structure of feeling' that Raymond Williams has stressed as linking social groups to a particular place and time—is changing." Friedland and Boden continue (10): "We live in a world where the territorial maps and temporal schedules that constitute modernity make less and less sense." This despite the equally modern, rational assumption that individuals can create a future in which progress has the capacity for both destruction of the old and reconstruction of the new (Berman 1988).

One of our early colleagues in the Religion and Urban America Program, Matthew Price, offered a piquant view of the modernist pursuit: "I do believe that there is social change, but I see it mainly coming out of attempts at preservation rather than transformation, acts of preservation that in the long run may turn out to be transformative, but which do not necessarily start with that intention" (personal communication, 1995). One of those "acts of preservation" is undoubtedly the effort to retain or rebuild community. As group size expanded in the move from rural to urban life, the forms of relationships changed (per Simmel) and reliable bonds had to be reconstituted in new conditions. As Berman noted, while industrial workers found a new basis for solidarity, the fleeting conditions in industry have shown the temporary nature of those collectivities and thrown people into perpetual flux. "How can any lasting human bonds grow in such loose and shifting soil?" asked Berman (1988, 104). Congregational communities provide one answer to his question.

The Distinctively Religious Form of Community in the New Urban Era

To be clear, we are also persuaded that the complexities of contemporary conditions have yielded diverse trajectories of change close to what S. I. Eisenstadt (2000) usefully terms "multiple modernities." Thus the relationship between religion and modern society takes different forms in different regions and cultures of the world, unlike the prediction that religion will decline with increasing economic and social modernity, as appears to be happening in Europe (Berger, Davie, and Fokas 2008). Since religion has not declined in the new urban era, we must ask what need it addresses for adherents, specifically through urban congregations. Since the generic human need for community can be satisfied by any number of local associations and arrangements, what is the distinctively religious component of congregational community that attracts individuals?

In our understanding, "religion" is a worldview grounded in perceptions of a reality that both transcends the material world and imbues it with sacred meaning and purpose. Thus, a religious perspective on urban life purports to come from somewhere beyond the metropolis, offering a larger significance to the adherent's urban experience and to the congregation's urban communal life. The Catholic, Protestant, Jewish, Muslim, and Hindu congregations in this book differ widely in many obvious respects, but they all apply a fundamentally religious perspective to the urban experience. This is the religious component of congregational community that distinguishes it from other communal entities that perform many of the same social functions.

The notion of sacred space or place in the phenomenology of religion field is helpful in this regard. Religions identify particular places as "sacred" or qualitatively different from other places. Such a place functions as a religious "focusing lens": "A sacred place focuses attention on the forms, objects, and actions in it and reveals them as bearers of religious meaning" (J. Brereton 2005, 7978, drawing on Jonathan Z. Smith). A sacred place can be constructed as such and thus obvious to outsiders—a church, synagogue, mosque, temple, and so on. An otherwise non-sacred place can also be designated as sacred through jurisdictional claims on the urban environment that are less obvious to outsiders, as in the Catholic understanding of a geographic parish or the Jewish notion of an *eruv*. Theologian John McCarthy (2013) extends the meaning of the *eruv* as sacred space by suggesting it is an inversion of urban space, that is, a suspension of conventional laws of motion. The space of the house is relocated for the period of Shabbat, thus permitting certain kinds of well-defined movement outside of the household. The *eruv* becomes a "hyperspace" in which symbolic representations are more real than the geographic reality of the city or neighborhood itself. McCarthy goes beyond our jurisdictional claim for the *eruv* by asserting that it makes a transformational one.

"To call a place sacred asserts that a place, its structure, and its symbols express fundamental cultural values and principles. By giving these visible form, the sacred place makes tangible the corporate identity of a people and their world" (J. Brereton 2005, 7984–85). From a sociological perspective, a sacred place brings together action and structure in a way that helps us understand how the political economy of the metropolis is produced and controlled through the culture work that individuals and groups do to make space for themselves and others (Eiesland 1997). Within their sacred spaces, congregations create moral communities and continually leverage them against the demands of the larger urban environment, such as new immigration, job insecurity, racism, consumerism, and various forms of political, social, and economic control. Hence, as McCarthy (2013) illustrates, "the holy continues to play a role within a variety of urban spaces."

In this way, congregational communities provide a distinctively religious answer to Marshall Berman's (1988, 104) question noted above: How can "any lasting human bonds" grow in the "loose and shifting soil" of the new metropolis? The answer lies in religion's potentially transformative power: "Because it is a place of communication with divine beings, the sacred place is also a locus for divine power, which can transform human life" (Joel Brereton 2005, 7981). Congregations thus provide religious resources—material and symbolic—for urban people to create a kind of community that can hold forth against the forces of late modernity.

Congregational Urban Impact

Chapter 2 proposed a set of variables with which to measure a congregation's effect on the urban environment along a continuum of weak to moderate to strong: *congregational spatial type* (neighborhood, area, metro), *congregational community traits* (common beliefs, the uniting function of ritual, enforcement of internal norms, mutual support, dense and demanding social ties, internal social similarities, stratification based on status or office, maintenance of boundaries with the outside world, types of disputes and their resolution, and internal versus external focus on needs), and *congregational action* (territorial claims, jurisdictional claims, public policy advocacy, programs or positions that challenge inequality, racial/ethnic composition, and mission activities). Table 8.1 (a reprint of Table 2.2) arranges our fifteen congregations along the urban impact continuum. The following sections analyze the variables that contribute to congregations falling at different points on this continuum.

The principal outcome of our analysis is revealed in the interpretation of the congregational community traits and congregational action indicators (arrayed across the horizontal bar at the top of Table 8.2). Both clusters of variables are related to the level of influence a congregation exerts on the urban environment. The congregations are listed vertically on the left side of Table 8.2 by level of impact from strong to weak. The "x's" identify factors that we consider salient in assessing the level of congregational impact and not simply present in a particular case. Of course, quantifying these factors, even in broad terms, will predictably raise questions regarding our assessment in specific

Table 8.1. Continuum of Congregational Urban Impact of Fifteen Case Studies

Weak	Low moderate	Moderate	High moderate	Strong
Ezra-Habonim (A)	Beth Shalom (A)	St. Jerome (N)	MCC (A)	St. Nicholas (N)
Calvary (A)		First Christian (N)	MEC (A)	Mosque Foundation (A)
Wheatland Salem (A)		New Covenant (A)	New Life (M)	Fourth Presbyterian (A)
HTGC (M)				Moody (M)

Abbreviations: Neighborhood (N), Area (A), Metro (M). Congregations listed in each column by order of appearance in Part II.

Table 8.2. Congregational Community Traits and Action Indicators

Congregation (in order by urban impact from strong to weak)	Urban impact scale	Chapter	Spatial type	Congregational community traits										Congregational action indicators					
				Common beliefs	Uniting ritual	Internal norms	Mutual support	Social ties	Social similarities	Stratification	External boundaries	Disputes	Focus on internal needs	Territorial claims	Jurisdictional claims	Public policy advocacy	Challenges inequality	Mixed race/ethnicity	Mission
St. Nicholas	Strong	3	Neighborhood	x	x	x				x	Low		Weak			x	x	x	
Mosque Foundation	Strong	4	Area	x	x	x	x				High		Strong	x		x	x	x	
Fourth Presbyterian	Strong	5	Area	x	x	x			x	x	Low		Moderate	x	x		x		x
Moody	Strong	7	Metro	x	x	x				x	Low		Moderate	x	x		x	x	x
MCC	High moderate	4	Area	x	x	x	x				High		Strong			x	x	x	
MEC	High moderate	4	Area	x	x	x	x				High		Strong	x	x	x	x	x	
New Life	High moderate	7	Metro	x	x	x	x	x			Low		Strong	x	x	x	x	x	x
First Christian	Moderate	3	Neighborhood		x	x	x				Low		Weak	x			x	x	
St. Jerome	Moderate	3	Neighborhood	x	x	x			x	x	Moderate	x	Moderate	x	x	x		x	
New Covenant	Moderate	5	Area	x	x	x	x	x	x	x	High		Strong	x	x	x	x	x	x
Beth Shalom	Low moderate	6	Area	x	x	x	x	x	x		Moderate	x	Strong			x			
Ezra-Habonim	Weak	5	Area	x	x	x	x	x		x	High	x	Strong	x					
Calvary	Weak	6	Area	x	x		x	x			High		Strong	x	x			x	
Wheatland Salem	Weak	6	Area	x	x		x	x	x		Low		Strong	x					
HTGC	Weak	7	Metro			x	x		x		Moderate		Strong	x				x	

instances. This is all to the good in that any analytical formula imposed on the complex reality of urban religious life will necessarily fall short. We offer our analysis as a stimulus toward advancing the empirical and theoretical questions regarding the interaction among religion, community, and urban structures that piqued our imaginations at the start of this research project.

Congregational Spatial Type

The three congregational spatial types (neighborhood, area, metro) are represented across the entire urban impact continuum. As discussed in chapter 2, spatial type may conduce to a certain degree of influence on the urban context but it does not predict the degree. The working hypothesis—that the greater the constituent residential diffusion, the more diffuse the awareness of a congregation's urban context becomes, thus neighborhood congregations tend toward relatively stronger urban impact whereas area and metro congregations tend toward relatively weaker urban impact—is contingent on other factors in our calculus, namely, the congregational community traits and congregational action indicators to be discussed below. Here we will explore the implications of our innovative spatial typology in some detail.

Neighborhood Congregations

The traditional urban neighborhood—which has a local identity and character, is small enough for many people to recognize each other in passing, and has a sense of neighborliness shared by many if not most residents— is increasingly threatened by the structural changes of the past fifty years. As noted in chapter 2, the decline in the number of neighborhood congregations can be detected even earlier, at least by the 1920s. But neighborhood congregations still exist as a necessity for observant Orthodox Jews, as an embodiment of the parish ideal for Catholics, and as a form of deliberate commitment to place-based community for some Protestants. The founders of Muslim Community Center took seriously the Islamic mandate to create a Muslim district in a non-Muslim land, which they envisioned as a self-contained neighborhood on Chicago's North Side, in many ways comparable to a classic immigrant Catholic parish or an Orthodox Jewish *eruv*.

In one sense, we can generalize that a neighborhood congregation invests in its neighborhood because of the geographic immediacy of its constituents. In other words, what a neighborhood congregation does for its constituents by definition affects the neighborhood, a formula that does not necessarily apply to area or metro congregations due to their constituents' residential distribution outside of the neighborhood.

Some Catholic churches in city neighborhoods close due to the out-migration of large numbers of their members; in such cases, the parish merges with a neighboring one. If the population remains high, as we saw with St. Nicholas of Tolentine and St. Jerome, the church may reconfigure both its membership and its relationship with the neighborhood and/or surrounding area as the location diversifies. St. Nick's anchors the Southwest Organizing Project, which bridges racial/ethnic boundaries and influences local economic development and real estate marketing practices to make the Southwest Side an area of choice where demographic diversity is associated with rising property values and economic opportunity rather than the opposite. This strategic partnering is a key factor in enhancing the urban influence St. Nick's exerts on its neighborhood and surrounding area. St. Jerome felt the pressures of the new urban era most acutely in the consolidation of its parochial school into the multi-parish Northside Catholic Academy. Although the demise of its school can be attributed in part to the church's inability to attract students from the exploding Hispanic population—unlike the period of classical European immigration, parochial schools are no longer affordable for a poor immigrant population—St. Jerome has developed a strong multiracial/ethnic identity, and the relationship between the parish and Rogers Park has become mutually supportive.

On the whole, the investments of St. Nick's and St. Jerome have benefited their respective neighborhoods, as well as their own long-term congregational viability. To some degree, the congregation's choices made the difference, though this was more pertinent to St. Nick's. In St. Jerome's case, the Northside Catholic Academy was the result of ecclesial interventions, even though the form the school eventually took was under the control of the parishes. The reforms of the Second Vatican Council have reduced the power of parish boundaries in shaping the identities of their respective parishes, within which ethnicity had historically reinforced who did and did not belong there. The battle over the Northside Academy demonstrated the sticking power of those boundaries.

In an examination of neighborhood characteristics and their contribution to community sentiment and attachment, Cynthia Woolever (1992, 112) found that "neighbourhood attachment depends on the level of social participation on the part of the individual resident as well as specific neighbourhood characteristics." Density and educational differences tend to deter attachment but class and racial/ethnic diversity does not. Despite earlier research suggesting that people prefer white and upper-income residential locations, Woolever found the opposite (111). Her thoughtful interpretation is that "once a person is settled in a neighbourhood the factors related to attachment may be different from those relevant to initial residential choice" (112). We suggest that congregations often function as mediating institutions providing opportunities for positive and meaningful social interaction that can foster attachment and accountability to neighborhoods.

Providing social services and programs for the neighborhood should not be understood simply as serving people in need or fulfilling an expectation of civil society. In providing such services and programs, congregations interact in face-to-face ways with the people who live nearby. The actual currency of the interaction—food pantries, clothing giveaways, health screenings, youth activities, and so on—is relatively unimportant. Much more important is that a social exchange occurs between the congregational community and the neighborhood even when the exchange is largely one-sided.

First Christian Church on Chicago's Southwest Side voluntarily created the geographic constraints of a parish structure, "building our church with whoever is here," as the board of elders put it. As the neighborhood and surrounding area became more black and less white, so did the congregation at First Christian, and their identity as a multiracial and inclusive church grew. Some non-white members found the church through immigrant religious networks, others while exploring churches closer to home. Each told a story of curiosity, surprise, some discomfort, and value choices that reflected losses as well as gains. First Christian shows evidence of the process of racial incorporation that Gerardo Marti (2009) found in his multiracial Los Angeles congregations: affinity with the congregation, identity reorientation, and ethnic transcendence. He invokes Goffman's (1961, 127) concept of "moral career" to illuminate the kind of progress interracial participation tracks in pursuit of new religio-ethnic identity. Marti (55) states that "Faithful members move toward moral conformity as a manifestation of their growth as religious persons, and their perception of personal progress toward that growth . . . ." Voices at First Christian converged to express a collective identity that sticking with one's "cultural preferences" is not "an adequate way to have church." We have assessed First Christian's urban influence as moderate, but we should emphasize that it has helped to stabilize a diversifying neighborhood.

Area Congregations

The majority of congregations discussed in this book are area congregations, an unsurprising consequence of urban mobility under late modern conditions. An "area" is bigger than a neighborhood—too big for most people to walk to their worship center—and has too many residents for more than a small fraction to know each other, or even to recognize each other in passing. But an area does have an identity, both a sense of place for residents and recognition as a place by the wider public.

We saw in the Muslim cases a gradual increase in local investment over time, due not merely to increasing Muslim residential concentration in their respective areas but also to an emerging sense of civic accountability and a need for civic self-advocacy. Local prejudices and traumatic national events like the 1995 Oklahoma City bombing and the attacks of September 11, 2001, served as catalysts for turning initially inward-looking congregational communities into more outward-looking ones. While some mosques nationally chose to remain inward-looking, research by Yvonne Yazbeck Haddad (2004; 2011) uncovered a strong transformation in civic consciousness propelled by these events. Haddad reported that many mosques and Islamic schools opened their doors to the general public in order to show that they do not teach hatred. There has been an increase in Muslim involvement in interfaith activities and collaboration, as well as cooperation with social service and human rights organizations in the United States. Also, more Muslim women and youth are engaging the public sphere than ever before. When Muslim Community Center began to provide health programs to local residents rather than exclusively to their Muslim constituents, the nature of the relationship with the local area changed both internally and externally. Mosque Foundation's responses to local tensions included establishing a speaker's bureau and initiating a relationship with their local congressional representative. These factors contribute to the high-moderate-to-strong urban impact of these area mosques.

Our other area congregations range across the entire urban impact continuum. The two Jewish congregations invest largely in the Jewish concerns of their constituents. The difference in the demographic makeup of their respective areas means that Congregation Ezra-Habonim's investment in Jewish concerns contributes to the larger Jewish infrastructure

in West Ridge and nearby suburbs. Congregation Beth Shalom's investment in Jewish concerns represents a minority voice in an increasingly
diverse Naperville. Beth Shalom's location combined with specific actions
it has taken thus factors into its slightly greater urban influence than
Ezra-Habonim. Beth Shalom's minority status in its area also helps to
explain its slightly greater urban influence than either Calvary Church or
Wheatland Salem United Methodist Church. Although Naperville's socioeconomic and cultural power tends to inhibit substantial congregational
influence, Beth Shalom's case illustrates the possibility of moving toward
the stronger end of the continuum.

New Covenant Missionary Baptist Church and Fourth Presbyterian
Church are also located in areas with powerful socioeconomic and cultural forces that impinge on congregational impact. Both congregations
invest substantially in their respective areas, creating communities of
resistance to the polarities of race and class and challenging the privati-
zation of religion and apathy toward the welfare of one's locale. The difference between their respective levels of urban influence can be partly
explained by the more powerful structural constraints of the South Side
that bear upon New Covenant Church.

Metro Congregations

Constituents of metro congregations reside throughout all or most of
the metropolitan region, which tends to weaken the connections to the
neighborhoods and/or areas in which their congregations are located. The
Hindu Temple of Greater Chicago's local civic investment is incidental
rather than integral and its relationship to Lemont cordial but distant,
based principally on legal matters of property ownership. Since HTGC's
constituency is metropolitan-wide, it does not need the neighborhood or
area to fulfill its institutional purpose to serve them. The Moody Church's
evangelical Protestant constituency is likewise metropolitan-wide, so it,
too, does not need the neighborhood or area to fulfill its institutional purpose to serve them. Yet Moody has chosen to invest more integrally in
its area, drawing upon its evangelical theology and past congregational
history, and thus advancing to the strong end of the urban impact continuum. New Life Community Church is a new form of urban church that
combines a straightforward evangelical message with an on-the-street
sensibility for the needs of its constituents. New Life Urban Impact, a
nonprofit organization that offers family support services, GED classes,
and the Urban Life Skills Program are programmatic responses to the

pastor's encouragement that members "get out of their shell and find the many needy people in the city." This contributes to New Life's high moderate urban impact.

The Moody and New Life cases illustrate how metro congregations can enhance their urban influence. The difference between these churches and HTGC is not in their respective religious or racial/ethnic identities but rather in their congregational choices regarding local investment. HTGC can draw upon its own religious and civic resources to increase its local investment, as have other Hindu temples in the United States (Bhardwaj and Rao 1998, 141).

The New Life case contains spatial complexity that points to the changing nature of the metropolis. One could argue that New Life's urban impact is locally grounded rather than an attribute of the church's metropolitan-wide reach. Our data do not permit us to validate this claim except to note that the church increases its membership by establishing new local sites rather than expanding its "home" facility on the Southwest Side, as would be more typical of megachurches. In contrast to an area megachurch like Calvary Church in Naperville or a metro megachurch like Willow Creek Community Church in South Barrington, New Life's new sites are dispersed and usually match the characteristics of the local population, for example, a multiracial congregation in a diverse community area or a Spanish-speaking congregation in dominantly Hispanic surrounds, mimicking a neighborhood rather than a metro spatial type. We could give it a hybrid designation such as neighborhood/metro, thus strengthening the hypothesis that neighborhood congregations tend toward greater urban influence. Less important than neat categorization is the glimpse of the changing spatiality of the city that New Life offers, reminding us to be attuned to the interactions of religion with living urban practices.

Spatial Type and Place Dependency

Recall Steven Brint's (2001) distinction between geographic and elective bases of social ties. We noted in chapter 2 that an urban congregation can function as a place-dependent community or as a dispersed community based on voluntary ties of beliefs or other kinds of shared identity, or it can combine functions.

Given what we knew about the increasingly weakened attachment to place in the new metropolis, we anticipated that our congregations on the whole would tend toward being more voluntary and less place-dependent.

Instead we were surprised at the tenacity of place-dependency across all three of our spatial types, though our understanding of place-dependency became more complex. On the one hand, we observed that the link between place and identity has been undercut by the circulation of people and symbols, intensifying a struggle to find a place in the new globality (Friedland and Boden 1994, 42). On the other hand, we also note Rhys H. Williams's (2004, 195) point that "everyday, lived religion—religion as the myriad cultural expressions of people as they move, grow, marry, died, and try to make sense of it all—depends crucially on place to constitute what it is."

Neighborhood congregations are place-dependent by definition. They do not locate "just anywhere" but specifically "somewhere"—the neighborhood—and they are unlikely to relocate outside of the neighborhood without compelling reasons. Some neighborhood congregations absorb and serve anyone who comes to their doors, and in the case of Catholic parishes in the city, they are often poor. Other neighborhood congregations attract a self-selected constituency that may or may not reflect the neighborhood's overall demographics. But even in such cases, the neighborhood as a "place" is integral to the congregation's self-understanding since a majority of its constituency live there. This is evident in all three of our neighborhood congregations.

A community area is the largest social-geographic unit with a meaningful sense of urban community, whether it is one of the seventy-seven official community areas in the city of Chicago or larger configurations in the city and/or suburbs. The greater geographic expanse of an area tends to reduce the social intimacy of its inhabitants. The place-dependency of our area congregations takes various forms.

Some area congregations are place-dependent by choice. Both of our synagogues chose their locations for reasons of affinity, though the kind of affinity differed in each case. Congregation Ezra-Habonim tenaciously kept its connection to its area, drawing upon the place-dependent model of a Jewish *eruv* despite the depletion of its own constituency base and a decreasing Jewish residential population and institutional infrastructure in the West Ridge community area. The place-dependence of Congregation Beth Shalom is qualitatively different since it is based on affinity with suburban Naperville rather than Jewish religious requirements or the support of other local Jewish institutions.

The other area congregations in Naperville likewise depend on Naperville for their identities. This is why relocations occur within the area (as with Beth Shalom, Calvary Church, and Wheatland Salem Church) and also why neither Calvary nor Wheatland Salem have shown any interest in becoming metro congregations despite their potential to do so. Naperville is an attractive place, but it is also a transient place for many who come and go for a variety of vocational and personal reasons. Although the lifespans of many of their constituents may be place-independent, while they live in Naperville, these congregations offer them a place-related community anchor.

For some area congregations, place-dependence is forced or reinforced by structural factors like class and race/ethnicity. Although New Covenant Church has occupied three sites in its history, all have been in predominantly black or racially transitioning areas. Both the residential concentration of its constituents and the racialized geography of the city have limited New Covenant's locational options. But a theology of the black experience has created a self-imposed geographic limitation as well. The only antidote to the dissolution and disempowerment of the black community, in the pastor's view, is black-only moral communities, principally the church and the family. New Covenant has created an enclave of resistance to the racism and secularism of the wider society by making black territorial and jurisdictional claims on the predominantly black South Side. This is not entirely dissimilar to Muslim Community Center's original vision of a Muslim neighborhood on the city's North Side. Moreover, both MCC and New Covenant were restricted in their locational options due to discriminatory obstacles, although the intractable nature of black disadvantage affected New Covenant in more serious ways. Despite local resistance, MCC was able to establish the Muslim Education Center in predominantly white Morton Grove in order to serve its expanding suburban constituency. A comparable extension of New Covenant's territory into non-black areas is unlikely for both structural and congregational reasons.

The place-dependence of our area mosques bears some similarity to Catholic parishes and Jewish *eruv*s in that they have created relatively dense constituent residential settlement close by their facilities. Thus, these mosques serve both area and neighborhood constituencies. Their geographical movement occurred within their respective areas, Mosque Foundation relocating along the southwest corridor of the metropolitan region, MCC establishing MEC in the northwest corridor. Both Mosque Foundation and MEC constructed significant religious facilities of traditional Islamic design that further bind them to their locations.

Two of our metro congregations have likewise bound themselves to their locations with heavy capital investments. The Hindu Temple of Greater Chicago is place-independent in terms of its constituency and incidental relationship with Lemont, yet its considerable temple complex would be difficult to abandon. The Moody Church's architecturally significant building ties it to its location in the Near North Side of Chicago, although its leaders pledged a perpetual theological—not just capital— investment in the city in the 1960s. Fourth Presbyterian Church has historically had a similar capital and theological investment in its strategic location on the Gold Coast but near the slums of the Near North Side. New Life Community Church's dispersed, low-capital campuses provide a more flexible connection to any specific site, supporting their search for people in need, which has taken them to all parts of the city and increasingly to the inner-ring suburbs. As we suggested above, New Life's method of expansion occurs through adding local sites rather than at the metropolitan level and therefore the church functions more like a network of neighborhood churches.

The foregoing discussion of spatial type and place-dependence suggests that urban congregations are participating in the emerging "new forms and combinations of social spatiality and territorial identity" described by Edward Soja (2000, 151–52). The fifteen cases in our study demonstrate place-dependency for various combinations of structural and cultural reasons, including theological and social justice commitments, class and race constraints and preferences, and capital investments. Yet even a congregation with little or no investment in the social geography in which it is located nevertheless establishes a site that draws its constituents together in a *particular* place.

Congregational Community Traits

Congregations on the high-moderate-to-strong end of the urban impact continuum avoid (or overcome, as in St. Nicholas of Tolentine and St. Jerome) serious internal disputes, the one trait found only in congregations on the weak-to-moderate end of the continuum. Congregations that exert relatively stronger urban influence place great emphasis on three traits: common beliefs, uniting rituals, and internal norms. Here, religious content (beliefs and rituals) is reinforced through group norms. Religious content can thus play a role in stronger urban influence, as when a congregation invokes Catholic social teaching and polity, certain

Protestant theological positions, or Islamic solidarity as an *ummah*. But the vastness and malleability of religions should be kept in mind. St. Nick's invokes Catholic social teaching but not all Catholic parishes do likewise. Fourth Presbyterian carries forward the Social Gospel stream but not all liberal Protestant churches do likewise, and evangelical Protestant theology does not always translate into relatively strong urban influence as it does with The Moody Church and New Life Community Church. Muslim Community Center has invoked the *ummah* ideal since its inception but not all mosques do likewise, while some (like Mosque Foundation) do so only gradually over time.

The fact that congregations with only weak-to-moderate urban influence can have the same three traits (common beliefs, uniting rituals, and internal norms) as congregations with stronger influence suggests that these traits enhance but do not guarantee a congregation's ability (or desire) to become a force for change in its surroundings. Such is the case with Calvary Church and New Covenant Church, both of which have affinities with Moody's evangelical theology, and St. Jerome Catholic Church, which practices Catholic social teaching particularly with regard to inequality. The Hindu Temple of Greater Chicago exerts a weak urban influence, but this cannot be attributed to its Hindu religious content in simplistic fashion, as we have seen with regard to Hindu temples nationwide. In like manner, the relatively weak urban influence of our synagogue cases should not be considered typical of all Jewish congregations, especially when considering the power of Orthodox synagogues to shape a Jewish neighborhood. As in all cases, the calculus of urban impact includes multiple factors.

Four congregational traits that indicate a robust internal community-building capacity—mutual support, dense and demanding social ties, internal social similarities, and stratification based on status or office—are more likely to be found among congregations with weak-to-moderate urban influence and appear to suggest that strong internal congregational communities work against making an external impact. The remaining two traits—maintenance of boundaries to the outside world and internal versus external orientation—involve congregations' outward positioning but do not display a clear pattern, although again, there is a slight tendency for congregations that focus on internal needs to exert weak urban influence. The mosques stand out in this regard in that they maintain both high boundaries with the outside world and a strong internal focus, yet they exert a strong influence on their urban contexts. An embattled minority status helps to explain this seeming incongruity, but, again, all mosques do not necessarily follow this pattern. Some may adopt a kind of enclave mentality that would weaken their urban influence. While the relationship between boundary maintenance and urban influence is not systematic, one question warrants further discussion— namely, what kinds of boundaries do congregations construct against the cultural challenges of the secular environment?

In general, congregations push against the negative moral implications of the late modern metropolis, albeit in decidedly different ways and by addressing different issues. In diverse Catholic parishes like St. Nicholas of Tolentine and St. Jerome, the respective racial/ethnic subgroups have different responses to larger social inequities, which is part of the internal tensions brokered by these congregations. In the predominantly white Catholic parishes of Naperville, resistance takes moral and doctrinal rather than racial/ethnic expressions since the constituents belong to the majority social group of the larger society. Those who wish a Catholic education for their children have three parochial schools from which to choose. And those who take seriously the pastor's homilies learn of a "countercultural" Christianity that offers real community for people who are "frayed at the ends" by the stresses of life in new growth suburbia.

At Fourth Presbyterian Church, racial and class barriers are only minimally crossed in worship and other internal programming, in contrast to the multiracial/ethnic and multi-class character of The Moody Church. Nonetheless, Fourth Church's intense and widespread commitment through preaching and programming demonstrates that the congregation's high-status position is inadequate to its self-understanding as a community of believers. They clearly stand inside the dominant culture; indeed, without the contributions of wealthy members, the church could not offer its programs for the poor. Ironically, Fourth Church critiques the larger society based on a theology of inclusiveness while class and racial stratification marks its congregational community.

For minority racial/ethnic groups, resistance can become a major emphasis in congregational cultures. New Covenant Church, for instance, creates an enclave community that resists the racism of the wider society and preaches racial separation over integration as the key to black self-determination. The possibility of integration existed in the 1950s when New Covenant relocated to then-transitioning Greater Grand Crossing, and it continues to exist despite white flight from the area. A few congregations on the predominantly black South Side have integrated, such as

St. Bride Catholic Church in South Shore and Masjid [Mosque] al-Faatir in Kenwood. Since the racial geography is the same, choices made the difference in the racial composition of these congregational communities.

Congregational Action

We also note some unexpected findings with regard to the congregational action indicators. Accepted wisdom seems to be that public policy advocacy is necessary for religion to exert strong urban influence. David Rusk (1999, 333–34), for instance, touts the power of church coalitions in regional urban politics. But of course advocacy can be more or less effective per se; furthermore, it is only one factor in determining a congregation's overall effectiveness in fostering urban change, improving urban conditions, or enhancing the quality of urban life. Although public policy advocacy is salient in five of our seven congregations on the stronger end of the urban impact continuum (high-moderate-to-strong), The Moody Church does not engage in it and Fourth Presbyterian Church has an ambivalent record in pursuing it, yet both congregations have a strong urban imprint.

Territorial claims also do not necessarily translate into relatively strong urban influence. Mosque Foundation and Calvary Church display equally imposing territorial presences, but their locations and symbolic meanings differ greatly. Calvary Church blends into its new growth suburban landscape with its familiar though minimalist exterior Christian symbolism. Even the largeness of its campus, which distinguishes it from most other Naperville churches, complements the ubiquitous light industrial parks and big box retailers of the area. Mosque Foundation stands out rather than blends into its suburban milieu, both architecturally and symbolically. The "sacred space" it has created by virtue of its own facilities and the dense residential, commercial, and institutional development it fostered around it gives Mosque Foundation a degree of urban influence comparable to large immigrant Catholic parishes in previous periods of American urban history. The relative substance of their territorial claims thus factors into the respective urban impacts of Mosque Foundation (strong) and Calvary Church (weak). Several of our congregations make significant territorial claims, but, like Calvary Church, these do not translate into relatively strong urban influence. The Hindu Temple of Greater Chicago, which we have likened to a "cathedral" in its architectural grandeur, is only the most striking case.

Jurisdictional claims and mission activities would also seem necessary to exerting substantial urban influence. However, the kinds of
claims and activities matter. Only three of our seven congregations on the
stronger end of the urban impact continuum make substantial jurisdictional claims and run significant mission programs (Fourth Presbyterian
Church, The Moody Church, and New Life Community Church). For the
other four cases, various other congregational actions factor into their
impact calculus. Interestingly, the mission activities indicator appears in
only one of the eight congregations on the weaker end of the urban impact
continuum, in contrast to three of the seven congregations on the stronger end, as we have seen. Of course, mission activities can be either adaptive or agentive vis-à-vis urban structures. In the former case, their urban
influence would be minimal.

The most salient action indicator for a stronger urban influence is
challenging inequality through programs or positions, which characterizes all of the congregations on the high-moderate-to-strong end of
the urban impact continuum. Not coincidentally, racial/ethnic composition also rates highly as all but one of the congregations that exert
relatively strong urban influence have racially/ethnically diverse com-
positions (Fourth Presbyterian Church being the exception). New Life
Community Church's spatial structure of racially/ethnically homogeneous home-based cell groups nested within geographically dispersed
campuses that are part of a larger church identity is a strategy for
addressing local needs while at the same time encouraging an outward
vision. Once again we note that neither of these indicators (challenging
inequality or racial/ethnic composition) guarantees a strong congregational effect on the urban context—in our pool, First Christian Church
is diverse and challenges inequality, but its urban influence does not rise
above a moderate level.

Space, Traits, and Action: A Summary

Our starting point was to claim, for theoretical and empirical reasons,
that congregations have a reciprocal relationship with their urban context,
both shaping and being shaped by it. Yet the evidence is clear that the
new metropolis limits the impact congregations could have, particularly
in their ability to create urban communities that provide recourse from
the negative circumstances of life in late modernity. Nevertheless, we are
able to offer some evidence that religious actors do push back and that

there are patterns in their ability to do so, which we summarize in the following three points.

First, our spatial types (neighborhood, area, metro) fall widely across the urban impact continuum and thus we cannot make a convincing case for a direct correlation between spatial type and extent of urban influence. In all instances, congregational traits and actions factor into this equation. That said, we note that neighborhood congregations do not appear on the lowest end of the urban impact continuum (see Table 8.2), which suggests the need for further research into the viability of the hypothesis that neighborhood congregations tend toward greater urban influence.

Second, we note that three traits are salient in those congregations that have a strong urban impact—common beliefs, uniting rituals, and internal norms. These traits provide a binding religious orientation that not only informs congregational choices but produces strongly shared norms. The kind of internal community that is formed has a bearing on the ability of a congregation to influence its surrounds—that is, the specific focus on building a congregational community may in fact reduce the likelihood of focusing its energies outward.

Third, public policy advocacy is unsurprisingly a salient, but still only one, factor in determining a congregation's overall effectiveness in fostering urban change, improving urban conditions, or enhancing the quality of urban life. We found, somewhat unexpectedly, that the most salient action indicator for a stronger urban influence is challenging inequality through programs or positions.

Are there factors we did not directly measure that might be a force in shaping the new metropolis? In considering Matthew Price's "acts of preservation" that we related earlier, we are compelled to think not only about the continuing efforts to seek community but also to notice the role of proximity in shaping people's choices about where to live. In the early twenty-first century, there is a dual housing trend in terms of location: both a continuing expansion away from the central city and a return to high-density urban life. Those residents seeking neighborhood rather than sprawl help neighborhood congregations remain viable, particularly as the troubling environmental consequences of the freedom to move further away are felt. Nonetheless, as we saw, a variety of congregational types are active players in the urban scene and they produce a variety of results. Hence, in the words of theologian John McCarthy (2013), we must continue to be "sensitive to the measure of the changing city" and "to measure the change in the holy city."

The Significance of the Religion Thing

We have made much of an insight of James Capraro, the Southwest Side activist who criticized Chicago business leaders for not grasping the importance of "the church thing," for a full understanding of the city. We expanded Capraro's indictment to urban studies scholars who do not grasp the importance of "the religion thing" for a full understanding of the new American metropolis, supporting Kathleen Neils Conzen's (1996, 114) plea that "first and foremost, the urban historian [and other urban scholars] must simply recognize that religion has been and remains a structuring and enculturating factor in American urban life and to ignore its power is to risk both misrepresentation and irrelevance."

Ignoring religion's urban power can mean giving religion no attention whatsoever or, more subtly, granting it relatively trivial weight vis-à-vis "primary objects of inquiry" like race and class (K. Conzen 1996, 109). Edward Soja's (2000) *Postmetropolis*, for instance, which has so helpfully informed our analysis of life in the new metropolis, pays more attention to religion's role in pre-modern cities (chapters 1, 2) than contemporary ones, the few references to the latter describing collaborations with other urban actors on social justice issues (410, 412, 415).

The City, Revisited (Judd and Simpson 2011), an important survey of classical and contemporary urban theories, illustrates the continuum of significance attributed to urban religion. On the one side, religious influences and contributions are downplayed or ignored. For instance, a discussion of Jane Addams and the settlement house movement includes only brief hints that Christian teachings might have played some role (Spain 2011, 56, 60). Yet the influence of the Social Gospel movement is well known (e.g., "Origins of the Settlement House Movement") and Addams herself (1912, 124) wrote eloquently about the Christian "renaissance" that helped to motivate the movement: "I believe that this turning, this renaissance of the early Christian humanitarianism, is going on in America, in Chicago, if you please, without leaders who write or philosophize, without much speaking, but with a bent to express in social service and in terms of action the spirit of Christ. Certain it is that spiritual force is found in the Settlement movement." Similarly, an analysis of the Justice for Janitors workers' rights campaign in Los Angeles in *The City, Revisited* makes no mention of religious participation (Bridges 2011), yet "support from the Catholic Church played a very important role throughout the conflict" (Erickson et al. 2002, 564). Churches have played a significant role in janitors' rights campaigns in other cities as well (Rudy 2004; Gangler n.d.). Looking locally, the community organization Arise Chicago was founded in 1991 by an interfaith group of clergy who sought faith-based strategies to address systemic poverty and workplace injustice (http://arisechicago.org/, accessed May 20, 2014).

On the other hand, *The City, Revisited* recognizes the importance placed on religion in the new Chicago School, specifically Terry Nichols Clark's work on Catholics (Clark 2011; Mollenkopf 2011, 178; Beauregard 2011, 193, 196; Sabatini and Salcedo 2011, 345–46). Most heartening, in their concluding chapter to the volume, Dick Simpson and Tom Kelly (2011, 359) include religious identity among the variables of "multiculturalism," one of six characteristics that must be included in any adequate urban theory today.

The authors of the present volume are scholars of religion—Numrich in the comparative study of religion, Wedam in the sociology of religion—and like many religion scholars, we tend to think religion is more important than it is. Most urban studies scholars, on the other hand, tend to think religion is less important than it is. The reality falls somewhere in-between these two tendencies. In this final section of the book, we seek to offer a realistic appraisal of religion's role in the contemporary American metropolis and why urban studies scholars and other urban observers should pay proper attention to it.

Early on in the Religion in Urban America Program, we were advised to make judicious claims about structural changes wrought by congregations. Sociologist R. Stephen Warner challenged a too-facile (and normative) perspective among our research team that congregations, especially socially liberal ones, should be dedicated to promoting structural change in their outreach missions. Furthermore, Warner asserted that few people (perhaps none) know what structural change should look like.

Indeed, Matthew Price mused openly that the reason nobody is really sure what structural change will look like is not due to lack of effort. "Therefore, I don't believe that [the Religion in Urban America Program] will be able to boldly go where Habermas and other mere mortals have not yet gone before" (personal correspondence 1995). Indeed, one of the constituent characteristics of social change is the element of indeterminacy (cf. Rubinstein 2001). Change is by definition transient; reality is continually in motion. And change may occur in the most unexpected ways and unpredictable places. Who foretold the Arab Spring? Or its violent aftermath? Who anticipated the decriminalization of marijuana in the United States?

Yet the evidence from Chicago supports the important claim that religious actors, including congregations and the individuals they influence and empower, both engage urban structures and effect change to varying degrees. Religion, as a cultural system, inspires different kinds of conduct than does the market (Geertz 1973; Rubinstein 2001, 156). And, when drawing on religious resources, congregations act with partial autonomy from the economic constraints that otherwise impinge on their choices. The evidence shows, in particular, that religion has been one of the resources by which place-based communities have resisted powerful centrifugal forces in the Chicago metropolitan region and have reconstituted themselves on a sustainable basis. It shows that religion has been a resource for diverse populations of local places to avoid racial tipping and to strike a viable balance between becoming segregated racial enclaves and losing the social support conducive to cultural identities. It shows that congregations make links to transnational movements and networks, enhancing the economic, multilingual, and technological capacities of their globally transient members. Perhaps most important, the evidence from Chicago shows that, while congregations function in many respects like secular nonprofit organizations, it is often in their explicitly "religious" work that they make their most profound impact.

In one sense, writing about the building and sustaining of urban congregational community seems routine and uninspired. Yet some of the most difficult questions in critical social theory revolve around issues of justice and genuine plurality in the emerging globalized world, and these problematics are constituted in the idea of the collective. In organizing the volume that emerged from the provocative discussion around Charles Taylor's *Multiculturalism and the "Politics of Recognition,"* Amy Gutmann (1992, ix) proposes that "Central among those questions is what kind of communities can justly be created and sustained out of our human diversity." Congregational communities are a locus for testing a form of sustained group engagement that has a traceable history in a particular place. We are reminded of an observation sociologist Mary Jo Neitz (2009, 352) made about rural churches that became "consumer driven" and minimized potentially off-putting traditional practices of more conventional churches in order to attract seekers who valued informality and contemporary styles. Practices in such low-commitment churches, Neitz (353) paradoxically observed, also generate some unease among members who compare them to older forms of knowing and caring: "These churches may leave some people, church members and not, nostalgic for ways of being together to which they do not wish to return." We can see here how such engagements are changeable, contentious, perennially fractious as well as fundamentally solidary. While examining the forms of community illustrated by our congregational cases, we kept in mind that this volume was never meant to be parochial (although it is entirely local), but a way to raise larger questions about social and moral order(s) and the role(s) of the sacred at the turn of the twenty-first century.

Sociologist Christian Smith's (2008, 479) summary of religion's importance for Christians is transferable to other religious people who are "interested in things like community belonging, moral bearings, forgiveness, subjectively meaningful worship, and significance in life, and who are affected by the emotions that religious beliefs and practices responding to those interests generate." It is noteworthy that community belonging tops Smith's list of religious people's interests. "Perhaps no social function of religion is more remarked upon than that of 'building community,'" observes sociologist Rhys H. Williams (2002, 256).

In "Doing Good in American Communities," sociologist Nancy Ammerman (n.d.) explains that the "primary task" of all congregations "is not the delivery of social services or supporting cultural organizations. Their primary task is the spiritual well-being of their members. Across every tradition and in every region, congregations agree—their highest priory is providing opportunities for vital spiritual worship. That is where leaders put the most energy, and that is the first thing members look for when they are seeking a place to join."

Ammerman immediately counters the criticism "that this spiritual activity is irrelevant to the larger community, that it is 'otherworldly.'" Although its effects are less measurable than programs for the poor, Ammerman argues that "worship services can make a real difference, too," for instance in placing people's lives in a larger perspective and providing moral bearings.

"Fellowship" is the second great work of congregations, according to Ammerman. "Across religious traditions, regions, class, and ethnicity people agree about what is most basic to congregational life. Leaders say they work hard at providing this family-like atmosphere, and members say they are looking for a warm, friendly community when they choose a congregation to join." Again Ammerman makes a case for this work's relevance to the larger community: "All of the work that congregations do at building up a caring, functioning internal community pays off for the larger community, even if indirectly." Indirect effects are difficult to quantify, but we have factored them into our calculus of congregational urban impact.

Sociologists of social movements have studied religion's impact on society through faith-based community organizing models (such as the Saul Alinsky-inspired PICO National Network and Industrial Areas Foundation), Homeboy Industries (a gang-intervention initiative in Los Angeles modeled on Latin American Christian base communities), and the Salvation Army. In *Claiming Society for God*, sociologists Nancy J. Davis and Robert V. Robinson (2012, 3) argue that the Salvation Army, the largest charitable organization of any kind in the United States, is one of several transnational religious organizations that seek a "fundamental transformation of communities and the larger society" through both religious and economic institution-building. Using a "communitarian logic which entails 'watching over' community members" (6), the Salvation Army has created a dense network of redistributive caring organizations that includes not just worship centers and thrift stores but hostels for the homeless, group homes, hospices for HIV patients, day care facilities, addiction dependency programs, domestic violence shelters, disaster assistance programs, outreach programs for released prisoners, career counseling centers, and medical facilities (9). While advocating morally conservative behavior regarding divorce, homosexuality, and abortion, the Salvation Army was also influenced by the Social Gospel movement of the 1890s and soon identified laissez-faire capitalism as the source of poverty and structural inequality (126). Through its International Social Justice Commission, the Salvation Army offers a "strategic voice to advocate for human dignity and social justice with the world's poor and oppressed" and supports the United Nations Millennium Development Goals (http://www.salvationarmy.org/isjc/about, accessed January 30, 2013). Davis and Robinson (5) maintain that while "success" in social movement activity is partial, "longevity," "reshaping national consciousness," and "providing an extensive array of services to their constituencies at the local level" are significant measures of it.

In this book we have documented cultural and economic relationships between congregations and their urban environments. Cultural relationships display the kinds of religious messages cultivated in the congregation and ways members are instructed to interact with the world outside the sanctuary doors. Economic relationships are established as a consequence of the gaps in the basic life needs of their own members at times, but more often those in the service and mission fields the congregations have identified. Congregations have often been criticized for their "band-aid" approach to the rising economic inequities of the last thirty years. Yet, because of the weak American welfare state, faith-based organizations have often been the first line of defense in recognizing and responding to this breach. The kinds of social services congregations offer are grassroots interventions that strengthen, more or less, local civil society institutions. Davis and Robinson (2012, 150) claim that the Salvation Army is one example of a "patient, entrepreneurial, under-the-radar strategy of rebuilding society, one institution at a time, from the ground up."

The Salvation Army and other major charitable organizations such as Catholic Charities and Lutheran Social Services provide a large share of the total social service output by religious groups. Mark Chaves (2004, 47) reported that 57 percent of congregations in the United States provide some kind of social welfare services, though most of this is done on a relatively small scale (consistent with Ammerman's assessment above). Less than 1 percent of congregations provide extensive welfare and institution-building work at the level of the Salvation Army. Hence, we must be careful not to overstate the value even of substantial congregational programs like New Life Community Church's Urban Impact, Fourth Presbyterian Church's Chicago Lights, or The Moody Church's By the Hand Club. In *Acts of Compassion: Caring for Others and Helping Ourselves*, Robert Wuthnow (1991) argues that caring behavior among volunteers supports a common social vision for a better society. Yet volunteering by Americans reveals mixed altruistic and individualistic motives. These volunteers do not appear to participate in a form of helping behavior that lobbies for larger social reforms that address systemic societal problems. Nonetheless, Chaves (2004, 51) emphasizes that congregations are much more likely to provide services than any other organization that is not specifically organized for charitable work. Furthermore, recent research has suggested that when nonreligious people have religious friends, that is, personal networks, they are more likely to volunteer in service activities (Lim and MacGregor 2012, 748).

The significance of "the religion thing" was recognized in the earliest days of American urban sociology. Recall that the Chicago School's Robert Park (1925, 115) placed churches ahead of schools, businesses, industries, and other entities in his "collection of institutions" that distinguish a community from "other social constellations." But we must not make the simplistic assumption that congregations constitute an unmitigated positive urban influence. We must also recognize that religious actors of all sorts can play a divisive role in civil society (Lichterman 2005), taking care not to leap from the fact that a congregation makes an investment in its urban context to the conclusion that the investment is necessarily positive.

Analogies to other urban actors are instructive in this regard. We recognize that political, economic, social, racial/ethnic, and other interests exert ambivalent influences on cities, sometimes to the betterment, sometimes to the detriment of urban life. We are advocating that religion be treated in the same fashion, as one of the ensemble of forces creating the new American metropolis and thus worthy of the same consideration given to the other forces in the urban ensemble.

Religion's ambivalence thus acknowledged, its potential for making the metropolis a more livable place should not be underestimated. In his review of two 2013 books on the status of cities, Harvey Molotch (2014) recommends "a very old-fashioned idea" for helping cities succeed against the "development derby" juggernaut: "rather than figuring out how mayors can make their cities better competitors, we should concentrate . . . on how to improve, as directly as possible, the lives of these cities' inhabitants." Molotch lists parks, good schools, bike lanes, museum walls, and free Internet access as modest but important contributions to "the public interest." Although Molotch could not add congregations to the list since he was advising public officials and policymakers, we will include them on our list of contributors to a livable urban existence, as exemplified by our Chicago congregations.

Afterword

A CASE FOR REPRESENTATIVENESS

WE HAVE EXAMINED congregations as diverse and complex cultural communities that, interlinked with geographic, socioeconomic, and political factors, built Chicago. Here we extend our discussion of religion and place beyond Chicago.

Recall Andrew Abbott's (1997, 1152, emphasis in original) summary of the Chicago School approach, cited in chapter 2: "the Chicago school thought—and thinks—that one cannot understand social life without understanding the arrangements of particular social actors in particular social times and places. Another way of stating this is to say that Chicago felt that no social fact makes any sense abstracted from its context in social (and often geographic) space and social time. Social facts are *located*." The Chicago School principle of located social-geographic facts raises questions concerning the generalizability of our conclusions: How representative is the new Chicago and its congregations? In such an endeavor, "It pays to be modest" by recognizing that American metropolises differ from metropolises elsewhere around the globe in significant ways (Judd 2011, 16).

Chicago and Other American Metropolises

In some ways, Chicago's iteration of the new metropolis comprises a set of located social facts that differ from other American metropolises. After all, the writer Nelson Algren (1951) called Chicago the "city on the make" filled with "hustlers and squares," "an infidel's capital six days a week." He hinted that there might have been room for Jane Addams and Dwight L. Moody on the seventh day. But Chicago and other American metropolises are alike in many structural aspects that characterize the new urban era. Here we find helpful Saskia Sassen's (2002, 49) distinction between structural dynamics of economics, globalization, and politics that impact all cities, and surface outcomes that differ due to their respective built environments and urban administrations (also see Clark 2011, 221).

The similarities have been recognized even in the debate between the Chicago School of urban sociology and the Los Angeles School of urbanism. Some Chicago School responses to the purported exceptionalism of Los Angeles delineate how Chicago and Los Angeles are very much alike in demographics, socioeconomic stratification, violence, and sprawl (e.g., Sampson 2002, 46–47), while the LA School has acknowledged that aspects of the new metropolis were anticipated by the classical Chicago School theorists, such as the growing importance of the urban periphery (Dear 2002b, 16). Since all urban social facts are "located," as the Chicago School reminds us, the new Los Angeles and the new Chicago differ in many surface-level iterations of the new metropolis. At the same time, as the Los Angeles School reminds us, the underlying and ubiquitous contemporary urban structures are sufficiently similar to qualify both metropolises as representative of the postindustrial urban configuration, even though Los Angeles may be arguably farther along in its postindustrial shift than Chicago.

We can cite evidence from other American metropolises to strengthen our claim that Chicago's urban structures are generally indicative of the new urban era, drawing upon research conducted by the director of our Religion in Urban America Program, the late Lowell W. Livezey (1943–2007), in the Metropolitan Congregational Studies Project housed at Harvard University Divinity School in Boston (2002–2004) and the Ecologies of Learning Project housed at New York Theological Seminary in New York City (2005–2007).

Lowell Livezey (2007) summarized the main contours of recent urban restructuring in New York City: the shift from a manufacturing-based to an information- and service-based economy, spatial mismatches of housing and employment that adversely affect minority populations, the demographic diversity and socioeconomic polarization of recent immigrant populations, and the growing influence of late modern thought. Other scholars have described such aspects of the new urban era as experienced in both New York and Chicago, helpfully identifying local variations in each case (e.g., Abu-Lughod 1999; Sassen 2004). Janet Abu-Lughod (1999, 274–84), for instance, notes the variable (but steadily rising) inequality of income and wealth across the two cities.

Boston has not attracted the same level of scholarly scrutiny as New York or Chicago, but it is certainly a restructuring metropolis. Livezey theoretically framed his 2004 "Faith in Boston" conference by the book *The Boston Renaissance* (Bluestone and Stevenson 2000). Part of the Russell Sage Foundation's Multi-City Study of Urban Inequality that included Atlanta, Detroit, and Los Angeles, the book posits a "triple revolution" in contemporary Boston: demographic change from predominantly white to racial/ethnic diversity, economic shift from "mill-based" to "mind-based" industries, and spatial reconfiguration from a central city hub to a regional metropolis. Again, with variations, the same triple revolution has hit Chicago. Differences between the two metropolises include particularities of history and physical geography that impact the current social geography, as seen, for instance, in Chicago's more extensive and concentrated residential segregation patterns ("Livezey Research Puts Urban Churches on the Map"). According to the oft-cited index of dissimilarity or residential segregation, the Boston metropolitan region had a white-black index of 64.0 based on 2010 census data, much lower than either the Chicago (76.4) or New York City (78.0) regions but still a relatively high degree of segregation (http://www.censusscope. org/2010Census/PDFs/Dissimilarity-Metros-Black.pdf, accessed March 8, 2014).

Descriptions of life in the new urban era coincide compellingly across the Boston, New York, and Chicago projects. At the 2004 "Faith in Boston" conference, Barry Bluestone pondered "the critical nature of community and neighborhood," a topic that has "gotten lost" in many discussions of urban restructuring. He spoke specifically about the deleterious effects on neighborhood community brought about by gentrification and the forced integration of Boston public schools. Rev. Ellis Clifton, Jr., pastor of St. Mary's Episcopal Church in Boston, spoke of threats to his immigrant constituents, particularly the youth, from today's "destructive society." An entire session of the conference was devoted to issues facing urban youth. Diane Rollert, a researcher from the Harvard project, spoke of the "toxic culture and violence" facing urban youth, while Rev. Omar Soto, associate pastor of Congregacion Leon de Juda, a predominantly Hispanic church in Boston, said that all urban youth are at risk today whether they affiliate with a congregation or not. Harvard's Allen Callahan spoke of the current "post-apartheid" period in which the legacy of America's racialized past burdens certain groups, particularly those of African descent, with "disproportionate difficulties" and "disabilities" in the renegotiation of urban territories and resources. David Carrasco, a joint faculty member of Harvard's Divinity School and Department of Anthropology, argued that all cities in all historical periods are founded on a social hierarchy that privileges some groups over others for whom the city is more of a place of risk. In American cities in the new urban era, at-risk racial/ethnic minorities want to tell their own stories because they have not been a part of the majority's story.

Life in the new urban era was also described by the Ecologies of Learning (EOL) Project in New York City, which changed its name in 2009 to the Center for the Study and Practice of Urban Religion. For instance, the topics of EOL's ongoing public forum program identified key social and economic tensions affecting congregations and religious groups, such as immigration policies and rights, affordable housing and gentrification, property development, and the criminal justice system (http://www.ecologiesoflearning.org/archives.html, accessed June 24, 2009). Five topics were covered at EOL's 2009 Mission Focused Faith Based Development Seminar: foreclosure prevention, housing counseling and development, personal financial management, family financial counseling, and community development and revitalization (EOL e-mail newsletter, June 23, 2009).

Congregations in Chicago and Other American Metropolises

This book has described some social facts about Chicago congregations in the new urban era. Can our observations and findings say anything about congregations in other American metropolises?

In one sense, the answer must be No. We agree with Mario Luis Small (2009) that ethnographic research such as ours does not conform to the standards of quantitative research that determine representativeness. We did not sample randomly; rather, we sampled on the dependent variable of congregations and the people associated with them. Thus, we cannot make statistical inferences from our case studies.

However, as Small (24) suggests, we can make logical inferences from our multiple case study approach, which should not be seen as a small-sample study. We identified a large research pool of 105 congregations with the intention of reflecting the racial/ethnic, historical, socioeconomic, demographic, and religious diversity of metropolitan Chicago—but this was not done according to some specious notion of representativeness. We then followed case study logic in selecting our primary congregational cases for their potential instructiveness on congregational communities and impact in the new urban era, refining our analysis case by case until we reached an analytical saturation point. Long before consulting Small, we discovered that "case study logic is probably more effective when asking how or why questions about processes unknown before the start of the study" (25). We also found that, "If the study is conducted properly, the very last case examined will provide very little new or surprising information" (25).

In a now-classic statement, *The Case for the Case Study*, Anthony Orum and his colleagues articulated several features of case studies that provide support for the representativeness of qualitative research. "The case study is usually seen as an instance of a broader phenomenon, as part of a larger set of parallel instances" (Orum, Feagin, and Sjoberg 1991, 2). Hence, cases encourage and facilitate "in practice, theoretical innovation and generalization" (7). As exemplars, Orum et al. call on the work of Helen and Robert Lynd and Howard Becker and associates to establish how cities and medical schools contain similar patterns. "The Lynds (1929), in their research on Muncie, argued that the city was representative of midsize American communities and that therefore its social and economic patterns could safely be generalized to the population of such places. Likewise, Becker and his associates (1961, chap. 4) went to great pains to argue that the University of Kansas Medical School, where they conducted their research into student culture, was similar to other medical schools in the United States. Hence, they argued, even though they were studying only one such school, claims about its student culture should hold true in other American medical schools." Orum et al. conclude that, "In general, . . . the nature of the phenomenon that one studies is the true gauge of the population to which one seeks to generalize. It is not merely a question of how many units but what kind of unit one is studying" (15). The characteristics of congregations we examined are not unlike congregations elsewhere, as are, in broad outlines, the neighborhoods, areas, and metropolitan regions of large, mixed-industry, late modern, urban agglomerations.

Another frequently raised question about qualitative research is to what degree the findings are reliable, or not idiosyncratic. To answer that charge, Orum et al. suggest that team and source verification provide the strongest guards against researcher bias, both in the collection of data and its interpretation. The multiracial and multireligious team assembled by the Religion in Urban America Program was designed to cross-check for these purposes.

Our Chicago congregational cases are thus generalizable in the following sense: they reveal certain processes, phenomena, mechanisms, tendencies, types, relationships, dynamics, or practices (terms adapted from Small 2009, 24) of Chicago congregations in the new urban era. This suggests a hypothesis that can be tested in other American metropolises: have seemingly similar congregations interacted with their new urban contexts in ways analogous to what we have reported from Chicago? If not, can the differences be explained by the respective urban contexts, by the respective congregations, or by a combination of these factors?

It is worth noting that the Midwest provides the closest composite picture of any of the regions in the United States. "Data from the 2000 census, including 34 categories detailing aspects of area, population, age, race, occupation, marital status, gender, and education, confirm that the Midwest more nearly than any other single region resembles the country as a whole" (Barlow 2004, 22–23). This Midwestern pattern follows for religious representativeness with the exception of having fewer Mormons and Asian religions, and more mainline Protestants (25). The state of Illinois is similarly positioned vis-à-vis the country as a whole: as historian Cullom Davis argues, "centrality, typicality, and middleness—terms commonly associated with the entire heartland region—apply with as much reason and sharper focus to Illinois" (cited in Barlow 2004, 41).

In his foreword to Robert J. Sampson's *Great American City*, William Julius Wilson (2012, viii) predicted that "A typical question will be raised about how representative Chicago is of other American cities." Although we have made an argument here for representativeness, we also think his answer is worth pondering: "That is the wrong question to ask. This is a theoretically driven study and Chicago happens to be an excellent laboratory for testing theoretically derived hypotheses."

Research Methods

The data for this book were collected by the Religion in Urban America Program (RUAP), originally housed at the University of Illinois at Chicago. The primary field work periods were 1993–1998 and 2001–2005, although we updated our principal case studies to the present. All the data were gathered by a diverse team of twelve field workers recruited for their expertise in different scholarly disciplines (religious studies, sociology, political science, anthropology) and holding various religious affiliations (Protestant and Catholic Christian, Jewish, Muslim, Hindu, and unaffiliated). Most of the researchers worked for approximately three years, in overlapping and somewhat discontinuous periods, dependent on funding. Numrich was a research associate with the project. Wedam was initially the project coordinator and then became the associate director.

We base the argument of this book on fifteen of the 105 congregational studies conducted by RUAP. We selected these cases mainly because we judged the data collected about them to be sufficiently broad and extensive to test our tentative guesses, in the Geertzian manner. We also wished to include a representative selection of the data in the RUAP database.

The data are of three types: congregational/organizational, demographic, and spatial. The program began by selecting seven social-geographic locations for study, six in the city of Chicago (Rogers Park/West Ridge, Loop/Near North Side, Pilsen, Near West Side, Greater Grand Crossing/Chatham, and Southwest Side) plus west suburban Naperville in DuPage County. (Pilsen and the Near West Side are not represented in this book but can be found in *Public Religion and Urban Transformation: Faith in the City* [L. W. Livezey 2000c].) These locations were selected to include the range of racial/ethnic, economic, religious, and geographic variation found in the Chicago metropolitan region. In addition, the program collected data from immigrant congregations in various parts of the city and suburbs, from several Christian and Jewish judicatories (principally the Catholic Archdiocese of Chicago), and from faith-based community organizations operating in various parts of the city and selected suburbs.

Field work in the study locations began with a windshield survey of all religious sites. Two researchers drove up and down all the streets of each community area, recording contact information for each site identified. A short questionnaire (appendix B) was mailed to each of these sites and a field worker was later sent to attend a worship service at those sites that responded, guided by a tailored field note instrument (appendix C). Based on information from these field notes as well as socio-demographic, religious, and size characteristics, between five and sixteen organizations in each study location were selected to become case studies. Upon gaining approval to research an organization during an entry interview that included informed consent in compliance with the university's human subjects institutional review board process, two field workers were assigned to each case. The field workers in the first year were teamed in order to provide diverse interpretive perspectives—different openness and different blinders—on the particular religious and racial/ethnic composition of the organization. So, for example, a Jewish/Catholic/Protestant team was assigned to study synagogues, Hindu/Catholic to study Hindu temples, black/white to study black Protestant churches, Protestant/Catholic to study Catholic parishes, Hispanic/white to study Hispanic congregations, and so forth. This was a methodological decision made by the principal investigator and director at the start of the program but was changed when it became unwieldy and time-consuming as the field workers sought to complete their assignments within the constraints of the grant. After the first year, a principal researcher was assigned to each congregation. The judicatory studies and faith-based community organization studies were only conducted by a principal researcher.

A "Protocol for In-Depth Study of Religious Congregations" was developed to guide field workers in collecting and analyzing the variety of data required by RUAP. The protocol included a summary of the general principles of the project as well as detailed descriptions of research procedures, such as gaining consent to conduct the case studies, recording field notes, compiling inventories of programs and activities, and writing an "exit" congregational or organizational narrative (appendix D).

Observing worship services provided significant but also easy entrée to the congregations. While houses of worship are private institutions, they are in most cases publicly accessible; RUAP researchers typically began a case study by showing up on worship day. Researchers were encouraged to be as "participatory" as feasible and to the extent they were comfortable with it. (Wedam, a Roman Catholic, can recount the experience of being prayed over by a Pentecostal preacher who exhorted the devil to "leave" her. The late director of RUAP, a Protestant, revealed how moved he was at attending Hasidic Jewish worship services.) It was our conviction that paying close attention to worship demonstrated respect for the congregation's central function. Religious communities express their religious and organizational culture, their urban orientation, and their collective identity primarily through worship. While interviews were necessary to obtain the "inventory," and interviews with both leaders and constituents were conducted in all cases, participant/observation data were at the center of our analysis. It is also important to add that RUAP strove to capture the broader role of religion's impact on its urban surrounds as an explicit contrast to a more "traditional" type of (Protestant-oriented) urban ministry (that is, community outreach) study. Some of the initial guiding questions particularly emphasized an inductive approach: What do the organization's activities have to do with being in an urban context? What does this organization do that is important to its urban context?

In addition to worship services, we also observed small groups meetings, committee meetings, holiday special events, prayer meetings, neighborhood activities, religious education classes, and social activities of various types. This emphasis was not meant to downplay the crucial role played by several religious nonprofit organizations in our analysis but rather to recognize that "religion" is principally represented by the great variety of congregations of all faiths in the United States.

Further narrative data included documentary evidence produced by the religious organizations. These included general information about their activities but also congregation constitutions and by-laws, membership directories, minutes of congregational meetings, information about schools, lesson materials used in religious education classes, copies or recordings of homilies and sermons, newsletters and other publications, and the like. The researchers also kept files of pertinent information from public sources such as newspapers, broadcast videos, and trade books.

A second type of data collected was the demographic information about the Chicago metropolitan community areas from the 2000 US census, Census Bureau estimates prior to the 2010 census, City of Chicago Data Portal, 2012, and ESRI Data & Maps, 2012. A third type of data was the home addresses (without names) of our congregations' constituents. In geocoding these addresses using ArcGIS Desktop by ESRI, we discovered the spatial types (neighborhood/area/metro) used in our analysis. The census and geographic data were layered under our constituent map data also using ArcGIS.

The data collected during the 1993–1998 period were incorporated into a NUD*IST database that helped researchers identify some of the initial findings of the project published in *Public Religion and Urban Transformation: Faith in the City* (L. W. Livezey 2000c). This current volume builds on those findings but relies heavily on data coded manually by each of us and guided by Barney Glaser and Anselm Strauss's (1967) grounded theory framework. At the conclusion of the 1993–1998 data collection period, RUAP held five "Neighborhood Forums" in which the principal researchers presented initial findings and benefited from responses provided by several of the congregational and organizational leaders from our research sites. Some of the feedback from these groups found its way into our current analysis.

Questionnaire

Religion in Urban America Program
Office of Social Science Research (m/c 307)
1007 W. Harrison St.
Chicago, IL 60607-7136
(312) 413-4117

Institution Name and Address

Pastor

Dear Pastor,
We at the Religion in Urban America Program would be most grateful for information about your church [other] which will help us to better understand your program and services.

1. What do you consider the most vital part of the life and work of your
   congregation?

2. Which of the following kinds of activities do you have? (Please check all that
   apply.)

   ____ Worship . . . number of services   ____ Prayer Meetings
                    each week _____
   ____ Religious education for children   ____ Religious education for adults
   ____ Scripture studies   ____ Literature distribution

   ____ Choir (s)   Counseling
                                                  ____ Individuals
                                                  ____ Families

Assist people in need
__ homeless
__ hungry
__ immigrants
__ others

Action on public issues
__ housing
__ education
__ job training and/or placement
__ neighborhood anti-crime issues
__ others

Work with outside organizations
__ community organizations
__ social service organizations
__ other religious institutions
__ others

3. Are there any other activities that your institution is involved in that you would like to tell us about?

4. What is the most important way you and your congregation serve your members?

5. What is the most important way you and your congregation serve the wider community (however you define it—neighborhood, city, country or world)?

6a. How many members are there in your congregation? _____

6b. What is the average worship attendance? _____

6c. What is the average religious education attendance for children?
_____

7. Would you be interested in talking with us about participating in the project?

THANK YOU VERY MUCH!

APPENDIX C

Field Notes on Worship Services

Religion in Urban America Program   Observer_____
Office of Social Science Research   Date of visit_____
University of Illinois at Chicago   Neighborhood_____

FIELD NOTES—Visit to a Worship Service
        Congregation Name _____
        Religious denomination/affiliation _____
        Address _____

Be concise when possible. Continue items as necessary on separate sheets.
Attach them.

Physical description, number, age of buildings		
Size of main bldg./ Style of architecture		
Appearance of surrounding neighborhood		

Clergy & Staff	Age	Gender	Race/Ethnicity	Other
Number of clergy				
Number and characteristics of other staff				

Order of service/mass		
Size and content of Bulletin	Attendance (#)	
Length of service:	Density (% filled)	

Composition of Congregation	Age	Gender	Race/Ethnicity	Other
Group 1 (children)				
Group 2				
Group 3				

Sermon/Homily (if any)	
Synopsis	
Noteworthy issues in relation to our project	
Other noteworthy issues	
Engagement of Congregation	
Seating placement	
"Hand of friends" / "of peace" / other physical contact	
Outreach to Visitors	
Personal/ From pulpit	
Forms to fill out?	
Music and Hymnals/Books	
Style (formal/informal)	
Choir/instruments	
Congregational participation	

Brief Description of Service (include any noteworthy issues and points that just strike you as interesting)

Post-Game Show

Planned activities	
Other interesting interactions	

People Met (put "keys" here and continue overleaf)

Names and Titles	
Brief synopsis of discussion	

Literature/pamphlets

Quantity and cost, if any	
Variety	
Topics	
Bookstore or table?	

Other Notes

Protocol for In-Depth Study of Religious Congregations

GENERAL PRINCIPLES

We will simultaneously try to pursue two objectives that are complementary, but somewhat in tension with each other. These are discussed in "Notes on Method" as follows:

(A) Attempt to understand thnle organization *in its own terms*, to grasp its internal logic, to describe and explain it in a way that most members and leaders would confirm (even if they wouldn't have come up with that description/explanation on their own). This involves seeking what is fundamental to the organization as a whole, not just what we think is "urban" or otherwise important.

This objective requires that the method be sufficiently open-ended that anything really important to the organization can be discovered, that our presuppositions and "research agenda" do not blind us to what is important from the organization's own point of view.

(B) Be sure, nevertheless, to get the information needed to see how the organization "serves urban people, addresses urban issues, and influences the quality of urban life" in terms that we, the researchers, consider important. (Comments on the meaning of "urban" are in "Notes.")

PROCEDURES

1. Introduction and agreement. The process of introducing the project and getting agreement to study the congregation consists of one or more interviews and a letter from the director. The director (or in some cases, a research

associate) will meet with the proper authority—usually the highest ranking clergy, the executive, or the head of the governing body. Additional presentation(s) to governing bodies or other membership-based units may be needed. Explain as fully as possible what the study will consist of, what cooperation is needed, what assurances can be given regarding the usage of information, and how the study might be beneficial to the congregation. It is desirable but not required that these discussions include the principal RUAP researcher for the congregation being studied.

The director's letter normally follows the personal presentation and reiterates the dimensions and purposes of the study, cooperation needed, and assurances about usage. However, the letter may be part of the request for the interview. The letter will also indicate the main personnel to be involved on behalf of the RUAP. If the organization wishes substantial changes in the terms proposed, any changes should be indicated in a subsequent letter. The project can go forward only when the organization indicates agreement to do so on the terms expressed in writing. If the organization's agreement is not in writing, we must keep notes of when it was expressed, by whom, and on what authority (e.g., clergy decision, board vote, etc.).

2. Initial research interviews. The introductory interview (above) can serve research purposes in addition to helping secure agreement. It should help us build the relationship needed to do the research and it should provide some of the information needed. Additional interviews with the same person or other leaders will probably be needed at the beginning of the research process. We should try to accomplish the following by means of this (these) interview(s):

a) The leader should have a basic understanding of RUAP and of the cooperation we need, and a positive acquaintance with the person(s) who will be doing the research.
b) We should get an overview of the organization's history and program, including as much as possible of the information needed for the "inventory" (see below). It is good to ask for basic documents (directories, annual reports, histories, lists of officers, PR material, etc.) at this time.
c) We should learn what the interviewee thinks is/are essential, central, and/or distinctive about this congregation. What is "really important" as this person sees it?
d) We should learn what this person thinks is most important about how this congregation "serves urban people and addresses urban issues."
e) We should find out who else in the congregation this person thinks we should interview and assure him/her that we will attempt to do so. Also, ask for whatever help we will need in contacting the various people we will want to interview.
f) We should establish a *protocol* for contacting people, observing meetings and events, and keeping in touch with the leader(s). In general, we can operate any way that they prefer—we can be very independent, or we can let them manage our schedule (make appointments for us, etc.).

3. A complete inventory of programs and activities.   A crucial early step is to make a complete inventory of programs and activities (not just of "urban" programs!), including formally established, perennial programs, occasional activities, and even informal activities of members if these are actively fostered by the congregation and acknowledged as integral to its common identity and purpose. Know *everything* this congregation *does* and everything its sub-units *do*.

Get basic descriptive information about all the programs and activities. Take either notes or the tangible evidence, depending on what the congregation permits and what is convenient. Talk to people involved if they can help get the big picture. For very big congregations with extensive programs, this detail may be unnecessary and too time-consuming, but such congregations are likely to have comprehensive annual reports or program directories that will meet many of our needs. Try whatever seems promising, remembering that different congregations will have different sources of information. These will include some or all of the following:

- Indicators of the organization's *structure*, such as directories, handbooks, lists, by-laws, constitutions, boards, staff, etc.
- Documents that list, or report on, past programs and activities: annual reports, minister's reports, minutes of governing bodies, etc.
- Indicators of current events: bulletins, bulletin boards, newsletters, etc.
- Interviews with clergy and/or lay leaders.
- Participation and observation of activities and discussions among the congregation's participants.

The *order* of using these sources, and the relative importance of each, depend on the organization. For example, if the organization is "print-oriented," start with the documents; if it is "oral," listen.

Write a *brief* description of each program (a sentence or a paragraph). Record the characteristics or functions of the program that indicate its importance in the congregation. This information will be used to determine whether to study the program in depth, and may be a basis for inter-organizational comparison.

But remember, the inventory is a relatively quick pass, and it should be done within a couple weeks of agreement to do the study.

4. Determination of which programs and activities to study in depth initially.   This decision should be made jointly by the staff doing the field study and the director. The programs to be studied must include:

(a) Programs that are central to the congregation's life—including worship and religious education.
(b) Programs that obviously have direct relevance and importance for "urban" people and issues.
(c) Programs and activities that the leaders tell us *they* think are important.

(d) Programs that involve institutional ties and relationships, e.g., with a larger religious body, with community organizations, with issue-oriented networks, etc. Especially look for connections with organizations and institutions of the city and urban systems.

This selection is preliminary. In big, complex congregations, we may have to exclude programs that would be interesting to study. Conversely, the most important areas may not be obvious at first, so always be looking for clues about other programs that ought to be studied in depth.

5. Collecting information about each program (What).   We are looking for the tangible evidence about what the program does (or did). This is the basis for understanding its fundamental purposes, the values it embodies, the agenda it pursues. We can't know in advance just what evidence will prove important. Moreover, different kinds of evidence will be important for different programs. We want to collect maximum information that is consistent for all programs and for all organizations. Therefore it is essential to collect "objective" data in categories that will be comparable across our whole study, and *also* as much information as may help us fully understand each program and organization—even if it doesn't come in our "preferred categories" or in categories comparable to other data.

In general, use your five senses and write down the data you take in. This does not exclude recording the ideas and values being expressed by the congregation, but it does mean that you should write down the observed indicators of those ideas and values. If the value is inferred, that should be obvious in the record. For each program or activity describe what happened as you experienced it.

Do not assume, however, that recording the data received through senses automatically makes your record objective. You will inevitably select, and selectively emphasize, data. You will inevitably put a "spin" on what you report. It is better to recognize this, even while you are minimizing it. This is one reason we are asking you to write more than one kind of field notes (see Section 7, below)—if you articulate your personal feelings and insights, the biases in the data will be more readily perceived.

Certain kinds of information are always needed and should always be recorded. About each and every program observed, try to learn:

(a) its stated purpose or function
(b) the means or instruments (e.g., sermons, gifts, boycotts, persuasion, etc.) used
(c) characteristics of the actors (including but not only leaders):

Employed or voluntary
gender
race, ethnicity, and nationality
age
whether members of the organization?

(d) characteristics of the participants and/or recipients (those affected by the program/activities)

Same as in (c)

(e) content, substance, ideas conveyed by the program

(f) resources available and used

AND

Your observations on everything you think relevant.

6. Collecting information about each program (How). The following general rules should be followed where they seem to be reasonable:

(a) Acquire, or at least see and take notes on, documentary evidence where it is available—not only "official" records like minutes of meetings, but things that illustrate what actually happened. Church bulletins, newsletters, flyers, lesson materials used in religious education classes, copies or recordings of homilies, etc., are potential sources of data. They may not be as precisely focused on our concerns as answers to interview questions, but they have the advantage of being undistorted by our intervention. No Hawthorne Effect is possible here.

(b) Observe in person the programs or activities.

(c) Observe/participate with persons/committees/etc. planning and responsible for the programs, as well as with those participating in them.

(For (b) and (c), see separate guidelines for "participant observer" roles, and other dimensions of ethnographic research.)

(d) Interview persons who are involved in these programs as actors, participants, recipients, and observers. Try to include a discussion with at least one "ordinary person" in each program you are trying to study in depth. If there seem to be differences among the participants, try to talk to people who reflect the variety. (See separate guidelines for interviews.)

(e) Additional means may be needed for congregations that are very informal or that generate little documentation. Group interviews, informal discussions, etc., may be helpful.

7. Recording information from field research. Write field notes and interview notes on all your observations. Do this the same day or the next day, and if that is not possible, *be sure to have very detailed informal notes to jog your memory when you do write them.*

On the first contact with a congregation, it is most useful to use the "Initial Visit Form," which helps to capture basic demographic information. All subsequent visits should be recorded in a "Field Notes" format, using the templates for observations or interviews as appropriate. There are three kinds of field notes: descriptive, self-reflexive, and analytic. All three can be included in the same report, and the template will prompt you for all three.

Descriptive field notes: You must always give a basic, objective description of the events you observe, giving as much as possible of the categories of information listed in Section 5, above. This is a "five senses" report. Most of the information you report will be the description. Often, however, you will have reactions to these events which go beyond description. Those reactions are also relevant data. There are two types:

Self-reflexive field notes: You will find yourself personally reacting to the event you are observing. For example, you might be reminded of a similar event in a completely different context which somehow bears on the current moment, or, the event you're observing evokes some kind of emotional response in you which strikes you as important or meaningful in some way. These thoughts should be recorded after the "Any self-reflexive observations?" prompt in the template, or (if brief) inserted in the text using square brackets [ ] so as to distinguish them from data strictly "observed."

Analytic field notes: In these you are recording thoughts, ideas, concepts and categories which include their properties, dimensions, relationships, variations, processes, and so forth, relevant to the event you are observing. In other words, you are beginning to interpret the data. Your interpretations may change over time, or you may later reject them completely, but these kinds of notes are very helpful in the thinking process prior to and at the point of preparing a narrative, as described below. These notes should be entered at the "Any analytic notes?" prompt, or if commingled with descriptive notes, must also be separated using square brackets.

8. Second interview with leader(s).   About one month after the first interview with the principal clergy or lay leader(s), interview the same person again. At this time, briefly review what has been learned so far, and then devote most of the interview to questions about the ways in which the congregation addresses urban issues and in which service ("ministry," etc.) to its members or other recipients are responsive to their specific needs and characteristics as "urban" people. This will primarily be an exploration of RUAP's "researchable questions."

9. For each program or activity studied systematically, enter data collected [in the program worksheet, and then] in the database.   At the beginning, at least, first enter the data on a worksheet that simulates the entry screen. Be sure the data are correct. Be sure the terms are defined as part of the database.

These are the directly observed data related to each program (mainly that which is listed in Section 5, a–e), above. These are *not* entered for every observation. There is one database record [or one program worksheet] per program. This is to be gleaned from all the field notes, interview notes, and documents collected from the congregation about that particular program. Put in only what you are sure of.

10. Write narrative statement about each program.   This is a very detailed description and an interpretation. The narrative should not be inconsistent with the data recorded (Section 8). However, the narrative is not just a restatement of

the data with verbs. It is our best judgment about what is really significant about the program, what its agenda or purpose is, why and how it matters. The self-reflexive and analytic field notes should be considered when writing the program narratives.

11. Congregational Narrative: description and interpretation of the congregation. The congregational narrative answers the question, How does this congregation serve urban people and address urban issues? It answers that question with emphasis on (a) what is the heart or "essence" of what the congregation is and does and how that relates to the urban context, and (b) what is "distinctive" about what the congregation is and does with respect to the urban context.

When we describe the "essence," we should expect our description to ring true to the clergy, lay leaders and ordinary members of that congregation. At the same time, our research perspective is inherently a critical one, that is, we may see things from an analytical viewpoint which is not obvious to those within the organization. Nevertheless, it is our goal that the congregation feel that in a fundamental or foundational sense, "RUAP really understands us. What they say in this paper really is what we are."

When we describe what is distinctive, we are locating the congregation on a "map" or within a classification system of the various ways religious organizations serve urban people and address urban issues. That "map" must make sense in terms of the available and relevant theoretical and empirical information, collectively known as "the literature." While the narrative need not refer extensively to the literature, and while the map we project will not be derived completely from the literature, the categories we use to describe and interpret each congregation should be used in a manner informed by the literature.

Each congregational narrative should include:

- A brief description of the congregation—its size, location, religious faith, leadership, primary mission (self-defined), etc.
- A brief description of the setting in which the congregation is located (the neighborhood) and with respect to which it locates itself (neighborhood, city, population group, audience, etc.).
- A summary of the primary identity and primary mission or purpose of this congregation as we understand them (that is, the understanding of the congregation that will inform this narrative).
- A list of the programs, activities, and other aspects of the life of the congregation that we have primarily studied. (Also, if major programs have been omitted, we should say why.) This makes public the basis of what we say about the congregation.
- A thematic presentation of what we find most significant about the congregation, particularly about its relationship to the urban context. This is the main body of the narrative. The themes depend on what we have learned about the congregations,

and therefore we can not say in advance what they will be. However, they should always include certain *kinds* of themes or subject matter. These would include responses to the following questions:

1. What is the religious or theological core of this congregation? How is its identity, and how is its mission or purpose, to be described in religious or theological terms?

2. What is it that connects this congregation with the urban context? This will depend upon, or entail, some assumptions about what "urban" means. The answer should include one or more of the subjects or issues identified in "Researchable Questions," but that may not be exhaustive.

Answers to these questions should be informed by the relevant literature, especially that in the areas of theology, ethics and religious studies; history; and the social sciences.

Notes

CHAPTER 3

1. This chapter contains verbatim excerpts from Wedam 2005, 212–14, used by permission.
2. As a result of complicated historical and ideological shifts in Catholicism, social doctrine regarding temporal issues such as economic policy and war, while distinctive and compelling, is not binding on Catholics, in contrast to matters of faith and morals that more directly affect individuals and families and on which the Church imposes sanctions (Burns 1992, 63; Ashley 1995, 81–82; Seidler and Meyer 1989, 26; cf. Komonchak 1995).
3. For our previous discussions of St. Nicholas of Tolentine, see Wedam 1996, 182–85; 2000b, 120–27; 2005, 213–21.
4. Jonathan Rieder (1985, 31) writes similarly about the experiences of Jews and Italians in Brooklyn.
5. LISC partners with the MacArthur Foundation to infuse financial support and intellectual capital into selected cities in the United States in order to expand community development activities, away from brick and mortar projects and toward programs for children, artistic expression, health care, safety, and public forums (see http://www.lisc.org, accessed July 1, 2009).
6. Information about Rogers Park here is taken from the *Local Community Fact Book, 1990*; Lewis et al. 2002; and Mooney-Melvin 2004a.
7. For our previous discussions of St. Jerome, see Numrich and Peterman 1996, 26–28; L. W. Livezey 2000a, 147–48; Wedam and Livezey 2004, 182.
8. This discussion of the restructuring process for Northside Catholic Academy relies heavily on D'Agostino 1996; 1997–98; 2000.

CHAPTER 4

1. Information about the communities discussed here is taken from the *Local Community Fact Book, 1990*; "Chicago Metropolitan Population"; Mooney-Melvin 2004b; Neary 2004; Solzman 2004; and Stewart 2004.

2. Information about the communities discussed here is taken from the *Local Community Fact Book, 1990*; "Chicago Metropolitan Population"; Pacyga and Skerrett 1986; Wedam 2000b; McKinney 2001; Knox 2004; McMahon 2004; Stockwell 2004; Vasile 2004; and Wedam and Livezey 2004.

3. The following history of Chicago's Arab Muslim community relies in part on Numrich 2012, 453–55.

4. This date is given in "The Mosque Foundation Project" [i], which also reports that Mosque Foundation was not incorporated as a nonprofit organization until 1976. For our previous discussions of Mosque Foundation, see Numrich 1996, 237; 2012, 453–55.

5. Personal communication, interpreting the statistics in "Data on the Organization, Resources and Activities of the Archdiocese of Chicago," 58.

CHAPTER 5

1. Information about Greater Grand Crossing here comes from *Local Community Fact Book, 1990*; Best 2004b; "Interpreting Neighborhood Change in Chicago"; American FactFinder.

2. Information about Chatham here comes from *Local Community Fact Book, 1990*; Best 2004a; "Interpreting Neighborhood Change in Chicago."

3. For our previous discussions of churches in and around Chatham, see Daniels 1996; 2000.

4. The history of New Covenant Church here comes from "Brief Chronological History."

5. With thanks to Judith Wittner for pointing this out.

6. With thanks to Michael O. Emerson for this suggestion.

7. Information about the Near North Side here comes from *Local Community Fact Book, 1990*; Seligman 2004b; 2004c; "Interpreting Neighborhood Change in Chicago"; American FactFinder.

8. The description of Cabrini-Green here relies on Seligman 2004a and the Chicago Housing Authority's website, http://www.thecha.org/housingdev/cabrini_green_homes.html, accessed May 1, 2009.

9. For our previous discussions of churches in the Near North Side, see Price 1996; 2000.

10. Information about Rogers Park and West Ridge here comes from Pacyga and Skerrett 1986; Cutler 2004.

11. For our previous discussions of Congregation Ezra-Habonim and the Jewish community in West Ridge, see L. W. Livezey 1996b, 46–51; 2000a, 139–46; Wedam and Livezey 2004, 183–84.

CHAPTER 6

1. Parts of this section generally follow Numrich 2000a, 188–92, revising and updating where necessary. Sources on DuPage County and Naperville include the following: "Economic Profile: DuPage County, Illinois"; "DuPage County Jobs/Housing Study"; "Profile: DuPage County Statistical Handbook"; Cormany 1996; Santana 1995; Leitner 1995; Edelhart 1995; Christiansen 1996; Krawzak 1997; "Annual Report 1995–96"; Reardon 1995; *Local Community Fact Book, 1990*; "Frequently Asked Questions Regarding DuPage County Planning Information"; Lemann 1989; Towsley 1975; Keating and Lebeau 1995; Fraser 1985; Ebner 1993; "Best Places to Live"; U.S. Census Bureau, Population Finder.
2. For our previous discussions of Calvary Church, see Numrich 1998; 2000a, 197–99.
3. The following description is based on three sources from Calvary Church: "Baseline Survey Dec. 29, 2002," "10 Year Attendance Comparison" (covering 1994–2003), and "Postal Code Status Report" (a mailing list dated March 2003). The "Baseline Survey" did not include data on the class status of Calvary's attendees, e.g., income, occupation, or education. A staff pastor explained that the church made a conscious decision not to include such questions on the survey but did not elaborate why.
4. For our previous discussion of Congregation Beth Shalom, see Numrich 2000a, 202–204.
5. The early history here draws from "A Brief History of Congregation Beth Shalom."
6. For our previous discussion of Wheatland Salem Church, see Numrich 2000a, 194–97.
7. Some of the historical information in the undated document "Inventory of the Wheatland Salem United Methodist Church" conflicts with our own sources, but we have done our best to reconcile the differences. Cf. Matile 2008.
8. "Route 59 Pedestrian Bridge." This is a composite of nine responses.
9. Historical information about Sts. Peter and Paul Catholic Church in this section comes from Towsley 1975; *150 Years of Sharing the Word*; "Ss. Peter and Paul Growth Parallels City's"; Hostert-Cassidy 1996; and Slykas 1996.
10. The official cathedral of the diocese is in Joliet in neighboring Will County.

CHAPTER 7

1. The demographic analysis in this section relies on Rangaswamy 2000, 78–93; Lal 2004; and US census data.
2. We did not receive constituent residential distribution data from HTGC. However, our interviewees confirmed the temple's metro status, which was also supported by census data and Rangaswamy's (2000, 248) observation: "Unlike Christian churches that serve a local parish and are built in the heart

of the community, the Indian temple [HTGC] draws its clientele from far and wide and does not betoken a heavy Indian population in Lemont."

3. For our previous discussions of The Hindu Temple of Greater Chicago, see Numrich 1996, 235–36; 1997; 2000b, 240–45.

4. Numrich 1997 and 2000b misidentified HTGC's location as Cook County. It is in DuPage County just north of the Cook-DuPage border.

5. The study released by the Wharton School of the University of Pennsylvania notes that the typical mall shopper drives twenty-three miles to a mall, while new shoppers travel even farther ("Mall Pall," 2).

6. This is somewhat speculative given the gaps in our comparative data. According to the 2000 census, seventy-five Asian Indians lived in Lemont Township and eighty-six lived in the same Zip Code as HTGC. According to Argonne's human resources department, 142 of Argonne's approximately 2,900 employees have a "Lemont home mailing address" (as of August 2006). Interestingly, more than that (two hundred) work in Argonne's Washington, DC, office, indicative of Argonne's non-local orientation, specifically its funding and oversight by the federal government.

7. Peter Jennings of ABC News used this phrase of Willow Creek (Sargeant 2000, 2); we made a similar claim for HTGC (see Numrich 2000b, 245).

8. For our previous discussion of The Moody Church, see Price 1996, 76–85.

Bibliography

"10-Year Attendance Comparison" (1994–2003). Calvary Church, Naperville, IL.

"40th Annual Report." Muslim Community Center. January 25, 2009. Accessed August 5, 2013. http://www.mcchicago.org/downloads/Annual_ Report_Jan_2009.pdf.

"41st Annual Report." Muslim Community Center. January 17, 2010. Accessed August 5, 2012. http://www.mcchicago.org/downloads/Annual_Report_Jan_2010.pdf.

150 Years of Sharing the Word. 1996. Sts. Peter and Paul Church, Naperville, IL.

"1938—November Ninth—1993, 55 Years Later, Remembering . . . Kristallnacht." Congregation Ezra-Habonim, Chicago, IL.

1994–1995 Parents Manual. Congregation Beth Shalom, Naperville, IL.

Abbott, Andrew. 1997. "Of Time and Space: The Contemporary Relevance of the Chicago School." *Social Forces* 75:1149–82.

———. 2002. "Los Angeles and the Chicago School: A Comment on Michael Dear." *City and Community* 1:33–38.

Abbott, Mark. 2007. "Suburbia and Post-Suburbia." In *The American Midwest: An Interpretive Encyclopedia*, edited by Richard Sisson, Christian K. Zacher, and Andrew Robert Lee Cayton, 1179–81. Bloomington: Indiana University Press.

Abu-Lughod, Janet L. 1999. *New York, Chicago, Los Angeles: America's Global Cities.* Minneapolis: University of Minnesota Press.

Addams, Jane. 1912. *Twenty Years at Hull-House, with Autobiographical Notes.* New York: Macmillan. Accessed February 2, 2014. http://digital.library.upenn. edu/women/addams/hullhouse/hullhouse.html.

Ahmed-Ullah, Noreen S., Kim Barker, Laurie Cohen, Stephen Franklin, and Sam Roe. 2004. "Struggle for the Soul of Islam: Hard-Liners Won Battle for Bridgeview Mosque." *Chicago Tribune*, February 8.

Alberts, Amy D. 1994. "Athens Marble: The Rise and Fall of a Building Stone." In *Looking for Lemont: Place and People in an Illinois Canal Town*, edited by Michael P. Conzen and Carl A. Zimring, 51–64. Chicago: Committee on Geographical Studies, University of Chicago.

Algren, Nelson. 1951. *Chicago: City on the Make*. Chicago: University of Chicago Press.

Alpert, Rebecca T., and Jacob J. Staub. 1986. *Exploring Judaism: A Reconstructionist Approach*. New York: Reconstructionist Press.

al-Tahir, Abdul Jalil. 1950. "The Arab Community in the Chicago Area: The Muslim Palestinian Community." MA diss., University of Chicago.

"Alternatives Analysis/Draft Environmental Impact Statement for the Southwest Transit Corridor." 1982. N.p.: U.S. Department of Transportation Urban Mass Transportation Administration and City of Chicago Department of Public Works.

American FactFinder. U.S. Census Bureau. 2000 Census Data. Summary File 1, Table P3; Summary File 3, Tables P77, P90. Accessed April 22, 2009. http:// factfinder.census.gov.

Amit, Vered, ed. 2002. "Reconceptualizing Community." In *Realizing Community: Concepts, Social Relationships and Sentiments*, edited by Vered Amit, 1–20. London: Routledge.

Ammerman, Nancy T. 1997. *Congregation and Community*. New Brunswick, NJ: Rutgers University Press.

———. N.d. "Doing Good in American Communities: Congregations and Service Organizations Working Together." Accessed September 3, 2013. http://hirr. hartsem.edu/orw/orw_cong-report.html.

Anderson, Benedict. 1991. *Imagined Communities: Reflections on the Origin and Spread of Nationalism*. London: Verso.

"Anniversary Update on Commission Activities Related to September 11." U.S. Commission on Civil Rights. September 2002. Accessed June 21, 2005. http:// permanent.access.gpo.gov/www.usccr.gov/pubs/tragedy/anniv02.htm.

"Annual Report 1995–1996." Indian Prairie School District 204.

Arredondo, Gabriela F., and Derek Vaillant. 2004. "Mexicans." In *Encyclopedia of Chicago*, edited by James R. Grossman, Ann Durkin Keating, and Janice L. Reiff, 532–34. Chicago: University of Chicago Press.

Ashley, Benedict M. 1995. "The Loss of Theological Unity: Pluralism, Thomism, and Catholic Morality." In *Being Right: Conservative Catholics in America*, edited by Mary Jo Weaver and R. Scott Appleby, 63–87. Bloomington: Indiana University Press.

Bagby, Ihsan, Paul M. Perl, and Bryan T. Froehle. 2001. "The Mosque in America: A National Portrait." Washington, DC: Council on American-Islamic Relations.

Bakke, Raymond J. 1997. *A Theology as Big as the City*. Downers Grove, IL: InterVarsity.

Balibar, Etienne, and Immanuel Wallerstein. 1991. *Race, Nation, Class: Ambiguous Identities*. London: Verso.

Barlow, Philip. 2004. "A Demographic Portrait: America Writ Small?" In *Religion and Public Life in the Midwest: America's Common Denominator?* edited by Philip

Barlow and Mark Silk, 21–48. Religion by Region Series. Walnut Creek, CA: AltaMira.

Barrett, James R. 1987. *Work and Community in the Jungle: Chicago's Packinghouse Workers 1894–1922*. Urbana: University of Illinois Press.

Barrett, James R., and David Roediger. 1997. "Inbetween Peoples: Race, Nationality and the 'New Immigrant' Working Class." *Journal of American Ethnic History* 16:3–44.

"Baseline Survey Dec. 29, 2002." Calvary Church, Naperville, IL.

Batterson, Mark. 2011. "Legacy." *aone:eight Annual Edition*, 2. Accessed October 2, 2013. http://www.aoneeight.org/download/a18mag-2010.pdf.

Bauman, Zygmunt. 2001. *Community: Seeking Safety in an Insecure World*. Cambridge, UK: Polity.

Beauregard, Robert A. 2011. "Radical Uniqueness and the Flight from Urban Theory." In *The City, Revisited: Urban Theory from Chicago, Los Angeles, and New York*, edited by Dennis R. Judd and Dick Simpson, 186–201. Minneapolis: University of Minnesota Press.

Becker, Penny Edgell. 1998. "Making Inclusive Communities: Congregations and the 'Problem' of Race." *Social Problems* 45:451–72.

———. 1999. *Congregations in Conflict: Cultural Models of Local Religious Life*. Cambridge, UK: Cambridge University Press.

Bellah, Robert N., Richard Madsen, William M. Sullivan, Ann Swidler, and Steven M. Tipton. 1985. *Habits of the Heart: Individualism and Commitment in American Life*. Berkeley: University of California Press.

Berger, Peter L., ed. 1999. *The Desecularization of the World: Resurgent Religion and World Politics*. Washington, DC: Ethics and Public Policy Center.

Berger, Peter L., Grace Davie, and Effie Fokas. 2008. *Religious America, Secular Europe? A Theme and Variations*. Farnham, UK: Ashgate.

Berman, Marshall. 1988. *All That Is Solid Melts into Air: The Experience of Modernity*. New York: Penguin.

Berube, Alan, Audrey Singer, Jill H. Wilson, and William H. Frey. 2006. "Finding Exurbia: America's Fast-Growing Communities at the Metropolitan Fringe." Washington, DC: Brookings Institution. Accessed January 10, 2009. http://www.brookings.edu/reports/2006/10metropolitanpolicy_berube.aspx.

Best, Wallace. 2004a. "Chatham." In *Encyclopedia of Chicago*, edited by James R. Grossman, Ann Durkin Keating, and Janice L. Rieff, 128–29. Chicago: University of Chicago Press.

———. 2004b. "Greater Grand Crossing." In *Encyclopedia of Chicago*, edited by James R. Grossman, Ann Durkin Keating, and Janice L. Rieff, 364–65. Chicago: University of Chicago Press.

"Best Places to Live." Accessed July 25, 2008. http://money.cnn.com/magazines/moneymag/bplive/2008.

Bhardwaj, Surinder M., and Madhusudana N. Rao. 1998. "The Temple as a Symbol of Hindu Identity in America?" *Journal of Cultural Geography* 17:125–43.

Binford, Henry C. 2004. "Multicentered Chicago." In *Encyclopedia of Chicago*, edited by James R. Grossman, Ann Durkin Keating, and Janice L. Reiff, 548–53. Chicago: University of Chicago Press.

Bluestone, Barry, and Bennett Harrison. 1982. *The Deindustrialization of America: Plant Closings, Community Abandonment, and the Dismantling of Basic Industry.* New York: Basic.

Bluestone, Barry, and Mary Huff Stevenson, eds. 2000. *The Boston Renaissance: Race, Space, and Economic Change in an American Metropolis.* New York: Russell Sage.

Bluestone, Daniel. 1991. *Constructing Chicago.* New Haven, CT: Yale University Press.

Brazier, Arthur M. 1969. *Black Self-Determination: The Story of the Woodlawn Organization.* Grand Rapids, MI: Eerdmans.

Brereton, Joel P. 2005. "Sacred Space." In *Encyclopedia of Religion*, 2nd ed., edited by Lindsay Jones, 7978–86. Detroit: Macmillan Reference USA.

Brereton, Virginia Lieson. 2004. "Religious Institutions." In *Encyclopedia of Chicago*, edited by James R. Grossman, Ann Durkin Keating, and Janice L. Reiff, 696–99. Chicago: University of Chicago Press.

Bridges, Amy. 2011. "The Sun also Rises in the West." In *The City, Revisited: Urban Theory from Chicago, Los Angeles, and New York*, edited by Dennis R. Judd and Dick Simpson, 79–103. Minneapolis: University of Minnesota Press.

"Brief Chronological History of New Covenant Missionary Baptist Church." 1993.

"A Brief History of Congregation Beth Shalom." 1995. August 6. Congregation Beth Shalom, Naperville, IL.

Brint, Steven. 2001. "*Gemeinschaft* Revisited: A Critique and Reconstruction of the Community Concept." *Sociological Theory* 19:1–23.

Brower, Sidney. 1980. "Territory in Urban Settings." In *Human Behavior and Environment: Advances in Theory and Research*, vol. 4, edited by Irwin Altman, Amos Rapoport, and Joachim F. Wohlwill, 179–203. New York: Plenum.

Bruch, Elizabeth E., and Robert D. Mare. 2006. "Neighborhood Choice and Neighborhood Change." *American Journal of Sociology* 112:667–709.

Bruegmann, Robert. 1993. "Schaumburg, Oak Brook, Rosemont, and the Recentering of the Chicago Metropolitan Area." In *Chicago Architecture and Design, 1923–1993: Reconfiguration of an American Metropolis*, edited by John Zukowsky, 159–77. Munich: Prestel-Verlag, and Chicago: Art Institute of Chicago.

Buchanan, John M. 1996. *Being Church, Becoming Community.* Louisville: Westminster John Knox.

Buerglener, Robert P. 1994. "Modern Life Comes to Lemont: Linkage and Infrastructure around 1900." In *Looking for Lemont: Place and People in an Illinois Canal Town*, edited by Michael P. Conzen and Carl A. Zimring, 139–48. Chicago: Committee on Geographical Studies, University of Chicago.

Burns, Gene. 1992. *The Frontiers of Catholicism: The Politics of Ideology in a Liberal World.* Berkeley: University of California Press.

Buschman, Barbara, ed. [1973]. *Lemont, Illinois: Its History in Commemoration of the Centennial of Its Corporation.* Des Plaines, IL: King/Mann Yearbook Center.

Byassee, Jason. 2009. "Ray Bakke and a School without Walls." *Christian Century,* February 24.

Cadge, Wendy, and Elaine Howard Ecklund. 2007. "Immigration and Religion." *Annual Review of Sociology* 33:359–79.

Cainkar, Louise. 1988. "Palestinian Women in the United States: Coping with Tradition, Change, and Alienation." PhD diss., Northwestern University.

———. [1997]. "The Deteriorating Ethnic Safety Net among Arab Immigrants in Chicago." Chicago: Arab-American Action Network Needs Assessment Project.

———. 2005. "Space and Place in the Metropolis: Arabs and Muslims Seeking Safety." *City and Society* 17:181–209.

Calhoun, Craig. 1980. "Community: Toward a Variable Conceptualization for Comparative Research." *Social History* 5:105–29.

Capraro, James F. 2004. "Community Organizing + Community Development = Community Transformation." *Journal of Urban Affairs* 26:151–61.

Cary, Joan. 1996. "Celebration of Diversity." *Aurora (IL) Beacon News,* December 20.

Castells, Manuel. 1989. *The Informational City: Information Technology, Economic Restructuring, and the Urban-Regional Process.* Cambridge, MA: Blackwell.

"Cat to Put More of Final Contract Offer into Action." 1996. *Aurora (IL) Beacon News,* August 25.

Cerulo, Karen A. 1997. "Identity Construction: New Issues, New Directions." *Annual Review of Sociology* 23:385–409.

Champion, A. G. 2001. "A Changing Demographic Regime and Evolving Polycentric Urban Regions: Consequences for the Size, Composition and Distribution of City Populations." *Urban Studies* 38:657–77.

Chaves, Mark. 2004. *Congregations in America.* Cambridge, MA: Harvard University Press.

———. 2006. "2005 H. Paul Douglass Lecture: All Creatures Great and Small: Megachurches in Context." *Review of Religious Research* 47:329–46.

"Chicago Metropolitan Population." 2004. In *Encyclopedia of Chicago,* edited by James R. Grossman, Ann Durkin Keating, and Janice L. Reiff, 1005–45. Chicago: University of Chicago Press.

Christiansen, Karri E. 1996. "Naper Counting on New Census." *Naperville Sun,* June 5.

Clark, Terry Nichols. 2004. "The New Chicago School—Not New York or LA, and Why It Matters for Urban Social Science." Paper presented at the annual meeting for the American Political Science Association, Chicago, Illinois, September 2–5.

———. 2011. "The New Chicago School: Notes toward a Theory." In *The City, Revisited: Urban Theory from Chicago, Los Angeles, and New York,* edited by Dennis R. Judd and Dick Simpson, 220–41. Minneapolis: University of Minnesota Press.

Clothey, Fred W. 1983. *Rhythm and Intent: Ritual Studies from South India*. Madras: Blackie.

"Coalition Tells 'Political Targets.'" 1983. *Chicago Defender*, January 11.

Coburn, Marcia Froelke, and David Zivan. 2007. "At a Crossroads." *Chicago*, June 29. Accessed November 24, 2013. http://www.chicagomag.com/Chicago-Magazine/September-2005/At-a-Crossroads/.

"Commercial Design Guidelines: Southwest Community Area, City of Naperville, Illinois." 2006. Naperville: City of Naperville and HNTB Corporation.

"Commuter Blues." 2004. U.S. Census Bureau News, February 25. Accessed September 23, 2008. www.census.gov/Press-Release/www/releases/archives/american_community_survey_acs/001695.html.

"Congregation Ezra-Habonim 55th Anniversary 1938–1993."

"Congregational Assessment Task Force Survey Data Pertaining to Affiliation and Choice of Prayerbook." 1993. Congregation Beth Shalom, Naperville, IL.

"Congressman Blunt during Muslim Visit." 1995. *The Star*, August 27.

Conzen, Kathleen Neils. 1996. "Forum: The Place of Religion in Urban and Community Studies." *Religion and American Culture* 6:108–14.

Conzen, Michael P. 1988. "The Historical and Geographical Development of the Illinois and Michigan Canal National Heritage Corridor." In *The Illinois and Michigan Canal National Heritage Corridor: A Guide to Its History and Sources*, edited by Michael P. Conzen and Kay J. Carr, 3–25. DeKalb, IL: Northern Illinois University Press.

———. 1994a. "Epilogue: Latest Lemont: Metropolitan Functions and Form." In *Looking for Lemont: Place and People in an Illinois Canal Town*, edited by Michael P. Conzen and Carl A. Zimring, 229–37. Chicago: Committee on Geographical Studies, University of Chicago.

———. 1994b. "Prologue: Lemont in Geographical Perspective." In *Looking for Lemont: Place and People in an Illinois Canal Town*, edited by Michael P. Conzen and Carl A. Zimring, 1–10. Chicago: Committee on Geographical Studies, University of Chicago.

———. 2004. "Global Chicago." In *Encyclopedia of Chicago*, edited by James R. Grossman, Ann Durkin Keating, and Janice L. Reiff, 340–44. Chicago: University of Chicago Press.

Corley, Cheryl. 2013. "In Chicago, Public Housing Experiment Enters New Phase." National Public Radio Morning Edition, June 24. http://www.npr.org/2013/06/24/188895584/in-chicago-public-housing-experiment-enters-new-phase.

Cormack, Bradin. 2007. *A Power to Do Justice: Jurisdiction, English Literature, and the Rise of Common Law, 1509–1625*. Chicago: University of Chicago Press.

Cormany, Michael. 1996. "Proof of Fox Valley's Growth Is in the Numbers." *Aurora (IL) Beacon News*, March 31.

Cotton, Jesse. 1988. "The Role of the Clergy in the Harold Washington Story." In *The Black Church and the Harold Washington Story*, edited by Henry J. Young, 67–72. Bristol, IN: Wyndham Hall.

Cresswell, Tim. 1999. "Place." In *Introducing Human Geographies*, edited by Paul Cloke, Philip Crang, and Mark Goodwin, 226–33. New York: Oxford University Press.

Cronon, William. 1991. *Nature's Metropolis: Chicago and the Great West*. New York: W. W. Norton.

"A Culture of Generosity: Creating a Place where Rich and Poor Share the Same Values." 2005. Accessed August 30, 2009. http://www.newlifechicago.mobi/News-articles/Leadership_2005.pdf.

Curran, Charles A. 1991. "Catholic Social Teaching and Human Morality." In *One Hundred Years of Catholic Social Teaching: Celebration and Challenge*, edited by John A. Coleman, 72–87. Maryknoll, NY: Orbis.

Cutler, Irving. 1995. "The Jews of Chicago: From Shtetl to Suburb." In *Ethnic Chicago: A Multicultural Portrait*, edited by Melvin G. Holli and Peter d'A. Jones, 122–72. Grand Rapids, MI: Eerdmans.

———. 1996. *The Jews of Chicago: From Shtetl to Suburb*. Urbana: University of Illinois Press.

———. 2004. "Jews." In *Encyclopedia of Chicago*, edited by James R. Grossman, Ann Durkin Keating, and Janice L. Reiff, 436–38. Chicago: University of Chicago Press.

———. 2006. *Chicago: Metropolis of the Mid-Continent*. 4th ed. Carbondale: Southern Illinois University Press.

D'Agostino, Peter R. 1996. "The Archdiocese of Chicago: Planning and Change for a Restructured Metropolis." In *Religious Organizations and Structural Change in Metropolitan Chicago: The Research Report of the Religion in Urban America Program*, edited by Lowell W. Livezey, 247–80. Chicago: Office of Social Science Research: University of Illinois at Chicago.

———. 1997/98. "The Crisis of Authority in American Catholicism: Urban Schools and Cultural Conflict, the Quest for Common Ground." *Records of the American Catholic Historical Society of Philadelphia* 108:87–122.

———. 2000. "Catholic Planning for a Multicultural Metropolis, 1982–1996." In *Public Religion and Urban Transformation: Faith in the City*, edited by Lowell W. Livezey, 269–91. New York: New York University Press.

Daniels, David D., III. 1996. "Chatham and Greater Grand Crossing: The Dominance of Religion and Race." In *Religious Organizations and Structural Change in Metropolitan Chicago: The Research Report of the Religion in Urban America Program*, edited by Lowell W. Livezey, 205–20. Chicago: University of Illinois.

———. 2000. "'Ain't Gonna Let Nobody Turn Me 'Round': The Politics of Race and the New Black Middle-Class Religion." In *Public Religion and Urban Transformation: Faith in the City*, edited by Lowell W. Livezey, 163–85. New York: New York University Press.

Danzer, Gerald A. 2004. "The Loop." In *Encyclopedia of Chicago*, edited by James R. Grossman, Ann Durkin Keating, and Janice L. Reiff, 493–94. Chicago: University of Chicago Press.

Dart, John. 1995. "Study Counts 500,000 Active North American Muslims." *National Catholic Reporter* 31:5.

Dashefsky, Arnold, Bernard Lazerwitz, and Ephraim Tabory. 2003. "A Journey of the 'Straight Way' or the 'Roundabout Path': Jewish Identity in the United States and Israel." In *Handbook for the Sociology of Religion*, edited by Michele Dillon, 240–60. Cambridge, UK: Cambridge University Press.

"Data on the Organization, Resources and Activities of the Archdiocese of Chicago: Facts and Figures for Year Ending 1996." 1997. Office of Research and Planning, Archdiocese of Chicago.

Davidman, Lynn. 1994. "'I Come Away Stronger': The Religious Impact of a Loosely Structured Jewish Feminist Group." In *"I Come Away Stronger": How Small Groups Are Shaping American Religion*, edited by Robert Wuthnow, 322–44. Grand Rapids, MI: Eerdmans.

Davis, Kevin. 2008. "Gentrification Hits Bump in Rogers Park." *Crain's Chicago Business*, July 28.

Davis, Nancy J., and Robert V. Robinson. 2012. *Claiming Society for God: Religious Movements and Social Welfare*. Bloomington: Indiana University Press.

Day, Graham. 2006. *Community and Everyday Life*. London and New York: Routledge.

Dear, Michael J. 2000. *The Postmodern Urban Condition*. Malden, MA: Blackwell.

———, ed. 2002a. *From Chicago to LA: Making Sense of Urban Theory*. Thousand Oaks, CA: Sage.

———. 2002b. "Los Angeles and the Chicago School: Invitation to a Debate." *City and Community* 1:5–32.

Dear, Michael J., and Nicholas Dahmann. 2011. "Urban Politics and the Los Angeles School of Urbanism." In *The City, Revisited: Urban Theory from Chicago, Los Angeles, and New York*, edited by Dennis R. Judd and Dick Simpson, 65–78. Minneapolis: University of Minnesota Press.

Dear, Michael J., and Steven Flusty. 2002. "Los Angeles as Postmodern Urbanism." In *From Chicago to LA: Making Sense of Urban Theory*, edited by Michael J. Dear, 55–84. Thousand Oaks, CA: Sage.

Delanty, Gerard. 2010. *Community*. 2nd ed. London and New York: Routledge.

"Directory of Masjids and Muslim Organizations of North America, 1994/1415." 1994. Fountain Valley, CA: Islamic Resource Institute.

Douglass, H. Paul. 1924. *The Saint Louis Church Survey: A Religious Investigation with a Social Background*. New York: George H. Doran Company.

Drake, St. Clair, and Horace R. Cayton. 1945. *Black Metropolis: A Study of Negro Life in a Northern City*. New York: Harcourt Brace.

Dreier, Peter, John Mollenkopf, and Todd Swanstrom. 2004. *Place Matters: Metropolitics for the Twenty-First Century*. 2nd ed. Lawrence: University Press of Kansas.

Drucker, Peter. 1969. *The Age of Discontinuity: Guidelines to Our Changing Society*. New York: Harper and Row.

"DuPage County Jobs/Housing Study." 1991. DuPage County Regional Planning Commission.

Durkheim, Emile. 1965 [1915]. *The Elementary Forms of the Religious Life.* New York: Free Press.

Eastman, Dale, Gretchen Reynolds, and Geoffrey Johnson. 1995. "Chicagoans of the Year." *Chicago Magazine*, January.

Ebaugh, Helen Rose, and Janet Saltzman Chafetz. 2000. *Religion and the New Immigrants: Continuities and Adaptations in Immigrant Congregations.* Walnut Creek, CA: AltaMira.

Ebaugh, Helen Rose, Jennifer O'Brien, and Janet Saltzman Chafetz. 2000. "The Social Ecology of Residential Patterns and Membership in Immigrant Churches." *Journal for the Scientific Study of Religion* 39:107–16.

Ebner, Michael H. 1993. "Technoburb." *Inland Architect* 37:54–59.

———. 2004. "Suburbs and Cities as Dual Metropolis." In *Encyclopedia of Chicago*, edited by James R. Grossman, Ann Durkin Keating, and Janice L. Reiff, 798–802. Chicago: University of Chicago Press.

Eck, Diana L. 1985. *Darsan: Seeing the Divine Image in India.* 2nd ed. Chambersburg, PA: Anima.

"Economic Profile: DuPage County, Illinois." N.d. DuPage County Development Department.

Edelhart, Courtenay. 1995. "Naperville Sprawls Contentedly." *Chicago Tribune*, November 30.

Eickelman, Dale F., and James Piscatori. 1996. *Muslim Politics.* Princeton, NJ: Princeton University Press.

Eiesland, Nancy L. 1997. "Comment on 'Sacred Space in Diverse Places in Three Different Faith Congregations.'" Paper presented at the annual meeting for the Religious Research Association, San Diego, California, November 7–9.

———. 2000. *A Particular Place: Urban Restructuring and Religious Ecology in a Southern Exurb.* New Brunswick, NJ: Rutgers University Press.

Eiesland, Nancy L., and R. Stephen Warner. 1998. "Ecology: Seeing the Congregation in Context." In *Studying Congregations: A New Handbook*, edited by Nancy Ammerman, Jackson Carroll, Carl Dudley, and William McKinney, 40–77. Nashville: Abingdon.

Eisenstadt, S. I. 2000. "Multiple Modernities." *Daedalus* 129:1–29.

Emerson, Michael O., and Christian Smith. 2000. *Divided by Faith: Evangelical Religion and the Problem of Race in America.* New York: Oxford University Press.

Emerson, Michael O., with Rodney M. Woo. 2006. *People of the Dream: Multiracial Congregations in the United States.* Princeton, NJ: Princeton University Press.

Erickson, Christopher L., Catherine L. Fisk, Ruth Milkman, Daniel J. B. Mitchell, and Kent Wong. 2002. "Justice for Janitors in Los Angeles: Lessons from Three Rounds of Negotiations." *British Journal of Industrial Relations* 40:543–67.

Evans-Cowley, Jennifer S., and Kenneth Pearlman. 2008. "Six Flags over Jesus: RLUIPA, Megachurches, and Zoning." *Tulane Environmental Law Journal* 21:203–32.

"Faith in Boston: How Congregations Matter in a Changing Metropolis." 2004. Accessed June 22, 2009. http://www.hds.harvard.edu/news/events_online/index.html.

Fawcett, James T., and Benjamin V. Carino, eds. 1987. *Pacific Bridges: The New Immigration from Asia and the Pacific Islands.* New York: Center for Migration Studies.

"Federal Jury Sides with Chicago Suburb in Mosque Dispute." Accessed June 18, 2005. www.fac.org/news.aspx?id=15306.

Fenton, John Y. 1988. *Transplanting Religious Traditions: Asian Indians in America.* New York: Praeger.

Fichter, Joseph. 1954. *Social Relations in the Urban Parish.* Chicago: University of Chicago Press.

Field, Scott N. 1991. "'Let My People Go!' Breaking the 200 Barrier at Wheatland Salem United Methodist Church through Lay Ministries." DMin diss., Asbury Theological Seminary.

Fischer, Claude. 1982. *To Dwell among Friends.* Berkeley: University of California Press.

Fish, John, Gordon Nelson, Walter Stuhr, and Lawrence Witmer. 1968. *The Edge of the Ghetto: A Study of Church Involvement in Community Organization.* New York: Seabury.

Franklin, Robert M. 2007. *Crisis in the Village: Restoring Hope in African American Communities.* Minneapolis: Fortress.

Franklin, Stephen. 1996. "40,000 at AT&T Now Await Word." *Chicago Tribune,* January 3.

Fraser, Helen. 1985. "Naperville." In *DuPage Roots,* Richard A. Thompson and contributors. Wheaton: DuPage County Historical Society. Accessed July 25, 2008. www.dupagehistory.org/dupage_roots/Naperville_15.htm.

"Frequently Asked Questions Regarding DuPage County Planning Information." Accessed July 24, 2008. www.dupageco.org/planning/generic.cfm?doc_id=565#14.

Friedland, Roger, and Deirdre Boden. 1994. "Introduction." In *NowHere: Space, Time, and Modernity,* edited by Roger Friedland and Deirdre Boden, 1–60. Berkeley: University of California Press.

Galef, Julia. 2010. "Gensler Finds God in Chicago." *The Architect's Newspaper,* September 15. Accessed December 2, 2013. http://archpaper.com/news/articles.asp?id=4819.

Gangler, Daniel R. N.d. "Clergy Take to the Streets for Janitors in Indianapolis." Accessed February 2, 2014. http://inumc.org/news/detail/755.

Garreau, Joel. 1991. *Edge City: Life on the New Frontier.* New York: Doubleday.

Geertz, Clifford. 1973. *The Interpretation of Cultures: Selected Essays.* New York: Basic.

Gems, Gerald R. 2004. "Jewish Community Centers." In *Encyclopedia of Chicago,* edited by James R. Grossman, Ann Durkin Keating, and Janice L. Reiff, 436. Chicago: University of Chicago Press.

Giddens, Anthony. 1984. *The Constitution of Society: Outline of the Theory of Structuration.* Berkeley and Los Angeles: University of California Press.

———. 1990. *The Consequences of Modernity.* Stanford, CA: Stanford University Press.

Gilbert, James. 2004. "Moody Bible Institute." In *Encyclopedia of Chicago,* edited by James R. Grossman, Ann Durkin Keating, and Janice L. Reiff, 541. Chicago: University of Chicago Press.

Girardi, Linda. 2004. "Tri-Cities Hoping to Establish Community Ties among Jews." *Aurora (IL) Beacon News,* May 26.

Girouard, Mark. 1985. *Cities and People: A Social and Architectural History.* New Haven, CT: Yale University Press.

Glaser, Barney G., and Anselm L. Strauss. 1967. *The Discovery of Grounded Theory: Strategies for Qualitative Research.* Chicago: Aldine.

Goffman, Erving. 1961. *Asylums: Essays on the Social Situation of Mental Patients and Other Inmates.* Garden City, NY: Anchor.

Goldberger, Paul. 1995. "The Gospel of Church Architecture, Revised." *New York Times,* April 20.

Gottdiener, Mark. 1983. "Understanding Metropolitan Deconcentration: A Clash of Paradigms." *Social Science Quarterly* 64:227–46.

"Governor Announces Opportunity Returns Grant to Fund Study Aimed at Identifying New Job Opportunities along I-88 Corridor." 2004. Press release, May 5. Accessed June 17, 2005. www.illinois.gov/PressReleases/ShowPressRelease.cfm?SubjectID=1&RecNum=3027.

Grant, H. Roger. 2004. "Transportation." In *Encyclopedia of Chicago,* edited by James R. Grossman, Ann Durkin Keating, and Janice L. Reiff, 826–32. Chicago: University of Chicago Press.

Greenblatt, Alan, and Tracie Powell. 2007. "Rise of Megachurches: Are They Straying Too Far from Their Religious Mission?" *CQ Researcher* 17:769–92.

Greer, Scott. 1962. *The Emerging City: Myth and Reality.* New York: Free Press.

Gregory, Mae. 1989. *Chatham 1856–1987: A Community of Excellence.* Chicago: Friends of the Public Library.

Grossman, James. 2004. "Great Migration." In *Encyclopedia of Chicago,* edited by James R. Grossman, Ann Durkin Keating, and Janice L. Reiff, 545. Chicago: University of Chicago Press.

Grossman, James, Ann Durkin Keating, and Janice L. Reiff, eds. 2004. *Encyclopedia of Chicago.* Chicago: University of Chicago Press.

Gutmann, Amy. 1992. "Introduction." In *Multiculturalism and "The Politics of Recognition": An Essay by Charles Taylor,* edited by Amy Gutmann, 3–24. Princeton, NJ: Princeton University Press.

Hack, Chris, and Allison Hantschel. 2003. "U.S. Investigating Mosque Foundation." *Daily Southtown*, September 21. Accessed June 21, 2005. www.religionnews-blog.com/4563-U.S._investigating_Mosque_Foundation.html.

Haddad, Yvonne Yazbeck. 2004. *Not Quite American?: The Shaping of Arab and Muslim Identity in the United States*. Waco: Baylor University Press.

———. 2011. "Becoming American: A Q and A with Yvonne Haddad." *Patheos*, September 20. Accessed August 18, 2013. http://www.patheos.com/Resources/Additional-Resources/Becoming-American-QA-with-Yvonne-Haddad-09-20-2011.html.

Hall, Matthew. 2010. "Racial Integration Rising in Chicago." *Chicago Sun-Times*, December 19. Accessed January 21, 2014. http://www.suntimes.com/opinions/letters/2900507-474/segregation-chicago-2000-neighborhoods-blacks.html.

Hall, Matthew, John Iceland, Gregory Sharp, Kris Marsh, and Luis Sanchez. 2010. "Racial and Ethnic Residential Segregation in the Chicago Metropolitan Area, 1980–2009." Changing American Neighborhoods and Communities Report Series, Report No. 2, December 14. Chicago: Institute of Government and Public Affairs, University of Illinois.

Hallenbeck, Wilbur C. 1929. *Minneapolis Churches and Their Comity Problems*. New York: Institute of Social and Religious Research.

Hammond, Phillip. 1992. *Religion and Personal Autonomy: The Third Disestablishment in America*. Columbia: University of South Carolina Press.

Hanania, Ray. 2005. *Arabs of Chicagoland*. Charleston, SC: Arcadia Publishing.

Hannaford, Katharine W. 1994. "Three New 'Rs' on the Expanding Metropolitan Fringe: Religious Retreats, Recreation, and Research as Objects of Farmland Conversion, 1920–1985." In *Looking for Lemont: Place and People in an Illinois Canal Town*, edited by Michael P. Conzen and Carl A. Zimring, 149–59. Chicago: Committee on Geographical Studies, University of Chicago.

Hattori, Akil, Ruopeng An, and Roland Sturm. 2013. "Neighborhood Food Outlets, Diet, and Obesity among California Adults, 2007 and 2009." *Preventing Chronic Disease: Public Health Research, Practice, and Policy* 10. Accessed July 29, 2013. http://www.cdc.gov/pcd/issues/2013/12_0123.htm.

"Havurot at Congregation Beth Shalom." [1996]. Congregation Beth Shalom, Naperville, IL.

Hayden, Dolores. 2003. *Building Suburbia: Green Fields and Urban Growth, 1820–2000*. New York: Pantheon.

Hayford, Sarah R., and S. Philip Morgan. 2008. "Religiosity and Fertility in the United States: The Role of Fertility Intentions. *Social Forces* 86:1163–88.

Hehir, J. Bryan. 1991. "The Right and Competence of the Church in the American Case." In *One Hundred Years of Catholic Social Thought: Celebration and Challenge*, edited by John A. Coleman, 55–71. Maryknoll, NY: Orbis.

Helgesen, Sally. 1998. *Everyday Revolutionaries: Working Women and the Transformation of American Life*. New York: Doubleday.

Hinkle, Bart. 2006. "Small Town Religion: How Megachurches Create Micro-Intimacy." *American Enterprise* 17:28–32.

Hirsch, Arnold. 1983. *Making the Second Ghetto: Race and Housing in Chicago, 1940–1960*. Cambridge, MA: Cambridge University Press.

"A Historical Review." 1994. In Ganesha-Shiva-Durga Temple Kumbhabhishekam Commemorative Souvenir booklet, The Hindu Temple of Greater Chicago, 19–21.

"History [of Muslim Community Center]." 2002. Accessed August 22, 2003. www.mcchicago.org/general/aboutus.aspx.

Hogan, Howard, and Gregg Robinson. [1994]. "What the Census Bureau's Coverage Evaluation Programs Tell Us about Differential Undercount." N.p.: Bureau of the Census.

Holt, Douglas. 1998. "Hindu Sect Enriches Community of Itasca: New Temple Part of Growing Presence." *Chicago Tribune*, November 6.

Hopewell, James F. 1987. *Congregation: Stories and Structures*. Philadelphia: Fortress Press.

Hostert-Cassidy, Judy. 1996. "Ss. Peter and Paul at 150: 'Meeting the Needs of Today, Tomorrow.'" *Naperville Sun*, June 16.

Hudson, John C. 2004. "Railroads." In *Encyclopedia of Chicago*, edited by James R. Grossman, Ann Durkin Keating, and Janice L. Reiff, 676–77. Chicago: University of Chicago Press.

Hunter, Albert. 1974. *Symbolic Communities: The Persistence and Change of Chicago's Local Communities*. Chicago: University of Chicago Press.

———. 1978. "Persistence of Local Sentiments in Mass Society." In *Handbook of Contemporary Urban Life: An Examination of Urbanization, Social Organization, and Metropolitan Politics*, edited by David Street and Associates, 133–62. San Francisco: Jossey-Bass.

Hunter, George G., III. 1987. *To Spread the Power: Church Growth in the Wesleyan Tradition*. Nashville: Abingdon.

Husain, Asad. 2004. "Bosnians." In *Encyclopedia of Chicago*, edited by James R. Grossman, Ann Durkin Keating, and Janice L. Reiff, 88. Chicago: University of Chicago Press.

Husain, Asad, and Harold Vogelaar. 1994. "Activities of the Immigrant Muslim Communities in Chicago." In *Muslim Communities in North America*, edited by Yvonne Yazbeck Haddad and Jane Idleman Smith, 231–57. Albany: SUNY.

"I-355 Heritage Corridor: Cumulative Effects of Local Plans." 1996. Chicago: Northeastern Illinois Planning Commission, October.

Ihlanfeldt, Keith R., and Benjamin P. Scafidi. 2002. "The Neighbourhood Contact Hypothesis: Evidence from the Multicity Study of Urban Inequality." *Urban Studies* 39:619–41.

"Interpreting Neighborhood Change in Chicago." College of Urban Planning and Public Affairs, University of Illinois at Chicago. Accessed April 18, 2009. http://

www.uic.edu/cuppa/voorheesctr/Gentrification%20Index%20Site/Main%20 Neighborhood%20Change%20Revised.htm.

"Inventory of the Wheatland Salem United Methodist Church." N.d. Northern Illinois Regional History Center. DeKalb, IL: Northern Illinois University.

"Islam in North America: Muslim Community Center, Accomplishments and Aspirations." N.d. Twenty-fifth anniversary commemoration booklet.

Jablonsky, Thomas J. 1993. *Pride in the Jungle: Community and Everyday Life in Back of the Yards Chicago*. Baltimore: Johns Hopkins University Press.

Jackson, Kenneth T. 1985. *Crabgrass Frontier: The Suburbanization of the United States*. New York: Oxford University Press.

Janowitz, Morris. 1952. *The Community Press in an Urban Setting*. Glencoe, IL: Free Press.

Janowitz, Morris, and David Street. 1978. "The Changing Social Order of the Metropolitan Area." In *Handbook of Contemporary Urban Life: An Examination of Urbanization, Social Organization, and Metropolitan Politics*, edited by David Street and Associates, 90–128. San Francisco: Jossey-Bass.

Jayaram, Smt. Sheela. 1997. "Celebrating 20 Years of Our Heritage: A Historical Review." The Hindu Temple of Greater Chicago. Accessed January 23, 2001. http://www.ramatemple.org/hisrevp1.html.

The Jewish Chicago Synagogue and Worship Directory. 2010. Accessed August 1, 2010. www.jewishchicago.com/directories/synagogues.html.

Johnson, Steve. 1986. "Hindu Temple Rising in Lemont Town's Newest House of Worship." *Chicago Tribune*, April 16.

Judd, Dennis R. 2011. "Theorizing the City." In *The City, Revisited: Urban Theory from Chicago, Los Angeles, and New York*, edited by Dennis R. Judd and Dick Simpson, 3–20. Minneapolis: University of Minnesota Press.

Judd, Dennis R., and Dick Simpson, eds. 2011. *The City, Revisited: Urban Theory from Chicago, Los Angeles, and New York*. Minneapolis: University of Minnesota Press.

Juergensmeyer, Mark. 2008. *Global Rebellion: Religious Challenges to the Secular State, from Christian Militias to Al Qaeda*. Berkeley: University of California Press.

Kamin, Blair. 2010. *Cityscapes*, August 16. Accessed December 2, 2013. http://featuresblogs.chicagotribune.com/theskyline/2010/08/abandoning-highrise-plans-fourth-presbyterian-ready-to-unveil-a-fivestory-mixeduse-addition-to-its-h.html.

Kantowicz, Edward R. 1983. *Corporation Sole: Cardinal Mundelein and Chicago Catholicism*. Notre Dame: University of Notre Dame Press.

Karnes, Kimberly, Wayne McIntosh, Irwin L. Morris, and Shanna Pearson-Merkowitz. 2007. "Mighty Fortresses: Explaining the Spatial Distribution of American Megachurches." *Journal for the Scientific Study of Religion* 46:261–68.

Katznelson, Ira. 1997. "Social Justice, Liberalism, and the City: Considerations on David Harvey, John Rawls and Karl Polanyi." In *Urbanization of Injustice*, edited by Andy Merrifield and Eric Swyngedouw, 45–64. New York: New York University Press.

Keating, Anne Durkin. 2002. *Building Chicago: Suburban Developers and the Creation of a Divided Metropolis.* Urbana: University of Illinois Press.

———. 2004. "Metropolitan Growth." In *Encyclopedia of Chicago*, edited by James R. Grossman, Ann Durkin Keating, and Janice L. Reiff, 524–31. Chicago: University of Chicago Press.

Keating, Anne Durkin, and Michael P. Conzen. 2004. "Economic Origins of Metropolitan Chicago's Communities." In *Encyclopedia of Chicago*, edited by James R. Grossman, Ann Durkin Keating and Janice L. Reiff, 526–27. Chicago: University of Chicago Press.

Keating, Ann Durkin, and Pierre Lebeau. 1995. *North Central College and Naperville: A Shared History, 1870–1995.* Naperville, IL: North Central College.

Kettani, M. Ali. 1986. *Muslim Minorities in the World Today.* London: Institute of Muslim Minority Affairs.

Kiang, Ying-cheng. 2004. "Chinatown." In *Encyclopedia of Chicago*, edited by James R. Grossman, Ann Durkin Keating, and Janice L. Reiff, 157–58. Chicago: University of Chicago Press.

Klowden, Kevin B. 1994. "Manufacturing in Lemont: The Fortuitous Rise of Industry in the Local Economy." In *Looking for Lemont: Place and People in an Illinois Canal Town*, edited by Michael P. Conzen and Carl A. Zimring, 99–108. Chicago: Committee on Geographical Studies, University of Chicago.

Kniss, Fred, and Paul D. Numrich. 2007. *Sacred Assemblies and Civic Engagement: How Religion Matters for America's Newest Immigrants.* New Brunswick, NJ: Rutgers University Press.

Knox, Douglas. 2004. "West Lawn." In *The Encyclopedia of Chicago*, edited by James R. Grossman, Ann Durkin Keating, and Janice L. Reiff, 871–72. Chicago: University of Chicago Press.

Komonchak, Joseph A. 1995. "Interpreting the Council: Catholic Attitudes toward Vatican II." In *Being Right: Conservative Catholics in America*, edited by Mary Jo Weaver and R. Scott Appleby, 17–36. Bloomington: Indiana University Press.

Kosmin, Barry A., Ariela Keysar, Ryan Cragun, and Juhem Navarro-Rivera. 2009. "American Nones: The Profile of the No Religion Population." Hartford, CT: Institute for the Study of Secularism in Society and Culture. Accessed January 5, 2014. http://commons.trincoll.edu/aris/publications/american-nones-the-profile-of-the-no-religion-population/.

Kostarelos, Frances. 1995. *Feeling the Spirit: Faith and Hope in an Evangelical Black Storefront Church.* Columbia: University of South Carolina Press.

Krawzak, Paul M. 1997. "Aurora, Naperville on the Way Up." *Aurora (IL) Beacon News*, May 23.

Kurien, Prema A. 2007. *A Place at the Multicultural Table: The Development of an American Hinduism.* New Brunswick, NJ: Rutgers University Press.

Lal, Vinay. 2004. "Indians." In *Encyclopedia of Chicago*, edited by James R. Grossman, Ann Durkin Keating, and Janice L Reiff, 410. Chicago: University of Chicago Press.

Lang, Robert E. 2003. *Edgeless Cities: Exploring the Elusive Metropolis.* Washington, DC: Brookings Institution.

LeGates, Richard T., and Frederic Stout. 2011. "Introduction to Part Two." In *The City Reader*, 5th ed., edited by Richard T. LeGates and Frederic Stout, 87–90. New York: Routledge.

Leinwand, Donna. 2004. "Muslims See New Opposition to Building Mosques since 9/11." *USA Today*, March 9. Accessed August 5, 2008. www.usatoday.com/news/religion/2004-03-08-mosque-opposition_x.htm.

Leitner, Jeff. 1995. "Naperville Planning for 135,000 in Next Decade." *Aurora (IL) Beacon News*, August 14.

Lemann, Nicholas. 1989. "Stressed Out in Suburbia." *Atlantic Monthly*, November.

Levine, Donald N. 1971. "Introduction." In *George Simmel on Individuality and Social Forms: Selected Writings*, edited by Donald N. Levine, ix–lxv. Chicago: University of Chicago Press.

Levitt, Peggy. 2001. *The Transnational Villagers.* Berkeley: University of California Press.

———. 2007. *God Needs No Passport: Immigrants and the Changing American Religious Landscape.* New York: New Press.

Lewis, James, Michael Maly, Paul Kleppner, and Ruth Ann Tobias. 2002. *Race and Residence in the Chicago Metropolitan Area 1980–2000.* Chicago: Roosevelt University and Northern Illinois University.

Lichterman, Paul. 2005. *Elusive Togetherness: Church Groups Trying to Bridge America's Divisions.* Princeton, NJ: Princeton University Press.

Lim, Chaeyoon, and Carole Ann MacGregor. 2012. "Religion and Volunteering in Context: Disentangling the Contextual Effects of Religion on Voluntary Behavior." *American Sociological Review* 77:747–79.

Livezey, Lois. 1998. "The Fourth Presbyterian Church of Chicago: One Congregation's Response to the Challenges of Family Life in Urban America." In *Tending the Flock: Congregations and Family Ministry*, edited by K. Brynolf Lyon and Archie Smith, Jr., 119–44. Louisville: Westminster John Knox.

Livezey, Lowell W. 1996a. "Introduction." In *Religious Organizations and Structural Change in Metropolitan Chicago: The Research Report of the Religion in Urban America Program*, edited by Lowell W. Livezey, 1–11. Chicago: University of Illinois.

———. 1996b. "The Jewish Neighborhood of West Rogers Park: Its Significance for the Jewish Community and the City." In *Religious Organizations and Structural Change in Metropolitan Chicago: The Research Report of the Religion in Urban America Program*, edited by Lowell W. Livezey, 37–59. Chicago: University of Illinois.

———. 1996c. *Religious Organizations and Structural Change in Metropolitan Chicago: The Research Report of the Religion in Urban America Program.* Chicago: University of Illinois.

————. 2000a. "Communities and Enclaves: Where Jews, Christians, Hindus, and Muslims Share the Neighborhood." In *Public Religion and Urban Transformation: Faith in the City*, edited by Lowell W. Livezey, 133–61. New York: New York University Press.

————. 2000b. "The New Context of Urban Religion." In *Public Religion and Urban Transformation: Faith in the City*, edited by Lowell W. Livezey, 3–25. New York: New York University Press.

————, ed. 2000c. *Public Religion and Urban Transformation: Faith in the City.* New York: New York University Press.

————. 2007. "Ministry when Urban Is Global: Connecting Church, City, and Seminary." Annual George W. Webber Lecture, New York Theological Seminary.

Livezey, Lowell W., and Mark Bouman. 2004. "Religious Geography." In *Encyclopedia of Chicago*, edited by James R. Grossman, Ann Durkin Keating, and Janice L. Reiff, 690–96. Chicago: University of Chicago Press.

"Livezey Research Puts Urban Churches on the Map." [2002]. Harvard Divinity School "News and Events" archive. Accessed January 23, 2009. http://www. hds.harvard.edu/news/article_archive/qa_livezey.html.

Local Community Fact Book, Chicago Metropolitan Area, 1990. 1995. Chicago: Chicago Fact Book Consortium.

Lombardi, Kate Stone. 2008. "In Curbing Walking Sprees, a Mall Sets Off Protests." *New York Times*, March 2. Accessed January 14, 2009. http:// www.nytimes.com/2008/03/02/nyregion/nyregionspecial2/02mallwe. html?pagewanted=print.

Lorch, Benjamin L. 1994. "From Here to There: Personal Mobility in Lemont, Illinois, 1848–1920." In *Looking for Lemont: Place and People in an Illinois Canal Town*, edited by Michael P. Conzen and Carl A. Zimring, 131–37. Chicago: Committee on Geographical Studies, University of Chicago.

Lyon, K. Brynolf, and Archie Smith, Jr., eds. 1998. *Tending the Flock: Congregations and Family Ministry.* Louisville: Westminster John Knox.

"The Mall Pall: Have America's Biggest Shopping Centers Lost Their Allure?" 2008. Accessed January 6, 2009. http://knowledge.wharton.upenn.edu/article. cfm?articleid=2111.

Maly, Michael T., and Michael Leachman. 1998. "Rogers Park, Edgewater, Uptown, and Chicago Lawn, Chicago." *Cityscape: A Journal of Policy Development and Research* 4:131–60.

Marciniak, Ed. 1981. *Reversing Urban Decline: The Winthrop-Kenmore Corridor in the Edgewater and Uptown Communities of Chicago.* Washington, DC: National Center for Urban Ethnic Affairs.

"Marketwatch." 2012. *Trib Local*, July 12–18.

Marler, Penny Long, and C. Kirk Hadaway. 2002. "'Being Religious' or 'Being Spiritual' in America: A Zero-Sum Proposition?" *Journal for the Scientific Study of Religion* 41:289–300.

Marti, Gerardo. 2009. "Affinity, Identity, and Transcendence: The Experience of Religious Racial Integration in Diverse Congregations." *Journal for the Scientific Study of Religion* 48:53–68.

Marty, Martin E. 2004. "Protestants." In *Encyclopedia of Chicago*, edited by James R. Grossman, Ann Durkin Keating, and Janice L. Reiff, 652–55. Chicago: University of Chicago Press.

"The Masjid and Community Development Project." 1977. Masjid Planning Committee, Muslim Community Center, January. Archived in the Islam in America collection, DePaul University Library, Chicago.

Massey, Doreen. 1994. *Space, Place, and Gender.* Minneapolis: University of Minnesota Press.

Massey, Doreen, and Pat Jess, eds. 2000. *A Place in the World? Places, Cultures and Globalization.* Oxford: Oxford University Press.

Masud, Muhammad Khalid. 1990. "The Obligation to Migrate: The Doctrine of *Hijra* in Islamic Law." In *Muslim Travellers: Pilgrimage, Migration, and the Religious Imagination*, edited by Dale F. Eickelman and James Piscatori, 29–49. Berkeley: University of California Press.

Matile, Roger. 2008. "Reflections: Settling a Rhubarb—and Rhubarb-Free Zone." *Oswego (IL) Ledger-Sentinel*, May 8. Accessed November 21, 2008. www.ledgersentinel.com/article.asp?a=7218.

McCarthy, John. 2013. "Configurations of Space in Contemporary Holy Cities." Paper presented at the "City of God/Towns for Humans" conference sponsored by the Hank Center for the Catholic Intellectual Heritage, Loyola University Chicago, April 26.

McClendon, Dennis. 2004. "Expressways." In *Encyclopedia of Chicago*, edited by James R. Grossman, Ann Durkin Keating, and Janice L. Reiff, 286–87. Chicago: University of Chicago Press.

McGreevy, John. 1996. *Parish Boundaries: The Catholic Encounter with Race in the Twentieth-Century Urban North.* Chicago: University of Chicago Press.

McKenzie, R. D. 1925. "The Ecological Approach to the Study of the Human Community." In *The City*, Robert E. Park, Ernest W. Burgess, and Roderick D. McKenzie, 63–79. Chicago: University of Chicago Press.

McKinney, Maureen Foertsch. 2001. "Hot Dogs and Hummus." *Illinois Issues*, June 14. Accessed October 26, 2013. http://www.lib.niu.edu/2001/ii010614.html.

McMahon, Eileen M. 1995. *What Parish Are You From? A Chicago Irish Community and Race Relations.* Lexington: University Press of Kentucky.

———. 2004. "Chicago Lawn." In *The Encyclopedia of Chicago*, edited by James R. Grossman, Ann Durkin Keating, and Janice L. Reiff, 143. Chicago: University of Chicago Press.

McRoberts, Omar M. 2005. *Streets of Glory: Church and Community in a Black Urban Neighborhood.* Chicago: University of Chicago Press.

"MEC Celebrates 4th of July with Morton Grove Residents." 2004. *Indian Reporter and World News*, July 9.

Mellen, Karen. 2002. "Council Approves Land-Use Plan for Naperville, Ill., Area." *Tribune Business News*, May 30.

Mendieta, Ana. 2004. "Village Reaches Deal on Mosque." *Chicago Sun-Times*, June 9. Accessed June 13, 2004. www.suntimes.com/output/news/cst-nws-mosque09.html.

Miller, Donald. 1996. *City of the Century: The Epic of Chicago and the Making of America*. New York: Simon and Schuster.

———. 1997. *Reinventing American Protestantism: Christianity in the New Millennium*. Berkeley: University of California Press.

Miller, Ross. 1993. "City Hall and the Architecture of Power: The Rise and Fall of the Dearborn Corridor." In *Chicago Architecture and Design, 1923–1993: Reconfiguration of an American Metropolis*, edited by John Zukowsky, 247–63. Munich: Prestel-Verlag and Chicago: Art Institute of Chicago.

Mills, C. Wright. 1959. *The Sociological Imagination*. New York: Oxford University Press.

"Missionary Preparation Program Handbook." The Moody Church. Accessed June 19, 2009. http://www.moodychurch.org/ministries/missions/MPP_Handbook_2008_09.doc.

Moberg, David. 2014. "Economic Restructuring: Chicago's Precarious Balance." In *Twenty-First Century Chicago*, rev. ed., edited by Dick Simpson, Constance A. Mixon, and Melissa Mouritsen Zmuda, 159–72. San Diego: Cognella.

Mollenkopf, John Hull. 2011. "School Is Out: The Case of New York City." In *The City, Revisited: Urban Theory from Chicago, Los Angeles, and New York*, edited by Dennis R. Judd and Dick Simpson, 169–85. Minneapolis: University of Minnesota Press.

Molotch, Harvey. 2002. "School's Out: A Response to Michael Dear." *City and Community* 1:39–43.

———. 2014. "Zero-Sum Urbanism." Review of *The Metropolitan Revolution: How Cities and Metros Are Fixing Our Broken Politics and Fragile Economy*, by Bruce Katz and Jennifer Bradley, and *Keys to the City: How Economics, Institutions, Social Interaction, and Politics Shape Development*, by Michael Storper. Public Books, February 1. Accessed February 3, 2014. http://www.publicbooks.org/nonfiction/zero-sum-urbanism.

Molotch, Harvey, William Freudenburg, and Kristen E. Paulsen. 2000. "History Repeats Itself, But How? City Character, Urban Tradition, and the Accomplishment of Place." *American Sociological Review* 65:791–823.

Mooney-Melvin, Patricia. 2004a. "Rogers Park." In *Encyclopedia of Chicago*, edited by James R. Grossman, Ann Durkin Keating, and Janice L. Rieff, 714–15. Chicago: University of Chicago Press.

————. 2004b. "West Ridge." In *The Encyclopedia of Chicago*, edited by James R. Grossman, Ann Durkin Keating, and Janice L. Reiff, 872–73. Chicago: University of Chicago Press.

"The Mosque Foundation Project: The Islamic Center for the Muslim Arabic Community in Southern Chicago." November 1978. DePaul University Library Archives, Islam in America Collection.

"Mosque Foundation Strategic Plan 2008–2012."

Muck, Terry. 1988. "The Mosque Next Door: How Do We Speak the Truth in Love to Muslims, Hindus, and Buddhists?" *Christianity Today*, February 19.

Mumford, Lewis. 1938. *The Culture of Cities*. New York: Harcourt Brace.

Murnion, Philip. 2000. "Parishes and the Public Arena: An Exploration." Commonweal Fall 2000 Colloquium. Accessed October 2, 2014. http://www. esosys.net/pew/papers/fall2000commonweal/murnion/murnionpaper.htm.

"Muslim Americans: Middle Class and Mostly Mainstream." 2007. Pew Research Center.

"Naperville Notice: Proposed Acquisition of the EJ&E Railroad." 2008. City of Naperville, Illinois. Accessed July 26, 2008. www.naperville.il.us/emplibrary/ EJENotice.pdf.

Narayanan, Vasudha. 1992. "Creating South Indian Hindu Experience in the United States." In *A Sacred Thread: Modern Transmission of Hindu Traditions in India and Abroad*, edited by Raymond Brady Williams, 147–76. Chambersburg, PA: Anima.

Neary, Timothy B. 2004. "Albany Park." In *The Encyclopedia of Chicago*, edited by James R. Grossman, Ann Durkin Keating, and Janice L. Reiff, 13–14. Chicago: University of Chicago Press.

Neitz, Mary Jo. 2009. "Encounters in the Heartland: What Studying Rural Churches Taught Me about Working across Differences." *Sociology of Religion* 70:343–61.

Nelson, Arthur C., and Kenneth J. Dueker. 1990. "The Exurbanization of America and Its Planning Policy Implications." *Journal of Planning Education and Research* 9:91–100.

Nelson, Timothy J. 1996. "Sacrifice of Praise: Emotion and Collective Participation in an African-American Worship Service." *Sociology of Religion* 57:379–96.

Newport, Frank. 2007. "Questions and Answers about Americans' Religion," December 24. Accessed July 16, 2008. www.gallup.com/poll/103459/ Questions-Answers-About-Americans-Religion.aspx.

Niebuhr, Gustav. 1995. "Where Shopping-Mall Culture Gets a Big Dose of Religion." *New York Times*, April 16.

Nisbet, Robert A. 1966. *The Sociological Tradition*. New York: Free Press.

" 'Nones' on the Rise." 2012. Pew Research Religion and Public Life Project, October 9. Accessed January 5, 2014. http://www.pewforum.org/Unaffiliated/nones-on-the-rise.aspx.

Numrich, Paul D. 1996. "Some Recent and Different Immigrant Religions of Chicago." In *Religious Organizations and Structural Change in Metropolitan Chicago: The Research Report of the Religion in Urban America Program*, edited by Lowell W. Livezey, 223–44. Chicago: University of Illinois.

———. 1997. "Recent Immigrant Religions in a Restructuring Metropolis: New Religious Landscapes in Chicago." *Journal of Cultural Geography* 17:55–76.

———. 1998. "A Pentecostal Megachurch on the Edge: Calvary Church, Naperville, Illinois." In *Tending the Flock: Congregations and Family Ministry*, edited by K. Brynolf Lyon and Archie Smith, Jr., 78–97. Louisville: Westminster John Knox.

———. 2000a. "Change, Stress, and Congregations in an Edge-City Technoburb." In *Public Religion and Urban Transformation: Faith in the City*, edited by Lowell W. Livezey, 187–210. New York: New York University Press.

———. 2000b. "Recent Immigrant Religions and the Restructuring of Metropolitan Chicago." In *Public Religion and Urban Transformation: Faith in the City*, edited by Lowell W. Livezey, 239–67. New York: New York University Press.

———. 2012. "Emergence of the Rhetoric of a Unified *Ummah* among American Muslims: The Case of Metropolitan Chicago." *Journal of Muslim Minority Affairs* 32:450–66.

Numrich, Paul D., and William Peterman. 1996. "Rogers Park: Congregations in a Changing Community Area." In *Religious Organizations and Structural Change in Metropolitan Chicago: The Research Report of the Religion in Urban America Program*, edited by Lowell W. Livezey, 19–35. Chicago: Office of Social Science Research, University of Illinois at Chicago.

O'Brien, David J., and Thomas A. Shannon, eds. 1992. *Catholic Social Thought: The Documentary Heritage*. Maryknoll, NY: Orbis.

Orfield, Myron. 2002. *American Metropolitics: The New Suburban Reality*. Washington, DC: Brookings Institution.

"Origins of the Settlement House Movement." N.d. The Social Welfare History Project. Accessed February 2, 2014. http://www.socialwelfarehistory.com/organizations/origins-of-the-settlement-house-movement/.

Orsi, Robert A. 1999. "Introduction: Crossing the City Line." In *Gods of the City: Religion and the American Urban Landscape*, edited by Robert A. Orsi, 1–78. Bloomington: Indiana University Press.

Orum, Anthony M., Joe R. Feagin, and Gideon Sjoberg. 1991. "Introduction: The Nature of the Case Study." In *A Case for the Case Study*, edited by Joe R. Feagin, Anthony M. Orum, and Gideon Sjoberg, 1–26. Chapel Hill: University of North Carolina Press.

Orum, Anthony M., and Xiangming Chen. 2003. *The World of Cities: Places in Comparative and Historical Perspective*. Malden, MA: Blackwell.

Oschinsky, Lawrence. 1947. "Islam in Chicago: Being a Study of the Acculturation of a Muslim Palestinian Community in That City." MA diss., University of Chicago.

Ostling, Richard N. 1993. "One Nation under Gods." *Time*, Fall (special issue).

Pacyga, Dominic A. 1995. "Chicago's Ethnic Neighborhoods: The Myth of Stability and the Reality of Change." In *Ethnic Chicago: A Multicultural Portrait*, edited by Melvin G. Holli and Peter d'A. Jones, 604–17. Grand Rapids, MI: Eerdmans.

Pacyga, Dominic A., and Ellen Skerrett. 1986. *Chicago: City of Neighborhoods: Histories and Tours*. Chicago: Loyola University Press.

Palmer, Ann Therese. 2003. "Port of Entry, Point of Interest: Albany Park Draws Immigrants, Housing Bargain Hunters." *Chicago Tribune*, November 9.

Paral, Rob, and Michael Morkewicz. 2003. *The Metro Chicago Immigration Fact Book*. Chicago: Roosevelt University.

Park, Robert E. 1925. "Community Organization and the Romantic Temper." In *The City*, Robert E. Park, Ernest W. Burgess, and Roderick D. McKenzie, 113–22. Chicago: University of Chicago Press.

Perella, Frederick J., Jr. 1996. "Roman Catholic Approaches to Urban Ministry, 1945–1985." In *Churches, Cities and Human Community: Urban Ministry in the United States, 1945–1985*, edited by Clifford J. Green, 179–211. Grand Rapids, MI: Eerdmans.

Pile, Steve. 1999. "What Is a City?" In *City Worlds*, edited by Doreen Massey, John Allen, and Steve Pile, 3–52. London: Routledge.

Portes, Alejandro, and Ruben G. Rumbaut. 1996. *Immigrant America: A Portrait*. 2nd ed. Berkeley: University of California Press.

"A Positive Outgrowth." 2003. *Chicago Sun-Times*, June 17.

"Postal Code Status Report." 2003. Calvary Church, Naperville, IL.

"Prayer Book Committee Report." 1995. Congregation Beth Shalom, Naperville, IL.

Price, Matthew J. 1996. "Chicago's Prestige Churches and Their Neighborhood." In *Religious Organizations and Structural Change in Metropolitan Chicago: The Research Report of the Religion in Urban America Program*, edited by Lowell W. Livezey, 61–105. Chicago: University of Illinois.

———. 2000. "Place, Race, and History: The Social Mission of Downtown Churches." In *Public Religion and Urban Transformation: Faith in the City*, edited by Lowell W. Livezey, 57–81. New York: New York University Press.

"Profile: DuPage County Statistical Handbook." 1992. DuPage County Development Department, Planning Division.

Rahner, Karl. 1958. "The Theology of the Parish." In *The Parish from Theology to Practice*, edited by Hugo Rahner, translated by Robert Kress, 23–35. Westminster, MD: Newman.

Rainey, Amy, and Whitney Woodward. N.d. "Rapid Change." *The Chicago Reporter*. Accessed May 1, 2009. http://www.chicagoreporter.com/index.php/c/Sidebars/d/Rapid_Change.

Rangaswamy, Padma. 1995. "Asian Indians in Chicago: Growth and Change in a Model Minority." In *Ethnic Chicago: A Multicultural Portrait*, 4th ed., edited by Melvin G. Holli and Peter d'A. Jones, 438–62. Grand Rapids, MI: Eerdmans.

———. 2000. *Namaste America: Indian Immigrants in an American Metropolis.* University Park, PA: Pennsylvania State University Press.

Rapoport, Amos. 2002. "Spatial Organization and the Built Environment." In *Companion Encyclopedia of Anthropology,* edited by Tim Ingold, 460–502. London: Routledge.

Rast, Joel. 1999. *Remaking Chicago: The Political Origins of Urban Industrial Change.* DeKalb, IL: Northern Illinois University Press.

Reardon, Patrick T. 1995. "The New Geography." *Chicago Tribune Magazine,* November 5.

Reed, Christopher R. 2004. "South Lawndale." In *Encyclopedia of Chicago,* edited by James R. Grossman, Ann Durkin Keating, and Janice L. Reiff, 769. Chicago: University of Chicago Press.

Renn, Aaron. 2014. "The Second-Rate City?" In *Twenty-First Century Chicago,* rev. ed., edited by Dick Simpson, Constance A. Mixon, and Melissa Mouritsen Zmuda, 173–80. San Diego: Cognella.

"Report to the Board of Moody Church." 1967. Copy provided by the Billy Graham Center, Wheaton College.

Richesin, L. Dale, ed. 1988. *Greater Chicago Religious Directory and Buyers Guide.* Chicago: Church Federation of Greater Chicago.

Rieder, Jonathan. 1985. *Canarsie: The Jews and Italians of Brooklyn against Liberalism.* Cambridge, MA: Harvard University Press.

Riemers, David M. 1992. *Still the Golden Door: The Third World Comes to America.* 2nd ed. New York: Columbia University Press.

Rodkin, Dennis. 2004. "Mondo Condos!" *Chicago Magazine,* October.

Roof, Wade Clark. 2001. *Spiritual Marketplace: Baby Boomers and the Remaking of American Religion.* Princeton, NJ: Princeton University Press.

Roozen, David A., William McKinney, and Jackson W. Carroll. 1984. *Varieties of Religious Presence: Mission in Public Life.* New York: Pilgrim.

Rosswurm, Steve. 2004. "Roman Catholics." In *Encyclopedia of Chicago,* edited by James R. Grossman, Ann Durkin Keating, and Janice L. Reiff, 717–21. Chicago: University of Chicago Press.

"Route 59 Pedestrian Bridge Questionnaire Public Input Totals." N.d. City of Naperville, Illinois. Accessed July 24, 2008. www.naperville.il.us/emplibrary/resultspub.pdf.

Rubinstein, David R. 2001. *Culture, Structure, and Agency: Toward a Truly Multidimensional Sociology.* Thousand Oaks, CA: Sage.

———. N.d. "Towards a (Truly) Multidimensional Sociology." Typescript.

Rudy, Preston. 2004. " 'Justice for Janitors,' Not 'Compensation for Custodians': The Political Context and Organizing in San Jose and Sacramento." In *Rebuilding Labor: Organizing and Organizers in the New Union Movement,* edited by Ruth Milkman and Kim Voss, 133–49. New York: Cornell University Press.

Rusk, David. 1999. *Inside Game / Outside Game: Winning Strategies for Saving Urban America*. Washington, DC: Brookings Institution.

Rydell, Robert W. 2004a. "Century of Progress Exposition." In *Encyclopedia of Chicago*, edited by James R. Grossman, Ann Durkin Keating, and Janice L. Reiff, 124–26. Chicago: University of Chicago Press.

———. 2004b. "World's Columbian Exposition." In *Encyclopedia of Chicago*, edited by James R. Grossman, Ann Durkin Keating, and Janice L. Reiff, 898–902. Chicago: University of Chicago Press.

Sabatini, Francisco, and Rodrigo Salcedo. 2011. "Understanding Deep Urban Change: Patterns of Residential Segregation in Latin American Cities." In *The City, Revisited: Urban Theory from Chicago, Los Angeles, and New York*, edited by Dennis R. Judd and Dick Simpson, 332–55. Minneapolis: University of Minnesota Press.

Samples, John. 1988. Introduction to *Community and Society*, by Ferdinand Tönnies, xi–xxvi. New Brunswick, NJ: Transaction.

Sampson, Robert J. 1999. "What 'Community' Supplies." In *Urban Problems and Community Development*, edited by Ronald F. Ferguson and William T. Dickens, 241–92. Washington, DC: Brookings Institution.

———. 2002. "Studying Modern Chicago." *City and Community* 1:45–48.

———. 2012. *Great American City: Chicago and the Enduring Neighborhood Effect*. Chicago: University of Chicago Press.

Santana, Rosa Maria. 1995. "Deep-Rooted: In the Midst of Subdivisions, a Farm Family Hold Its Ground." *Chicago Tribune*, November 12.

Sargeant, Kimon Howland. 2000. *Seeker Churches: Promoting Traditional Religion in a Nontraditional Way*. New Brunswick, NJ: Rutgers University Press.

Sassen, Saskia. 2001. *The Global City*. 2nd ed. Princeton, NJ: Princeton University Press.

———. 2002. "Scales and Spaces." *City and Community* 1:48–50.

———. 2004. "A Global City." In *Global Chicago*, edited by Charles Madigan, 15–34. Urbana: University of Illinois Press.

Schroeder, John D. 2004. "Lemont, IL." In *Encyclopedia of Chicago*, edited by James R. Grossman, Ann Durkin Keating, and Janice L. Reiff, 475. Chicago: University of Chicago Press.

"A Sector of a Metropolis: A Study of Radial Corridor Development for the Chicago Metropolitan Region." 1964. Urbana: University of Illinois College of Fine Arts.

Seidler, John, and Katherine Meyer. 1989. *Conflict and Change in the Catholic Church*. New Brunswick, NJ: Rutgers University Press.

Seligman, Amanda. 2004a. "Cabrini-Green." In *Encyclopedia of Chicago*, edited by James R. Grossman, Ann Durkin Keating, and Janice L. Reiff, 115. Chicago: University of Chicago Press.

———. 2004b. "Gold Coast." In *Encyclopedia of Chicago*, edited by James R. Grossman, Ann Durkin Keating, and Janice L. Reiff, 345. Chicago: University of Chicago Press.

————. 2004c. "Near North Side." In *Encyclopedia of Chicago*, edited by James R. Grossman, Ann Durkin Keating, and Janice L. Reiff, 561–62. Chicago: University of Chicago Press.

Selman, Robin R. 1994. "A History of the Lemont Quarry Industry." In *Looking for Lemont: Place and People in an Illinois Canal Town*, edited by Michael P. Conzen and Carl A. Zimring, 65–77. Chicago: Committee on Geographical Studies, University of Chicago.

Sewell, William H., Jr. 1992. "A Theory of Structure: Duality, Agency, and Transformation." *American Journal of Sociology* 98:1–29.

Simmel, Georg. [1903] 1950. "The Metropolis and Mental Life." In *The Sociology of Georg Simmel*, translated and edited by Kurt H. Wolff, 409–24. New York: Free Press.

————. [1908] 1971. "Group Expansion and the Development of Individuality." In *George Simmel on Individuality and Social Forms: Selected Writings*, edited by Donald N. Levine, 251–93. Chicago: University of Chicago Press.

Simpson, Dick, and Tom Kelly. 2011. "Studying Twenty-First Century Cities." In *The City, Revisited: Urban Theory from Chicago, Los Angeles, and New York*, edited by Dennis R. Judd and Dick Simpson, 356–66. Minneapolis: University of Minnesota Press.

Sinha, Jill Witmer, Amy Hillier, Ram A. Cnaan, and Charlene C. McGrew. 2007. "Proximity Matters: Exploring Relationships among Neighborhoods, Congregations, and the Residential Patterns of Members." *Journal for the Scientific Study of Religion* 46:245–60.

Skerrett, Ellen. 1993. "Sacred Space: Parish and Neighborhood in Chicago." In *Catholicism, Chicago Style*, edited by Ellen Skerrett, Edward R. Kantowicz, and Steven M. Avella, 137–69. Chicago: Loyola University Press.

Sklare, Marshall. 1974. "The Conservative Movement: Achievements and Problems." In *The Jewish Community in America*, edited by Marshall Sklare, 175–92. New York: Behrman House.

Slattery, Michael, and William Droel. N.d. "Christians in Their Neighborhood." Chicago: Southwest Catholic Cluster Project, Sponsored by the Southwest Cluster of Catholic Parishes and the Office for the Ministry of Peace and Justice, Archdiocese of Chicago.

Slosar, Jennifer. 2010. "Fourth Presbyterian Unveils New Addition." *Skyline Newspaper*, August 18. Accessed December 2, 2013. http://www.skylinenewspaper.com/News/In-The-Paper/08-18-2010/Fourth_Presbyterian_unveils_new_addition.

Slykas, Jennifer. 1996. "Ss. Peter and Paul at 150: 'A Community Builds a Church.'" *Naperville Sun*, June 9.

Small, Mario Luis. 2009. "'How Many Cases Do I Need?' On Science and the Logic of Case Selection in Field-Based Research." *Ethnography* 10:5–38.

Smith, Christian. 2008. "Why 'Why Christianity Works' Works." *Sociology of Religion* 69:473–88.

Smith, Christian, Brandon Vaidyanathan, Nancy Tatom Ammerman, Jose Casanova, Hilary Davidson, Elaine Howard Ecklund, John H. Evans, Philip S. Gorski, Mary Ellen Konieczny, Jason A. Springs, Jenny Trinitapoli, and Meredith Whitnah. 2013. "Roundtable on the Sociology of Religion: Twenty-Three Theses on the Status of Religion in American Sociology—A Mellon Working-Group Reflection." *Journal of the American Academy of Religion* 81:903–38.

Smith, David A. 1995. "The New Urban Sociology Meets the Old: Rereading Some Classical Human Ecology." *Urban Affairs Review* 30:432–57.

Soja, Edward W. 1989. *Postmodern Geographies: The Reassertion of Space in Critical Social Theory.* New York: Verso.

———. 2000. *Postmetropolis: Critical Studies of Cities and Regions.* Malden, MA: Blackwell.

Soja, Edward W., and Allen J. Scott. 1996. "Introduction to Los Angeles: City and Region." In *The City: Los Angeles and Urban Theory at the End of the Twentieth Century*, edited by Allen J. Scott and Edward W. Soja, 1–21. Berkeley: University of California Press.

Soja, Edward W., Rebecca Morales, and Goetz Wolff. 1983. "Urban Restructuring: An Analysis of Social and Spatial Change in Los Angeles." *Economic Geography* 59:195–230.

Solzman, David M. 2004. "North Park." In *The Encyclopedia of Chicago*, edited by James R. Grossman, Ann Durkin Keating, and Janice L. Reiff, 576–77. Chicago: University of Chicago Press.

Sorkin, Michael, ed. 1992. *Variations on a Theme Park: The New American City and the End of Public Space.* New York: Hill and Wang.

Spain, Daphne. 2011. "The Chicago of Jane Addams and Ernest Burgess: Same City, Different Visions." In *The City, Revisited: Urban Theory from Chicago, Los Angeles, and New York*, edited by Dennis R. Judd and Dick Simpson, 51–62. Minneapolis: University of Minnesota Press.

Spear, Allan H. 1967. *Black Chicago: The Making of a Negro Ghetto, 1890–1920.* Chicago: University of Chicago Press.

"Ss. Peter and Paul Growth Parallels City's." 1981. *Naperville Sun*, June 5.

Stamper, John W. 2005. "Magnificent Mile." In *Encyclopedia of Chicago*, edited by James R. Grossman, Ann Durkin Keating, and Janice L. Reiff, 503. Chicago: University of Chicago Press.

Steffes, Tracy. 2004. "Chinese." In *Encyclopedia of Chicago*, edited by James R. Grossman, Ann Durkin Keating, and Janice L. Reiff, 158–59. Chicago: University of Chicago Press.

Stevens, Darlene Gavron. 2000. "Meeting Set to Settle Dispute over Mosque." *Chicago Tribune*, July 13.

Stewart, Adam H. 2004. "Wilmette." In *The Encyclopedia of Chicago*, edited by James R. Grossman, Ann Durkin Keating, and Janice L. Reiff, 881. Chicago: University of Chicago Press.

Stockwell, Clinton E. 2004. "Gage Park." In *The Encyclopedia of Chicago*, edited by James R. Grossman, Ann Durkin Keating, and Janice L. Reiff, 322. Chicago: University of Chicago Press.

Suttles, Gerald D. 1972. *The Social Construction of Communities*. Chicago: University of Chicago Press.

"Temple Annexation Brings 'Prestige.' " 1991. *Chicago Tribune*, February 4.

Thumma, Scott Lee. 1996. "Megachurches of Atlanta." In *Religions of Atlanta: Religious Diversity in the Centennial Olympic City*, edited by Gary Laderman, 199–213. Atlanta: Scholars Press.

Thumma, Scott Lee, and Dave Travis. 2007. *Beyond Megachurch Myths: What We Can Learn from America's Largest Churches*. San Francisco: Jossey-Bass.

Thumma, Scott Lee, Dave Travis, and Warren Bird. 2005. "Megachurches Today 2005: Summary of Research Findings." Accessed January 11, 2009. http://hirr. hartsem.edu/megachurch/megastoday2005_summaryreport.html.

Tomasi, Silvano M. 1975. *Piety and Power: The Role of the Italian Parishes in the New York Metropolitan Area, 1880–1930*. New York: Center for Migration Studies.

Towsley, Genevieve. 1975. "A View of Historic Naperville from the Sky-Lines: A Collection of Articles of Historic Significance." Naperville, IL: Naperville Sun.

Travis, Dempsey J. 1989. *"Harold" The People's Mayor: An Authorized Biography of Mayor Harold Washington*. Chicago: Urban Research Press.

Trueheart, Charles. 1996. "Welcome to the Next Church." *Atlantic Monthly*, August.

U.S. Catholic Bishops. 1983. "The Challenge of Peace: God's Promise and Our Response." In *Catholic Social Thought: The Documentary Heritage*, edited by David J. O'Brien and Thomas A. Shannon, 492–571. Maryknoll, NY: Orbis, 1992.

U.S. Catholic Bishops. 1986. "Economic Justice for All." In *Catholic Social Thought: The Documentary Heritage*, edited by David J. O'Brien and Thomas A. Shannon, 572–680. Maryknoll, NY: Orbis, 1992.

U.S. Census Bureau. Population Finder. Accessed July 25, 2008. www.census.gov.

USDA. 2009. "Report to Congress: Access to Affordable and Nutritious Food: Measuring and Understanding Food Deserts and Their Consequences."

Vaillant, Derek. 2004. "Midway Airport." In *Encyclopedia of Chicago*, edited by James R. Grossman, Ann Durkin Keating, and Janice L. Reiff, 536. Chicago: University of Chicago Press.

Vasile, Ronald S. 2004. "Bridgeview, IL." In *The Encyclopedia of Chicago*, edited by James R. Grossman, Ann Durkin Keating, and Janice L. Reiff, 93–94. Chicago: University of Chicago Press.

Vasquez, Manuel A. 2005. "Historicizing and Materializing the Study of Religion: The Contribution of Migration Studies." In *Immigrant Faiths: Transforming Religious Life in America*, edited by Karen I. Leonard, Alex Stepick, Manuel A. Vasquez, and Jennifer Holloway, 219–42. Walnut Creek, CA: AltaMira.

Vaughan, John N. 1993. *Megachurches and America's Cities: How Churches Grow.* Grand Rapids, MI: Baker.

Vergara, Rowena. 2010. "Close Summons Old Memories for Prairie Parishioners." *Fox Valley Villages Sun,* July 1.

Waldinger, Roger. 1989. "Immigration and Urban Change." *Annual Review of Sociology* 15:211–32.

Walton, John. 1980. Review of *Handbook of Contemporary Urban Life. Social Forces* 59:312–14.

Warner, R. Stephen. 1998. "Approaching Religious Diversity: Barriers, Byways, and Beginnings." *Sociology of Religion* 59:193–215.

———. 2000. "Epilogue: Building Religious Communities at the Turn of the Century." In *Public Religion and Urban Transformation: Faith in the City,* edited by Lowell W. Livezey, 295–307. New York: New York University Press.

———. 2006. "The De-Europeanization of American Christianity." In *A Nation of Religions: The Politics of Pluralism in Multireligious America,* edited by Stephen Prothero, 233–55. Chapel Hill: University of North Carolina Press.

Warner, R. Stephen, and Judith G. Wittner, eds. 1998. *Gatherings in Diaspora: Religious Communities and the New Immigrants.* Philadelphia: Temple University Press.

"Washington Announces 'Blue Ribbon' Team." 1982. *Chicago Defender,* December 14.

Waters, Mary C. 1990. *Ethnic Options: Choosing Identities in America.* Berkeley: University of California Press.

Wedam, Elfriede. 1996. "The Southwest Side: Its Catholic Churches, Community Organizations, and Other Religious Institutions." In *Religious Organizations and Structural Change in Metropolitan Chicago: The Research Report of the Religion in Urban America Program,* edited by Lowell W. Livezey, 177–202. Chicago: Office of Social Science Research, University of Illinois at Chicago.

———. 1999. "Ethno-Racial Diversity within Religious Congregations in Indianapolis." *Research Notes from the Project on Religion and Urban Culture* 2. Accessed November 1, 2009. http://www.polis.iupui.edu/RUC/Newsletters/Research/vol2no4.htm.

———. 2000a. "Catholic Spirituality in a New Urban Church." In *Public Religion and Urban Transformation: Faith in the City,* edited by Lowell W. Livezey, 213–37. New York: New York University Press.

———. 2000b. " 'God Doesn't Ask What Language I Pray In': Community and Culture on Chicago's Southwest Side." In *Public Religion and Urban Transformation: Faith in the City,* edited by Lowell W. Livezey, 107–31. New York: New York University Press.

———. 2002. "The Predicament of Race." *Visions* 5:1–4.

———. 2005. " 'If We Let the Market Prevail, We Won't Have a Neighborhood Left': Religious Agency and Urban Restructuring on Chicago's Southwest Side." *City and Society* 17:211–33.

————. 2008. "Structure, Agency, and Adaptation in Congregations." *Cross Currents* 58:363–68.

Wedam, Elfriede, and Lowell W. Livezey. 2004. "Religion in the *City on the Make.*" In *Religion and Public Life in the Midwest: America's Common Denominator?* edited by Philip Barlow and Mark Silk, 159–86. Walnut Creek, CA: AltaMira.

Weinstein, Deena, and Michael Weinstein. 1989. "Simmel and the Dialectic of the Double Boundary: The Case of the Metropolis and Mental Life." *Sociological Inquiry* 59:48–59.

Weinstein, Richard S. 1996. "The First American City." In *The City: Los Angeles and Urban Theory at the End of the Twentieth Century*, edited by Allen J. Scott and Edward W. Soja, 22–46. Berkeley: University of California Press.

Weiss, Jonathan D., and Randy Lowell. 2002. "Supersizing Religion: Megachurches, Sprawl, and Smart Growth." *Saint Louis University Public Law Review* 21:313–30.

Wellman, Barry, ed. 1999. *Networks in the Global Village: Life in Contemporary Communities*. Boulder, CO: Westview.

Wellman, James K., Jr. 1999. *The Gold Coast Church and the Ghetto: Christ and Culture in Mainline Protestantism*. Urbana and Chicago: University of Illinois Press.

Wievel, Wim. 1988. *The State of the Economy and Economic Development in the Chicago Metropolitan Region*. Chicago: Metropolitan Planning Council.

Williams, Raymond Brady. 1988. *Religions of Immigrants from India and Pakistan: New Threads in the American Tapestry*. New York: Cambridge University Press.

————, ed. 1992. *A Sacred Thread: Modern Transmission of Hindu Traditions in India and Abroad*. Chambersburg, PA: Anima.

Williams, Rhys H. 2002. "Review Essay: Religion, Community, and Place: Locating the Transcendent." *Religion and American Culture: A Journal of Interpretation* 12:249–63.

————. 2004. "Religion and Place in the Midwest: Urban, Rural, and Suburban Forms of Religious Expression." In *Religion and Public Life in the Midwest: America's Common Denominator?* edited by Philip Barlow and Mark Silk, 187–208. Walnut Creek, CA: AltaMira.

Williams, Robert J. 1994. "A Social Profile of the Community in 1900." In *Looking for Lemont: Place and People in an Illinois Canal Town*, edited by Michael P. Conzen and Carl A. Zimring, 215–20. Chicago: Committee on Geographical Studies, University of Chicago.

Wilson, William Julius. 1987. *The Truly Disadvantaged: The Inner City, the Underclass, and Public Policy*. Chicago: University of Chicago Press.

————. 2012. Foreword to *Great American City: Chicago and the Enduring Neighborhood Effect*, by Robert J. Sampson, vii–xiii. Chicago: University of Chicago Press.

Wind, James P., and James W. Lewis, eds. 1994. *American Congregations*, 2 vols. Chicago: University of Chicago Press.

Wirth, Louis. 1928. *The Ghetto*. Chicago: University of Chicago Press.

———. 1938. "Urbanism as a Way of Life." *American Journal of Sociology* 44:1–24.

Wolfe, Christopher. 1995. "Subsidiarity: The 'Other' Ground of Limited Government." In *Catholicism, Liberalism, and Communitarianism*, edited by Kenneth L. Grasso, Gerard V. Bradley, and Robert P. Hunt, 81–96. Lanham, MD: Rowman and Littlefield.

Woolever, Cynthia. 1992. "A Contextual Approach to Neighborhood Attachment." *Urban Studies* 29:99–116.

Worland, Gayle. 2003. "Cultures Melding in Albany Park." *Chicago Tribune*, October 22.

Wuthnow, Robert. 1988. *The Restructuring of American Religion: Society and Faith since World War II*. Princeton, NJ: Princeton University Press.

———. 1991. *Acts of Compassion: Caring for Others and Helping Ourselves*. Princeton, NJ: Princeton University Press.

———. 1998. *After Heaven: Spirituality in America since the 1950s*. Berkeley: University of California Press.

Yates, Jon. 2001a. "Hindu Group Finds Acceptance in Addison." *Chicago Tribune*, July 4.

———. 2001b. "Hindus Build Monuments to Their Faith: A Growing and Affluent Indian Population Fuels Temple Boom." *Chicago Tribune*, January 19.

Young, Iris Marion. 1990. *Justice and the Politics of Difference*. Princeton, NJ: Princeton University Press.

Zaghel, Ali Shteiwi. 1976. "Changing Patterns of Identification among Arab-Americans: The Palestinian Ramallites and the Christian Syrian-Lebanese." PhD diss., Northwestern University.

Zelinsky, Wilbur, and Stephen A. Matthews. 2011. *The Place of Religion in Chicago*. Chicago: The Center for American Places at Columbia College Chicago.

Zhou, Min. 2008. "Are Asian Americans Becoming 'White'?" In *The Contexts Reader*, edited by Jeff Goodwin and James M. Jasper, 279–85. New York: W.W. Norton with the American Sociological Association.

Zinnbauer, Brian J., Kenneth I Pargament, Brenda Cole, Mark S. Rye, Eric M. Butter, Timothy G. Belavich, Kathleen M. Hipp, Allie B. Scott, and Jill L. Kadar. 1997. "Religion and Spirituality: Unfuzzying the Fuzzy." *Journal for the Scientific Study of Religion* 36:549–64.

Zorbaugh, Harvey Warren. 1929. *The Gold Coast and the Slum: A Sociological Study of Chicago's Near North Side*. Chicago: University of Chicago Press.

Zotti, Ed. 1990. *Chicago River Urban Design Guidelines: Downtown Corridor*. Chicago: Chicago Plan Commission.

Index